THE JAVIER PLAYS

DIAGRAM OF A PAPER AIRPLANE

A THICK DESCRIPTION OF HARRY SMITH (VOL.1)

YOUR NAME WILL FOLLOW YOU HOME

53SP 24

April 2016

ISBN no. 978-0-9897393-4-4

53rdstatepress.org
© Carlos Murillo 2016

THE JAVIER PLAYS

Carlos Murillo

53rd State Press
Brooklyn, NY

TABLE OF CONTENTS

Deluge: A Preface to *The Javier Plays*

Carlos Murillo

"Beware the things you find behind file cabinets in musty basements. Rather — beware the things someone else finds in such places that you take it upon yourself to steal."

— *American playwright Javier C., from the introduction of his unpublished manifesto "To Murder Whimsy: Bi-Polar Realism and the Future of American Playwriting" (1984)*

THE ORIGINS OF *THE JAVIER PLAYS*

Some time in the last decade of the last century, I became acquainted with a young woman who briefly had worked as a summer intern at New Dramatists — we'll call her "Nicole" for the purposes of this preface — 1) to protect the innocent, and 2) to confess that I can't recall with certainty her actual name.

New Dramatists, housed in a former house of worship on West 44th Street in Hell's Kitchen, is a New York City based organization "Dedicated to the Playwright" — or so read the fading gold letters stenciled on the transom window above the entrance. The organization provides a select group of playwrights seven-year residencies designed to help develop their craft, work within a community of likeminded professionals, and provide a home for folks pursuing a profession in which the specter of homelessness — both literal and figurative — looms large. Most of the organization's activity takes place in the months between September, when a new crop of writers are inducted as members, to June, when writers who have completed their seven years get "kicked to the curb," as one former resident described his experience to me over beers at Rudy's, a nearby watering hole and holdout from the darker, seedier days of Hell's Kitchen.

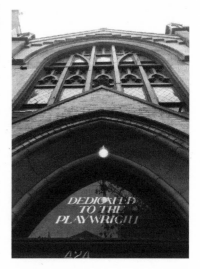

Summer is a quiet time at The Church (as playwrights and staff affectionately call the place) so "Nicole," our intern, was tasked with preparing boxes of archival material for shipment to the Beinecke Library at Yale University, which houses New Dramatists' storied archives. For the interplanetary visitor wishing to unearth the trajectory

of late 20th century American drama, there hardly exists a better place to start. Among the artifacts in the collection: seminal works in draft form by some of the country's finest, most successful and legendary playwrights, as well as countless lost plays by obscure and forgotten ones. "Nicole" spent a good deal of her summer entombed in the dank basement, combing through dozens of file cabinets, dusting off their contents, cataloguing, organizing and packing them away for future theatre scholars. The tedium of her task was tempered by the glimmer of possibility: she'd heard tales of past interns striking gold while excavating the ruins, unearthing lost treasures. Past discoveries included an early draft of a Pulitzer-winning play by August Wilson, a lost James Baldwin work, complete with handwritten marginal notes, among many others.

In mid-August, after emptying the contents of a brown metal file cabinet tucked in a far corner of the basement, "Nicole" discovered an unopened package in a large manila envelope behind the bottom drawer. The envelope piqued her curiosity – battered, wrinkled, torn and mended with layers of clear packing tape, blotched with stains of indeterminate origin, it had been reduced, reused and recycled by its sender frequently enough as to render it almost useless. Covered with dozens of labels with different addresses, cross-outs made with magic marker and numerous strata of "Return to Sender" stamps and post markings worthy of an archaeological dig, the envelope had traveled great distances over the course of its life before landing in its final resting place behind the drawer. The sender had clearly "pushed the envelope" of this envelope, as it were, with his presumably penny-pinching reuse of it. Or perhaps the sender meant to create

a low-rent, Rauschenberg-esque assemblage – a reminder to himself and to its recipients of the cycles of hope and rejection inherent to the playwriting profession, and of the porous line between gold and garbage, the permanent and the ephemeral.

All alone in the dank basement, "Nicole" hesitated opening the envelope. She felt foreboding that the artifact's exterior strangeness must conceal something dark, cursed, perhaps evil. Indeed, the contents were alarming.

Enclosed in the envelope, "Nicole" found an unread, unevaluated application for one of New Dramatists' coveted residencies by the obscure Colombian-born American playwright Javier C. Though none of the material inside was dated, "Nicole" deduced from the faded, top layer postmark that the applicant mailed the package a full seven years before, on September 11, 1991 – a full four days before the submission window closed on September 15th (and a full twenty years before the New Dramatists application process went paperless.) Had Javier's application been accepted, he would have completed his residency around the time "Nicole" graduated from Bennington College and moved to New York to start her internship.

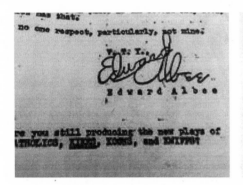 

The application contained all the requisite materials: a cover letter, two copies of two complete plays, a resume, a statement of purpose, and a letter of recommendation from Pulitzer Prize winning playwright Edward Albee (later declared a forgery).

In addition, the sender included a number of unrequested supplementary materials: an incomplete, handwritten, mostly illegible draft of a manifesto entitled "To Murder Whimsy: Bi-Polar Realism and the Future of American Playwriting," fragments of a third play (perhaps "play" is too generous a description – the sender himself described it as a "bucket of vomit" in the form of dialogue, impossible stage directions, descriptions of unwritten scenes, unsent hate mail, proposals for unwieldy practical jokes), a Ziploc bag containing a half dozen crumpled paper airplanes, a photocopy of what appeared to be a page from an original copy of Giordano Bruno's *Ars Memoriae* (1582), an unopened package of Little Debbie cakes, a half smoked cigarette, a series of cut-outs from milk cartons featuring images and descriptions of missing children, and an unopened fortune cookie that had been crushed to dust under the weight of all this material. (The fortune itself, legible through the plastic wrapper and shards of cookie, read: "Trust him, but still keep your eyes open. Lucky # 3, 23, 25, 31, 34, 46."

As "Nicole" delved deeper into the required materials, they revealed an eccentricity that matched the supplementary ones. The typo-ridden cover letter, a model of incoherence, argued that the long history of political violence in Javier C.'s native land Colombia – a violence which cost him his father's life, prompting his mother to whisk her two year old son into exile in the US in 1960 – justified his choice to become a playwright bent on examining "the unfinished nature and dark underbelly of the American experiment from the perspective of a reluctant immigrant from the other America – where your coffee, bananas and cocaine comes from." The two plays – *Death of a Liberal* (1977) and *The Rich Also Cry* (1979) – evidenced an undoubtedly unique (and some would say abrasive) voice. More drafts-in-progress than finished works, the manuscripts were riddled with handwritten marginal notes, cross outs, index cards stapled to various pages, and pornographic doodles. The handwritten resume said little about his dramatic output, production history or educational background – instead it read as a catalogue of misdeeds: his petty crimes, the various drugs he took, and the names (when he could recall them) of women and men that "co-piloted" his numerous and varied sexual escapades, including dates, locations and brief notes on the duration, quality and psychic cost of these experiences. The Statement of Purpose was equally

inappropriate to the application. Rather than describe his plays, his work, his theatrical vision, his influences, what he hoped to accomplish over a seven-year residency, the Statement goes to considerable length to describe his mother's hands and the hundreds of matchbooks she collected from every restaurant she visited in her adult life – a collection he discovered in a linen closet while cleaning out her apartment after her sudden and unexpected death in 1981.

While not a discovery as significant as an early, lost August Wilson work, for "Nicole" it had enough value as a curiosity to break the monotony of that August.

After squandering half the afternoon peeling away the spooky layers of this strange artifact, "Nicole" did what any industrious intern would do: she went to the office of Todd London, New Dramatists' recently appointed Artistic Director, to ask him what to do with it. Mr. London had no idea who Javier C. was, nor could he explain to "Nicole" why the package had never been opened and the materials enclosed in it never evaluated. As to what to she ought to do with it, he told "Nicole" to "Go to town with it, sweetheart." (In an interview I conducted with Todd London in 2012, he recalled neither the incident nor the intern in question, and denied with uncharacteristic bite "I actually used a phrase like that, despite this 'Nicole person's' claim that I did.")

Javier C.'s unevaluated application package was not included among the items sent to Yale that summer. Thus, the chances of his work being resurrected by an intrepid scholar seeking to fill in the potholes in the accepted evolutionary trajectory of American drama, were reduced, for all practical purposes, to nil. Faced with the choice of condemning it in the dustbin or restoring the package to its purgatory behind the drawer, "Nicole" followed Todd London's advice: she took it home, where it languished on her bookshelf, forgotten.

HOW *THE JAVIER PLAYS* CAME INTO MY POSSESSION

That December, at the New Dramatists annual holiday party, I met "Nicole."

Like many American playwrights, I coveted membership in the organization. Being only a few years into a fledgling theatre career at that point, and knowing tales of now well-established playwrights applying multiple times before gaining admittance (I understand from organizational lore that Pulitzer-winner Paula Vogel holds the record for number of attempts before acceptance), I acknowledged that it might be some time (in my case, more or less a dozen years) before I might be anointed a congregant of The Church. In the meantime, I contented myself with attending the occasional play reading and crashing holiday celebrations, where, as a young, struggling artist on the prowl, I happily helped myself to the copious amounts of free booze, pounced on networking opportunities and sought out potential partners for "no strings attached," consequence-free dalliances.

It was the '90s. I was in my 20s. In that period of my life I was marked with twin character flaws: kleptomania and promiscuity. My kleptomaniac impulses focused exclusively on the accumulation of books. I lifted them everywhere — bookstores, public libraries, the various places where I was employed, off of shelves in the apartments of friends, acquaintances and strangers. If I happened to find myself an overnight guest at someone's home, I never left without a souvenir volume. I had read Edmund White's exhaustive 1993 biography, *Genet* (NB: I actually paid the $35 it cost to acquire it) — which chronicled, among other things, the novelist and playwright's obsessive book thieving. I love Genet's work. As a young writer seeking models in the work of my predecessors, both Genet's self-reflexive dramaturgy and his thieving criminality served to justify my own.

My promiscuity, on the other hand, was driven by the privilege of being a poor, young and randy aspiring-artist-on-the-make in a city filled with poor, young and randy aspiring-artists-on-the-make. While I mostly acted on these twin traits separately, I found myself, on occasion, in circumstances where these flaws dovetailed into an admittedly neurotic, criminal compulsion. Forensic science provides ample documentation of cases where criminals either leave behind or remove artifacts from the scenes of their crimes. While it would be wrong to characterize my consensual amorous escapades as criminal, being raised Catholic, they might as well have been. That I could never leave a "crime" scene without removing a book from it, well that, friends, is indeed criminal.

My library, as long as it existed (past tense, yes, more on that soon), not only embodied much of my accumulated knowledge (a substitute for my failure to complete a college education), but encoded in the volumes was my personal history: the places I visited, friends, colleagues and acquaintances I associated with, establishments where I worked, retail outlets at which I shopp(lift)ed, and people with whom I slept.

That said, beyond the accumulation of books and sexual experience, by chasing this criminal compulsion I hungered for something deeper: an anthropological knowledge I could only acquire visiting the apartments of strangers. Many of the greatest museum collections in the world are concentrated in the 469 square miles of New York City. But in my opinion the richest treasures aren't housed in obvious places like The Met, the MOMA or the Museum of Natural History. No. The greatest museum treasures in New York City — or any metropolis for that matter — exist in the private realm, inside the apartments of anonymous dwellers of the city. For me, being taken to a strange apartment by a sweet young thing was to gain entry to a museum for one. What artifacts does she possess? What books sit on her shelves? What images hang on her walls? What unpaid bills sit neglected on her night table? What garments (and skeletons) hang in her closet? And footwear? What rots inside her refrigerator? Are unspoken hopes and fears written into the tchotchkes she collects and the manner in which she arranges them? Is there a story all this stuff tells? Of her life? Of the city? Of the culture inside which we're condemned to live? It was in these unofficial museums where I believed I might unlock a thick description of American life in the 20th Century. For years I toyed with the idea of writing a history of the United States as revealed by the artifacts people accumulate in their apartments. As with so many ideas, this one never came to fruition.

A DIGRESSION ABOUT MUSEUMS

The stranger's-apartment-as-museum paradigm struck me for the first time in 1992 while housesitting for a "friend with benefits" in the Prospect Heights section of Brooklyn. The owner of the apartment was a divorcee in her 30s who worked in the development office of a well-known, now defunct not-for-profit off-Broadway theatre. She left town regularly to visit her ailing mother in Ottawa. When she traveled, knowing I was hard up for a consistent place to live, she generously handed over the keys to her place so I could get the mail and tend to her Ficus tree. The apartment was beautifully appointed – large south-facing windows overlooking a Brownstone – and tree-lined Brooklyn street, high ceilings and spacious, airy, tastefully furnished rooms that took up the entire second floor. For all its beauty, I couldn't help but sense that something fundamental was missing. Her apartment was a museum with phantom wings. Something had been removed, amputated from the place. The artifacts she had accumulated seemed to enclose absence – like when you remove a photograph from a wall and it leaves a clean rectangle of color fresher than the paint surrounding it.

She had lived in the apartment for nearly a decade with her ex-husband, a French

Canadian attorney who relocated to Montreal after their divorce. The apartment appeared as if he removed half its contents when he left, and she never bothered to makeover the apartment in her own image. I don't mean to convey that she was a sad, lonely or forlorn person, pining away for her lost husband. On the contrary, she voraciously enjoyed her post-marital life. She possessed razor-sharp intelligence and head-turning good looks, worked in a profession she loved and was very good at, lived in a fantastic apartment, had lots of friends and a healthy stable of gentlemen (and women) with whom she indulged in life's pleasures.

A small alcove off the living room served as a library. Built into it were floor to ceiling Mahogany bookshelves framed by a pair of expensive leather wingback chairs. One afternoon, on my third stint house sitting, I went into the library alcove to browse titles and choose a souvenir. I found wedged in a section devoted to serious, thick historical and legal tomes three paperback books of Magick spells – their titles barely decipherable. The cheap bindings were cracked from heavy use. Opening one of the volumes to a dog-eared page revealed instructions for a fertility spell. Combing through all of the spell books, it became clear: fertility spell after fertility spell after fertility spell. Having seen her naked on dozens of occasions, I never expected to see her so naked as this. I quickly returned the spell books to their place on the shelf – feeling ashamed that I had violated her most hidden, private self.

It struck me then and strikes me any time I am in a stranger's apartment: encoded in the artifacts the dweller accumulates (and in their juxtaposition to each other) is the psychic DNA of the being that occupies the space. Everything about them – what's visible and invisible, their past, present and future wishes and anxieties, their triumphs, disappointments, love and hatred, the ache they feel for people and things they've lost – is written in invisible ink in the white spaces between words.

How *The Javier Plays* came into my possession, part two

But back to "Nicole."

We met at the New Dramatists holiday party that December and immediately hit it off. We were roughly the same age, shared a common pursuit (she also aspired to be a playwright). We liked many of the same plays, books and films. I laughed at her jokes, she laughed at mine. I was struck by her contrarian nature, which she backed up with her sharp powers of observation, brutal honesty and deft use of language. Not to mention she looked irresistible in the green 40s vintage flower print dress she wore – presumably one specimen of many vintage garments I fantasized hung in her closet. As festivities wound down at The Church, we fell into a taxicab on 9th Avenue. Half an hour later, on Bedford Avenue in the Greenpoint section of Brooklyn, we fell out of it, and stumbled up the four flights of stairs to her studio apartment.

A few hours later, we lay silent, wide awake, post-coital on her bed, black sky outside morphing into pale blue, the constant dull whoosh of late night New York City giving way to early morning bird chirps, joggers and garbage trucks making their dawn rounds. We'd arrived at a moment familiar to anyone who has indulged in such escapades – when the unspoken question hovers in the air: Should I stay or should I go?

"You should go," she said, just as the question began to form in my mouth.

"Oh." Torn between disappointment and relief, I asked if I could call her, maybe hang out some night, go see a show. She shrugged, wrote her number down on the back of a ConEd envelope, and left it at the foot of her bed.

She watched me dress, expressionless, which made me uneasy. Her gaze made me feel like I might be a forged artifact intruding on her museum. To defuse my discomfort, I confessed my book thieving guilty pleasure, hoping it would amuse her. She stared back at me blankly, pointed to the bookshelf. "Go to town, kid," she said. So I did.

Combing through the titles I noted a lot of overlap between her book collection and mine. One title caught my interest – a paperback copy of *Famous All Over Town* by a writer named Danny Santiago. While skimming through it, my eye caught the manila envelope I described earlier, wedged between her copies of Thomas Mann's *Doctor Faustus* and *Open Secrets* by Alice Munro. I replaced the Santiago book, and pulled the manila envelope off the shelf. "What's this?" I asked. She told me the story. I asked if I could take it as my souvenir. She shrugged, and repeated: "Go to town with it, kid."

I left her apartment, walked the two miles down Bedford Avenue to the apartment where I was crashing in Williamsburg, which at the time was still an urban war zone. I wedged the envelope on my own bookshelf between Camille Paglia's *Sexual Personae* and Plutarch's *Lives of the Noble Greeks and Romans*. It languished there for a decade.

I tried calling "Nicole" the next weekend. I couldn't bring myself to punch in the last digit of her telephone number. I never saw her again.

DELUGE: CHICAGO, 2007

In my family's history, triumph and catastrophe often share the same bed. I'll spare you the catalogue of examples that go back generations. Suffice to say that when things are looking up, it's always a good idea to keep an eye over your shoulder for the rabid dog, cancer tumor, federal agent or assassin that's inevitably stalking your heels.

In 2007, I spent a good part of the winter in Louisville, KY where my play *dark play or stories for boys* premiered at the Humana Festival at Actors Theatre of Louisville. The production was a huge success, and though it did not receive the blessing or invitation to come to New York by *Times* theatre critic Charles Isherwood (who dismissed the entire slate of plays that year as "dispiriting"), the play has enjoyed a fruitful life with many productions in the US and eastern Europe, and continues to be produced with some frequency, at least at the time of this writing, seven years after its premiere.

After the opening, I returned on a high to Chicago – where I live with my wife and two children (I'd successfully sublimated my promiscu-klepto compulsions eight years earlier). I bustled with renewed energy, optimism and a fearless hunger to climb the next mountain, as it were, to write my next play.

We live in a tiny house in Bridgeport, an historic neighborhood in the South Side of Chicago. Built in 1878, seven years after the Great Chicago Fire decimated the city, the house was originally inhabited by Lithuanian immigrants employed by the nearby Union Stockyards (see Upton Sinclair's *The Jungle* for a colorful portrait of the place.) A previous owner of the house illegally converted a detached garage into a livable apartment, complete with kitchenette and bathroom. This was one of the main amenities that at-

tracted my wife and I when we house hunted in 2005 – I could use this space as an office and guests could stay there, affording me (and them) privacy from the child dominated main house. The morning after I returned from Humana, emboldened by my success, I grabbed my keys off the kitchen table and headed back there to write. I unlocked the door, looked inside, muttered to myself "huh" – or something equally idiotic – closed the door and returned to the house. My wife sat in the kitchen working at her computer. She spotted me swaying in the threshold. She must have noticed the dead, faraway look in my eye – she asked, "Carlos, what's wrong." My response: "It's raining in there."

While in Louisville, the hot water heater failed, turning my office into a 400 square foot sauna/terrarium – how long it had been that way, God knows. Long enough for the drywall to warp and buckle. Long enough for a steady rain to drip from every surface. Long enough for a rainforest-like haze to permeate the air. Long enough for horror movie-sized chunks of mold to feed on the futon, the vintage wooden sewing table I used as a desk, the bookshelves. Long enough for boxes and file cabinets filled with drafts of plays, notebooks, files, newspaper clippings I collected and rejection letters I saved, to sweat their ink rendering them illegible. Long enough for entire continents to peel off the globe my wife gave me as a wedding present. Long enough for the accordion file containing every letter ever written to me to disintegrate in my hands when I tried to rescue it from the closet. Every shred of evidence of friendships, relationships, love affairs that

16

shaped me in my twenties – in other words, my personal history – the museum of my life on Earth up to that point – disappeared forever as if my life never happened.

Water doesn't discriminate. It decimated the 2000-plus volumes in my library. Every book – the ones I acquired legitimately, ones I stole, the ones I inherited or were given to me as gifts – lost their angular shape, thickened, bulged. Bindings peeled. Mold spores devoured words. The handful of rare and very pricey volumes (a beautiful, mint English-language first edition of Le Corbusier's 1923 *Towards a New Architecture* that I stole from a previous employer comes to mind) reduced to worthlessness. The external manifestation of my pursuit of knowledge, bloated like the victim of a drowning.

I wrote before about one's accumulated things being a personal museum – a form of psychic DNA. The utter destruction of all the material objects that mattered to me split the double helix of my identity, leaving each strand to blow aimlessly in the wind. If a stranger wanted to visit my museum, they would be chagrined to discover that my life pre-2007 ceased to exist anywhere except inside my deeply flawed memory. If a stranger visited my museum, they would think I came into existence at the age of 36.

A firm that deals with catastrophic fire and water damage gutted the space, tossing my collection of artifacts in a pile on the parking platform behind the house. The pile looked like the ruins left behind by a devastating Midwest twister. My things. A pile. Destined for a landfill somewhere. Waiting for the insurance adjustor to assess it, and assign a dollar amount to an incalculable personal loss.

When I could muster up the courage to bear it, I would sneak to the parking podium out back hoping I could salvage something. One day digging through the wreckage, I broke into tears when I came upon a cheap paperback copy of Edward Albee's *Zoo Story*, given to me by a former lover from many years before. The inscription she'd written on the title page had been smudged into near illegibility: the only words that survived – "You," "I," "inspired." Shaking off this flood of emotion, my eyes landed on the manila envelope with Javier C.'s ill-fated New Dramatists application. Beneath the decimated cheap paperback copy of *Zoo Story*, this resilient little artifact somehow survived. The layers of packing tape waterproofed the contents.

A PHONE CALL DELIVERS GOOD NEWS

In a narrative symmetry usually reserved for novels, plays and films, and almost never the stuff of actual life, two months after the deluge Emily Morse, the Director of Artistic Development at New Dramatists, telephoned me. I'd known Emily for a long time — early in the roaring 90s, we both interned at the legendary but sadly defunct Circle Repertory Company. She also had a hand in the production of my very first play *Subterraneans* in 1994, at Todo Con Nada, a tiny, resource-free but seminal performance space on Ludlow Street, where she served as Associate Artistic Director. Emily was calling with good news: I had been accepted, after five failed attempts, as a New Dramatists resident playwright, with a graduating date of June 2014. Unlike Javier C., I know my applications never got lost, because until that moment the rejection letter arrived like clockwork every May.

Seven years in residence at the finest playwright development organization in the United States seemed ideal. Seven years to dream up new worlds, to bask in the brilliance of my fellow residents, seven years to build on my body of work and take it to a whole new level, seven years of having what so many artists in the field lack — a place to call home. My elation lasted 48 hours. All emotions, like coins, have two faces. If elation was "heads" then dread, fear of failure, and self-loathing lived on the flipside. On that side of the coin, seven years seemed like a mountain of time waiting to be squandered.

I had no question where this dread was coming from.

I was wounded — not that anyone looking at me would know it. I went about life wearing a mask of calm that concealed grief — I lost nearly everything, but there had not been funeral rites to transition me from a life with my things to my life without them. (Only later did I come to understand the function and value of funerals when my mother passed away suddenly and unexpectedly in December of 2009.) I taught my playwriting courses at DePaul University, directed a play by a young student playwright named Ike Holter (on my birthday the cast thoughtfully gave me a box full of books to begin rebuilding my collection), played with my kids, took meetings, ate two and a half meals a day. Inside, though, I lived with a persistent, drone-like ache that wouldn't go away. I had no words. I was in mourning. I'd try to ridicule my empty materialism – it was all just stuff, after all. Compared to the day-to-day catastrophes in the world, my loss amounted to nothing. But looking at it that way that didn't help. All that "stuff" was my history, my *identity*. If my museum was obliterated, who was I anymore – as a think-er, a writer, as a male human in his thirties wandering the earth searching for scraps of meaning? In some ways it felt as if I'd survived an irreversible brain injury. I was alive, I could function, but some fundamental capacity had been wrenched from my grasp. Part of me was dead – robbed of the things that expressed my being, my history existed only as memories in my head. But memory decays, perpetually rewrites itself, invents out of whole cloth entire episodes of life that never actually happened. My history might as well have been a figment of my imagination.

A lot of my writing was destroyed. In those days I wrote mostly by hand. I had electronic copies of the completed versions of my plays (that they survived encoded in 1s and 0s provided little comfort – if solid things can perish so easily, surely flimsy 1s and 0s offer no safety) – but the notebooks, drafts, scribbles on napkins (all of which I hoarded) – all the work that went into the finished plays gone, gone, gone. And being gone, morbid questions about the worth of dreaming up fictions for the stage haunted me and nearly paralyzed me. Was Emily Morse's good news really good news, then? Would the gift of seven years help resurrect what I had lost? Would I reconnect with my lost sense of purpose? Or would it presage more destruction?

Turning my eyes away from the abyss, I carved out a week in July for a self-imposed writing retreat at New Dramatists. I reserved a room in 7th Heaven (one of the great amenities of the organization: the building has three modest rooms up on the third floor where out of town resident writers can stay free of charge). In the face of all the uncer-tainty and anxiety I was feeling, I hoped being there for a spell would help me overcome my grief and point me in a direction of renewal.

I can't explain what compelled me, but on the eve of my trip to New York as I fin-ished packing, I grabbed the envelope containing Javier C.'s ill-fated New Dramatists application and stuffed it in my suitcase.

I spent my first three days in the Church avoiding the task at hand. The writing went nowhere. Everything I set down rang hollow, false. Instead of facing the blank page, I squandered hour after hour chain-smoking on the stoop of New Dramatists. Late night on the second day I tried the last number I had of an ex-girlfriend, expecting that it would be long disconnected. To my surprise, she answered. I apologized for breaking up with her by phone on Christmas Eve in 1997. She accepted my apology, then told me to fuck off and hung up.

At dusk on the third day, butt firmly planted on New Dramatists' stoop, my eyes landed on an elderly man on the sidewalk across the street. He must have been in his 80s. Rail thin, his plaid shirt and khaki pants hung off him like his body was a coat hanger. His shoulders were so hunched it appeared as if his head was a cancer growing from his sternum. He moved at a sloth's pace, heading west – a creature moving in slow motion trapped in a world where everything else moved at warp speed. At the pace he moved, it would take him half an hour to reach Tenth Avenue. I imagined his arrival to his run down tenement and his slow, pained assault of the five-flight Mount Everest separating him from the safety of his apartment. Who was this man? Did he have family? Friends? Did he have anyone to look after him? (I suspected, because of his advanced age, most of the dramatis personae in his life either were dead or near death.) What had he done with the time he'd been given? What would he do with the little time he had left? Had he chased after some vision for his life, only to realize too late that he painted himself into a corner chasing pipe dreams? If he died in the night, how long would it take for someone to notice? And what in God's name was he doing still living in a crappy neighborhood in an unforgiving city that reserves its most cruel indifference for its oldest, weakest and least productive citizens? What did *his* museum look like? Would any of it survive him? Would I become him some day?

He haunted me for the rest of the day.

Late that night, after several frustrating hours trying to write, I packed it in for the night. I headed up to my room in 7th Heaven. As I prepared for bed, the strange manila envelope on the desk caught my eye. I'd only ever given the most cursory glance at its contents – when I did, it filled me with dread – so I can't say for certain what compelled me to open it and dig inside. I spent the rest of the night in the library looking through all the materials and reading the plays, exceptional works which were written in the vein of "Bipolar Realism" (Javier C.'s description). What happened to this guy? Why had his work been ignored? The application materials revealed a brilliant mind offset by a healthy dose of insanity lurking in the shadows, waiting to pounce. Was he still writing? Does he still live at the return address on the envelope (just five blocks from New Dramatists)? Does he live in New York City anymore? What did his museum look like? Was this envelope his museum? If so, what kind of life could I infer from it? I felt a door open inside me.

At dawn, I strolled up to 49th Street to the building where Javier lived. His name was not on the buzzer panel. Listed next to apartment 4C, a woman's name. I buzzed on the off chance he might still live there. A woman's groggy, bothered, Puerto Rican accented voice answered. I asked if Javier was around. No one here by that name, followed by a shower of curses for waking her up.

Google searches for Javier and his plays proved that even in this day and age there exist those few that leave no footprints behind. I visited the website Doollee.com, a free online guide to modern English-language playwrights from 1956 to the present. Javier C.'s name does not appear among the 47,000+ playwrights. His plays are absent from the 160,000+ works accounted for. I called Morgan Jenness, my mentor from my days working in the literary office of The Public Theater in the 90s. She's a living encyclopedia on everything to do with contemporary plays and playwrights. Morgan knew nothing of Javier or his work.

Curiosity devolved to obsession. I needed to know who this man was, if more of his work existed somewhere, if I could find him, if I could rescue these works from obscurity. For the next seven years – the full duration of my residency at New Dramatists – incapable of writing anything of my own, I set aside my theatrical ambitions and explorations in order to excavate everything I could about Javier's life, his work and the loss he suffered, and to build, in the pages of this book, a small museum to document it.

Every museum needs a curator – who is either blessed or cursed by the task of organizing a museum's contents into an assemblage that conveys something resembling meaning. Whether it is a blessing or curse depends in some measure on the comprehensiveness and quality of the material left behind for the curator to assemble. I've visited world-class museums that seek to convince us that its version of history's grand sweep is correct because they possess the goods to prove it. I've also visited many small town museums in the most out of the way places, built on artifacts acquired at estate sales, replicas and forgeries – their narratives sag like skin hanging from a skeleton missing most of its bones, their placards obfuscate, riddled as they are with questionable facts, discrepancies and misspellings, and their message speaks less about the grand sweep of history, but more to a cry for help, a shout against a gale force headwind to a world that doesn't care: "We existed!"

Javier himself, in *A Thick Description of Harry Smith*, his final viable work, addresses this dilemma through the character of the Curator, a woman driven to the brink of madness and despair trying to make heads or tails of the seemingly random artifacts left behind by the very real Harry Everett Smith. The artifacts in and of themselves may or may not mean something. That they exist together in boxes suggests a web of relationships waiting to be deciphered. Often in the process of digging up Javier's bones and attempting to reanimate them, I've looked to her struggle for guidance, inspiration and plain old commiseration.

As curator of the small museum that exists within these pages, I relied on the scantest of materials to lay its foundation: a battered envelope with three half written plays, a manifesto both literally and figuratively illegible; a series of maddening, and in the end, frightening interactions with one Professor Emiliano Kurtz, whose book, *The Mystique of*

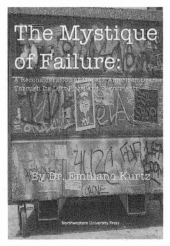

Failure: Reconsidering Modern American Drama Through its Lost Playwrights and Plays, contains a chapter on Javier based on dubious research; and a handful of other clues that led me to dead end to discovery to dead end. A curator faced with such insurmountable obstacles has two choices: 1) give up, or 2) play archaeologist and infer a civilization from the pottery shards and bones you've dug up. During my seven years at New Dramatists, I built the museum contained in these pages. The thought of giving up was not infrequent. In the end, however, the shards Javier left behind were too important to me to leave buried in the dirt. The picture still remains woefully incomplete. Perhaps, however, the existence of this small museum will spur readers to pick up where I leave off to embark on a more thorough excavation.

Chicago, January 2015

7   Transom window above the entrance of New Dramatists. Photo by Carlos Murillo.

8   Exterior of Rudy's Bar & Grill on 9th Avenue between 44th & 45th Streets. Photo by Carlos Murillo.

Basement of New Dramatists, scene of the discovery of Javier C.'s lost New Dramatists application. Photo by Carlos Murillo.

9   Low-quality reproduction of forged Edward Albee signature. Photo by Carlos Murillo.

Bronze statue of Giordano Bruno (1548-1600) by Ettore Ferrari at Campo de' Fiori, Rome. Bruno was an Italian Dominican friar, philosopher, mathematician, poet and atrologer who was tried for theological heresy and burnt at the stake in 1600. Photo in public domain.

10 The Fortune. Photo by Carlos Murillo.

11 Todd London, New Dramatists' Artistic Director from 1996-2014. Courtesy Todd London. Photo by Susan Johann.

13 Row houses on Prospect Avenue in Prospect Heights, Brooklyn. Photo in public domain.

16 Exterior of my home in the Bridgeport neighborhood in Chicago. Photo by Carlos Murillo.

The guest house that doubles as my writing space in the rear of the property. Photo by Carlos Murillo.

17 Insurance company photos of gutted office space. Photo by Carlos Murillo.

18 Exterior of 167 Ludlow Street, former site of Todo Con Nada, a legendary basement performance space that was evicted to make way for The Dark Room Bar. Photo by Michael Minn.

Entrance to The Dark Room Bar, which occupies the former site of Todo Con Nada. Photo by Michael Minn.

21 Exterior of the apartment building where Javier C. lived on West 49th Street between 9th and 10th Avenues. Photo by Carlos Murillo.

The buzzer outside the building where Javier C. lived, according to the return address on the envelope. Photo by Carlos Murillo.

22 Birgit Huppuch as The Curator in A Thick Description of Harry Smith presented by P73 at The Culture Project in June 2012. Photo by Carlos Murillo.

23 Cover image of Emiliano Kurtz's 2007 book. Photo by Carlos Murillo.

DIAGRAM OF A PAPER AIRPLANE

INTRODUCTION

Kip Fagan, Freelance Director

Carlos Murillo likes to drive people insane.

It's sometimes intentional, sometimes un-, but he derives great pleasure from it either way. In polite company he'll profess the opposite, but his mad cackle as someone's eyes spiral inward when confronted with a particularly vertigo-inducing plot revelation gives him away. He wants you to live in the insanity that his characters live in. He wants you to feel as unsteady, as unstable, as unsure of what's real and what's bullshit as the recurring cast of his nightmare-logic trilogy are forced to feel. I think he feels bad that he makes his characters feel so insane, so he wants you to keep them company.

The thing about this particular brand of Murillo insanity, though: *it's an immensely pleasurable place to live.*

Carlos' plays trap you in their logic and don't let go, in the way that Martin Scorsese's *After Hours* traps you, or a Roberto Bolaño novel, or the first season of *Twin Peaks*. And once you're trapped, you become a co-conspirator with his characters in trying to solve their existential mysteries, finish their Sisyphean collaborations, reconcile their irreconcilable feuds. And once you're trapped inside this trilogy, you'll probably start to feel a mixture of resentful admiration, fond exasperation, and hopeless love for its central character: the elusive and obscure playwright Javier C.

But at first you'll be on the outside looking in.

Diagram of a Paper Airplane is the first play in the trilogy, though in true Carlos fashion, it's the last sequence of events in a strict chronological sense. He starts at the end, with the fallout and the ruins. The play begins with a man named Alvaro talking to an unseen academic interlocutor about Javier C.'s unfinished *magnum opus*:

> You askin me
> if it survived? If it
> still exists somewhere out in the big bad world?
> *Shit.*

Maybe the question you *should* be askin,

Mistah P. Aitch.D Candidate, Columbia University: Did *Diagram of a Paper Airplane* exist at *all*?

And so the play named after an imaginary, unfinished play begins by questioning the existence of the imaginary, unfinished play in question. This opening announces that the world isn't solid under our feet. And as we meet the other collaborators and fellow-travelers — Herman, sputtering paranoically into a recording device, and Valerie, the den mother full of compassion one second and volatility the next — we begin to piece together the group's splintered past, and present.

The past: a combustible, anarchic ensemble of theatre artists idealistically committed to the irascible, unpredictable maybe-genius at its center. Javier C. and his notion of a new and dangerous theatre of "bipolar realism." Alcohol-fueled fights, polemical screaming-matches, bursts of bewildering inspiration. And, finally, a disappearance so shattering it splinters the group irretrievably.

The present: a reunion of sorts on the occasion of Javier C.'s death. A cosmic practical joke where the dead author assembles his former compatriots, now wrecked and haunted, to read his lost play. And a damaged young woman who begins to learn the truth behind the wreck and the haunt.

Formally and structurally, *Diagram of a Paper Airplane* (Carlos' version, not Javier's) hews closer to traditional play-making than the freewheeling *Your Name Will Follow You Home* or the mad, rambling medicine show *A Thick Description of Harry Smith*. This allows Carlos to sink deep emotional talons into a reader or viewer. We are compelled to mythologize the absent Javier and the (brilliant? crackpot?) work the group created together. This mythology both deepens and breaks apart in the dizzying meta-narratives of the other two pieces, so *Diagram* is crucial as a lodestar for the trilogy. It's as *firma* as Carlos' *terra* gets.

If some mad and inspired theatre company were to ask me how to most ideally produce the trilogy, the only true answer is an insane one. Though the plays function brilliantly as individual entities, to really grasp the ferocious imaginative reach of the trilogy one would have to experience a same-day marathon of all three plays, starting with *Diagram*, followed by *Harry Smith*, and concluding with *Your Name*. And after the nine or so hours of living with this crazed assemblage, the audience would be fed a strong cocktail and told to get comfy, because the actors were demanding to perform *Diagram of a Paper Airplane* again.

I can already hear Carlos' cackle from behind the risers as the shell-shocked audience settles back into their seats and the actor playing Alvaro meanders on stage to ask:

You askin me

if it survived? If it

still exists somewhere out in the big bad world?

Shit.

Maybe the question you *should* be askin, Mistah P.Aitch.D Candidate, Columbia University: Did *Diagram of a Paper Airplane* exist at *all?*

Norfolk, Nebraska 2014

NOTES ON IMAGES, BY PAGE

27 This image is in the public domain in the United States because it is a work prepared
by an officer or employee of the United States Government as part of that person's
official duties under the terms of Title 17, Chapter 1, Section 105 of the US Code.
See Copyright.

28 Kip Fagan during a music rehearsal for a workshop of The Javier Plays at New Dramatists in March 2014. Pictured left to right: Lucas Papaelias, Kate Ferber, Kip
Fagan and Joe Jung. Hidden behind Joe Jung – Paul Whitty. Photo by Carlos Murillo.

DIAGRAM OF A PAPER AIRPLANE

Characters

(in order of appearance)

Alvaro	49
Herman	53
Valerie	50
Lila	28
Mario	29

A minor character, the FedEx Man, is played by the same actor that plays Mario.

Setting

Various kitchens in tenement apartments in NYC. Hells Kitchen, Lower East Side, Washington Heights.

1. The Lonesome Death of Javier C.

ONE

Morning. The kitchen table in Alvaro's tenement apartment in Washington Heights. On the table, an unopened pack of Kools, an empty ashtray, a microphone, a digital recording device. Alvaro talks to an unseen interviewer.

ALVARO: You askin me
    if it survived? If it
    still exists somewhere out in the big bad world?

Shit.

Maybe the question you *should* be askin,
Mistah P. Aitch. D Candidate, Columbia University:
Did *Diagram of a Paper Airplane* exist at *all*?

TWO

The wee hours. The kitchen table in Herman's Hell's Kitchen tenement apartment. On the table: an old telephone — the kind with a dial and obsolete ring, and a portable cassette recorder, also obsolete. Herman in his pajamas presses the record button.

HERMAN: Valerie *P.*

telephoned at 2:35 this morning.

My telephone hardly rings anymore —
People stopped calling long ago.
To most people,
A telephone call that time of night —
How *intrusive*. How *thoughtless*. How *rude*.
But not me, no.
I sleep very little these days.
For all practical purposes
2:35 in the morning is quarter past noon is six forty five pm is three minutes to midnight.

What *did* arouse my curiosity vis-a-vis the phone call
Was the fact that Valerie P. bothered to make it.
You see:
Two and a half decades have passed since Valerie P., Javier C. and I
Played at being *pioneers*. Co-*colonists*
Inhabiting a tiny but shared slice of
Terra Incognita.
In other words:
We stopped being friends.
A long.
Time.
Ago.
Furthermore
When we were friends,
If Valerie P. and I ever *did* speak *telephonically*,
It was because *my* digits reached for hers.

Yes,

Valerie P. telephoned at 2:35 this morning

To inform me that

Javier C.

Her estranged husband

(and father to their mutually estranged daughter

Lila

Hhhhhhhh

Lila

Herman clicks off the recorder, gathers himself, clicks it back on.

Valerie P. telephoned at 2:35

To inform me that Javier C.

Her estranged husband

(father to their mutually estranged daughter

Lila C. dash P.)

"Left the building" as it were.

This past Tuesday.

Javier C. *drowned.*

In a *freak.*

Flash.

Flood.

Somewhere in the wilds of Northern New Mexico,

Where *supposedly*

he was

immersed (forgive the pun)

in "*research*"

for a play he first

threatened to write

Two and a half decades ago

A play he *claimed* to have been *actually* writing

For the last seventeen years:

Diagram of a Paper Airplane.

Long awaited follow up to his *oeuvre* of lost plays:

The *seminal Death of a Liberal*, the genuinely *spooky*

The Rich Also Cry, the complete *mind* fuck,

A Thick Description of Harry Smith,

And his unpublished, book-length manifesto

To Murder Whimsy:

Bipolar Realism and the Future of American Playwriting.

Works for the theatre noteworthy for their undeserved

obscurity.

Works which have not been performed in

many, many years.

When they *were* performed,

they appeared in venues only the most generous would call *theatres*.

Yes,

once upon a time

We pursued the quixotic endeavor of putting on *plays*.

Which I expect surprises you:

That before I became an historian,

Before I built my formidable reputation,

And *long* before said reputation endured a gang rape by a cabal of

Certain powerful, well-connected individuals,

I.

Did.

Theatre.

I was the *dramaturge*.

(If you have no idea what that means, *Google* it.)

Yes, once upon a time, Javier dreamed we could "resurrect a dying animal."

We believed in him. He was *that. good*.

But like so many dreams,

Ours was rudely interrupted by certain crimes of omission.

Anyway. Hearing the news from Valerie P., the tips of my fingers went cold.

Montage of images exploded in my brain: Moonless night. Arctic Circle.

Japanese fishing boat torn in half by an iceberg.

Japanese fishermen slaughtering each other over pieces of flotsam

While their flag burned against the night sky.

A small child sinking under the surface of the sea.

Haunted, Herman clicks off the recorder. The haunt passes. He resumes recording.

Valerie P. had more on her *agenda*:

Following her account

of the freakish circumstances surrounding Javier C.'s *death,*

She proceeded to ask me a *favor.*

Would I telephone *Alvaro M.*, tell *him* the news.

Alvaro M., American playwright (of *Latin* American descent)

Fellow traveler-slash-casualty of our colonial exploits of yore.

I told her under no circumstances would I do such a thing.

I told her: "For all I know Alvaro M. could be dead too,

Besides: I don't have his telephone number."

"*Liar,*" she said. "Liar, liar, *liar.*"

Don't think I've forgotten Herman, about your *habits*."

"Habits?"

"The date books, the recordings, the index card files, the *lists*, the *address books* — "

I tried to reason with her:

"Valerie, Val Valie The likelihood Alvaro M. hasn't *moved*

In the mountain of time that's passed between — "

"Where are you sitting, Herman?"

"In my kitchen."

"You made a meal for me in that kitchen once upon a time."

"Point. being?"

"The kitchen I'm sitting in is the same one you wept in ten days straight when Maria

R. left you. Once upon a —"

"*Point. being.*"

"You haven't moved. I haven't moved. In that *'mountain of time'*

So there's every reason to believe Alvaro *M.* is festering away in his kitchen too."

Pause.

Then Valerie *reeeaaalllly* crossed the line:

"Besides … It's what *Javi* would have *wanted*."

Javi.

Which was *cheap*.

For her to play the "what-the-dead-guy-would-have-wanted" card.

I told her as much, I said:

"Valerie that is just plain cheap I would have expected more from you."

Valerie appears in her own kitchen talking on a cordless telephone.

VALERIE: You don't really know me anymore, do you … Herman?

The sound of a telephone click. Valerie disappears.

HERMAN: That fucking passive aggressive

Herman hits the record button on his tape recorder. Herman clicks off the recorder.

HERMAN: So yes, I dug out

The *address book*.

Dialed Alvaro M.'s telephone number.

THREE

The wee hours. A young couple asleep on a beat up fold out couch in a tenement apartment in Greenpoint, Brooklyn. The young man snores. The woman stirs and mutters in her sleep. An alarm clock on the side table reads 2:34 am.

YOUNG WOMAN: No.

    Please.

    Go away.

    I don't want you here.

    I won't listen.

    I won't go

    I won't —

When the time on the clock changes to 2:35 am, the young woman darts upright. She looks at the young man next to her. She rises from the bed as if under a spell.

FOUR

The wee hours. Valerie's kitchen in her Lower East Side apartment. On the table a large mag-nifying glass on a stand, a cloth with strands of human hair on it, tweezers, scalpels and other surgically precise instruments. A half-eaten bowl of Cheerios. In front of the magnifying glass a metal stand on top of which is an object barely visible to the naked eye. Valerie's face appears huge, distorted by the lens. She works on the minuscule object with her instruments while talking on a cordless phone.

VALERIE: Yes, *that* Herman.

Come on, Josephine, how many Hermans are there?

Herman The Human Sledgehammer.

Herman The Human Sandpaper Machine.

Herman The Human Box Cutter.

Yes, if you want to resort to vulgarities, he's that too.

But you know something?

Truth be told Herman's one thing to me he isn't to anyone else.

He's sweet.

No no no no no no no … listen:

He calls.

Couple of hours ago.

Right, who calls that time of night?

He calls to tell me he "heard." About Javier.

Wanted to

"check in"

See how I was taking the news.

If I "needed" anything —

Right? Talking as if I was still married to that prick, as if there was some sort of feeling some sort of I don't know what

Anyway

After assuring him I'm "okay," I don't "need" anything

— that I'm *relieved* —

(No of course I didn't say that can you imagine?) —

There's this silence

Followed by that Herman sigh …

Herman appears in his kitchen, recorder off, staring at nothing.

HERMAN: Hhhhhhhhhh

Herman disappears.

VALERIE: That's right *THE* Herman sigh

That says "I've got a lot more on my *mi-ind*, get ready for the *on-slaaaaught*."

You know me

I took the bait.

Herman's a Human Sledgehammer, I'm a Human *Fish*.

Always spellbound by the worm on its hook,

Always subject to a bunch of idiotic fishermen celebrating their catch.

And when the fisherman (or woman – you know that story) sees I'm not fat enough?

They toss me in the sea to sink beneath a trail of my own blood.

No I'm not self-dramatizing, Josi. It's true. But I recover, I recover, cause that's who
I am that's what you *do* that's what you're supposed to *do*.

Anyway, he sighed. That Herman sigh.

Herman appears in his kitchen, recorder off, staring at nothing.

HERMAN: Hhhhhhhhhh

Herman disappears.

VALERIE: I said, "Herman? You okay?"

He said: "Were you intending to keep me in the dark?"

"You found out on your own, you didn't need me to break the news."

You know what he said?

"That's just *mean*.

Valerie."

Followed by a tirade,

Catalogue of wrongs *I'd* done *him*.

All that concern, am I okay, do I need anything

Next minute –

Know what he called me?

A passive aggressive, self-involved, dried up *orifice*.

Oh, I told him

"Eat me, Herman, I'm hanging up!"

"No no no no no no

Please. Valerie Val Vali I'm

Sorry I"

That's right one second shock and awe, next he's raining sweetness on me.

No, he *is* sweet –

That's my point –

In fact, he can be downright maudlin –

Herman on the telephone. The earpiece has a suction cup wire tap attached.

HERMAN: Valerie?

VALERIE: Yes, Herman?

HERMAN: Do you think?

Javier's in heaven or in hell?

The sound of Valerie choking on cereal.

HERMAN: Valerie?

Are you okay?

Wait: Are you *eating*?

Herman disappears. Valerie's phone conversation with Josephine continues.

VALERIE: Yes, Josephine, I fixed myself a bowl of cereal when he called

I'd been working, it was late I have deadlines I was hungry phone calls with Herman

can become

Epic

Hearing *Herman* ask that:

Do I think Javier is in heaven or hell?

I choked on my Cheerios, okay?

Heaven? Hell? Javier? *Herman?* What the *fuck?*

But sweet, right? In that awkward? Wooden? Herman-like way?

No, I didn't answer I did that thing *teachers* do?

What do they call it? Made it a "teachable moment"?

You know, when some little fucker of a student asks a question you don't know the answer to? Throw the question right back.

Herman and Valerie back on the phone.

VALERIE: What do *you* think, Herman? Do *you* think Javier's gone to heaven or hell?

HERMAN: *Hhhhhhhh …*

Herman disappears. Valerie back to conversation with Josephine.

VALERIE: Yeah. He answered.

Although …

I have no idea what he said.

Soon as he started yammering

my mind wandered off, Josi

like I was

walking down a hallway with three million doors.

Each with a different question written on it:

Is he in heaven?

Is he in hell?

Or somewhere between?

What was he doing in New Mexico, was he still —

Nothing.

Nothing, Josephine.

Looking. I was going to say "looking," "was he still looking," *okay?*

I'm sorry I didn't mean to it's just …

Wait: are you seriously asking me that?

Let me put it this way, Josephine:

Long time ago?

Javier wrote a fragment of some play he never finished

something about

paper airplanes

It was about visiting purgatory. After his death.

All I can tell you, sweetie? if he landed in some kind of purgatory?

God help him if it was like the one he imagined.

Herman appears again.

HERMAN: What are they going to do with his body?

VALERIE: What do you mean?

HERMAN: The body.

Javier's body?

What are they going to do with it?

VALERIE: "They." What are "they" going to do // with his

HERMAN: That's what I am ask//ing

VALERIE: What are you implying?

HERMAN: Nothing?

VALERIE: Because what I hear lurking underneath that "*they,*" Herman, is "*you*"

HERMAN: I mean to imply no // such

VALERIE: That's always the substitute "*they,*" right? Meaning "*You.*"

"What are *you,* Valerie, going to do with the body?" What about "*we*" Herman? No, of course, that would be too *painful,* would mean having to *dig,* right?

HERMAN: I'm just asking // a

VALERIE: My god you really are a motherfucker. You think I'm still tethered to him. You think I *owe* him something. "*What are they going to do with // his body?*"

HERMAN: I was simply asking a // question …

VALERIE: I don't know what *they* are going to – For all I know he has another family to take care // of

HERMAN: Unlikely

VALERIE: I've got to // go

HERMAN: Look, Valerie … Val … Valie …

All I am saying is
I know any obligation you had to him
ended
When
It *ended*
But at the same time certain bonds

VALERIE: God you're an ass//hole

HERMAN: *Certain bonds*
Do transcend failed marriages.

VALERIE: Good bye Her//man

HERMAN: Wait: does Alvaro know?

VALERIE: Christ, how the hell would I // know if Alv

HERMAN: Don't you think Alvaro
Of all people
Should know?

VALERIE: Herman …

HERMAN: Shouldn't someone call him?

VALERIE: "Someone." First "they," now "someone"
For all we know, Alvaro could be dead too.

HERMAN: True,
But if you were him … And you were alive
Would you want to be kept in the dark?

VALERIE: Um. Yeah.

HERMAN: Someone has to call him. It's the *humane* thing to // do.

VALERIE: You're like a dog with a bone.
Go ahead. Call him.
But don't say I didn't warn you.
Last time I saw Alvaro he was

Sick.

HERMAN: All the more reason someone should call him, don't you think?

VALERIE: Frankly, I could give a shit.

HERMAN: Wow. Valerie. I would have expected more from you.

VALERIE: You don't really know me anymore, do you … Herman?

HERMAN: I'm calling him.

VALERIE: That tone worries me, Herman.

HERMAN: What tone?

VALERIE: I hear morbid glee in your voice.

HERMAN: What kind of person do you think I am?

VALERIE: I think …

    For the most part? You,

    Herman, are a decent human being.

    But I know Herman well enough to know

    He can be a twelve-year-old boy.

    That's captured a little frog in a jar.

    Dying to know what kind of

    Stresses

    Its little body can take.

HERMAN: Are you comparing Alvaro to a helpless animal?

VALERIE: Oh, // god.

HERMAN: Because I wonder how Alvaro would // feel

VALERIE: One thing I know about Alvaro? He's more civilized than some savages I know.

HERMAN: I'm calling him.

VALERIE: Go ahead.

HERMAN: Valerie … one more question, I'll leave you alone …

    What about Lila?

    Does Lila know?

    Or do you plan on keeping your daughter in the dark about this one too?

VALERIE: Good bye Herman.

Herman disappears. Valerie continues her conversation with Josephine.

VALERIE: And that was that, Josi.

What?

Lila?

Of course she knows. Josephine: what kind of person do you think I am?

FIVE

The apartment in Brooklyn. The clock reads 3:17 am. The young man still deep in sleep. The young woman, fully clothed, watches the sleeping man. She leans down, touches his chest, caresses his face and kisses him. She takes her cell phone from the side table and slips it into her bag. She leaves.

SIX

Herman's kitchen. He talks into the recorder.

HERMAN: So yes, I dug out

> The *address book*
>
> Dialed Alvaro M.'s telephone number.

Herman attaches a suction cup wire tap to his receiver, plugs it into his recorder, presses record and dials. Alvaro answers the phone in his kitchen.

ALVARO: Ahhhl-*Oh.*

HERMAN: I hear a voice I'll be damned

> It's *Alvaro M.'s* voice
>
> Sounds older –
>
> Little less …
>
> *Alive*
>
> Than I remember …
>
> But then: we're all a little less alive every day, aren't we?

> Alvaro? Is that you?

ALVARO: Who's calling?

HERMAN: Herman.

ALVARO: Herman // *Fin—*

HERMAN: Yes.

ALVARO: Shit.

HERMAN: It's

> good to hear your voice.

ALVARO: Wish I could say the same.

HERMAN: Soooo … are you well? How's the … scribbling?

ALVARO: Scuse me?

HERMAN: The writing. How's // the … ?

ALVARO: I was just pullin my next Play out my ass when you called.

> Hey, didn't I read something bout you? Like what?
>
> Nine? Ten years ago?
>
> In *The Post? Weekly World News? National Enquirer?*

HERMAN: Alvaro …

ALVARO: No no no that's right,

> *New York Times.*
>
> What they call it? The *pay-puh* uh record?

HERMAN: Alvaro …

ALVARO: Didn't they sack you from some fancy pruh-fessuh-ship cause // like

HERMAN: For heaven's sake // Alvaro

ALVARO: Didn't they sack you cause

> You became like a
>
> Holocaust denier or some // shit like that?

HERMAN: Oh. Please. Alvaro // that's just

ALVARO: I read that I was like "Man,

> Always knew Aitch was one fucked up individual // but … "

HERMAN: Alvaro …

ALVARO: Cause I didn't know PhD meant Pruh-fessuh, Holocaust Denial

HERMAN: *Stop it.*

ALVARO: Least you got a nice settlement out of it – always wondered how many dollar bills are in an "undisclosed sum a // money"

HERMAN: *Alvaro …*

ALVARO: *That's* living the American Dream, right? – wish somebody'd pay me an undisclosed sum a money // to go away

HERMAN: *ENOUGH.*

ALVARO: Why you dialing my number after all these years?

> You getting nostalgic cause you about to die or something?

You thinking: "While I'm countin the days I got left on this piece a shit planet

Why not make some phone calls? Right some a my wrongs in case there *is*

a Man // Upstairs?"

HERMAN: Hhhhhhhhh//hhh

ALVARO: *Big* sigh. *Heavy* sigh. I remember that sigh, Aitch,

An I distinctly remember never liking what came out your mouth *after* // that sigh.

HERMAN: Alvaro. Look: I didn't want to call.

I'm calling because

I just received a telephone call – out of the blue – from Valerie.

ALVARO: Name don't ring a bell.

HERMAN: Valerie // you know who

ALVARO: I might a known a *Mallory* once, but a // Valerie?

HERMAN: *Valerie*. Javier's // ex –

ALVARO: Cut to the chase, Aitch.

HERMAN: Hhhhhh//hhh

ALVARO: For motherfucking // sake stop it with that *sighing*

HERMAN: Okay okay okay.

Are you sitting down?

ALVARO: No I'm riding the final stage a the Tour de France, Aitch.

Out with it.

HERMAN: Valerie called

To tell me that Javier

Passed

on Tuesday.

ALVARO: *"Passed."*

HERMAN: That's correct.

ALVARO: What'd he pass? Kidney stone? The ketchup?

More a them warped motherfuckin genes a his – now *that* would be a // tragedy.

51

HERMAN: Alvaro …

ALVARO: Cause what's the saying? First time a mistake? Second time bad luck? Third time—

HERMAN: Alvaro!

ALVARO: *Ohhhhh* … you mean he *died*. Why didn't you just come out an say // that?

HERMAN: *Hhhhhhhhhh//hh*

ALVARO: That sigh, man, that *fucking* sigh —
    Wait: are you recording this?

HERMAN: No of course not.
    Look, Alvaro, I know how you must // feel

Shift. Alvaro's kitchen. Early afternoon. Alvaro recounts the phone call to the unseen interviewer.
Alvaro smokes.

ALVARO: An I'm like …
    That why you calling me? Tell me *that?*
    An he's like

HERMAN: I thought you of all people   ALVARO: "I thought you of all people
    Would want to know   would want to know."

ALVARO: In that motherfucking patronizing voice a his.
    I'm like: "Thankyouverymuch for ruining my day."
    An he's like …

HERMAN: Tragic isn't it   ALVARO: "Horrible, isn't it?"

ALVARO: I'm like …
    Sorry.
    That's just not something that registers on my horror-meet-uh
    I'm glad that motherfucker is dead.

HERMAN: If you're so glad he's gone

ALVARO: He said "*gone*." Not "*dead*." // What an asshole

HERMAN: If you're so glad he's gone
    How is it I ruined your day?

ALVARO: By telling me that bitch was still alive til last week.

    Cause far as I'm concerned?

    Javier died a *looooong* time ago

    The *thought*

    He was still out there

    Slithering around somewhere

    That he still *existed* in the world

    Til Tuesday?

    That just fucks me up like you wouldn't believe.

HERMAN: His reaction was so

    Shocking

    I was dumbstruck I said something

    feeble like

    "Alvaro, I

    I'm dumbstruck I

    Didn't know you felt // that way."

ALVARO: Now you do, Mr. Herman F. Dumbstruck.

HERMAN: Look, I wouldn't have called if Valerie hadn't asked // me to …

ALVARO: What? Yoko Ono too delicate to dial the phone all by herself?

HERMAN: That's just …

ALVARO: Look Aitch:

    In like three seconds?

    You an your tape recorder gonna hear a click, // okay?

HERMAN: I'm not // rec

ALVARO: When you hear that click

    I want you

    An your tape recorder

    To understand in no uncertain terms what I mean:

    Bye Bye. Fuck off.

    Don't

Ever. call this number again.

Comprende, *compadre?*

One

Two …

Three.

HERMAN: The line went dead.

Herman disappears. Alvaro talks to the unseen interviewer.

ALVARO: I used to smoke Kools.

I loved smoking.

Sometimes? I'd sit in my kitchen all day?

An just smoke.

But I quit cold turkey like a year ago.

Woke up one morning

Went in the kitchen do my first chore a the day

Which was like

smoke five Kools drink a pot a coffee stare out the window?

But that day I was like …

"E-nuff. No more. I'm tired.

Gotta find me something else to look forward to than the next Kool."

Cause that's how bad shit had got — sit in my kitchen all day

Only time I left the apartment was to replenish my pack.

So I light up, thinking:

This is my last. Kool. *ever.*

I start thinking about all the Kools I ever smoked

I look at the Kool I'm smoking

"You're the last one, baby … "

Kind a like breakin up with someone?

But trying to let em down gentle?

Like, "Aw, yeah, we had some good times, right?

Remember that time we went to Coney Island in like

December?

That time I got in a fight with my brother on Thanksgiving

I came over you made me potato salad?"
But inside you're thinking
"Taxi meter's runnin, Gotta split."
I *stubbed* that last Kool out.
Cause in the end you gotta be *hard*
You gotta be like
Japanese about it.

I pick up the pack,
Zippo, ashtray,
Go over to the kitchen window
Which has like a million dollar view uh the airshaft?
Pile a garbage at the bottom of it?
I'm like:
"Bye Kools. Nice knowing you.
Bye ashtray. Have a good life.
Bye Zippo. You be cool now."

I been clean since.
I keep myself honest.
Five minutes after I threw my paraphernalia down the airshaft?
Went down to the corner bought me one last pack.
Brought it back in my kitchen.
put it in the drawer where I keep the knives.
Temptation's three feet away in my knife drawer —
But I *don't* succumb
Willpower, baby. I am the master a my own twisted desires.

Sometimes?
When shit gets real bad?
I open that knife drawer
Take out that pack a Kools
Lay it on the table
Gentle
I look at it

Touch it

Sometimes —

I take one a the Kools out the pack

Smell it slip it in my mouth

Roll it round my lips

Got the Zippo in my hand

Thumb on the flint wheel all twitchy

like I'm Christopher Walken playin Russian Roulette

Then I'm like

HA! Motherfucker

You don't own me bitch.

Lonely, isn't it? All alone in the dark with the knives?

A year.

Then that bitch Herman calls?

To tell me Javier "*passed*"?

I hang up I'm like

Night a the Living Dead.

Zombie-beeline to the knife drawer.

Take out my Kools.

Light one up.

First Kool in a year

"Hi old friend. Nice to see you. I missed you, baby."

Five Kools later?

My head starts trippin out —

How'd Javi die?

Not like it matters — you die you die,

Don't matter if it's by heart attack or shark attack.

But how'd Javi die?

Was Javi sick?

Was Javi alone?

Did Javi do it to himself?

Did Javi have a place to live or was he in the streets?

Was someone gonna bury him? Or was Javi gonna end up in Potter's Field?
And why the fuck am I still calling him Javi?

His little girl ... Lila ... (though she must not be so little no more)
Does she know?
She even care?

An what the fuck did Javi mean by that?
"*Whimsical.*"
Last motherfucking thing he said to me before he split — "*whimsical.*"
What. the *fuck*. did he mean by that?

Bitch was like that. Always had at the tip a his tongue
The one word that could pull that thread
Unravel the whole muthafuckin sweater ...
"*Whimsical*" ...

Next thing I know? I reach for a Kool, pack is empty.
Year I been away from this shit.
That bitch Herman calls?
Two hours later whole pack is gone.

Now I got two questions for *you*, Mistuh Pee. Aitch. Dee Candidate, Columbia University ...

One: How'd you find me?
An two:
Where the *fuck*
Did you find his plays?

SEVEN

The wee hours. The young woman by the front entrance of a Hell's Kitchen tenement. She is about to buzz an apartment, but instead reaches for her cell phone and dials.

YOUNG WOMAN: Hi, sweet one. It's me.

I

know you won't get this?

Not til … Much later. But …

I need you to know that

I love you.

That's the first thing the *important* thing …

I didn't want to wake you I

I know you'll wonder –

How can I love you

When you'll wake up

On a fold out couch

in some strange apartment

Me not next to you …

Martha and Bonnie'll be there –

they'll see you they'll see the empty …

You'll think

"She can't possibly love me.

She drags me to New York

No reason

On some random *Tuesday,*

makes me stay on some couch in some

hole in the wall in the ass end of Brooklyn

with her weird lesbian friends then

disappears."

Mario: I need you to know: I love you with all of my heart.

But that's the uh …

hhhhhhhhhh

See: there's ... *my* heart

And there's an

other heart.

Shit.

Bad service cuts her off. She dials again.

It's me again I got cut off ...

I was

Trying to explain ...

Sometimes?

I feel a *heart*.

Other than my own. Beating inside me.

Like I have two hearts.

One that's mine.

Another that's ...

Someone else's.

Squeezed next to mine.

Like having

twin hearts?

Trapped in

Some kind of fucked up cradle? made of ribs and muscle?

I'm not being metaphoric I know you sometimes think I talk in ...

but this heart this

second heart?

It's been there since I can remember ...

Sometimes it speaks for me. Moves for me. Thinks for me ...

Like having the ghost of a stranger inside you.

I love you, Mario.

I woke up at 2:35.

I thought it was your heartbeat that woke me.

But no.

It was his. That stranger inside ...

He told me to slip out of bed. Get dressed.

Leave Martha and Bonnie's place. Come here.

I could hear my own heartbeat

Faint in the background begging me

Don't listen. Get back in bed. Leave tomorrow.

Forget you ever came back to this godforsaken city.

But the other heartbeat ... He always wins ...

I can't tell you where I am ...

I'll explain it to you some time. I promise.

But please believe me: It's the last time I will ever come here.

When I'm done, I'm coming back, Mario.

I love you ...

Please understand.

I love you.

She clicks off the phone.

LILA: *Hhhhh*

She waits, then presses the buzzer.

EIGHT

The wee hours. Herman's kitchen. He changes tapes and resumes recording himself.

HERMAN: Four thirteen am
    I've got the Willies.

    I'll wager, oh listener —
    That if you endured the
    Ickiness
    Of that last tape —
    The
    disastrous exchange of *un*-pleasantries with my *Latin* friend —
    I'll wager two questions come to mind.
    One:
    Why does this Herman "F" use only first initials of surnames?
    Two:
    What is up, Mister Herman F. with this monstrous accusation of Holocaust denial?

Quick shift to VALERIE's place. She rubs her head, as if suffering an excruciating headache.

VALERIE: What are they gonna do with his body …
    Herman, you fucker.

She downs some aspirin, picks up her phone and dials. Herman's phone begins to ring.

HERMAN: Ah! The telephone! Guess who's calling? Guess who won't pick up? Anyway:
    why initials in place of names? Cryptic, no?
    This Herman fellow must be *hiding* something.
    But that would make no sense, would it?
    For you to have requested these tapes from the Special Collections Librarian
    (a woman I fantasize about obsessively)
    You would have to:
        1) Know the tapes exist, therefore
        2) Know the identity of the man who recorded them, and
        3) Knowing his identity, you must have at least an inkling of his *notoriety*.

In other words: you already have an *agenda*.

But maybe you're that rare, genuinely curious, agenda-free person
lured into the constipated bowels of The New York Public Library
not to seek what you already know,
but to journey across the vast terra incognita of human knowledge.
In your quest you stumble on a man named Herman. With a Jewish sounding last
name.
You learn the library's holdings include all eleven of his published books.
You learn he bequeathed tapes ... hundreds of hours of his own testimony ...
Curiosity aroused, you dust off a voice unheard for years ... ? Decades ... ?
Centuries ... ?

The telephone stops ringing. Quick jump to Valerie's kitchen.

VALERIE: Fucker.

She dials another number.

ALVARO: Ahhhl-
    Oh?

VALERIE: Alvaro?
    It's Valerie.

ALVARO: Coño! What is this?
    Fuckin' *Night a the Living Dead?*

Back to Herman's place.

HERMAN: It is for you, virgin listener,
    I use initials in place of surnames.
    You see: In spite of the ongoing *threats* – from time to time
    I leave my apartment, head to the Library. To use the computer.
    Maybe
    Oh, I don't know
    Look up a recipe?
    On occasion I'll permit myself
    A petty indulgence:
    I "google" myself.
    My full name.

No quotations.

18 million results.

I try again — my name. In quotes.

Four million results.

Less unwieldy but still needing refinement.

I add "historian"

Ah! A manageable 350,000 results!

A number that remains somewhat stable when I add, oh,

The title of one of my books, say, *The Peace Delusion* or

Towards a Gentler Means to an End: Reconsiderations of Machiavelli for the Age of Globalization.

Then,

Indulgence devolves into morbid curiosity …

I add the dreaded "H.D." words

Lookee there!

One hundred twenty thousand results!

My my look at all those places where the crime of Holocaust Denial

And my name live in wedded bliss.

Morbid curiosity becomes self-laceration:

I replace "Holocaust Denier" with

Terrorist.

Fascist.

Murderer.

Friedmanite.

Rapist.

Abortionist.

Child molester.

Genocidal maniac.

Results! Results!

Thousands of results.

I reside among the pantheon of untouchables.

You understand now why I keep names secret?

Was just last week I subjected myself again to this assault.

For reasons that still baffle me, I typed one. last. combination: My name. In quotes. Followed by Javier C.'s name.

"Your search did not match any documents."

Herman clicks the recorder off. He sits silently. He clicks the recorder on.

HERMAN: As to question Two — this Holocaust Denial business

Where to begin …

The apartment intercom buzzer sounds. Herman leaps to the defensive: he turns out the light, moves to the knife drawer, where he removes a handgun. Next, he goes to a cabinet and removes a periscope-like device — a car mirror attached to a tv antenna. He moves to the window, extends the mirror outside to see who is down below. The intercom buzzes again.

HERMAN: God …

He goes to the intercom, presses a button. Sounds of the street outside.

HERMAN: Who is it?

YOUNG WOMAN'S VOICE: Herman … ?

It's me.

Herman hesitates, then buzzes her in.

He opens the front door slightly. The echo of women's shoes ascend the four flights stairs.

During the ascent, we pop in on Valerie. She's just getting off the phone. Her headache seems to have gone away. She dials another number.

Back at Herman's. The young woman's footsteps stop outside the door. She pushes it open, stands, a silhouette in the threshold. A silent standoff. The telephone begins to ring.

HERMAN: Lila … What are you …

LILA: You gonna answer that?

HERMAN: No.

LILA: Herman … ?

Do you believe in ghosts?

He says nothing. She says nothing. The phone continues to ring.

HERMAN: Lila … I am so, so sorr—

LILA: Shhhhh.

A moment. They fall into an embrace. It is uncertain who initiates. Herman still has the gun in his hand. The last thing we see: the red light of the tape recorder recording. The telephone continues to ring.

2. Deus FedEx Machina

ONE

Herman's kitchen the next morning. Herman and Lila in bathrobes. Lila absorbed in the crossword puzzle. The gun is still on the table. Herman fixes his gaze on Lila's finger, which sports a modest engagement ring.

HERMAN: I spoke to your mother last night.

    This morning, actually

    She telephoned.
    At 2:35.

Lila looks at him quickly, then returns her attention to the crossword.

HERMAN: Does your mother know you're in town?

LILA: What's up with the gun, Herman?

HERMAN: This? Oh, well …

    You know.

LILA: No.

HERMAN: Protection.

LILA: From … ?

HERMAN: Neighborhood …

    The city …

LILA: I read in some magazine it's become one of the most livable places in America.

HERMAN: Perhaps but

    Certain *people*

LILA: Want to see you dead.

HERMAN: That's right.

LILA: They make threatening calls at all hours –

HERMAN: 24/7. I have tapes, I could // play them for

LILA: They want to find you so they can kill you. Slowly.

HERMAN: That's right.

LILA: You're nuts.
  You'd think, if "those people" wanted you dead?
  They'd have done it a long time ago.

HERMAN: When it mattered, you mean.

LILA: No …

HERMAN: When I mattered, is that what you're say//ing?

LILA: Forget it.

HERMAN: Aside from that
  Things happen. Door to the street.
  Doesn't lock properly.

  So: you're not interested.

LILA: In why you have a gun? I'm plenty // interested in

HERMAN: No.
  Your mother …
  She telephoned // last night.

LILA: Your conversations with my mother are none of my business.

HERMAN: She doesn't know you're in town … ?

LILA: If she does, it's not because I told her. She say anything to you?

HERMAN: About …

LILA: Me being in town …

HERMAN: No.

LILA: Cause she has a way of knowing things like that that just …
  Drives me up the fucking // wall

HERMAN: Do you plan on *contacting* her

LILA: No.

HERMAN: She seemed to *suggest*
  she'd like to
  touch base // with you

LILA: That would be novel.
  Why would she tell you that?
  She doesn't *know*, does // she

HERMAN: Christ NO, God, no.
  Imagine?

  What exactly are you doing in town?

LILA: What's with the questions? I'm in town. I come I go I

HERMAN: I know

LILA: When I come I come see you, right? I don't ask anything, you don't ask anything,
  complication free. That should make you happy, // right?

HERMAN: It does …

  It's just that
  I got the sense that she's
  Looking for you // and

LILA: She has my *cell*.

HERMAN: I think you should call // her.

LILA: Oh for fuck's sake
  Ground rules, Herman. Remember ground rules?
  I walk through that door –

HERMAN: –Your mother // your fa–

LILA: – Does not exist. She lives in the world out there. What we do happens in the
  world in here. And never the two worlds –

HERMAN: – Shall meet I know I know I'm // only –

LILA: Herman!

Silence.

HERMAN: You look well.

LILA: Thank you.

HERMAN: It's been what? Six months // since

LILA: Eight.

HERMAN: Right ...

>   But you.
>   Standing at my door.
>   Arriving unannounced –

LILA: I'm sorry about // that

HERMAN: No ...

>   I
>   Just
>   *You.*
>
>   I forget to breathe.
>   You
>
>   *Move*
>   Me.

She places her hand – the one with the ring – on his, and gives it a squeeze.

LILA: What do you say we get out of here, go somewhere?

>   It's a beautiful day.

HERMAN: Somewhere ...

LILA: I don't know. Coney Island?

>   The park? The zoo?

HERMAN: Not in the mood.

LILA: You won't take me to the zoo?

HERMAN: Lila ...

LILA: You like taking me to the zoo ...

HERMAN: *LILA.*

LILA: Whoa. Tone, Herman.

> You do not have the permission to use that // tone with

HERMAN: I'm sorry I'm just

> confused.

LILA: By … ?

HERMAN: You come here

> In the night
>
> At the end of a week that,
>
> Fuck. I can't even talk about this.

LILA: What is it?

HERMAN: You come here. God knows what time.

> We hardly say a word – I know:
>
> Not unusual.
>
> But now it's morning. And last night
>
> certain questions
>
> I should have asked …

Lila's cell phone rings loudly. The ring tone, some kind of "ironic," Lila-appropriate song.

HERMAN: What is that?

LILA: My phone? Hold on.

> Shit.

HERMAN: You're not going to answer it?

LILA: Nope.

HERMAN: Who was it?

LILA: A friend.

HERMAN: Why don't telephones sound like telephones anymore?

LILA: Cause the future happened last Thursday, Herman. You missed it.

> You were saying …

HERMAN: You need to call your mother.

LILA: Jesus // Christ

HERMAN: And what is that thing?

LILA: What thing?

HERMAN: On your finger – // that *thing*.

LILA: Which finger oh // *this* finger *this* thing

HERMAN: *That* finger, yes, *that* thing, // yes yes yes

LILA: What does it look like?

HERMAN: I told your parents?
    Years ago I told them:
    "Why all of a sudden are you
    dabbling in having *babies?*"

LILA: Babies

HERMAN: I told them:
    Two of the biggest narcissists ever to walk the earth
    What do you want a *baby* for?
    Now there's a a a a
    thing on your finger

LILA: Herman. Settle down. Let's get dressed. Go to the park. I'll tell you all about it.

HERMAN: And what's this insanity you were talking last night, this business about ghosts?

LILA: Nothing. Something stupid // that's all

HERMAN: What did you // mean?

LILA: *Nothing.*

HERMAN: You need. to call. your mother.

LILA: Herman! I am not calling my mother, now drop it or I'm out // of here

HERMAN: Do you know your father died this week?

LILA: Excuse me?

HERMAN: Do you know.

    Your father.

    Died.

    this week.

LILA: Why would you say such a horrible thing?

HERMAN: So you don't know.

LILA: He's not dead.

HERMAN: According to your mother, he is.

LILA: What the fuck would my mother know, she doesn't talk to him she // hasn't

HERMAN: And you do?

LILA: I talk to Tina. I talked to Tina on Monday // I

HERMAN: Who's Tina?

LILA: I talked to her, she said everything was fine

HERMAN: Who's Tina?

LILA: His *friend*.

HERMAN: In New Mexico?

Pause.

LILA: How do *you* know he's in // New

HERMAN: You talked to this Tina woman Monday?

LILA: Yes, Monday.

HERMAN: Your mother told me he died on Tuesday.

LILA: No.

HERMAN: He drowned. In a freak

    flash // flood

LILA: Herman … why are you saying // this —

HERMAN: Call your mother. Ask her.

LILA: She was telling you the truth?

HERMAN: I haven't spoken to your mother in –

When we do speak it's mercifully brief

Mention of your father *rare,* and no,

Neither she nor I make a habit of telling fibs about people dying,

let alone your father dying.

What are you doing?

LILA: I'm calling Tina. She would have called she

Lila dials Tina. She waits. What she hears puzzles her. She tries again. Same thing. Hangs up.

LILA: What the fuck …

HERMAN: What?

LILA: You knew this. Last night.

You didn't think this would be // something I'd want

HERMAN: That's what I've been trying to tell you, Lila. I'm sorry // that …

LILA: "Do I tell her?" "Do I fuck her?" Hm. "Fuck her. Tell her in the morning // if I ever get around to

HERMAN: It was not like that, Lila, // it was

LILA: That's just *FUCKED* Herman …

HERMAN: Where are you going?

LILA: They were right about you – everything they *said*, everything they *wrote* – they were right.

HERMAN: Please. Don't. // go.

LILA: Go to hell, Herman.

She begins dressing. The intercom buzzes. Herman freaks, grabs his gun and moves into a defensive position aiming it at the door.

LILA: What the fuck …

HERMAN: See who it is.

LILA: No.

HERMAN: Please!

LILA: For Chrissake!

She goes to the buzzer.

LILA: Who is it?

VOICE: Fed Ex.

LILA: Fed Ex. What do you w— Herman, don't point that thing // at me

HERMAN: Ask him what he wants.

LILA: You'd guess he's delivering a package?

HERMAN: *Ask him what he wants.*

LILA: What's this is in reference to?

VOICE: Uhhhh FedEx package for Herman Fi--- ?

The sound of a sidewalk argument obscures the last name.

HERMAN: Ask who it's from.

LILA: For God's sake // Herman …

HERMAN: *Ask* him.

LILA: May I ask who the package is from?

VOICE: Lady …

LILA: Please …

VOICE: Christina Sanchez … Gallup, New Mexico.

HERMAN: I don't know a Christina San—

LILA: *Tina.* Herman. *Tina.*

Lila buzzes and opens the door slightly. Footsteps rising up floor by floor. Lila lights a cigarette, and stares down Herman. The Fed Ex Man reaches the door, knocks. It opens. The Fed Ex Man is baffled by what he sees — the half naked young woman smoking and the older man crouching in his robe with the gun.

FED EX MAN: Whoa. Uhhh … Either of you wanna sign for this?

Hello?

Lila signs for the package. The Fed Ex Man is taken aback by her half nakedness and her seeming not to care. He leaves. She deposits the package on the table.

LILA: You gonna open it?

HERMAN: Open it for me?

LILA: Fucking coward.

She exits, still dressing, shoes in hand.

HERMAN: Lila … please, don't go …

Herman goes to the table. He opens the box and removes a manuscript.

HERMAN: God …

Herman's telephone rings. He picks up the phone as if in a trance.

HERMAN: Hello?

Valerie's kitchen. On the table an open Fed Ex box and a manuscript.

VALERIE: It's me. DON'T hang up. Did you … ?

HERMAN: The Federal Express man was just here.

VALERIE: Here too.

He hangs up the phone. A moment. The phone rings again. Herman doesn't answer. It rings and rings and rings. Herman goes to the package. He nudges it. It doesn't explode. He gingerly opens the package. He removes from it a huge manuscript. He looks at its cover.

HERMAN: *Hhhhhhhhhhhhh* …

He clicks on the recorder.

HERMAN: I have on my kitchen table
A practical joke from a dead man.
Javier C.
Lifeless at the bottom of a river in the wilds of Northern New Mexico
Could not be content to just
Sink Into oblivion.

Fucker.

75

Herman clicks off the recorder.

Calm.

He clicks the recorder back on again.

A box arrives this morning –
I sign for it and the *attitude*. The
self-importance of the Federal Express Man,
with his *hat* his
uniform that
little electric *thingy*
For all I know the package could be some kind of
improvised explosive device sent by my enemies
But I open it:
Inside, a manuscript. By Javier C.

My first impulse: burn the damn thing
But curiosity – oh curiosity …
That whore always wins in the end doesn't she.

The title …
Diagram of a Paper Airplane. Rotten bastard made good on his decades old threat
Actually *wrote* the fucking thing.
Of course, Javier C. could never leave a title alone, noooo
There had to be an "or" or a colon followed by a subtitle – some corrosively stupid,
incomprehensible description of the play's "form." This one is no exception:
Diagram of a Paper Airplane COLON *A last will, testament and indictment in the form of a
tragical metatheatrical fantasia (with songs)*. Parentheses around "with songs."

Pompous cocksucker.

Next page:
Dramatis Personae – seven principals in all HA! I know where *this* is going! Long list
of minor characters – the Goat Herder, the German Innkeeper, Consuela – the
German Innkeeper's wife, Japanese Fishermen … and *hhhhhhhh*
A Chorus of Children Disappeared …
Jesus.

And the *setting:*

Herman reads from the manuscript. Valerie and Alvaro in their kitchens do the same.

HERMAN: "Setting:

VALERIE: Various kitchens in New York City tenement apart//ments.

ALVARO: A roach infested unit of a flea bag motel outside Gallup, New // Mexico.

HERMAN: A disgraced history professor's office on the campus of an unnamed major Catholic university in a very large Midwestern city. Haha!

VALERIE: Various locations in the small fishing village of Puerto Angel, Oaxaca, Mexico, including: a German-run bed and breakfast, a police station, a Japanese fishing boat anchored in the bay, a goat herder's shack, a morgue.

ALVARO: A potential future sinkhole near downtown Albuquerque, New Mexi//co?

VALERIE: A garbage strewn dead end street by the Domino's Sugar plant, Williamsburg, Brook//lyn.

HERMAN: A mental asylum in Middletown, Connecti//cut

VALERIE: A New Age emporium in Portland, Oreg//on.

HERMAN: A burning Japanese fishing boat that has struck an iceberg in the North Atlan//tic.

ALVARO: An illegal sex club in Barri Xinès, Barcelona, // Spain.

VALERIE: An abandoned nuclear power plant in an unspecified coun//try?

HERMAN: "Red Herring's Bar and Grill" outside Mahagonny, USA.... ?

HERMAN/ALVARO/VALERIE: The moon.

HERMAN: Listen to this:

"Given the number and variety of locations, // no attempt

VALERIE: no attempt shall be made when // staging the play

ALVARO: staging the play to recreate these environments literally."

HERMAN: I love that.

The dedication:

"For the Puerto Angel Seven and the Innocent Bystanders Caught in the Crossfire."

Valerie's kitchen. She's on the phone with Josephine.

VALERIE: Josephine, sorry, I forget you're three hours behind.
Call me when Fed Ex –

I got one. Herman got one. Alvaro got one.
Dedication says "To the Puerto Angel Seven –

I know you weren't there – would you
Hush for a second, Josephine? The *pages* –
They *skip*. Seven pages at a time.
Mine goes: 2, 9, 16, 23, 30 and so on.
I don't know what pages Herman got, bastard won't talk to me

HERMAN: 1, 8, 15, 22, 29, // 36, 43, 50 …

VALERIE: but Alvaro talked, he got pages

ALVARO: 3, 10, // 17, 24

VALERIE: and so on to 600 something so one would assume –

I KNOW YOU WEREN'T THERE! IT'S NOT ABOUT YOU, JOSI,
HE'S POINTING FINGERS AT ALL OF US …

Silence.

I'm sorry … Josi, I didn't mean …
Don't cry Josephine … Jesus.
Look: there's a letter
Do *you* know who this Tina person is?

Look, Josi –
I'm throwing darts here, blindfolded

I *know* it's a can of worms. How *dare* you even say that to me.
Shame on you.

Anyway, the letter:
Barely read this Tina person's *scrawl*

the grammar

the *presumption*

Okay. I won't editorialize

Can I just fucking read it to you?

ALVARO: *(Reading the letter.)* "To Whom It May Concern.
You don no me from Atom."

VALERIE: Spelled like Atom bomb

ALVARO: "And I don no you from Atom Ether?"
Either.

VALERIE: "I m cool keepin it that way. Im jus the messenyer so don shut me.
I just wut he says I am: the 'companyun' – I'm only doin what Havi axt me"

ALVARO: "In cace bad shit wen down. Bad shit wen down so Im doin like he axt."

VALERIE: "I do not no wuts incide the Onvelup?"

HERMAN: *Envelope.*
"Alls I no he wanned u to haf it
I learned eons ago never to seek the light of reason behind Javier's dark, subterranean impulses."
What?

VALERIE: That's right Josephine,
A complete sentence.
I mean, what the *fuck?*

ALVARO: "I hop wuteverz in the onvelup meens sumthin good to you, cuz he wuz actin all freekie at the en an wen he wuz lyk that u never noo wut wuz cumin next."

HERMAN: "Pleez don contac me. Im only the mesenyer. Lik I sed. I don't wan get shoot."

ALVARO/HERMAN/VALERIE: "Sinseerlee. Tina"

VALERIE: Doesn't that weird you out? Who is this fucking illiterate bitch?

Alvaro folds the letter into a paper airplane. He goes to the window, sets the plane on fire with his Zippo and tosses it into the airshaft.

Herman folds the letter and clicks off the recorder. He picks up the phone and dials.

VALERIE: Josphine, can you hold on a second? Call waiting. Hello?

HERMAN: Who is Tina?

TWO

Alvaro's kitchen. Late afternoon. A pile of cigarette butts in the ashtray. A carton of Kools, open. The microphone and digital recorder. Alvaro lights up a Kool and resumes his conversation with the unseen interviewer.

ALVARO: After that Night a the Livin Dead?

Week later? Invitation comes in the mail –

"Your presence is requested for a Memorial Celebration of our fallen friend Javier"

"Friday, October 8, 9pm. Bring pictures, poems, memories."

Hosted by

What do you call her?

Ex-wife in mourning? Reluctant mother a his offspring?

If you don't know what to call her,

What you gonna call me?

Ex-friend?

Ex-barrier-between-his-sorry-ass-an-the-streets?

Ex-other-woman-who-happens-to-have-a-pi-pi-between-her-thighs?

Make sure you write *that* shit down, in your book diss-uh-tation whatevuh …
Memorial.

To go or not to go, that was the question, right?

Alvaro goes to a kitchen cabinet. Inside, notebooks, wedged between plates and bowls. He removes a small stack of handwritten pages and returns to the table.

ALVARO: Javi left a bunch a shit behind when he split,

Most of it garbage I got rid of.

But I kept a couple a things …

First two pages a *Diagram of a Paper Airplane*. Original. Hand written.

Bitch wrote – five, 600 pages? Split it up, sent it to all the people that were there.

All that for what? When all he had to do was mail these pages to his daughter.

"Whimsical."

Looks like you salivatin' Mista PhD Candidate, Columbia University …

3. Memorial

ONE

Valerie's apartment. Night. In the kitchen, Mario and Herman. Mario drinks a beer. Herman sips tea. Awkward silence.

MARIO: Weird, cause ... I didn't even know Lila *had* parents.

    I mean yeah

    Everyone's got parents –

    It's just

    Weird.

    See: cause Lila?

    She like

    Never mentioned?

    Her mom?

    Her ...

HERMAN: Father?

MARIO: Right, cause she's fierce

    You meet her you're like

    "Man, were you born fully formed?"

HERMAN: You went to Harvard?

MARIO: Yes and no.

    Did three semesters then

    Life

    Happened like a

    fork in the road?

    Harvard? Or the swirling chaos of life.

HERMAN: And swirling chaos ...

MARIO: Exactly. But no regrets ...

HERMAN: And your family's Irish?

MARIO: That's right.

HERMAN: Then why'd they name you "Mario"?

MARIO: Ha! *That's* a story ...

Herman does not take the bait. Pause.

MARIO: Like I was saying,

 Cool she's

 Reconnecting?

 Lila's not used to ...

 See: like my family?

 We're like the Kennedy's?

 If they were ass broke and lived in south Boston?

 We're tight, touch football, booze –

HERMAN: Assassinations?

MARIO: What? Oh. No no no Ha – there's been tragedy but ...

 Any time I bring Lila there she's

 Overwhelmed

 Like she can't deal with the

 We can get pretty sentimental sometimes? like

 We'll get into fisticuffs over who loves who more –

HERMAN: Fisticuffs?

MARIO: My family – not Lila and me – god no, we never fight. But like my brother and me? We'll kick the living crap out of each other to prove something stupid, like who's more loyal, who's more – Lila's not used to people automatically treating her like family, like – okay, I love someone? I bring that person home? My family? Second they walk in the door. Instant part of the tribe.

 Freaks Lila out sometimes.

Long silence.

MARIO: Totally sucks about her father.

HERMAN: How did you and Lila meet?

MARIO: That's an awesome story.

HERMAN: I bet you're dying to tell it to me.

MARIO: Totally – wait.
Are you being
Sarcastic?

HERMAN: No.

MARIO: Cause reading you's like reading ancient Egyptian hieroglyphs –
But yeah, it's an awesome story –
See: She was doing the Car Crash Prom Queen thing in Harvard Square –

HERMAN: Car what *what?*

MARIO: Car Crash Prom Queen …

That's what's so hard to get used to – cause like my family? You can't
Screw in a light bulb without everyone gossiping about it, takes getting used to her
family not

HERMAN: I'm not Lila's family.

MARIO: Well no, but …

HERMAN: Enlighten me. Car crash … ?

MARIO: Prom Queen. It was like a
Living-statue-slash-performance-art-type-thing, SO cool to watch.
She would deck herself out? in this pink prom dress? Corsage of thorns around her
wrist. Face painted all white – blood red tears on her cheeks. She'd stand on this
podium. That was *covered* with paper airplanes.

HERMAN: Paper airplanes.

MARIO: Weird, right? She has tons of them at her place. She *finds* them. On the street.
She has this theory? that if you look at the ground all the time? you find paper airplanes everywhere. She'll walk around Boston, find like twenty of them. I thought:
crackpot, but I started looking? They're everywhere –

Anyway, she'd stand on the paper airplanes, for hours, striking these poses. And the
climax … She'd unzip the back of her dress? Expose her back, her –

HERMAN: Scars?

MARIO: You know about her scars?

HERMAN: I was there when they happened.

MARIO: Holy shit.

HERMAN: Indeed.

MARIO: Wow ... I don't mean to pry // but

HERMAN: Then don't.

MARIO: Okay ... Anyway

At the end she'd set fire to the paper airplanes burn herself in effigy. Not really – it was theatre ... It was un.be.lievable. Thing was, no one knew who she was – people rumored she was the Provost's illegitimate daughter, castoff of the Kennedy clan –

Jangle of keys opening the front door interrupts. Valerie enters carrying bags of Chinese food.

MARIO: Let me get those for you Mrs. P.

She kisses his cheek.

VALERIE: Such a sweetie – thank you – here, there's a couple more outside.

MARIO: Chinese! Awesome!

During the following Mario unloads the Chinese food bags and groceries.

VALERIE: Herman! My // God!

HERMAN: Valerie ...

VALERIE: My. *God* ...

HERMAN: Likewise ...

VALERIE: You're
early.

HERMAN: I

VALERIE: No no no no it's fine I'm
I should hug you shouldn't I?

HERMAN: Not necessary.

MARIO: Mrs. P. – should I just set this stuff out?

VALERIE: Please, no, Mario – you're a guest, // just …

MARIO: Not a problem Mrs. P. – where's // Lila

VALERIE: My god you
    You look the same only

HERMAN: Different?

VALERIE: Have you met Lila's fiancé // Mario

HERMAN: Indeedie

VALERIE: Isn't he just delightful?

MARIO: You're too kind // Mrs. P

VALERIE: Can I get you something, Herman? Drink?

HERMAN: I'm fine.

Valerie goes to the freezer and removes a bottle of vodka. She pours herself a drink.

VALERIE: So …
    How's the scribbling? Oh, I got us Chinese – meat *and* vegetable dishes of course – // you

HERMAN: I'm back to meat.
    Relapsed carnivore since …

VALERIE: Really.

HERMAN: As to the scribbling –

VALERIE: Pardon?

HERMAN: You asked if // I

VALERIE: Oh right right – my mind – three hundred different places // at a

HERMAN: I remember

VALERIE: I read the last one, what was it called? *Billions of Feet* or // some

HERMAN: *A Billion Fewer Footprints: A Case for Accelerating Climate Catastro* // *phe*

VALERIE: Rightrightright. Scary stuff. I still don't understand, though, why it caused you so // much …

HERMAN: Trouble? // Well —

VALERIE: I assume, though, that you
What's the expression?
"Got back on the horse that 'throwed' ya?"

HERMAN: You're asking if I got back on a horse.

VALERIE: That's what you do, right?

HERMAN: Well, no. The horse threw me. I tried to get up. The horse kicked me. While I was down? Horsie pooped on my head, galloped off into the sunset.

VALERIE: I'm sorry, Herman. But the job situation —
Surely you must be back in de//mand

HERMAN: I'm toxic. Unhireable.

VALERIE: Shame. You were such a good teacher.
So how are you … ?

HERMAN: How am I … ?

VALERIE: Living.

HERMAN: Settlement.

VALERIE: Oh, right, I read about that, undis//closed sum?

HERMAN: Undisclosed sum of money.

VALERIE: Must have been some undisclosed sum, living all these // years.

HERMAN: I'm frugal.

VALERIE: Hey, at least you get to live, right?

HERMAN: Goodbye. Nice seeing you Valerie, call me in another // twenty years

VALERIE: Oh, Herman, I'm teasing, so sensitive … for the record, I never believed for a moment that Holocaust denial business

HERMAN: Oh, goody.

VALERIE: I even considered writing a letter to the *Times* in your defense, but who am I?

HERMAN: And you? How's the
> Mashing together of very large, incongruous objects to create "new sculptural forms" going?

VALERIE: So. Mean.

HERMAN: Really, I'm curious.

VALERIE: I've gone miniature.

HERMAN: They were getting so *Big*

VALERIE: That was twenty years ago. I've *evolved*. Besides,
> I lost my space. Real estate in this fucking city
> So I work here. In my kitchen.
> But more importantly I've become obsessed with things barely visible to the naked eye.
> I'm working on a series I'm showing at a gallery in Toledo.

HERMAN: Is it just us?

VALERIE: Hm?

HERMAN: Here. For this
> Reunion? Memorial? Posthumous play // reading?

VALERIE: Mario's here.

HERMAN: I don't mean Mario.

VALERIE: That's not nice – Mario please don't take offense, Herman is // just

MARIO: No offence taken – I'm just the fiancé.

VALERIE: Lila

HERMAN: Lila's coming?

VALERIE: She'd be here now if // she

MARIO: Mrs. P.? You mind if I?

VALERIE: Of course not – there's an ashtray out on the fire escape.

MARIO: The view out there isn't half bad.

VALERIE: Sweetie.

Mario goes out the window to smoke on the fire escape.

VALERIE: I've known him a day and a half
    Already he's like a son.

Pause.

HERMAN: You haven't answered my question.

VALERIE: Which question.

HERMAN: Are we it?

VALERIE: If I said it was just us would you stay or go?

HERMAN: Valerie, Val, // Valie

VALERIE: If I said all of us will find ourselves cramped in this tiny kitchen
    Would you run screaming for the hills?

HERMAN: Is it just you. And me.

VALERIE: There's Alvaro

HERMAN: He's coming?

VALERIE: He said he was intrigued but noncommittal.

HERMAN: Doesn't sound like something he would say.

VALERIE: People *evolve,* Herman.

Shift to Alvaro's apartment. He wears a black pinstripe suit with a carnation in the buttonhole and bold red tie. He holds a bouquet of roses and looks into a mirror.

ALVARO: "Whimsical"

He folds the hand written pages of Diagram of a Paper Airplane and slips them in his jacket pocket. Back to Valerie's place.

HERMAN: Nero? Is he // coming?

VALERIE: Nero's dead.

HERMAN: Shut up.

VALERIE: It's been ten years

HERMAN: Let me guess: blew his brains out?

VALERIE: Warm.

HERMAN: He jumped off of something. Big. Like a suspension bridge.

VALERIE: Cold

HERMAN: Knowing him it had to have been something spectacularly vengeful –

VALERIE: Hot.

HERMAN: Did he take Lina and the kids out with him?

VALERIE: God, Herman, // that's

HERMAN: You said "Hot"

VALERIE: He *stabbed* himself –

HERMAN: *Fuck.*

VALERIE: Talk about vengeful, he did it right in front of Lina.

HERMAN: Shit.

VALERIE: At breakfast one morning at the B&B.

HERMAN: The what?

VALERIE: You didn't know? They ran a charming little B&B in Burlington, Vermont.

HERMAN: You're joking.

VALERIE: I know, weird, right? Actors … *Anyway* – they were making breakfast for guests – one second he's chopping onions next he impales himself.

HERMAN: God.

VALERIE: Awful, no?

HERMAN: And Lina?

VALERIE: Poor woman. Week after they buried Nero they found her one night. Wandering naked on some country lane. Screaming she'd murdered her children — that she was the murderer of all children.

HERMAN: Did she?

VALERIE: Murder her children? Of course not.

HERMAN: Long overdue confession?

VALERIE: Don't. Even.

HERMAN: I'm sorry.

VALERIE: Last I heard she was in a nut house up in Connecticut.

HERMAN: How do you know all this?

VALERIE: How do you *not* know this?

HERMAN: Your evil twin.

VALERIE: Josephine?

HERMAN: Dead? Institutionalized? Witness Protection Pro//gram?

VALERIE: She lives in *Portland*. Runs a *shop* — one of those places that sells candles? Incense?
"Crafts" by local artists. Those *"books."*

HERMAN: Lordy.

Mario reenters from smoking.

HERMAN: Portland, Maine or Portland, Oregon?

VALERIE: Oregon.

MARIO: I love Oregon.

HERMAN: I fucking hate it.

MARIO: Whoa   VALERIE: Herman!

HERMAN: Forgive me Mario I didn't // mean

MARIO: No sweat – I say tomato you say toe-mah-toe

    Mrs. P.? Table cloth?

VALERIE: Linen closet – door just to the right of the // bathroom

HERMAN: Is Josephine coming?

VALERIE: You know I offered to scrounge up money to pay half her airfare? Chintzy little bitch.

HERMAN: You talk to her.

VALERIE: All the time.

HERMAN: Doesn't surprise me.

VALERIE: Ha! Well fuck you Herman, eat me while you're at it.

    I'm furious with her. I begged her to come. You know what she said? "I'm *content* living in the *present*." Selling candles, incense, those "*books*."

HERMAN: The latest in hemp fashion?

VALERIE: And *hats*

HERMAN: The cow.

VALERIE: That's right, that fucking hysterical cow has gone New Age.

HERMAN: Moo.

VALERIE: Moo.

HERMAN: MOOOO

VALERIE: MOOOO Ha HA Fucking right MOOOOOOOOO

They laugh as they once used to. Valerie affectionately touches Herman's face.

VALERIE: Herman I've missed you.

No response from Herman.

VALERIE: Anyway despite her hippie cow-dom

    She was kind enough to FedEx her part of the manuscript.

Valerie goes to pour herself another vodka.

VALERIE: I wonder if Maria got one.

    Herman – I wonder if Maria // got one.

HERMAN: I heard you the first time.

VALERIE: You think … ?

HERMAN: Unlikely.

VALERIE: He found the rest of // us.

HERMAN: Maria's

    Elusive.

    You haven't …

VALERIE: No. Lord, no not since a long time.

HERMAN: Because you're like the Associated Press on everyone's misfortunes.

VALERIE: I can't help it if people think I'm still Queen Bee – not that I asked for that –

HERMAN: What about the goat herder? Think he'll put in // an appearance?

VALERIE: Go to hell, Herman –

HERMAN: Or is he still languishing in a Mexican prison?

VALERIE: Fuck you.

Lila enters – a very different Lila than we've seen before. She wears a simple dress with a nautical themed print. It is as if her mother chose the outfit but forgot her daughter is in her late 20s. Something childlike, unsettling about it. On the one hand, it might seem that Lila is attempting irony, on the other, there's something deadly serious about it that is unnerving. Lila carries shopping bags, one with supplies for the party, the other filled with paper airplanes.

VALERIE: Lila! Where on *earth* did you go? I waited for you at the Chinese // place –

LILA: I apologize mother. I got distracted.

MARIO: Hey, baby.

LILA: Sweetie –

MARIO: Man, you lookMm.

LILA: Mother bought it for me. Isn't it sweet?

MARIO: Sweeet.

Lila goes to Mario, kisses him —

LILA: I missed you.

MARIO: I missed *you*.

LILA: I love you.

MARIO: I love *you*.

LILA: No, I *love* you.

MARIO: Baby.

LILA: What are you up to?

MARIO: Helping your Ma set up.

VALERIE: I told him not to – he's a // guest

MARIO: No sweat Mrs. P … Like Ma always says: best way to handle a situation you're not totally comfortable with? Put on an apron, bake a cake.

LILA: Mother, you haven't introduced me to this gentleman.

VALERIE: Oh. You remember Herman. He's known you since you were a baby.

LILA: I'm afraid, mother, I have no recollection of meeting him. How do you do, sir? My name is Lila Anne. But you may call me // Lila.

VALERIE: When was the last time you saw each other?

HERMAN: Another lifetime – I understand you not

LILA: I'm enchanted to make your acquaintance.

HERMAN: Likewise Lila Ann

LILA: Please: Lila. Daddy had so many interesting friends. I learn so many things meeting them—

HERMAN: I'm
Sorry to
Hear the news about your father.

LILA: Tragedy, isn't it.

    If you'll excuse me, I'm going to help my fiancée.

    Pleasure to make your acquaintance.

She goes to Mario to help. They stand close to each other and talk in whispers.

HERMAN: What is the point of all this, Valerie?

VALERIE: Point of

HERMAN: Do the math: We have only four sevenths of *Diagram of a Paper Airplane* how do you // expect

VALERIE: You think that's why I asked you here?

HERMAN: Of course it is. Why else would any of us come?

VALERIE: To pay respects? To honor a man who —

    None of us would be who we are without him.

HERMAN: Suicides, mental asylum inmates, estranged mothers —

VALERIE: Lila and I are not estrange//ed.

HERMAN: — amnesiac daughters, failed writers, disgraced professors. What. a. legacy.

VALERIE: So you came out of what? Morbid curiosity? Want to know what the "mad playwright" had to say before kicking // it?

HERMAN: He *could've* sent each of us our own copy — No, he wanted us all in a room together.

VALERIE: Does that frighten you?

HERMAN: Does it frighten you?

MARIO: Smoky time!

VALERIE: Pardon?

MARIO: Didn't mean to interrupt.

    Lila and I are going out for a smoke.

LILA: *You're* going for a smoke, I'm just joining you.

MARIO: Right, for the *view.*

LILA: You're incorri//gible.

VALERIE: May I join you?

LILA: Mother!

MARIO: Mrs. P. Didn't know a fine lady like you partook in such filthy habits, but I'm happy to indulge. I promise I won't tell anyone.

VALERIE: So naughty … such a sweetie.

They exit to the fire escape. Herman alone. The intercom buzzes, startling him. He instinctively goes to a kitchen drawer to find his gun, but realizes he's not in his own apartment. Momentary panic. The intercom buzzes again. He goes to it.

HERMAN: … yes? …

ALVARO'S VOICE: Shit.

HERMAN: Alvaro? That you?

ALVARO'S VOICE: Yeah, it's me.

HERMAN: Are you … alone?

ALVARO'S VOICE: No I got Javier's rotting corpse with me.

Herman buzzes him in. He opens the door and waits. Sound of Alvaro's shoes ascending the stairs. Alvaro arrives at the door, carrying the flowers but no Fed Ex box.

HERMAN: Well

After our little tete-a-tete the other night —

I wouldn't have expected you to grace us with your presence

Lovely flowers the *suit*. My word. You look

ALVARO: Where's Valerie?

HERMAN: They're out on the fire escape.

ALVARO: They?

HERMAN: Valerie, Lila. Her *boyfriend*.

ALVARO: Lila's here?

HERMAN: Yes.

ALVARO: Hm.

HERMAN: What's that supposed to mean?

ALVARO:

HERMAN: So how are your theatrical endeavors?

ALVARO: How your Holocaust Denier friends?

HERMAN: *Hhhhhhhh*

    I caught the last one, ten years ago was it? –

    It *was* the last one, right?

    I flew in for the occasion – in the midst of my "troubles" – Couldn't miss Alvaro's great triumph after years in the trenches ... I have to say I disagree with those that *opined* that you sold your soul to the expectations of your ethnicity.

    What was the title again? *Maria–something and a Ward // robe?*

ALVARO: *Mariposa Duarte and Her Cabinet of Broken Dreams.*

HERMAN: Right.

    Astonishing. So much heart. So much charm. So whimsical.

ALVARO:

HERMAN: Okay your health?

ALVARO:

HERMAN: No? Alright

    Looks like you forgot something.

ALVARO: What'd I forget.

HERMAN: I assumed, with a certain express package conglomerate making recent visits –

ALVARO: Do I smell Chinese?

Valerie and Mario return from the fire escape, laughing. Lila follows.

VALERIE: OH. MY. GOD.

    Alvaro, you *saint.*

ALVARO: Valerie.

VALERIE: Are these for me? You shouldn't have …

Lila, come say hello to Alvaro.

ALVARO: You've grown.

VALERIE: Alvaro was also a friend of your father's …

LILA: Enchanted to meet you. My name is Lila Ann. But you may call me Lila.

ALVARO: Your father woulda been proud – little girl grown up into a beautiful señorita.

LILA: Why // thank you

VALERIE: This is Lila's fiancé Mario.

MARIO: Pleasure to meet you Alvaro. I'm uh

So sorry for your loss.

ALVARO:

VALERIE: Let's sit down, I got us Chinese – anyone like a drink?

She goes to one of the kitchen cabinets and opens it – liquor.

ALVARO: You got tequila?

VALERIE: Sure Lila?

LILA: I'd love a glass of Chardonnay, please, if you // have –

VALERIE: Herman?

HERMAN: Water's fine.

VALERIE: Mario?

Mario has already gone to the refrigerator and gotten himself a beer.

MARIO: I picked up a twelve pack – hope you don't mind, Mrs. P.

Assorted autumn brews. Anyone want one go right ahead.

During the following Valerie and Mario serve the Chinese food. At a certain point, Valerie sits, while Mario finishes the job.

VALERIE: So

Mario

Are you and Lila planning some kind of honeymoon?

LILA: Mother, I'm sure our guests are not int//erested in

VALERIE: Of course they are, // right Herman?

MARIO: To answer your question Mrs. P. // I

VALERIE: I love that you call me that no one's ever called me that

MARIO: At first we wanted to do something simple, road trip somewhere. Vermont? Adirondacks? No plans, just get in the car, stay in weird motels, maybe do a little fishing

HERMAN: Fishing

MARIO: You fish, Herman?

HERMAN: Can't say I do.

MARIO: Alvaro?

Alvaro looks at Mario like he's just seen an extraterrestrial.

MARIO: What about you Mrs. P., you ever fish?

Herman and Alvaro exchange glances and crack up.

VALERIE: Ha. Fucking HA.
    I'll have you know, Mario, that yes, I have gone fishing.

HERMAN: When did you go fishing?

VALERIE: My father took me. All the time. When I was a child.

MARIO: Must be in the genes —Your daughter, Mrs. P.? Is a regular ace with the pole — you should see some of the monster fish I seen her catch. Effortless, like she's got a fish finder wired // into her

LILA: That's an exaggera//tion

HERMAN: Fish what?

MARIO: Fish *finder.*

HERMAN: What is that?

MARIO: Like GPS, for finding fish.

HERMAN: I have no idea what you're talking about.

MARIO: Sonar. Sends sound waves underwater

So like when a school of fish goes by?

It detects em // whammo!

HERMAN: Isn't that cheating?

MARIO: Right? I'm with you on that one. Whole *point* of fishing — least to me — you can't see what's under the water, right?

Mario notices Valerie crying softly.

MARIO: Jeez. Mrs. P … you okay?

HERMAN: I think the water image —

MARIO: God, I'm an idiot

Mrs. P. I wasn't thinking what with your // ex-hus

VALERIE: No. Please. Go on

MARIO: How'd I get off on fishing?

HERMAN: Fishing Lila honeymoon …

MARIO: Sure you're gonna be okay, Mrs. P?

Valerie gathers herself. She pours herself another vodka.

VALERIE: I'm fine. I do love that you call me that.

MARIO: Honeymoon — so yeah, first we figured road trip. But *then*

One morning? Lila wakes up, she's like —

LILA: Mario

MARIO: What?

LILA: Nothing. If you'll excuse me

MARIO: Where are you going?

LILA: I need some air.

Lila exits to the fire escape.

MARIO: Okay

Anyway, one morning she's like "I want to go to Mexico."

Valerie, Herman and Alvaro stop eating and focus their attention on Mario. Mario suddenly feels on the spot.

MARIO: I had the same reaction like, "Yeah, baby, you want to go to Mexico? We'll go but, why Mexico? Never heard you mention the place let alone express some secret desire to go there."

She's like "Because."

Lila, one word answer

You learn pretty quick not to dig,

let her come round if she wants to.

Couple of days later she's like, "Okay. I'll tell you why I want to go to Mexico, but promise me you won't think I'm a freak."

Lila reenters.

MARIO: Hey baby, I was just about to tell them your Mexico dream.

Lila exits out the window again.

MARIO: What?

Anyway – She has this dream. She's on this balcony? Of this small hotel. Looking down at this little fishing town – boats in the bay, with names in Mexican –

ALVARO: Spanish.

MARIO: Right. Anyway she senses this "presence"? And this "presence", whispers the name of the town. That she has to go there someday. Next morning she googles it. This town? – that came to her in a dream? *actually* exists.

Valerie, Herman and Alvaro are clearly taken aback.

HERMAN: The name of this town?

MARIO: *(Using the Anglo pronunciation, AYN-jel.)* Puerto Angel.

Herman and Alvaro exchange a look. Valerie leaves the table for the bathroom.

MARIO: Whoa. Way to clear the room, Mario

Anyway. That's where we're going.

Did I say something to?

HERMAN: No, Mario, it's just that

    Lila's father and "Mrs. P."

    For that matter Lila herself — went there once upon a time.

MARIO: *(Saying it again using Anglo pronunciation.)* Puerto Angel?

ALVARO: *AN*-hel.

HERMAN: She was just a baby.

ALVARO: Leave it, Aitch.

MARIO: That's incredible! That's Un.be.liev//able!

HERMAN: In fact, Mario, Alvaro and I went there with them.

ALVARO: *Coño.*

MARIO: When was this?

HERMAN: Long time ago. Twenty years.

Mario, excited, goes to the window.

MARIO: Yo, Lila! Come inside, you won't believe —

Lila enters. As she does, Valerie returns from the bathroom wiping her mouth.

MARIO: I was telling them? About Puerto AN-hel? You've already been been there!

LILA: No I haven't.

MARIO: You have! You, your father, your mother. Herman and Alvaro too. Isn't // that —

LILA: Mother, is this true?

    Mother?

HERMAN: I know a little *pension* you might consider staying —

ALVARO: *Aitch.*

VALERIE: Cut it, Herm//an.

HERMAN: Run by a German fellow and his Mexican wife — what was her name? Anita?
    Gabri//ella

ALVARO: *Consuela*

VALERIE: For Chris//sake

LILA: What were we doing there?

HERMAN: Your father led us down there. He was plotting the murder of whimsy —

LILA: What does *that* mean?

HERMAN: How'd he phrase it in the manifesto?

VALERIE: Herman, I'm warn//ing you —

HERMAN: "Deadly serious times demand a deadly serious // theatre … "?

VALERIE: *ENOUGH*.

Pause.

LILA: Mother, will you please tell me what // he's

VALERIE: We were on vacation.

LILA: *Mother*

VALERIE: We were *on. vacation.*

LILA: But —

VALERIE: End of discussion.

Valerie moves to the table, sits, pours a vodka and eats in silence. Lila, exasperated, heads to the bathroom.

VALERIE: Where the hell do you think you're going?

Lila slams the bathroom door shut. Mario heads to the door and knocks.

LILA: Leave me alone mother!

MARIO: Baby, it's me.

Pause. The door opens. Mario slips in. Pause. Tense silence.

ALVARO: Ever cross your mind
    Maybe Javi's not dead?

VALERIE: He's dead.

ALVARO: Wouldn't put it past him,

Him flingin that door open, "April Fool's."

VALERIE: Hm.

No.

He's dead.

HERMAN: So what now, Valerie.

VALERIE: We read.

HERMAN: Valerie, Val // Valie.

VALERIE: Christ, what is Lila doing in there? I'm going to –

HERMAN: Let them be.

The bathroom. Lila sits on the toilet bowl smoking. Mario sits at the edge of the bathtub.

MARIO: Fuckin weird, huh?

Stick a pin in the map, bang, you've already been there. Weird.

You okay?

You

Wanna leave?

LILA: No.

MARIO: Say the word, stay, go – whatever makes you happy.

Talk to me, baby. Say something.

LILA: Why did you tell them that?

MARIO: What?

LILA: Forget it.

MARIO: Lila I'm

Sorry.

Pause.

LILA: You always stayed put.

MARIO: Meaning?

LILA: Always Boston. Never anywhere else.

MARIO: We went places, vacation. Nothing too far, but yeah,
    whole tribe's pretty much right there.

LILA: I don't know what that's like. Staying put.

MARIO: It's okay, I guess. I like knowing my tribe's nearby.

LILA: Being here? It's been … forever. But

    I walk through that door, things …

    You think you're doing something that's *you*. Dabbling in school. Car Crash Prom
    Queen. Playing in a band. *You*. But I come back — you realize you're life's already
    been lived by someone else.

MARIO: Lila, baby. You're not gonna end up like them.

    Anyhow, couple of years down the road? You and me? We'll start our *own* tribe …

Pause.

LILA: When I was out on the fire escape? I
    Remembered something I
    Hadn't thought about in …
    But there it was.
    Like it happened yesterday.

MARIO: What'd you remember?

LILA: Nothing.

MARIO: Come on Lila, talk to me.

The kitchen.

HERMAN: Seriously, Valerie. How can we possibly read it when we only have three parts —

VALERIE: *Four* parts.

HERMAN: Are you going to tell her, Alvaro?

ALVARO:

VALERIE: Tell me what?

HERMAN: Seems Alvaro neglected to bring his —

VALERIE: What? Why not?

ALVARO: I burned it.

VALERIE & HERMAN: You *what?*

ALVARO: I burned it.

HERMAN: Jes//us

VALERIE: What the fuck did you do *that* for?

ALVARO: Con Ed bill's killin me, figgad I'd try eco-friendly alternatives to heat
my apart//ment

VALERIE: Wait: Tell me you didn't. Tell me you're making a sick joke —

ALVARO:

VALERIE: You motherfucker!

ALVARO: Did you read it? Shit was an embarrassment. You wanna remember him for that?

VALERIE: It was out of context.

ALVARO: You see it makin sense in any con//text?

HERMAN: Regardless, Alvaro, he was our friend.

ALVARO: *Friend.* You sanctimonious motherfucker that why you're here? Celebrate
your "friend"?

VALERIE: You had no right to burn it.

ALVARO: He addressed it to me. Way I see it?
Green light to do whatever the fuck I wanted.

VALERIE: So you came here because

ALVARO: I don't get out much, figgad I could use some enta-tainment.

VALERIE: You selfish son of // a bitch

ALVARO: You calling me selfish? I took Javi in when none a you would give him the
time of day. Right when things started turning for me — finally, years a me pluggin
away, getting nowhere, an yeah, you can say I put on my lipstick, sequin miniskirt,
tacones whatever

HERMAN: Huh?

ALVARO: Whored myself, Aitch. –

But I earned that shit. He shows up. Broken little dog. I fed him. Made sure he took his meds. *Paid* for those meds. Cradled him in my arms, calm him down when he had night//mares.

VALERIE: Boo fuck//ing hoo

ALVARO: Sat through him reading me bullshit plays he wasn't ever gonna finish, when I shoulda been finishin my own. When I do finish? Follow up to *Mariposa*? Bitch reads it. "*Whimsical.*" You want a list a all the shit I gave up to keep him alive?

VALERIE: Yet despite all your heroic efforts

ALVARO: Yeah, he ended up in the streets. Yeah, maybe best I could do, delay the inevitable. But I didn't turn my back on him.

VALERIE: No. You got your hero to finally fuck you.

He was more than you bargained for.

You got rid of him.

ALVARO: Fuck you, Valerie.

VALERIE: What on earth is she doing in there? LILA!

HERMAN: Valerie, Val, Valie just let them be.

The bathroom.

LILA: I can't stand it when she yells.

MARIO: Lila, talk to me. Please.

LILA: I was 3.

It was summer.

We were in a house I forget where –

an *actual* house, with a yard …

Just me and my father.

He used to read me this book.

About this little girl who loved the moon so much,

Her father brought it down from the sky for her.

One night, middle of the night,
I left the house.
Went into the yard.
To look at the moon.

I don't know how long I was out there
I remember feeling cold,
But I couldn't get back inside

I shouted: "Daddy! Daddy!"
He didn't hear me.
He was asleep.

I was so. Scared.
out there by myself,
no way to get back in …

When they went away they used to tell me
"Mommy always comes back, Daddy always comes back."
When they did, they came through the front door.
So I thought Front door.

In the yard there was a gate to an alley.
God that alley was so frightening
Shadows,
Cold concrete
I walked down the alley to the sidewalk.
To the front door
Curled myself into a ball,
Waited til morning.

Morning came, I hear my father out back.
"Lila! Lila!"
"Please, god, no, please god no"
He came running up the alley.
Naked except for his boxers.
When he got to the sidewalk,

He collapsed. "Fuck you God, Fuck you God"
Punching the pavement with his fists
I'd never seen him like that he was so
Terrifying
I went to him
Put my hand on his shoulder
"Daddy, you came back!"

He looked at me,
like he'd seen a ghost.
He grabbed my whole body,
Like he was going to crush me
The look in his eye – god just thinking about it …

Pause.

MARIO: What?

LILA: The look in his eye like
he loved me
And hated me
more than anything else in the world.

Silence.

After that
He was around less and less
Until he never came back …

Mario strokes her hair.

LILA: I'm afraid, Mario.

MARIO: Lila, baby? I promise you: I will always come back.

LILA: That's not what I am afraid of.

MARIO: Then what?

LILA: That I won't.

Back in the kitchen. Tense silence.

HERMAN: Alvaro: I don't think you realize what it is you burned.

ALVARO: Oh no?

HERMAN: No.

    I saw him. Not long after that.

ALVARO: You saw him?

HERMAN: Day I moved back to New York. After my "troubles." I'd taken the train from Chicago. On the 8th Avenue side of Penn Station, I see a homeless man outside the entrance. Cardboard sign hanging from his neck. Photograph taped to it. The word "missing" written in scrawl.

    I didn't recognize him.

    On 44th, half a block from my apartment, it hits me. Javier. And the photo Pablo.

VALERIE: Oh, god …

HERMAN: I went back to Penn. He was gone.

    Few days later I start getting hang up calls late at night.
    One night, the intercom buzzes. It's him.
    He'd cleaned up —
    Still a little worn, but
    he had that glimmer.
    Of his old self.

VALERIE: He was so beautiful

HERMAN: We talked. Like old days. He'd read about my "troubles."
    Told me he was working on a new play

    Then without warning, something shifted. He got
    Edgy. Saying he had new "leads." That the
    Japanese fishermen had done it. That the boat sank
    Iceberg. That if he could find them, he could finish the play.

ALVARO: Shit …

HERMAN: Pure nonsense …

 I told him so. He broke down …

 Said he'd been drinking the night before.

 Dive on 9ᵗʰ by the Port Authority. Said he wanted to die because

 He "left it there"

VALERIE: Left what there?

HERMAN: *Diagram*, Valerie. *Diagram of a Paper Airplane.*

 Next day he went back, it was gone.

 He had to write the whole goddamn thing over again, Alvaro.

VALERIE: And you burned it …

Silence. Valerie rises from the table.

HERMAN: Where are you going?

VALERIE: I'm getting Lila. So goddamn rude of her to lock herself in there.

She pounds on the door.

VALERIE: LILA!

Lila flings the door open.

LILA: What do you *want?*

VALERIE: In the kitchen. Now. It's time.

LILA: For what?

VALERIE: We're reading your father's play.

Lila emerges from the bathroom, followed by Mario. Valerie brings the parts of the manuscript to the table. Mario helps make room by moving dishes away. Everyone sits.

VALERIE: Well?

HERMAN: I have page one. Guess I'm first. *Hhhhhhh.*

 "Author's Note: You will note reading *Diagram of a Paper Airplane* that many narrative threads remain mysterious, and unwoven in any way one can characterize as quote neat. This is my intent, and not evidence of me being a sloppy hack. The play's open-ended nature stems from my conviction that it truthfully reflects the condition of being alive. To that end, I invite you to take a long hard look at your own fucking life – all that you've done (and not done), people you know (or once knew), things you wish you said (but didn't) – in short, all your own mysteries and unwoven threads – and see for yourself the countless paper airplanes you tossed into the sky, only never to see them land. – Javier C., Gallup New Mexico."

Who wants to read stage directions?

MARIO: I'll read. Okay: here goes.

"Prologue: Ferry to Purgatory. A massive iceberg in the middle of the North Atlantic. Floating in the sea beneath – detritus of a shipwreck: shards of a hull, dead bodies, a burning Japanese flag. In the distance, an ancient FERRYMAN rows a lifeboat towards the iceberg.

"A naked man, OUR DEAD WRITER, stands atop the iceberg."

Who's reading DEAD WRITER?

VALERIE: Alvaro.

ALVARO: *I'm* reading him? Shit

"Hello. I was not expecting you. An audience. I imagine you are wondering: who is this man wearing nary a stitch, standing butt nekkid on a massive tabular dome iceberg out in the middle of the North Atlantic. Allow me to introduce myself: I am Your Dead Writer. I'm delighted you could make an appearance on the occasion of my death. Yes, folks, I died. Just before the lights went up, in a landscape far removed from this Arctic nightmare. My death has freed me to point my finger at you in cruel indictment. Alas, decades of agony have taught me that to point a finger at you is to point a finger at myself."

MARIO: *"The FERRYMAN's boat reaches the foot of the iceberg."*

ALVARO: "Hark! I spy a Ferryman! A crotchetyoldsonofabitch Ferryman approaching my iceberg."

I told you this shit was an embarrassment.

VALERIE: Come on Alvaro.

ALVARO: That's where it skips. Anybody got page two?

VALERIE: Here.

ALVARO: "Does he bring word of my estranged bride? Of my friends turned bitter enemies? Has he come to explain why I feel no cold though my butt is nekkid and the air Arctic? ..."

Why we reading this mother//fucking bullshit?

VALERIE: Godddamnit, Alvaro, SHUT UP and READ

ALVARO: *Coño*

"Will he usher me through the gates of heaven? Or hurl me into the fires of hell? Or worse: lead me to my greatest terror? Oh, cursed destiny! Purgatory! No! The foreboding!"

MARIO: "*Ominous feedback fills the stage — generated by the CHORUS OF CHILDREN DISAP-PEARED playing electric guitars.*"?

ALVARO: "State your business, wicked Ferryman!"

MARIO: "*The FERRYMAN, smiling dementedly, folds a piece of paper into a paper airplane and tosses it. It lands at the feet of OUR DEADWRITER.*"

ALVARO: "Do I read this wicked Ferryman's aeronautic missive? Or do I ignore it? Curiosity, like St. George, has vanquished my dragon will"

HERMAN: He's right, Valerie. This really is a piece of shit.

VALERIE: Indulge me.

MARIO: "*OUR DEADWRITER unfolds the paper airplane.*"

ALVARO: "What's this? A form letter? 'Dear Author: Thank you for submitting your manuscript. We regret to inform you that we have no use for your work. Please know that our decision pains us too: we don't like to think we're driving another nail into your coffin.
'Sincerely,
God in Heaven'"

MARIO: "*The FERRYMAN tosses another airplane, beaming with toothless delight. It lands, bursting into flames.*"

Is there a page three?

VALERIE: Here —

ALVARO: "'Dear Author: Why do you insist on sending us piece of shit after piece of shit manuscript? What the fuck is wrong with you? Are you a masochist? Or a fucking moron? Please! No mas.

'Sincerely,

The Prince of Darkness'

"Oh! The dread! Rejected by Heaven and Hell! I fear the next paper airplane will seal my Purgatorial fate!"

MARIO: "*The FERRYMAN tosses a third airplane, his toothless grin an abyss of demented joy.*"

ALVARO: "'Dear Sir: It gives us great pleasure to inform you we accept your submission. Please find enclosed a check for an astronomical sum of money. Enjoy the pleasure that awaits! Booze, drugs, women, cannibalism, necrophilia, etc Our Ferryman is at your disposal.

'Yours,

Purgatorio Repertorio Tay-Atch-Roh'"

MARIO: "*The FERRYMAN beckons. OUR DEAD WRITER hangs his head, climbs down to the boat. The FERRYMAN hands him a smelly blanket and broken life preserver. The FERRYMAN rows, humming a vaguely familiar show tune as they disappear in the distance.*"

ALVARO: Can we stop?

VALERIE: There's half a page before it breaks.

MARIO: "*The iceberg melts, whimsically, revealing:*

"*SCENE ONE*

"*A filthy motel room in Gallup, New Mexico. Dirty clothes, empty liquor bottles, cigarette butts, cockroaches. On the desk a battered Smith-Corona next to a monumental unfinished manuscript. OUR DEAD WRITER lies in bed, naked, next to a naked, functionally illiterate New Mexican Woman, TINACONSUELA.*

"*A LITTLE BOY, 4, creeps through the window. He's beautiful — head of blonde curls, large brown eyes. OUR DEAD WRITER wakes abruptly. The LITTLE BOY reaches out his hand.*"

Uh who's reading LITTLE BOY?

There are no takers.

LILA: I'll read …

VALERIE: Lila

LILA: What?

VALERIE: Never mind.

LILA: "Daddy Let's take a walk. I want you to take a walk with me."

ALVARO: "Where have you been all this time?"

LILA: "I been far, far away … Daddy, don't be afraid … "

MARIO: *"The LITTLE BOY takes his father's hand, leads him to the window and"*

HERMAN: And …

MARIO: That's it. From there it skips to page

Everyone notices Valerie softly crying.

MARIO: You okay Mrs. P.?

VALERIE: I'm

　Fuck.

　Don't mind me I

HERMAN: This might be a

　good place to stop?

VALERIE: No. A dead man has a wish. We grant it.

The lights shift. Passage of time. They continue reading in dumbshow. They pass pages back and forth. Valerie drinks. The lights return to normal when they reach the end of the play.

MARIO: *"Dusk. OUR DEAD WRITER and LITTLE BOY stand in Potter's field by a stack of wooden caskets. The CHORUS OF CHILDREN DISAPPEARED sing the Anagram Chant:"*

HERMAN: "Paper Airplane

　Plan a Ripe Pear"

ALVARO: "You have shown me the graves of my friends.

　"The graves of men and women I knew in passing."

HERMAN: "Pal Reaper Pain

Pear Apple Rain"

ALVARO: "The graves of strangers I never knew."

HERMAN: "Rare Papal Pine

Plain Raper Ape."

ALVARO: "But when will you show me the grave where I might finally rest?"

MARIO: "*He turns and sees the LITTLE BOY has gone. He kneels by the caskets and covers his face. Lights fade. End of Play.*"

Long silence.

MARIO: Wow that was …

VALERIE: Not necessary, Mario. It's okay.

Pause.

HERMAN: I'm

Sorry, Valerie. I'm truly sorry.

Pause.

HERMAN: What time is it?

ALVARO: Quarter past two.

Silence. No one seems to know what to do.

ALVARO: "Makes you think about all your own trees."

VALERIE: What?

ALVARO: Last line of *Death of a Liberal*?

Frank's eulogy at Jim Barrie's funeral?

VALERIE: Right, right. "What's the saying? If a tree falls in the forest?"

HERMAN: "Makes you think about all your own trees. The trees in the forest of your heart."

ALVARO: *That* was some incredible shit.

HERMAN: Hm.

ALVARO: Shit My compadre lost the plot

HERMAN: Lost more than that.

LILA: I thought it was beautiful.

Pause.

ALVARO: Well

    Guess this party's over ...

VALERIE: NO.

Pause.

    We. Are not. Finished ...

    Memories I asked all of you to bring something
    Did anyone ... ?
    Anyone?
    Fine, I'll go.

    I have memories.
    I can think of a hundred off the top of my head that
    made me want to slit his throat in his sleep // HA

HERMAN: Jesus, Valerie

VALERIE: Oh, Herman, I'm just being *truthful*
    In spite of all the
    Shit
    My fondest memory?
    First time I laid eyes on him.
    He couldn't have been more than 17 // 18

ALVARO: 22.

VALERIE: Noooo

ALVARO: I was there, Valerie, he was 22.

VALERIE: Oh, go to hell, Alvaro -
    What difference does it make if he was 15 or 35 I'm talking about what I *experienced*,
    what I *felt*, God // you a –

HERMAN: Just go on, Valerie

VALERIE: First time I laid eyes on him, God, he was

Amazing.

This magical, demonic, scary, little urchin

You're right, Alvaro, he was 22, you *were* there, *mea culpa.*

I was just a kid – directionless, too afraid to

Throw myself completely into anything –

but Javi

Way he talked, those *eyes* – I was a little frightened of him,

It's like he knew who you were supposed to be before you had any idea.

He was so ... *Convincing.*

ALVARO: Like a snake oil salesman.

VALERIE: Shut up, Alvaro

ALVARO: I didn't mean nothing by that – I was convinced too.

VALERIE: A lot of people thought that – all talk,

But then we read *Death of a Liberal* –

My god This kid wrote *this* when he was 19?

ALVARO: 22.

VALERIE: If he'd been 60, Alvaro, it would have been an achievement, // so eat me.

MARIO: You ever read it, Lila?

LILA: No.

MARIO: I'd love to read it ...

ALVARO: Doesn't exist anymore. Plays disappear.

VALERIE: That night, I knew I had to be with him ...

The fucker.

Long pause.

Who's next? Herman?

HERMAN: I'll pass this round.

VALERIE: So infuriating — Alvaro?

ALVARO: Pass.

VALERIE: Oh, come on, why can't —
Lila. Lila, it's your turn.

LILA: Mother

VALERIE: Mario, please *instruct* my daughter // to —

LILA: Mother!

MARIO: Dying to hear this woman I love, who knew, right?

VALERIE: As his flesh and blood, // as his

LILA: Fine.

VALERIE: If you're going to be that way // never

LILA: I'm not being any // "way"

VALERIE: First thing that pops in your head. // Pop!

LILA: Beluga whales.
Daddy took me weekends to the aquarium on Coney Island, to see the beluga whales. I remember holding his hand. Our reflections in the glass. The whale's big, ghostly shape

MARIO: That's beautiful kinda chokes me up …

VALERIE: Beluga whales, what else?

LILA: You wanted a memory, I gave you a memory.

VALERIE: That image — like Mario says — beautiful

LILA: What are you getting at, mother?

VALERIE: Nothing. What else do you remember?

LILA: All sorts of things — more flashes than // full blown

VALERIE: That's the nature of things, sweetie Go ahead, we'd love to hear more.

LILA: I remember the rubber alligator. The convoluted bed time stories he made up.

VALERIE: Like which ones?

LILA: I just remember they were funny … Oh, the times it snowed, and Daddy took me to Central Park to make snow angels.

VALERIE: Snow angels?

LILA: In Sheep Meadow. We'd plop down in the snow, make snow // angels

VALERIE: Weird, I don't have any recollec//tion

LILA: It was just me and him.

VALERIE: Right.

LILA: The Paper Airplane Quests.

VALERIE: Mario, will you be a pumpkin, hand me that bottle? No – the tequila …

MARIO: Sure Mrs. P.

Alvaro shoots Mario a warning glance. Mario hesitates.

VALERIE: Is there an issue, Mario?

MARIO: No, Mrs. P …

Alvaro shrugs. Mario hands Valerie the tequila bottle. She pours herself a glass.

VALERIE: You were saying. Paper Airplane what?

LILA: I'm done talking.

VALERIE: Please finish. Not for my sake, for Mario I'm sure // he'd

HERMAN: Valerie Val Val//ie

VALERIE: Don't "Val Val Val" me.
    Paper. Airplanes.

LILA: I'm done.

MARIO: Come on Lila

LILA: Jesus, Mario, what the // fuck

VALERIE: See? Mario'd love // to know

HERMAN: *Hhhhhhhhhhh*

LILA: Fine. Once we were in the Park. By the Carousel.

    Daddy said if I kept my eyes fixed on the ground I'd find paper airplanes everywhere. He said we should have a contest whoever found the most paper airplanes would win a prize.

VALERIE: A prize

LILA: I remember thinking how silly it was – But he was right. They were everywhere. I must have collected a dozen that day.

MARIO: That's how it started? What a cool story –

VALERIE: Astonishing, isn't it Mario.

MARIO: Yeah, unbeliev / / able –

VALERIE: Fucking Beluga whales.

LILA: Excuse me?

VALERIE: *Fucking*. Beluga whales.

HERMAN: Valerie … Val / / Valie

VALERIE: What else, Lila? What other *magical* moments do you remember?

    He buy you strawberry ice cream / / cones?

HERMAN: Valerie.

VALERIE: Eat me, Herman.

    Beluga whales fucking *snow angels?* Fucking paper airplanes …
    Jesus Christ, the way you tell it
    You'd think that cocksucker deserved the
    Daddy of the Millennium Award.

HERMAN: Valerie, Lila let's

VALERIE: He was *terrified of you,* Lila
    God, you've taken an eraser to your childhood
    Scrubbed out all the *shit* all the *sickness*
    Let me tell you something you little ingrate:

ALVARO: Valerie, come // on

VALERIE: Shut it Alvaro.

Weekends. He took you to see the beluga whale *once*.

Paper *air*planes. How bucolic, daddy and his little girl in the park —

You know what that was?

His way of telling you to *shut up*.

Leave him alone so he didn't have to really *be* with you, *father* you.

Look how ridiculous you are with your shopping bags full of them

Years later, still collecting them, still obsessing over one stupid afternoon he *tricked* you,

Contest what was the prize, Lila?

LILA: I don't remember.

VALERIE: There wasn't one.

You'd bring him piles of them, like a little cat carrying in dead birds "I want your love so bad I'll do the most idiotic things to get it" — you know where they ended up? The *garbage,* Lila —

HERMAN: That's enough, Valerie.

VALERIE: You are one sick little girl. You are just like him.

LILA: That has to be the nicest thing you've ever said to me, Mommy. Thank you.

VALERIE: Forget everything.

The violence.

The contempt.

The endless silences.

The parade of "assistants" he used in *my* bed.

Because I know

Staring it in the face

Would confirm every ugly suspicion you have about yourself

Make you want to slit your // wrists.

MARIO: Mrs. P that's *enough*.

Silence. Lila holds back any emotional reaction to Valerie's attack.

VALERIE: Mario. May I have one of your cigarettes.

Mario offers his pack. Valerie takes it and heads out to the fire escape. Mario places his hand on Lila's shoulder. She shrugs it off.

MARIO: I could uh

Use a cigarette too …

Lila?

No response. He exits to the fire escape. Lila, Herman and Alvaro sit in awkward silence. Alvaro heads to the fire escape. Lila begins to cry. Herman reaches his hand to Lila's.

LILA: Don't touch me.

HERMAN: Your mother, she

LILA: Don't. I know.

Pause.

HERMAN: You don't look like you.

LILA:

HERMAN: You don't seem like you.

What is going on, Lila, you're diff//erent

LILA: What do you think of him?

HERMAN: Who?

LILA: Mario.

HERMAN: Depends on what // you

LILA: Don't

HERMAN: Are you asking me if I'd like to go *fishing* with him some week//end?

LILA: Forget it forget I asked.

HERMAN: Because honestly, Lila, I have no idea what my approval would mean to you.

LILA: You're approval, Herman, means everything to me.

Outside on the fire escape, Valerie, Alvaro and Mario smoke in tense silence.

ALVARO: You keep her in the dark about him all this time?

VALERIE: Excuse me?

ALVARO: Lila. You keep her in the dark. All this time.

Silence.

Shit. That's deep.

Back in the kitchen.

HERMAN: Do you love him?

LILA: I *do* // love him

HERMAN: Then what I say shouldn't matter.

LILA: He's not what you would expect, right? For me, I mean.

HERMAN: That pleases you.

LILA: Yes. It does. To know that
We're much bigger than we think we are.

Why are you smiling that way?

HERMAN: What way?

LILA: Like I'm some
Charming imbecile in one of your seminars I remember that look
Someone would raise their hand, say something they thought was bright,
You'd smile in that crushing way,
"How sweet, how idiotic."

The fire escape:

ALVARO: Why would you do that?

VALERIE: Do what?

ALVARO: Keep her in the dark.

VALERIE: She was too young to remember. Why fill her head up with
heartache
That happened long before she could remember

MARIO: Mrs. P.? If you don't mind me asking ...

VALERIE: Would you be a sweetie Mario and give me another cigarette?

MARIO: Sure

ALVARO: You don't think she remembers

VALERIE: She was 14 months old.

ALVARO: She remembers

VALERIE: I'm her mother. I would know // if she —

ALVARO: She *remembers*.
　　All you gotta do is take one hard look at that girl
　　She's walking around like the whole world's some
　　Haunted house

MARIO: Can I please ask —

VALERIE: It's a phase. She'll get over it.

ALVARO: How old is she?

VALERIE: Twenty-five, twenty // six?

MARIO: Twenty-eight.

ALVARO: Little late for her to be going through "phases" // don't you

VALERIE: Tell me something: Did you ever ask my husband these // questions?

ALVARO: Oh, he's your *husband* now that's com//ical.

VALERIE: Did you ever *judge* my husband the way you're // judging me

ALVARO: Yeah. I asked him. He gave me the same motherfuckin bullshit answer.

MARIO: Somebody please tell me what you're talking about.

VALERIE: Nothing, sweetie. Nothing.

The kitchen.

HERMAN: Truth be told, Lila.
　　I'm
　　envious.

LILA: Herman, that's not what I

HERMAN: No no no

> I knew long ago the day would come you'd
> Find someone your age. Someone uncompromised.
> Am I sad you won't ever come visit me again? Yes.
> But my envy isn't from wanting you for me. No.
> I'm envious of a *feeling* I haven't felt in a very
> Long.
> time.

LILA: I don't understand.

HERMAN: You go around when you're young

> With a picture in your head
> of the person you think you're supposed to love.
> That person doesn't exist.
> So it takes an
> Abitrary look across a room.
> Your eyes land on someone
> Who doesn't look like, talk like, think like,
> smell like the person you imagined
> But there they are. You love them.

> I'm envious, Lila, because I'm long past the point in my life
> Where even faking that feeling is a possibility.

Pause. Lila puts her hand on Herman's.

HERMAN: Last time I felt that?

> Was that day eleven years ago
> when you walked into my seminar.

LILA: Are you trying to manipulate me?

HERMAN: No.

> Maybe a little,

> No.

LILA: Tell me something, Herman.

Promise me you'll tell me the truth.

Did you know who I was that day?

HERMAN: I'm not sure I under//stand

LILA: Did you know I was my father's daughter.

Herman?

HERMAN: No.

I didn't.

Not until it was too late.

LILA: I love you Herman.

HERMAN: I love you.

LILA: Kiss me?

HERMAN: No.

LILA: Please?

She kisses him. At first he's reluctant. Reluctance becomes a longing, final farewell kiss. The window opens, Alvaro, Valerie and Mario return from the fire escape. They freeze seeing Herman and Lila kissing.

VALERIE: What.

The *fuck.* //

Is going on in here.

MARIO: Lila Jesus, // Lila

ALVARO: Shit.

VALERIE: *What the fuck is going on here?*

HERMAN: Valerie, please let me explain

Mario calmly walks up to Herman. They stand eye to eye.

HERMAN: Mario … Why don't we all sit down and

Mario lands a powerful right hook to Herman's face, knocking him down.

MARIO: Let's go Lila.

Lila: I said: Let's. *Go*.

Lila: *Now*.

LILA: No.

The quiet conviction in her voice suspends the room. Alvaro reaches into his pocket and removes the handwritten pages of Diagram of a Paper Airplane.

ALVARO: Lila? You don't know me. But
I knew your father.

Sometimes? Your father?
Wasn't so good at
making distinctions.
Between what mattered, what didn't.
This mattered.

VALERIE: What is it?

ALVARO: Please. Take it.

LILA: Is this his handwriting?

ALVARO: Yeah.

VALERIE: What is it?
Alvaro, goddamnit, what is it?

Lila sits and reads.

LILA: "Unsent Letter to My Daughter Lila Anne:
A Prologue to *Diagram of a Paper Airplane*."

"Sweet Lila:

"I don't know if you will ever read this. I suppose when I finish writing it, I could put it in an envelope, and send it to you. But I'm not sure I have the courage.

"I wish we lived in a universe where I could fold these pages into a paper airplane, toss it into the sky and have faith it'd reach you wherever you may be.

"I wasn't a good father to you. Offering parental advice might seem at worst, a betrayal, at best, a not very funny joke. But I want to share with you something I learned which might help you someday if you have children of your own: the greatest danger to a child is not a wall socket. Crossing the street. A swimming pool with no one watching. No. The greatest danger to a child is the father and mother that brought you into the world.

"Two and a half years before you were born, your mother and I had a son. We named him Pablo. A beautiful boy. Wild blonde curls. Impish smile. Your mother's eyes."

Lila looks at Valerie. Valerie closes her eyes.

"When he was four – you were 14 months – we took you to Puerto Angel, a village by the sea in Mexico. We traveled there with our friends – fellow artists, to dream up a theatre we believed in. A theatre we planned to make when we returned to New York.

"We were young.

"At night, after your mother and I put Pablo and you to bed, we left you. To meet our friends in the hotel's courtyard. We talked, drank, dreamed late into the night. Taking turns to check on you.

"That night, we were reckless. I left with Consuela, the Mexican wife of the man who ran the hotel. Your mother left with my close friend – a man who later abandoned the theatre to become an historian.

Lila looks at Herman. He looks away. She looks at Valerie. Valerie looks away.

"In the wee hours, a voice tore open the night. "HE'S GONE" It was Alvaro. The raw, the brilliant Alvaro. He was the last to look in on Pablo and you. We returned to find him. Holding you, so small, so innocent, asleep. But Pablo was gone.

"We never found him.

"For years, your mother and I lived a purgatory of not knowing, of shame, of recrimination; as your mother and father, we tried to see only you, not the shadow of a boy who'd gone missing. We failed.

"Needless to say, we never made our theatre.

"I dream of your brother often. In my dreams Pablo appears exactly as he did the day he left us. That morning, on the beach, I taught him to make paper airplanes. I'll never forget the ecstatic delight in his eyes watching them circle in the air

Pause.

"Forgive me, Lila. Please forgive me.

"Love,
Your father."

Lila folds the sheets of paper, rises from the chair. She moves to Alvaro. She places the pages in his inside jacket pocket. She presses her hands against his chest and looks him in the eye.

LILA: *(A whisper — so soft as to be barely audible.)* Thank you.

She turns to Mario. She looks him in the eye. She removes her ring, takes his hand, places the ring on his palm and closes his fingers.

LILA: I can't.

She turns to Herman. She moves very close to him.

LILA: Denier.

She turns to Valerie. She moves towards her, thinks better of it, turns to leave the apartment.

MARIO: I guess I should uhhh

It was a

pleasure meeting you all.

He exits. Alvaro, Valerie and Herman. Alvaro goes to the door. Before he exits he turns to them.

ALVARO: Good night.

Herman and Valerie alone, not looking at each other.

TWO

Dawn. Valerie and Herman on the rooftop, sitting on crappy outdoor furniture. The FedEx boxes with Diagram of a Paper Airplane *rest on a table between them. They both fold pages of the manuscript into paper airplanes and toss them into the sky. This continues through:*

Night. Alvaro's kitchen. The carton of Kools is dead. Microphone and digital recorder still going. Alvaro talks to the unseen interviewer.

ALVARO: Did *Diagram of a Paper Airplane* survive?

    Far as I know? Mistuh PhD Candidate,

    Columbia University,

    It didn't.

    But you never know, right?

    Could be out there somewhere,

    Like the plays a his you found.

    I'm tired. Gotta sleep.

    But lemme ask you one question: his plays …

    what are you gonna do with them?

Alvaro fades. Valerie and Herman continue tossing paper airplanes. After several airplanes, their hands touch. They hold hands. They do not look at each other.

VALERIE: Shall we walk in the park?

Slow fade to black.

End of play

A THICK DESCRIPTION OF HARRY SMITH (Vol.1)
(or Do What Thou Wilt Shall Be the Whole of the Law)

INTRODUCTION

Tamsen Wolff, PhD. Associate Professor of English, Princeton University

A Thick Description of Harry Smith, Volume 1 (or, Do What Thou Wilt Shall Be the Whole of the Law) is the second play of the trilogy entitled *The Javier Plays*, and it is the hallucinogenic heart of the matter. The play is a kaleidoscopically theatrical, deeply funny, razor-sharp take on the overlapping concerns that run through all three plays, including: authorship, how, when, and whether it matters; the slippery relationship between reality and fiction; and the lifecycles of art forms and artists, especially the question of what gets left behind and what to do with it.

The play begins with three beginnings, immediately establishing its multiple points of entry, and its sly, gleefully non-linear, choose-your-own trip sensibility. The first scene, "An Overture," is an introduction to the emphatically aural world of the play, since

all we see is a figure, "Perhaps it is Harry Smith," who is recording and listening – as we do too – to an assortment of American sounds, from regional songs to street noise to fireworks. According to Professor Emiliano Kurtz, who arrives in the second scene to present the play, *A Thick Description of Harry Smith* is an unfinished drama he discovered, written by forgotten playwright Javier C. The play is a surreal live radio variety show, with folk and traditional musical guests, storytelling segments, and barely tongue-in-cheek "old-timey" advertisements for fictional products. The Stranger Emcee introduces the radio show in what might be considered the third opening scene. He may or may not also be Harry Smith and Professor Kurtz, since the same actor plays all three figures. The Emcee/Harry introduces, comments on, and possibly engineers aspects of the radio show. Kurtz, not quite managing to bookend the show authoritatively, returns in the penultimate scene to discuss the drama's putative ending. But we really end where we started: with sound, this time the final musical performance of the guest band on the radio show, Blank Marlowe and the Red Herrings singing a rendition of Bob Dylan's "A Hard Rain's A-Gonna Fall."

The composite figure of Harry Smith and the form of the variety show, with its seemingly haphazard collection of recycled pieces of Americana, reflects the question that drives the alleged playwright, second-generation American Javier C.: what does it mean to be American? This is plainly an artistic as well as a national question; how can disparate peoples and histories and materials cohere into a recognizable country, or a piece of art? At the same time, the grab bag format of the variety show is a front, since the work has a strict methodical structure. The play braids together three separate radio performance segments, each in turn with three parts, reflecting the larger trilogy form and a recurring insistence on threes. These segments are: Mystery Radio Theatre: The Curator's Folly; The Darkest Heart of America: The Never-Ending Tour of Blank Marlowe and His Band, The Red Herrings; and Shadow of the Shining City: Chronicles of the American Underground. (A fourth promised segment – the confounding radio act of the Albuquerque Youth Ballet's adaptation of a Harry Smith film – turns out, after all, to be a will-o-the-wisp, a lower case red herring, a no-show.) Songs and music punctuate and shape the show. Like the segments, the musical choices appear to be a) unrelated, stand-alone performances and b) critical to collectively forming the thick description of the title. Characters, songs, and segments, like the sounds of the initial scene, summon one another out of the ether, interjecting, elaborating, confirming, merging, competing, and colliding. This babel steadily, and only apparently circuitously, builds a partial picture of Harry Smith.

Through the story of Smith, the play makes a deft, witty case for the concomitant survival and evolution of art, for memorializing without totalizing. To kick off the radio variety show, Marlowe and the Red Herrings sing Blind Lemon Jefferson's "See

That My Grave is Kept Clean," which leads the Emcee/Harry to wonder, "Will someone see *my* grave's kept clean?" Of course the answer is yes: the play is grave-tending as well as grave-robbing. It introduces the wildly eccentric avant-garde visual artist, musicologist, and experimental filmmaker Harry Smith (1923-1991) to an audience who by and large will never have heard of him. He and his work are exhumed here, brushed off, and given their due. But the play refuses to lionize Smith. The suggestion is not that he is an overlooked genius – or even necessarily any kind of recognizable genius – but that his work and life are deeply fruitful and deserve some play. His tale here remains hilariously, messily resonant, neither mythical nor definitive. This Harry Smith is a chameleon of reinvented identity, a hard act to document, let alone follow.

Late in the play in a piece of background action, Smith is giving an interview to a music journalist that illustrates his undoubtedly paranoid but also creative desire to elude a single, defining account of his life. He lies freely, transparently, zealously. The play mirrors his example in this. In the playful spirit of Harry's invention and reinvention, the real and the imaginary are so tightly and thoroughly imbricated in the play that it is nearly impossible to sort out the difference between fact and fantasy. Besides, as the material makes patently clear, the real is fantastical (you can't make this stuff up, or you can try, but you may well find that real life has already done it better). The confusion that the playwright Javier C. expresses early on in a recorded voiceover on this point – which came first, the egg (the real Harry Smith), or the chicken (his play about Harry Smith) – is not as far-fetched as Kurtz suggests. This is a legitimate question too about what constitutes the creative process: where do ideas originate? The relationship between an artist and an idea or creation is rarely simple or one-directional. The play's authorial instability repeatedly begs the question, in the immortal words of Aretha Franklin's lesser work, "Who's zoomin' who?" What's more, if we can't tell with any real specificity where ideas begin, to whom do they belong? And how much does that matter, anyway?

Even when the figures, facts, or history in the play are "real" (Allen Ginsberg, Richard Nixon, the history of recording devices), that reality is simultaneously interlaced with invention to the point where it's disconcertingly hard to know if you know what you think you know. Navigating the play's facts and fictions is an unsteady but exhilarating enterprise, like trying to stand up in a tippy boat, or attempting to complete a simple task while high. In other words, the play compels an audience to experience the joyful, liberating vertigo that comes from acknowledging that at  bottom very little if any boundary exists between what is real and what is invented, and, moreover, energy expended trying to differentiate cleanly between "true" and "not true" is probably wasted energy. Whereas *Your Name Will Follow You Home* in particular offers a more literal examination of what it means to cross the line from fact to fiction – in that play, specifically to claim another identity as your own – *A Thick Description of Harry Smith* obliterates any meaningful distinction between the two.

The giddy, unruly convergence of the real and the fictional together with the multiple stories and modes of storytelling means too that the audience is both constantly surprised and tickled, and constantly attempting to piece together a narrative. An

 audience has to make sense of the information being doled or spewed out, even though – and because – this information is clearly always incomplete and unreliable. Such is the Curator's ongoing lament (or Folly, as the play would have it) as she struggles to put together the Harry Smith Museum and Interpretive Center: what can she make of the hard evidence, the actual stuff, that Harry made or owned and left

behind? What does it amount to and what story does it tell? Because Smith, it turns out, was an unusual combination of hoarder – amassing enormous, odd collections of items like paper airplanes, Ukrainian Easter eggs, 78s – and its opposite – selling or destroying works and possessions whenever necessary or on a complete whim.

Harry's central lost masterpiece is his unfinished movie about Oz. Marlowe's doomed search for it, on and off the roads in the official Rand McNally map, mirrors the original journey on the Yellow Brick Road. The story of the Wizard of Oz ripples lightly outward through the whole trilogy, present particularly in the band of four slightly grudging compatriots who appear in each play (Jorge/Martin/Annie/Marlowe here, flanked by Alvaro/Herman/Valerie/Javier in the first and last plays). Like Dorothy and her crew, each group is searching for meaning/the Wizard and all will be disappointed. As the Curator repeatedly discovers, there is no *there* there, only an empty box or more of the same unfathomable stuff. About this apparently random pile of material floating in his wake, the Voice of Harry offers this key refrain: "I'm uhhh/Leaving it to/Future generations to uhhh/Figure out the purpose of all this *stuff*." What this comment extends is a blessing to future artists to have their way with his remains. What the play proposes, in its use of Oz and all things Harry, is that a vital purpose of art lies in its repurposing.

Music is the play's most important and consistent demonstration of repurposing with a purpose. Music – in the form of the vast, influential compilation *The Anthology of American Folk Music*, which Smith published in 1952 – may also be the single solid, irrefutable artifact that remains of Harry. Moreover, since he eventually won a Grammy Award

in 1991 for his efforts, music marks his one moment of public recognition and celebration, his entry into the official annals of American culture. When he won the Grammy shortly before his death, Smith stated, "I'm glad to say my dreams came true. I saw America changed through music." His dream about the potentially social transformative power of music is matched by a profound comprehension of how music itself changes. The play uses songs as constant practical examples of adoption and adaptation in art, as well as the perfect grounds for corresponding ideological artistic debates about memory, virtuosity, loss, and change. For example, Harry's determination to press recordings of perhaps the last Orthodox cantor to sing certain ancient Jewish liturgical songs is at once absurd, affecting, and illuminating. This segment, which is not long, manages to encompass questions of cultural and generational change, what it means to capture art and pass it along, and the vagaries of critical reception. In prac-

tice, all the songs that are sung throughout the play rely to greater or lesser degrees on the "originals" from Smith's anthology (which are of course not any more original than any other version), but at the same time the songs range widely and may be freely altered and reinterpreted.

In this way, "Do What Thou Wilt Shall Be the Whole of the Law," the philosophical maxim of early twentieth-century English occultist and writer Aleister Crowley, may be the play's subtitle and the motto of the town –

the Darkest Heart of America — in which Marlowe eventually finds Harry Smith and his motley crew of hangers-on. But "Do What Thou Wilt" is not the whole of the law in this play, or in the trilogy. "Do What Thou Wilt" may be the bulk of the law of artistry in *The Javier Plays*, but with the mild caveat, "Do It With a Modicum of Appreciation and Recognition for the Material and Lives at Hand" (obviously not nearly as catchy). This means that although the Curator's efforts to organize Harry Smith's artifacts to create a museum and a cogent narrative about his life and art are highly entertaining, even ludicrous, and thwarted at every turn, they are nonetheless presented as worthy of respect. Indeed, the Curator is matched by complementary, counterpart characters in the first and third plays in the trilogy, Lila in *Diagram of a Paper Airplane* and Alex in *Your Name Will Follow You Home*. All three women are truth seekers, trying, to the best of their abilities and not without self-interest, to make sense of the flotsam and jetsam of information they receive. The trilogy would never mock this effort; it depends upon it. It celebrates actively remembering and remaking art, artists, and artists as art. That action is itself wizardly. In the end, the Curator's pressing question, "What should a Harry Smith museum look like?" and Javier C.'s shadow question, What should an American artwork look like?, has a short answer: exactly like this play.

Princeton, NJ

133 *A Mechanical Device for Playing a Bagpipe, by Kaspar Rötel, 1624.* Courtesy Deutsche Fototek of the Saxon State Library. Image in the public domain.

134 As a teenager, Harry Smith documented Lummi rituals. This photo was taken in 1938 by Bill Holm. Photo in public domain.

135 Only surviving photograph of the famed Texas bluesman Blind Lemon Jefferson taken some time between 1927 and 1929. Jefferson died at the age of 36 in Chicago. Accounts of his death vary: some claim he was murdered during a robbery, others that he was attacked by a dog. The most likely scenario was that he became disoriented during a snowstorm and died of a heart attack. Photo in public domain.

136 Portrait of Allen Ginsberg and Bob Dylan backstage at a concert in 1975. Photo by Elsa Dorfman.

137 On December 21, 1970, Elvis Presley arrived in D.C. on a mission: to obtain a Federal Bureau of Narcotics and Dangerous Drugs badge. After being rebuffed at the Bureau, he visited the White House where a spontaneous meeting with President Richard Nixon was captured by White House photographer Ollie Atkins. Elvis brought a gift: a Colt .45 revolver. Elvis told the president he believed The Beatles were an anti-American influence and promoters of drug culture in the U.S., and that he wanted to do everything in his power to help the president combat these forces. Elvis left the White House with his badge. United States government – public domain.

138 Blank Marlowe and the Red Herrings, the house band of Harry Smith rehearsing during a New Dramatists Creativity Fund workshop in March 2014. Pictured left to right: Lucas Papaelias, T. Ryder Smith, Paul Whitty, and Joe Tippet. Photo by Carlos Murillo

Aleister Crowley bathing naked. Photograph was taken by Jules Jacot-Guillarmod during Crowley's 1902 expedition to K2. Photo in Public Domain.

A THICK DESCRIPTION OF HARRY SMITH (Vol.1)

(or Do What Thou Wilt Shall Be the Whole of the Law)

CHARACTERS

Dr. Kurtz/Stranger Emcee/Harry Smith, a man of indeterminate age
The Curator, a woman in her 40s
Merry Andrew

The Band, Blank Marlowe and the Red Herrings are:

Blank Marlowe, who also plays:	The Voice of Javier C.
Annie, who also plays:	Testimonial Voice #1
	Voice of *Time* Magazine
	Voice of *Rolling Stone* Magazine
	Smithsonian Receptionist
	Pat Nixon
	Octogenarian Widow
	Frankie
Martin, who also plays:	Testimonial Voice #2
	Victor Dealer
	Announcer's Voice
	Göteborg Ethnology Museum Curator
	Allen Ginsberg
	Ken Burns-esque Documentary Voice
	Alger Crimus, Pop Culture Theorist
	Rabbi
	Journalist
	'40s Newsreel Sounding Voice
Jorge, who also plays:	Smithsonian Automated Recording
	Voice of the *New York Review of Books*
	Thelonious Monk
	Jonas Mekas
	Bob Dylan
	Richard Nixon
	Lionel Z.
	Dr. Wilder Penfield

NOTES FROM THE AUTHOR

On the Music:

The presence of a live band, Blank Marlowe and the Red Herrings, is crucial. In addition to playing the songs, they serve as the acting ensemble. They are the third greatest bar band that ever was.

The songs in the play, with the exception of The Fugs' "I Couldn't Get High" and Bob Dylan's "A Hard Rain's A-Gonna Fall," are loosely adapted from songs that appear on Harry Smith's *Anthology of American Folk Music*. In certain cases, the lyrics are written by me using the original melodies and lyric fragments ("My Name is Merry Andrew," "The Bible Salesman's Daughter," "White House Blues"). In other cases, the lyrics are mostly from the original versions with some of my own words and tweaks. Some of these stray considerably from the originals ("Coo-Coo Bird"), and others remain closer to the originals ("See That My Grave is Kept Clean," "House Carpenter" and "Frankie"). This is intended to reflect the notion of the "folk process" – where songs are passed down, altered and rearranged, by the interpreter – acknowledging and honoring the source, yet re-crafting them for new and unforeseen purposes.

In production, I encourage the collaborators to discover as many opportunities to utilize the band even when it is not called for explicitly in the script – whether to underscore sections, aid and abet the storytelling, or create moments of delight for the audience.

Lastly, I would encourage avoiding slickness where the band is concerned. Rather, they should lend a scrappy, homespun, DIY feel to the proceedings.

On Sound:

The play functions in many respects as a radio variety show performed before a live audience. The spoken language of the play is intended to entice the audience's imagination – to have them "see" things in their minds that are not actually depicted on stage. To enhance this effect, I suggest the use of Foley work. There are places where this is indicated in the script, and like the use of the band, production collaborators are encouraged to find other places in the play for live sound effects. Again, the more homespun and actor-generated this is, the better. Slickness is strongly discouraged.

On the Performance:

This is more of a performance than a play – sort of a medicine show, or live radio play. The way I have described it to folks is: imagine an episode of *The Prairie Home Companion* in which Garrison Keillor's soul has been overtaken by Aleister Crowley, and where Lake Wobegon is a Mystery Spot, the center of a psychedelic universe.

AN OVERTURE

A stage that is a stage and nothing more, as it would appear between productions.

Hovering in the air between the audience and the stage are twin "Applause" lights — which light at appropriate moments in the performance.

A man sits on a crappy folding lawn chair. He's ancient looking, gnome-like — simultaneously benign and sinister, like grandpa. He wears large, plastic rimmed glasses with thick lenses that distort his eyes. He has a grey beard, and wears his grey hair long and scraggly. He sports a large, clunky pair of headphones attached to a portable cassette recorder, which is connected to an omnidirectional microphone.

Perhaps it is Harry Smith.

The man records sounds, which we hear through the theater's sound system. At first the sounds are of the theater itself — backstage noise, the chatter of the audience. Over time the sounds shift. We hear the ghostly, scratchy, low fidelity sounds of Depression-era 78 records — ancient sounding blues, Appalachian ballads, Negro spirituals, sounds of a lost America. The sounds evolve — Times Square at midnight. Atmosphere of a bus terminal waiting room. A children's playground in the city. Nature sounds in the city. An Orthodox Rabbi singing liturgical music. A street poet's incantation. Hot bebop jazz played live in a tiny nightclub. A Kiowa Indian ritual. A speed freak preacher's prophecy of doom.

The sounds culminate with the atmosphere of a 4th of July gathering. Patriotic music, fireworks, burnout.

AN INTRODUCTION TO *A THICK DESCRIPTION OF HARRY SMITH (VOL.1)*
BY DR. EMILIANO KURTZ, PROFESSOR OF THEATER HISTORY AND
DRAMATIC CRITICISM, UC BERKELEY

In the darkness we hear a voice on the theater's public address system.

VOICE: Ladies and gentlemen, please welcome UC Berkeley Professor of Theater
   History and Dramatic Criticism, Dr. Emiliano Kurtz.

*The Applause light goes on. Applause — both real and recorded. Kurtz, a man in his 40s,
appears on stage. His style: professorial slick — in other words, overly styled and unnervingly
confident.*

KURTZ: Thank you.

   Bronislaw Slowik was in his late seventies when, as a graduate student, I assisted
   him in the preparation of the tenth and final volume of his seminal *Lives of the American Dramatists,* colloquially known as *Lives* — an ironic riff on Plutarch's *Lives of the
   Noble Greeks and Romans.*

   The final volume — which Slowik affectionately referred to as "The Ugh-Known
   Vitals" — profiled a series of minor writers — that were criminally underproduced,
   lost their marbles, starved to death, killed themselves, or simply vanished off the
   face of the earth — writers who, in spite of their anonymity, influenced the dramatists that came after them.

   Slowik kept index cards on these writers — he began compiling them after serving
   as an Air Force test pilot during World War II. You can imagine, over sixty years,
   how many "Ugh-Known Vitals" he collected. Sorting through them was a thank-
   less bitch — information on these writers was scant, their extant plays few and the
   quality of their work — not to mention influence — dubious at best.

   In the midst of this monumental — and I must say, *sad* — undertaking, I stumbled on
   this index card, written in Slowik's barely legible shorthand:

   *"Javier C. b. April 10, 1958, Bogota, Colombia, d. date uncertain, Gallup, New Mexico.
   Little is known about Javier C. — immigrated to the US in '64, settled in Jackson Heights,
   Queens. Studied Dramatic Writing at NYU for 2.5 semesters. Body of work includes: 3
   full length plays,* Death of a Liberal, The Rich Also Cry *and* A Thick Description

of Harry Smith; *a collection of thematically related short plays titled,* Revenge Fuck: A Chronicle of Schadenfreude in the Bedroom; *and an unpublished manifesto,* To Murder Whimsy: Bipolar Realism and the Future of American Playwriting. *Rumors persist about the existence of a fourth play, his magnum opus,* Diagram of a Paper Airplane, *though it is likely apocryphal.*

Of all the index cards documenting the shattered lives of lost playwrights, this one...

Shifted my insides.

Slowik died before completing Volume 10.

Javier never made it into *Lives.*

This index card set me on a journey

to discover this "Ugh-known Vital."

A journey that culminates

in tonight's performance of Javier's final work —

The *only* work he completed after the disappearance of his son ...

Several years ago I unearthed a recording Javier made — notes for an introduction. Listen:

A recording of Javier's voice. The voice sounds broken.

JAVIER'S VOICE: Twenty-two months into writing this play, I suffered a near terminal case of writer's block when I discovered its subject, Harry Smith — the musicologist, filmmaker, painter, anthropologist, occultist, magician, editor of *The Anthology of American Folk Music* — was not my own fictional creation, but an actual person. A cosmic joke: how could a figure so emblematic yet enigmatic, so ... *American* be anything but a figment of an overheated imagination ...

DR. KURTZ: None of this is true, of course. Javier's archives reveal his *monomania* in unearthing the facts and many fictions surrounding Harry's life and work. One might misread Javier's introduction as an *apologia* for his play. A later passage reveals his true intent ... Javier's own words:

JAVIER: *A Thick Description of Harry Smith* is my folly. My attempt to solve a riddle that has confounded me since childhood. Since immigrating from the *other* America, the Latin one, from a place one might call a "Banana Republic," I've wrestled with the question: what does the word, the idea, "American" mean? My obsessive listening to *Prairie Home Companion* provided occasional insight. Ginsberg, Whitman, Ralph Ellison helped. Elvis Presley? The Dionysian whippersnapper of '55, yes, but in my heart I want to believe: America must not end at the foot of a toilet, pants rolled round its ankles, face down on a shag carpet – If these failed me, what about the Founding Fathers, the great Presidents? – No, I needed a creature of the underground, an unknown American genius of self-invention. I needed to invent my own American. Alas, Harry Smith, America already invented you.

– Javier C., Chippewa Falls, Wisconsin, 1993

DR. KURTZ: I confess: first time I read *Thick Description,* I believed Harry Smith to be Javier's invention. His triumphant solution to the riddle of America. His demented *Citizen Kane* for the tired, poor huddled masses – I wanted Harry to embody Javier's brilliance, recklessness, invention – a naked self-revelation through the creation of an impossible "other," his penance for what he called his "great crime of omission."

What Javier never grasped was that he himself – like Harry – was an invention of the America he claimed not to understand.

Before we begin tonight's performance, I want to offer my deepest gratitude to Berkeley Repertory Theater for their tremendous support in my reconstruction of this almost-lost play.

Ladies and gentlemen, *A Thick Description of Harry Smith (or Do What Thou Wilt Shall Be the Whole of the Law...*

Applause sign lights. Real and recorded applause. Lights out. Collage sound of train whistles, iron horses, the steady rhythm of steel wheels powering along steel rails that crescendos to:

PART ONE

THE BEGINNING OF THE SHOW

A live band kicks into a rocking, swinging, celebratory version of Blind Lemon Jefferson's "See That My Grave Is Kept Clean." They are the centerpiece of a space that should have the feel of a Rauschenberg assemblage or scrap junk sculpture or post-Millennial medicine show.

SONG: "SEE THAT MY GRAVE IS KEPT CLEAN"

MARLOWE: *(singing)* Well there's one kind favor I ask of you
　　　There's one kind favor I ask of you
　　　Lord there's one kind favor I'll ask of you
　　　Please see that my grave is kept clean

　　　Lord it's two white horses in a line
　　　Lord it's two white horses in a line
　　　Well it's two white horses in a line
　　　Take me home to my burying ground

　　　My heart stopped beating, my hands got cold
　　　My heart stopped beating, my hands got cold
　　　My heart stopped beating, Lord my hands turned cold
　　　I believe now what the Bible told

　　　Have you ever heard that coffin sound
　　　Have you ever heard that coffin sound
　　　Have you ever heard a coffin sound
　　　Then you know another poor boy's in the ground

　　　Will you dig my grave with a silver spade
　　　Please dig my grave with a silver spade
　　　Won't you dig my grave with a silver spade
　　　You may lead me down with a ball and chain

　　　There's one last favor I'll ask of you
　　　Just one small favor I'll ask of you

> There's one last favor I'll ask of you
>
> Please see my grave is kept clean …

They perform a rousing finish. Applause light — real and recorded applause. The band plays a theme for the entrance of the Stranger Emcee (who may be Harry Smith in disguise).

STRANGER EMCEE: Evening friends, Americans, countrymen

> Ole Garrison couldn't make it tonight,
>
> Body snatchers got him
>
> Ice fishing on Lake Wobegon, Minnie-sotie
>
> But like they say in the bizness they call *show*
>
> "War must go on … "
>
> Ladies and gentlemen:
>
> Let's hear it for the third best bar band in the world
>
> Blank Marlowe and the Red Herrings,

Applause light. Real and recorded applause.

> Performing Blind Lemon Jefferson's
>
> "See That My Grave Is Kept Clean"
>
> Last song ol Lemon committed to acetate 'fore he uhhh
>
> *Froze* to death
>
> Or got shot on 47ᵗʰ and Wabash, Bronzeville, south side Chicago …
>
> Details hazy like so many things …
>
> Any case wasn't a white horse but
>
> An iron horse hauled his coffin down
>
> To the Wortham Black Cemetery, Wortham, Texas …
>
> You told me back stage, Marlowe,
>
> That you, the boys and the *fine* young lady on piano
>
> Did a little grave tending on your way here …

The band members trade uncomfortable glances behind MARLOWE's back.

MARLOWE: Indeed.

STRANGER EMCEE: Quite the detour

> Speed fueled beeline from New York City to Berkeley, Cali-4-nye-A?

Wortham, Texas ... not a

Conventional stop on the triple A guide ...

MARLOWE: We got

You know,

Waylaid.

Detours ...

Circuitous routes ...

The road ...

STRANGER EMCEE: Sure sure.

Any case

Mighty kind of you to go down there

Fulfill Blind Lemon's final wish ...

You did fulfill his wish ...?

MARLOWE: Swept the headstone.

Tossed the dead flowers.

Laid down some fresh ones.

STRANGER EMCEE: Long time?

There was no head stone.

Ol Lemon lay there, grave unmarked

Wasn't til '67, '68,

Folks lobbied State of Texas to place a marker.

MARLOWE: I did not know that.

STRANGER EMCEE: By '96,

Nature reclaimed it

But in marched an Outfit called the

Scandinavian Blues Association

(Blues and Swedes, now *that* is some free association)

Wrote a check

Installed a proper headstone

LEMON JEFFERSON 1893-1929

Epitaph reads:

MARLOWE: "Lord it's one kind favor ..."

STRANGER EMCEE: dot dot dot ...

>   Makes you wonder
>
>   Will someone see *my* grave's kept clean ...?

MARLOWE: I hope so, sir ...

STRANGER EMCEE: That a favor I might ask of you?

MARLOWE: If I don't end up in the grave before you do.

STRANGER EMCEE: Anyway, ladies and gentlemen, we got a show for you tonight,
   Merry Andrew's here with his Death Machine.

Applause light. Live and recorded applause.

>   Latest installment of
>   *Darkest Heart of America: The Never Ending Tour of Blank Marlowe and The Red Herrings*

Applause light. Live and recorded applause.

>   Musical guest, the late Rabbi Nuftali Zvi Margolies Abulafia

Applause light. Live and recorded applause.

>   The Albuquerque Youth Ballet's performance of *Heaven and Earth Magic*

Applause light. Live and recorded applause.

>   Mystery Radio Theatre Presents: *The Curator's Folly*

Applause light. Live and recorded applause.

>   *Shadow of the Shining City: Chronicles of the American Underground* ...
>   Featuring special guests Allen Ginsberg and Richard and Pat Nixon

Applause light. Live and recorded applause.

>   Course no evening's complete without a trip to Mahagonny, USA
>   And everyone's favorite watering hole-in-the-wall, Red Herring's Bar and Grill,
>   Where the rotgut's cheap, the men are creeps, and the women even creepier.

Applause light. Live and recorded applause.

>   And Ladies and Gentlemen ...
>   Mr. Harry Smith's in the house

Applause light. Wild live and recorded applause.

Rumor has it

as part of our series "Dangerous Experiments in American Film"

Harry's screening his rarely seen masterpiece *Oz* ...

The applause light goes crazy. Live and recorded applause. Recorded oohs and ahhs.

... that is, if you're all good, now.

so sit back, re-lax, cause off. We. Go ...

The band kicks into a raucous reprise of "See That My Grave is Kept Clean"

But first, a word from our sponsor: Dr. Smith's American Balsam

The band strikes up a self-consciously old-timey instrumental. The Merry Andrew appears. He wears a fat suit underneath a garish, careworn costume that conjures the image of a lost Merry Prankster or a medicine show that went bust eons ago.

MERRY ANDREW: Invalid Americans! This is for YOU!

Best cure for all diseases – including asthma, bronchitis, consumption, indigestion, skin eruptions, heart troubles, obesity, swine flu, female complaints, rheumatism, diarrhea, kidney stones, flatulence, offensive breath, insomnia, chronic fatigue, scurvy, premature ejaculation, constipation, jaundice, anorexia, and chronic boredom.

TESTIMONIAL #1 (ANNIE): I have been a chronic sufferer of a number of diseases over the years – liver complaint, female weakness, not to mention manic depression. They've kept me fairly wild day and night. I tried Dr. Smith's American Balsam – in no time, my symptoms disappeared! – Mrs. Mary Anne Baxter, Boise, Idaho

TESTIMONIAL #2 (MARTIN): I am 65 years old. For the past thirty years I've endured long periods of flatulence, indigestion, catarrh of the heart. I'm also prone to road rage, sadistic and suicidal thoughts. I've taken lots of medicines over the years – Dr. Smith's American Balsam is by far the best. Dr. Smith: you changed my life. – Mr. Harold Dean Wilson, Wichita, Kansas.

MERRY ANDREW: Guaranteed remedy for every ailment known to man, Dr. Smith's American Balsam contains no narcotic, hypnotic, or hallucinogenic ingredients.

Side effects may include inexplicable euphoria, phantom limb sensation, mild paranoia, increased libido, speaking in tongues, delusions of grandeur, and in rare cases, cosmic insight. Dr. Smith's American Balsam – it's your own damn fault if you don't use the remedy that cures.

Sold in large bottles for 50 cents. Prepared by Dr. Harry E. Smith, Anacortes, Washington.

The band finishes the song. The Stranger Emcee returns, wearing ceremonial regalia: old worn trousers, an Ordo Templi Orientis t-shirt, a seersucker suit jacket and a black satin cape. He's barefoot. On his head, he wears an object that at first glance might appear occultish, but is actually constructed of cardboard paper towel tubes and paper flowers.

STRANGER EMCEE: Before we go on ... in the name of full disclosure uhhhh

Back in the greenroom

Management

Kindly provided us with free Leinenkugels.

Myself I consumed Three, four ... Six?

Also partook in our pre-performance ritual

The

Communal sharing of Mr. Fattie, a.k.a a generously rolled marijuana cigarette.

Helps with

Passing through the limn

Between

Life *off* stage and life *on.*

Speaking of Mr. Fattie

First made his acquaintance

In Berkeley, California, 1947? '46?

Applause light. The band underscores following with a Jefferson Airplane-esque psychedelic instrumental.

Beginning of a beautiful friendship.

My

Initiation

Occurred on what was supposed to be a

Decompression weekend third semester of my

Anthropological studies at the University of Washington

This was uhhh

'fore I came to the realization that

Levi-Strauss was the greatest novelist that ever lived.

Trip coincided with the

First time I saw Woody Guthrie play,

Mr. Fattie

Woody Guthrie

The uhhhh

Air?

There?

In the Bay Area?

Combined with

The

Atmosphere bourgeois people call

B'hemian – Man, I just call it American –

Red White and Blue blooded *invisible* American –

One could rightly say that weekend was a

Formative experience.

In addition to the twelve Leinenkugels, Mister Fattie

I have also ingested a couple of valium, a fistful of bennies, a few other assorted flavors from the candy dish, as part of an ongoing anthro-pharmacological self-study.

I tell you this as a friendly warning:

Anything I say or do is

Uhhhh subject to theeee

Influence of my self-medication.

That said:

Let's go on with the show –

MYSTERY RADIO THEATRE: THE CURATOR'S FOLLY, PART ONE

The band kicks into an intense, creepy version of Clarence Ashley's "The Coo Coo Bird." A wall of boxes appears, as does The Curator.

STRANGER EMCEE: Ladies an Gentlemen, it's time for *Mystery Radio Theatre: The Curator's Folly Part One ...*

Please give a warm welcome to The

Curator of the future Harry Smith Museum and Interpretive Center, Mahagonny, USA, Ms. Pa—

The Curator interrupts with her rendition of "The Coo-Coo Bird." As the song progresses, The Curator's bookish exterior slowly unravels to reveal the sensuous, somewhat naughty, woman that's hidden inside.

SONG: "THE COO COO BIRD"

CURATOR: *(singing)* Gonna build me a temple
On a hilltop so high
So you can see Harry
As he walks on by

Oh the Coo-coo is a pretty bird
She warbles as she flies
She never hollers coo-coo
Til the 4th of July

We've played chess in New York
We've played chess on the Plains
Won't bet you ten dollars
Cause you beat me every game

There's a white Queen, there's a white Queen
I know her from old
She's robbed my shallow pockets
Of my bishops and my gold

Gonna build me a temple

On a hilltop so high

So you can see Harry

As he walks on by

Oh the Coo-coo is a pretty bird

She warbles as she flies

She never hollers coo-coo

Til the 4th of July …

The song ends, applause light goes on. Applause, live and recorded. The Curator, catching herself having gone to this very sensual place, takes on her "curatorial" persona.

CURATOR: Thank you, thank you …

Behind me you see a wall of boxes,

Contents of which are the collections left behind by Harry Everett Smith

When he died in 1991 … 160 boxes in all,

Which I, as the curator of the Harry Smith Museum and Interpretive Center,

Am immersed in the

Complex task of

Cataloguing,

Organizing and …

Interpreting …

Allow me to demonstrate …

She removes a box and opens it. The lighting changes, so the Stranger Emcee is in silhouette. He becomes the Voice of Harry and speaks into the microphone. The Curator is aware of the voice and disconcerted by it.

HARRY: This uhhh's

One of those things I

Don't like being touched …

People touching

Never know the uhhh

Danger of hand washing, hazardous chemicals on your fingers uhhh

The Curator removes items from the box.

CURATOR: Box One Forty Seven: Realia, Items Seven Thousand One to Seven Thousand Twenty-Five.

Or, what I call "Things that are shaped like things they are not."

HARRY: I'm uhhh

Leaving it to

Future generations to uhhh

Figure out the purpose of all this *stuff*

CURATOR: Plastic mechanical bank shaped like Uncle Sam.

Plastic toy phone shaped like Mickey Mouse.

HARRY: The uhhh

Rotten Easter eggs,

Paper airplanes

CURATOR: Metal mechanical bank shaped like Elvis Presley.

Metal mechanical bank shaped like the State of Oklahoma.

HARRY: The uhhhhh ...

String figures,

Seminole patchwork I never look at —

CURATOR: Plastic Halloween horn shaped like Pocahontas.

Plastic mechanical bank shaped like the Statue of Liberty.

HARRY: I will say that the uhhhh *collections* are

Justifiable as any other type of

Research.

CURATOR: Yo-yo shaped like a UFO.

Dog squeak toy shaped like a hot dog.

1991 Chairman's Merit Grammy Award for Lifetime Achievement

HARRY: What was it I said at the ceremony? "I have arthritis,

I uhh flew in from Colorado so ...

Thank you."

CURATOR: *1991 Chairman's Merit Grammy Award —*

HARRY: And uhhh

"I'm Glad to say my dreams came true

That I saw America change through music ... "

CURATOR: You see my dilemma ...

Charged with organizing these materials into a museum.

Like Harry used to say ...

HARRY: I'm uhhhh

Leaving it to future generations to uhh

Figure out the purpose of all this *stuff*

CURATOR: Is there rhyme is there reason ...

Is all this

Some secret, invisible map of the universe waiting to be deciphered?

Or a third rate, lunatic Dadaist's practical joke?

HARRY: But you'll wanna watch your step, see, cause uhhh

I'm an expert in Black Magick ...

CURATOR: How about a song.

Reprise of "Coo-Coo Bird."

STRANGER EMCEE: Ladies and gennelmen ...

We'll come back later in the show for more

Mystery Radio Theatre, but right now it's that time again ...

DARKEST HEART OF AMERICA: THE NEVER ENDING TOUR OF BLANK MARLOWE AND HIS BAND THE RED HERRINGS, PART ONE

A montage of sounds created by using the instruments and Foley work, mirrors the sounds described by the Stranger Emcee.

STRANGER EMCEE: It's two minutes to midnight somewhere in America ...

Hear the campfire crackle?

Crickets? Forlorn coyote howl?

Night critters lookin for a meal and a mate ...

Whoosh of Goodyear tires rolling down the Innerstate

So dark you can hear the Milky Way ...

Sounds of the lonesome American Outback

That three thousand mile wilderness between

East Coast Sodoms and West Coast Gomorrahs ...

Ugh-knowable landscape you see

Out the window of your transcontinental flight

Fills you with wonder, dread ...

Endless prairies

Lonely deserts

Rocky Mountain Donner Family Picnics

In the middle of this nowhere we find

Blank Marlowe and his band The Red Herrings:

VW bus broken down on route to their gig ...

Listen: Martin toys aimlessly with Annie's *dulcimer* ...

Watch: pretty little Annie builds her house of cards

Knocks em down, starts all over ...

Jorge sips his Miller Lite,

readin a paperback bout UFOs ...

And Blank Marlowe.

Blowin all his yearning and pain into that harmonica

Cause Marlowe's always de-tourin

Leaving the Interstate for those forgotten two lane ribbons of asphalt,

Chasin the faded jewels strung along them:

Abandoned towns, where mysteries wait
in junk shops, last chance taverns,
gravestone etchings of vanished musical forebears
And the bedrooms of lonely widows ...

Yes, Blank's got a story on his mind,
Hopes by telling it, his fellow troubadours'll
forgive this latest detour into
The Darkest Heart of America ...

MARLOWE: Once upon a time
Darkness ruled here too ...

MARTIN: *(Stops playing the dulcimer, addresses the audience.)* Always an "Oh shit" moment,

ANNIE: Oh shit

JORGE: *Mierda*

MARTIN: when Marlowe pulled something out like that

MARLOWE: Once upon a time the darkness ruled here too.

MARTIN: Just like Marlowe to throw the gauntlet down —

JORGE: Even before the first hand of poker was dealt

ANNIE: Never bent me out a shape
Half the shit came out Marlowe's mouth?
Was just that
Shit.

MARTIN: "Once upon a time" ... meant Marlowe had
Something buried in his heart dying to crawl out.
Been a year since our last tour.
Tour ends, we got homes to go to,
Beds to lie in, dogs to walk, kids to play with,
Other halves to endure,

But not Marlowe ...

He still ...

MARLOWE: "Follows the sea"

MARTIN: That's what he says, "Follow the sea."

Marlowe's got no home –

MARLOWE: Makes you wonder

What the darkness was like

When Eisenhower passed through.

1918? '19?

Army caravan crawling East coast to West

Testing how fast the war machine'd move

If the enemy invaded ...

Sixty two days took to cross –

Might as well have crossed the darkest heart of Africa ...

Only this was the United States of America

One nation under God, indivisible –

JORGE: Don't go there ...

MARLOWE: What.

JORGE: Part about liberty and justice – don't get me // started

MARLOWE: Crossing the continent

Ol' Eisenhower felt the Dread.

Saw this wasn't one nation, no!

But a *granfalloon* of exiles, criminals, desperadoes, snake oilmen, heyoka

JORGE: Hey-oh-//wha?

MARLOWE: Sharing nothing but that vague identifier ...

American ...

If this "nation"? was under "God"?

Wasn't indivisible cause

God kept his eye only on certain parts.

ANNIE: *(Sigh.)*

MARLOWE: When ol Ike signed the bill made the Interstates? '55? '56?
    Sure as hell had those dark places etched in his head,
    Made damn sure those concrete blood vessels'd bypass
    The white spaces in your Rand McNally …
    Cause you know what's in those white spaces?

MARTIN: No …

MARLOWE: Darkest heart of America, that's // what

ANNIE: Oh. My. Lord.

MARLOWE: Cause once upon a time the darkness ruled // here too.

ANNIE: What in God's name are you talking about, // Marlowe?

MARLOWE: Suspicious? Course I'm suspicious, it's downright idol worship …

ANNIE: HhhhhhhohmyGod.

MARLOWE: The singer.

ANNIE: From the interstate to the singer, here we go.

MARLOWE: Should be the singer singing the song and not the song, right?
    Or should it be the other way around –
    The song, not the singer singing it.

JORGE: Huh?

MARLOWE: Should the singer singing the song outlive the song
    or
    Should the song outlive the singer singing it
    OR:

MARTIN: Or …?

MARLOWE: Are the singer and the song abominations against the Heavenly Creator …

ANNIE: Now he's talking Heavenly Crea//tor

MARLOWE: Least that's what I think *he* was trying to tell me …

ANNIE: Any idea what's he's talking about Jorge // cause I

JORGE: No idea, I just work // here

MARTIN: Shhhhhh – Marlowe?

You were saying … "least that's what I think he was trying to tell me?"

MARLOWE: I said that?

MARTIN: Um. Yeah.

Who was trying to tell you?

MARLOWE: Andrew.

MARTIN: Andrew …

MARLOWE: *Merry* Andrew.

ANNIE: Merry? Andrew?

MARLOWE: It's what he said, even sang it. *(Half sings.)* "My name is Merry An-drew, I come from … "

Pause. Crickets.

The Stranger Emcee interrupts.

STRANGER EMCEE: Ladies and gentlemen, please give a warm welcome to Merry Andrew and His Death Machine

Applause light. Wild applause. Merry Andrew appears, with a bull horn and pulling a large, heavy wooden box with a long rope. This should be painful and comical to watch, sort of like Lucky in Waiting for Godot, *only American. He completes the journey — looks at the audience, striking a pose of a tired and low rent showman. He begins his song —*

SONG: MY NAME IS MERRY ANDREW (BASED ON "STATE OF ARKANSAS")

MERRY ANDREW:

My name is Merry Andrew I come from Tupelo town
For 20 years I've traveled this sad, wide world aroun'
Bumps, dead ends, and miseries, maybe one good day or two
But I never knew what misery was til Harry I met you.

I walked down to the depot saw the ticket counter man
Asked me where I want to go, said far away's I can
He took my last ten dollars, pointed to the track
Ride that Iron Horse one way, don't bother comin' back.

Got off at Mahogany where I chanced to meet a man
Told me "Call me Harry Smith, or you can call me Cain"
Wore bottle-bottom glasses, had rows of rotten teeth
Said he knew a good motel where I could catch some sleep.

Harry led me down the road to this establishment
Wasn't a motel at all, but a squalid tenement
In his room he had no food, in his milk the roaches crawled
He cast a wicked spell on me, for soon I was enthralled.

Late that night he showed me films, strangest I ever seen
Colors, shapes, vibrations leapt off the movie screen
He told me that he painted them, by hand and frame by frame
If they hadn't mesmerized me, I'd have thought this man insane.

He showed me his collections, paper airplanes, 78s,
Easter eggs, string figures, books stacked up high in crates.
He pointed out connections, fired up another joint
My mind confused and reeling I began to see his point.

Sunrise Harry turned to me, asked for fifty cents
Told me even shamans have got to pay their rent
For six long weeks he taught me to spin gold into straw
He emptied out my pockets sent me down to Wichita.

Now I wander town to town, I sell his medicine
Haunted by the memory of his demon eyes and grin
Hardly any takers except for one or two
I curse and bless the day that Harry I met you.
I curse and bless the day that Harry I met you.

At the camp fire.

164

MARTIN: Marlowe ... ?

>You okay ... ?

MARLOWE: He said to me:

MERRY ANDREW: Mister? I don't know you from Adam, what your business is ...

>You gotta pass the test 'fore I let you take one step further.

MARLOWE: Test?

MERRY ANDREW: Pass, I let you in.

MARTIN: "Let you in" where?

MERRY ANDREW: Fail, push that hunk a junk back in the direction you came

MARLOWE: Look I don't want no trou//ble

MERRY ANDREW: PSSSHT!

Merry Andrew hides behind the box. Drum roll. He prepares for a cheap magic trick. He leaps out from behind the box, cane in hand, and lands, striking a carnival barker pose and gesturing with his cane. Nothing happens.

He repeats this. Nothing happens.

He repeats it again. Nothing. Frustration mounts.

Again. Nothing. Explosion: Merry Andrew attacks the box with his cane, his fists, his feet and string of four letter words punctuated by the occasional "Sonofabitch Harry Smith." Nothing, nothing, nothing. He's furious. Humiliated. A performer hung out to dry. He exits. As he disappears offstage, the walls of the box collapse revealing a 1920s Victor Talking Machine. Merry Andrew pops his head out from offstage. He reenters, back in performance mode.

MERRY ANDREW: Son, you have any idea what your godforsaken eyes are a-gazin' upon?

MARLOWE: Uhhh, 78 record play//er?

MERRY: WRONG!

>Yeah, it plays 78s, but NO!
>
>You have before you
>
>A miracle of forward thinking American know-how:
>
>1927 VV-830-X *Credenza* Victor Talking Machine
>
>Known to those of us on the *inside*

As the pre-Depression iPod …

Imagine, mister,
It's 1927. You walk into the wonderland of a Victor Dealership
Dealer makes a friendly suggestion —

VICTOR DEALER (MARTIN): Step right over here, feller …

MERRY ANDREW: Voice turns you into the obedient customer he wants you to be
And at heart you are —

Leads you down a path flanked by these beautiful machines,
To the Holy of the Holies, top of the line
1927 —

VICTOR DEALER: VV-830-X *Credenza* Victor Talking Machine —
This elixir can be yours for 300 pre-Depression Dollars … Listen: this'll knock
your socks off …

MERRY ANDREW: Dealer slips a 78 on the turntable,
Lays the needle on the grooves …

A loud pop. A symphony of eggs frying. Merry Andrew closes his eyes in eargasmic reverie. A song begins: "You Must Be Born Again" by Reverend J.M. Gates. The recording — scratchy, ghostly, unnerving — sounds impossibly ancient, yet terrifying in its immediacy. It plays through the scene.

MERRY ANDREW: Listen to that … Reverend JM Gates …
You see Mister:
Your iPod might hold quarter million songs in a box smaller'n a pack of Lucky
Strikes,
But this Machine,
Un-portable as she is, ain't no dummy.
Lasts longer too — no built-in self-destruct-in-four-years mechanism …
Yep, she features the latest in Orthophonic sound reproduction technology,
Developed in that great laboratory for advances in science, business, art, and Democ-
racy:
World. War. I.

Yep: 20 million corpses not only made the world temporarily safe for democracy,
All them bodies made possible the accurate, affordable reproduction of sound
To enjoy in your living room.
No 20 million dead, no Elvis.
No dead, no Bobby Dylan.
No dead, no Sly and the Family Stone, no Hannah Montana.

ANNIE: Hannah Montana?

MARLOWE: It's what he said.

MERRY ANDREW: Ready for the test?

MARLOWE: Uhhh –

MERRY ANDREW: Good: now

    Some folks, Mister,
    Call it the Death Machine
    Unrepentant Murderer of American Music ...
    Others kneel in reverence,
    Pronounce it Birth Mother of American Music.
    Others'll tell you it's The Wicked Messenger
    Abomination against the Creator and all that is Holy ...

MARLOWE: Is there like a ... question you want me to answer?

MERRY ANDREW: Yeah, I got a question ... Where do you stand?

MARLOWE: Ummm ... could you elaborate?

MERRY ANDREW: Mister: advocates of the Death Machine Theory'll tell you
    'fore this machine? Everyone sang. Didn't have to be a musician proper,
    You just sang. To your children. Layin rails, tilling fields. Little taste of joy
    After a hard day in the coal mine.
    Old songs, pieces of ancestral memory
    In a land that demands amnesia ...

    Nowadays people spend good money on psychiatrists, Yoga lessons
    When all they need's a good song, sung from the heart ...

Death Machine killed that — gave birth to a thing called *virtuosity*

Split the world in two: those that sang, those that listened …

Those that sang got themselves on records

Those that *listened*

Turned deaf to the natural sound of their voice yearning to sing out …

Those songs on record? Sound the same every time you listen …

Back at the campfire. Marlowe directs the following few exchanges between Merry Andrew and the band.

MARLOWE: I'm asking you — is it not natural to be suspicious

Of those that kneel at the altar of infinite reproduction?

ANNIE: *What?*

MARLOWE: Like etching a name on a gravestone —

Wax cylinders

78s

Vinyl 45s, 33 and a third

8-track,

Cassette,

Pure evil compact disc.

Now what they call it … MP3?

Criminal.

Squeezing all those singing voices into ones and zeroes

Like squeezing an elephant into a cricket's cage …

MARTIN: There was a long pause.

MARLOWE: How's a song supposed to change when it's endlessly reproduced?

How's it supposed to *evolve?*

MARTIN: There was another long pause.

ANNIE: We all wished he was over and done with …

MARLOWE: How's a song // supposed

ANNIE: Mother//fucker …

MARLOWE: to learn to walk talk say momma sing the alphabet song

> Keep secrets talk back lose its virginity go off to the college uh hard knocks ...
> How's its heart supposed to grow when it's got a million identical twins running round?

MARTIN: I —

MARLOWE: HOW's a song supposed to find its woman, its man

> Birth a brood of children that look a little, sound a little like mama and daddy
> But have to grow up alone. Get Hurt. Have a one night stand.
> Maybe die a lonesome death.

MERRY ANDREW: Slow down there, Mister ... you ain't heard the other side ...

> Those that believe this machine's the Birth Mother'll tell you
> Sure, everyone sang,
> But all those songs?
> Woulda died by the campfire ...
> But for this machine keeping them alive.
> With all them songs floating around?
> Eventually they'd copulate.
> Indulge in polysexual orgiastic rites.
> Presto: a Love Child —
> Rock n Roll, baby:
> Some call it Bastard Child of musical miscegenation,
> But in my humble opinion?
> After Democracy? And the McDonald's French Fry?
> Greatest gift this country ever gave to the world ...

Band plays a '50s rock and roll riff — Merry Andrew gyrates like a demented Elvis.

MARLOWE: Right on ...

MERRY ANDREW: While you contemplate that

> Let me tell you bout those that call it The Wicked Messenger ...
> They'll have you believe this here machine is a Demon
> Violator of the Cosmic Order —

MARLOWE: Yeah. That's bullshit …

MERRY ANDREW: Yeah. Pay em no mind.

Cause in America?

Violatin' the Cosmic Order is the Lost Amendment to The Bill of Rights …

So: Death Machine? Birth Mother? Wicked Messenger?

Where do you stand?

From the Victor we hear, quietly, the beginning of Clarence Ashley's version of "The House Carpenter" from the Anthology. *Marlowe strums, aimlessly, to the music. Both sounds underscore the following.*

ANNIE: What'd you answer, Marlowe?

JORGE: Yeah, what did you answer?

MARTIN: Marlowe?

MARLOWE: I had a nightmare …

All the Mommas of the world

Stopped singing songs to their little children.

Instead they bought em iPods

Stuck them ear buds in their little ears,

Hit shuffle, let them little babies cry themselves to sleep alone in the dark …

I had another nightmare …

Where no one ever heard the cosmic roar

Of "Voodoo Chile," or Dylan ask

"How does it *feel* to be on your *own*

No direction *home* … "

MERRY ANDREW: Mister? You gonna answer the question?

MARLOWE: What's that music?

ANNIE: What music …

MERRY ANDREW: That…? Little present Harry made.

MARLOWE: Who's Harry?

MARTIN: Again. Silence. *Long* silence …

MARLOWE: I'm getting ahead of myself …

    I'm starting in the middle when I

    Should be starting at the start …

ANNIE: Shit.

STRANGER EMCEE: Listen: you hear that?

    Marlowe's aimless strumming

    Catches a melody …

In the stillness of the night, recognition of the song sets in. Annie begins to sing, almost to herself.

SONG: THE HOUSE CARPENTER

ANNIE: *(singing)*

    Well met, well met said my old true love

    Well met well met said he

MARLOWE: *(singing)*

    I've just returned from the cold grey sea all for the love of thee

ANNIE:

    Come in, come in my old true love

    Have a seat with me

MARLOWE & ANNIE:

    It's been three fourths of a long long year since together we have been

MARLOWE:

    I can't come in, I can't sit down

    I haven't but a minute's time

    They say you're married to a house carpenter, your heart will never be mine

ANNIE:

    He said: "I could've married a king's daughter there

    And she would have married me"

ANNIE & MARLOWE:

> But I've forsaken her jewels and gold all for the love of thee

MARLOWE:

> Will you forsake your house carpenter
>
> Leave this hell with me
>
> I'll take you where the palm trees grow on the banks of the turquoise sea

ANNIE:

> I lifted up my newborn babe
>
> And kisses gave him three
>
> Said stay right here my little darling boy, keep your daddy company

MARLOWE & ANNIE:

> We hadn't been on ship but about two weeks
>
> I'm sure it was not three
>
> His true love began to weep and mourn as she gazed at the lonesome sea

MARLOWE:

> Are you weeping for your house carpenter
>
> Are you weeping cause we're poor?

ANNIE:

> I am weeping for my darling little boy whose face I'll never see anymore

MARLOWE & ANNIE:

> We hadn't been at sea but about three weeks
>
> I'm sure it was not four
>
> When a leak sprung in the bottom of the ship and we sank to the ocean floor …

The song ends. Silence. The sounds of the night.

JORGE: There any more beer?

The crickets fade up, the harmonica theme closing the segment begins. Applause light.

STRANGER EMCEE: Folks we'll come back in a spell

> For more *Darkest Heart of America.*
>
> Little ditty you just heard was "The House Carpenter" —

Light shift. The silhouetted Harry overtakes the Stranger Emcee.

HARRY'S VOICE: Appears as track number uhhh 3

> Volume One of the *Anthology*
>
> Clarence Ashley, 1930, Original issue Columbia Records, Number 15654D
>
> Based on the Scottish Ballad, "The Daemon Lover"
>
> The uhhhh
>
> Supernatural theme in early versions
>
> Is virtually nonexistent in its American descendents ...

Light shift, silhouetted Harry replaced by the Stranger Emcee.

STRANGER EMCEE: Speaking of records,

> Let's hear another word from our sponsor.

Music. Recording of a rabbi singing ancient Jewish liturgical music.

ANNOUNCER'S VOICE (MARTIN): *Time* magazine calls it:

VOICE OF TIME MAGAZINE (ANNIE): "A landmark in the annals of recording..."

ANNOUNCER'S VOICE (MARTIN): *The New York Review of Books* describes it as:

VOICE OF THE NEW YORK REVIEW OF BOOKS (JORGE): "A once-in-a-generation musicological event ... "

ANNOUNCER'S VOICE (MARTIN): *Rolling Stone* creams:

VOICE OF ROLLING STONE (ANNIE): "A cosmic mind-fuck. If Harry Smith's *Anthology of American Folk Music* was the Rosetta Stone for the '50s Folk revival, these recordings are an esoteric time bomb" —

ANNOUNCER'S VOICE (MARTIN): Smithsonian Folkways, K-Tel and Zohar Records present *East Broadway Tree of Life: The Jewish Liturgical Songs of Rabbi Nuftali Zvi Margolies Abulafia.* This never-before-released 18 record set contains digitally remastered recordings of a Lower East Side legend: Rabbi Nuftali Zvi Margolies Abulafia. Recorded by noted ethnomusicologist Harry Smith, this set contains the only existing recordings of Rabbi Abulafia and his encyclopedic knowledge of Jewish liturgical music, sung by heart, from memory ... Own this miracle of music history. Available wherever records are sold ...

MYSTERY RADIO THEATRE: THE CURATOR'S FOLLY, PART TWO

STRANGER EMCEE: Time once again for *Mystery Radio Theatre*. Please welcome back
   The curator of the future Harry Smith Museum and Interpretive Center Ms. Pa—

The Curator removes two more boxes from the pile.

CURATOR: Box 158: Tarot and Playing Cards.
   I won't show you each of the two hundred fourteen items in this box —
   but to give you a sense ...
   Golden Dawn Tarot
   Tree of Life Tarot
   Tarot of the Cat People
   Old Maid
   Mickey Mouse Playing Cards
   Pioneers of Country Music Cards by R. Crumb
   Watergate Scandal Trading Cards
   Iran-Contra Scandal Trading Cards
   And so on ...

HARRY: I'm uhhh
   Leaving it to
   Future generations to
   Figure out the purpose of all this stuff

CURATOR: A thought experiment:
   Tonight when you go home to your *Tepee*,
   Pretend it's not you that lives there,
   That the *stuff* surrounding you
   Is the detritus of someone else's life.
   Walk through the rooms as you'd
   Walk through a museum.
   Could you infer a life from the accumulation of things?
   Would the life in any way resemble the one you lived?
   Could you extract anything resembling *meaning?*

There are 160 boxes.

The contents of which are ...

Not what one would expect.

One would *think,*

That the man responsible for assembling the *Anthology of American Folk Music* —

A recording that forever altered the course of American music —

Compiled from a collection of 20,000 78 records

One would *think* he might have a few 78s lying around ...

No. Not a single 78 in all these boxes.

HARRY: The

Anthology was intended to uhhh

Span six volumes.

I finished 1, 2, 3, middle of 4 I uhhh

Lost interest.

Same reason I

Put it together in the first place I uhh

Needed money

To

Finance

Certain

Cinematical alchemical chemical alch'olical endeavors.

CURATOR: There are records ... hundreds, mint condition. But all LPs purchased after 1965.

HARRY: I sold the 78s to the uhhh

It's another collection among collections collecting dust in

The constipated bowels of the New York Public Library —

Librarian lost my documentation

So regardless of the uhhh

Collection's *comprehensiveness,* their

Worth as a

Thick description of American life to extraterrestrial invaders,

Without documentation the records —

Are just that. Records.

CURATOR: Okay, no 78s ...

HARRY: I'm uhhh

Leaving it to

Future generations to

Figure out the purpose of all this *stuff*

CURATOR: What about the paper airplanes?

It's said Harry assembled the largest collection of found paper airplanes in the world ...

HARRY: Donated them to the Gnash-Null Air/Space Museum, Smithsonian Institution, Washington, D.C.

The Curator picks up a phone and dials. Ringing. A click.

SMITHSONIAN RECEPTIONIST #1 (JORGE): Space Museum, please hold.

Muzak version of David Bowie's "Space Oddity" underscores the following:

HARRY: The paper airplanes I was

Deciphering uhh

Patterns.

Paper airplanes you find on the streets of Greenwich Village possess characteristics —

Aerodynamics, paper quality, fold precision, unique to that geography

Compared to paper airplanes in Spanish Harlem ...

Cross-classification of the different varieties reveals a —

The Muzak is interrupted by someone picking up the phone.

SMITHSONIAN RECEPTIONIST #2 (ANNIE): Space Museum, can I help you?

CURATOR: I explained what I was looking for.

SMITHSONIAN RECEPTIONIST: Paper airplanes?

No, ma'am.

CURATOR: Nothing bequeathed by Harry Smith?

SMITHSONIAN RECEPTIONIST: Nope. But we have some other neat things ...

Ever hear of the Wright Brothers?

The Receptionist cackles and hangs up.

CURATOR: Okay, no paper airplanes ...

HARRY: I'm uhhh

Leaving it to

Future generations to –

CURATOR: What about the Ukrainian Easter eggs?

HARRY: Göteborg Ethnography Museum, Stockholm, Sweden ...

CURATOR: I email my counterpart there ... Email back:

Sound of email arriving in inbox.

GÖTEBORG CURATOR (MARTIN): Madam,

I'm sorry to say the Göteborg Museum has no Easter eggs in its collections and no objects donated by Harry Smith.

Regards,

Olle,

Head of Collections

CURATOR: Okay, no Ukrainian Easter eggs,

Except for seven rotten ones in the boxes.

HARRY: I'm uhhh

Leaving it to

Future generations to

Figure out the purpose of all this –

CURATOR: What about the films? *Early Abstractions? Mirror Animations?*

Heaven and Earth Magic? Mahagonny? The Oz film?

Not an inch of celluloid in the boxes ...

HARRY: Give Jonas Mekas a call at Anthology Film Archives. He'll hook you up.

CURATOR: I left a message ...

Waiting for the call back ...

Okay. Films? Archived.

What about the paintings – the "wild cosmic monsters" Allen Ginsberg // refers

HARRY: I have a habit of tearing out the canvases

    When I have too much to drink and I uhhhh

    Turn into Rumpelstiltskin.

    Others I traded for illuminated manuscripts, beer,

    If you uhhh track down the

    Hungarian fellow, midget –

    He'll point you to

    Fresh Kills Landfill on Staten Island where you'll uhhhh

    Find your uhhh

    "Harry Smith Museum"

CURATOR: Is there rhyme, is there reason ...

    Is all this

    Some secret, invisible map of the universe waiting to be deciphered?

HARRY: I'll say though that uhhhh

    It's as justifiable as any other type of uhhh

    Research.

CURATOR: Or some third-rate Dadaist's practical joke?

HARRY: It's a cross-sectional index to a variety of thoughts

    You can piss away your time reading *The Oxford English Dictionary*

    Or you can

    collect paper airplanes,

    Easter eggs –

    Designs are thirty thousand years old

    Making them superior to any book

    Because reason I make films, reason I paint,

    Reason I jack off or –

    It just occurred to me, saying "jack off," that Jack,

    Kerouac, that is – his favorite sex act also was uhhh

    Masturbation, specially of the mutual kind, we'd spend hours discussing it

    Though we uhhhh

    He, I never uhhhh I mean he wanted to, I wanted to but we didn't like the idea of

Offending

Anyone's religious sensibilities — what was the question?

CURATOR: Question becomes:

What should a Harry Smith Museum look like?

How about a song?

Short "Coo-coo Bird" reprise. At the end of the song, the applause light goes on. Real and recorded applause.

DARKEST HEART OF AMERICA: THE NEVER ENDING TOUR OF BLANK MARLOWE AND HIS BAND THE RED HERRINGS, PART TWO

STRANGER EMCEE: Ladies and gennelmen ...

    Hear the crackle of the campfire?

    Time once again for a detour into

    The Darkest Heart of America ...

MARLOWE: I'm getting ahead of myself

    I'm starting in the middle

    When I should be starting at the start

ANNIE: Shit ...

MARLOWE: Outside every town there's a

    "Welcome to..." sign

    Name of the place, town motto,

    picture of the thing town's famous for –

    Minor Civil War skirmish ... Giant Ball of Yarn ...

    Town I met Merry Andrew was no different

    Only –

    "Welcome" sign?

    Moved.

During the following, Jorge plays the Theremin, a spooky underscore.

MARLOWE: First time I saw it – couldn't tell how far it was –

    That time a night, nowhere two-lane country road?

    Mile could be ten,

    Ten miles, a hundred ...

    Looked like a

    Drive-in movie screen on the horizon.

    "Welcome to MAHAGONNY," sign read.

    Spelled like that Brecht play

    (Learned the hard way,

    With a price I'm still paying,

Locals call it Mahogany — like the wood —
Nowhere towns like that all over your Rand McNally —
Americanized foreign names
KAY-roh for Cairo, Ver-SALES for Versailles ...)

ANNIE: Where's this town?

MARLOWE: Place on my Rand McNally where it should've been?
Just white space ...

"Welcome to 'Mahogany'"
Against a strange background —
Hand breaking through the clouds,
plucking a celestial monochord ...

ANNIE: Celestial what?

MARLOWE: Monochord.
Fuckin' celestial monochord.

MARTIN: Marlowe'd never gotten over his
Decade old declaration of love for Annie,
Her brief acceptance and subsequent rejection of him,
So they had a tendency to be short with each other times like // this ...

ANNIE: Pray tell, what's a celestial monochord?

MARLOWE: Break it down.

ANNIE: Mono, one. Chord, stringed instrument. One stringed instr//ument.

MARLOWE: There you go.

ANNIE: It's the celestial part you're losing // me ...

MARLOWE: In relation to the string?

ANNIE: Yeah, jackass, "in relation to the // string."

MARLOWE: Pythagoras.

ANNIE: Oh, for crying out // loud.

MARLOWE: 580-500 // BC

ANNIE: BC blah // blah

MARLOWE: BC that's // right

ANNIE: I know who Pythag//oras ...

MARLOWE: Studied mathematical patterns
    Made by vibrating string.
    Saw evidence of an underlying plan,
    Might even say *Rand McNally*
    Of the universe ...
    That the universe is like
    one infinite musical instrument –
    If you figure its harmonies?
    mathematically – ?
    You can listen to the mind of god ...

MARTIN: There was a long silence while we
    Contemplated that.

MARLOWE: May I go on ... ?

    Sign: "Welcome to Mahagonny, Celestial Monochord,"
    Underneath: town motto ...

HARRY'S VOICE: "Do what thou wilt shall be the whole of the Law."

ANNIE: Shit.

CURATOR: Quotation from *Liber AL vel Legis*, also known as *The Book of the Law.*
    Main sacred text of the Law of Thelema. Dict//ated

HARRY'S VOICE: Dictated to my poppy, Aleister Crowley, 1904, in KAY-roh, Egypt
    by Aiwass, Minister of Hoor-par-crat, central deity of the Law of // Thelema ...

MARTIN: None of us needed an explanation where that came from ... We'd all,
    in our younger days,
    Dabbled.
    Crowley. Magick. *Sex* magick.

MARLOWE & HARRY: "Do what thou wilt shall be the whole of the Law."

JORGE: Sounds like a good law to me.

MARLOWE: Folks in town lived by it ...

> I get out the car to get a closer look.
> My eyes weren't playing tricks. Sign moved ...
> Morphing colors, shapes, patterns, vibrations ...
> Like some invisible projector was projecting on it.
> Then I hear a voice behind me.

The Merry Andrew theme plays on a toy piano.

MERRY ANDREW: Who the fuck are you?

MARLOWE: Man's standing there – dressed in this far-out drag

> Like some lost carnival geek, dragging on a rope this huge wood box.
> I say:
> Me?

MERRY ANDREW: No. The eight foot tall Chinese dude standing next to you ...

> Yeah, I'm talkin to you.

MARLOWE: I was just ...

MERRY ANDREW: Just ...

MARLOWE: Admiring the sign here.

MERRY ANDREW: Better get movin

> If you know what's good for you.

MARLOWE: Don't wanna ruffle the man's feathers

> Get back in the car, stick the key in the ignition

Jorge makes the sounds of a car ignition failing to catch.

MARLOWE: Won't turn on.

> No idea what to do – I'm in the car,
> Sign's pulsating,
> Mr. Every-Day-Is-Halloween's glaring at me

Finally, I get out ...

Um.

Car won't start.

MERRY ANDREW: That so.

MARLOWE: There a gas // statio

MERRY ANDREW: What do you think this is? New York City?

MARLOWE: Huh?

MERRY ANDREW: I don't like the look of your license plates.

MARLOWE: Look, there at least

A place I can lay my head til morning?

MERRY ANDREW: Lay your head ...

MARLOWE: Motel, // hotel

MERRY ANDREW: Town's closed for the night.

I'd think twice, buster, bout camping by the side of the road.

MARLOWE: Look, I'm just passing through, I // don't

MERRY ANDREW: "Passing through," huh?

Through what?

To what?

From what? And why?

MARLOWE: Decided wasn't gonna talk to him no more,

went to the car,

Locked the door,

Closed my eyes.

Don't know if it was minutes or hours passed but I hear tapping,

Against the window. High school ring, "Mahagonny High, Class of '68"

It's him. I roll down the window:

What?

MERRY ANDREW: Um ... sorry ...

> Did I ... wake you?

> I was
> Watching you sleep?
> Started feeling like,
> where'd my hospitality go?
> My
> Sense of humanity?

MARLOWE: I just stared at him.

MERRY ANDREW: Town's closed.

> Most of it, anyhow ... but
> One place's open. Red's.

MARLOWE: Red's.

MERRY ANDREW: Red Herring's Bar, Grill

> And Happy Bottom Riding Club
> Might get yourself a room there.

MARLOWE: I'm thinking:

> This guy for real?
> Or is he settin a trap...

MERRY ANDREW: Tween you me and the lamppost:

> Rumor round town Harry's screening *Oz* tonight ...

MARLOWE: Huh?

MERRY ANDREW: I intend you no harm

> just that people
> claimin to be "passing through"
> Come here with *motives* ...

> I got a mandate to protect Harry.

MARLOWE: Who's Harry?

MERRY ANDREW: Nevermind.

MARLOWE: I'll be fine here til morning.

MERRY ANDREW: Suit yourself.

MARLOWE: Off he went, dragging that wood box behind him …
But Curiosity … Oh, Curiosity.
Five dollar hooker always wins in the end, didn't she?

MARTIN: You followed him?
Marlowe went silent … looked up at the sky then:

MARLOWE: Once upon a time the darkness ruled here too …

Harmonica theme music. Applause light.

STRANGER EMCEE: Ladies and gentlemen,
Let's leave our traveling troubadours for a spell, cause
It's time for
Shadow of the Shining City: Chronicles of The American Underground …
Part One: The Ballad of Harry and Allen (Ginsberg that is)

SHADOW OF THE SHINING CITY: CHRONICLES OF THE AMERICAN UNDERGROUND, PART ONE

The band strikes up the "Coo-coo Bird" theme. The Curator appears.

CURATOR: I comb through indexes.

> An example:
> *I Celebrate Myself: The Somewhat Private Life of Allen Ginsberg*
> (Bill Morgan, Viking, 2006)
> Entry for "Smith, Harry":
> "pages 278, 384, 580, 596, 607, 615-619"
> Followed by subheadings
> "Death of, 619
> Bob Dylan and, 587
> Fish design by, 371
> As Ginsberg's houseguest, 586-588"
>
> A significant number of references, yes,
> But miniscule compared to
> Burroughs, William
> Kerouac, Jack, etc.
> Which begs the question:
> What is Harry's place
> In the hierarchy of significance?

STRANGER EMCEE: Ladies and gentlemen, it gives me great pleasure to bring you
> Live from the Bardo Plane,
> Poet Laureate of the Beat Generation,
> Mister Allen Ginsberg ...

Applause light goes on.

ALLEN GINSBERG: Thank you, so nice, thank you ...

STRANGER EMCEE: Welcome to the show, Allen ...
> Two words:
> Harry. Smith.

ALLEN GINSBERG: Harry ... what do you say about Harry. I weep for Harry. I laugh my ass for Harry ... Harry was a genius on the realm of Leonardo

STRANGER EMCEE: You don't say —

ALLEN GINSBERG: Biggest pain in the ass ever walked the earth ...
I love Harry Smith.

First heard about him in San Francisco from a mutual filmmaker friend
Described Harry as a painter slash filmmaker slash alchemist slash magician
That Harry was descended from Aleister Crowley

Cut to 1960. '61. I'm at the Five Spot in New York listening to Thelonious Monk.
I see this old guy

Bebop Jazz underscores the next.

CURATOR: Old guy ...?
In '60 Harry was 37.
Ginsberg 34.

ALLEN GINSBERG: ... at a table drinking milk
(He was terrified of being poisoned)
Making tiny marks in a notebook —
For some inexplicable reason I think:
This must be Harry Smith.
I'd been at the Five Spot every night to see Monk
I gave him a copy of *Howl*, to Monk cause ...
I wanted to know what he thought
One night I ask Monk,
Did you read it? Did you read *Howl*? What do you think?

Music abruptly stops.

MONK (JORGE): Makes sense.

Jazz kicks in again.

ALLEN: Which was pure pleasure to hear Monk say that,
But anyway —
I ask him: "Are you Harry Smith?"

HARRY: Who wants to know?

ALLEN GINSBERG: Which I take to mean Yes.
"Wow! What are you doing here?"

HARRY: I'm
Deciphering theeeeuuuuh
Mathematical patterns theeeee
Recurrent syncopations in Monk's solos —

ALLEN: Far out ...
What are you doing that for?

HARRY: I'm using his music as background to films I'm making.

Jazz music cuts out.

ALLEN: Harry lived like a hermit
One night
He invites me to his room,
401 ½ East 70th — *Tiny,*
Every inch covered with books, Easter eggs, records, paper airplanes

HARRY: It's a work-in-progress examination of uhhh
Cross-disciplinary investigations into
Visual, anthropological, musicological phenomena.

ALLEN: That's exactly what I'm thinking, room is some kind of
Museum, map,
Of what I couldn't tell you but —

HARRY: Step right over here uhhh

ALLEN: He shows me a closet — stuffed with Seminole Indian dresses
One point I got too close to a cabinet? Sign said // keep off?

HARRY: KEEP OFF! THOSE'LL BLOW UP IF YOU GET TOO CLOSE!!

ALLEN: That's where he kept the Ukrainian Easter eggs, which he donated to a museum in Scandinavia.

CURATOR: Ha!

ALLEN: Second later he's immersed,

Playing what looks like a solitary version of Cat's Cradle

HARRY: I'm the world's leading authority on string figures

ALLEN: Far out, how'd you get to be the world's leading authority on –

HARRY: I've mastered hundreds of forms from around the world

I'm working on a manuscript that uhhhh –

ALLEN: Then he showed me his paintings ... *Jesus*

These

Amazing Cosmic Monsters

HARRY: They're not paintings they're uhhh

Doodles of formulaic triangulations of Pythagorean calculations –

Ones over there are uhhh

Note for note visual transcriptions of the music of Dizzy Gillespie

Here, I'll demonstrate

ALLEN: He sat me down ...

Handed me a beer from the fridge, (had only a six pack, yogurt, cat food, dead birds he found on the street) put Dizzy's "Manteca" on the record player ...

Harry appears before an empty frame dressed like a professor but wearing shades, cigarette dangling from his mouth. Opening drums of Gillespie's "Manteca." Harry does a little jig. When the horns kick in, he uses a telescopic pointer to point out spots that correspond to the notes. At a certain point it should appear he is no longer motivating his own movements. It's as if puppet strings from the sky manipulate him. The song cuts off.

ALLEN: Then he got me high.

Turned on his movie projector

Showed me his films ...

HARRY: My uhhh

Cinematic excreta comes in four delicious flavors:

Batiked abstractions, painted directly on cellulouid – made 1939 to '46.

ALLEN: He painted them by hand, frame by frame ... intricate like you wouldn't believe.

HARRY: Next: semi-realistic animated collages made as part of my alchemical labors, 1957-62.

ALLEN: Movie called *Heaven and Earth Magic //* which

HARRY: which depicts the heroine's toothache consequent to the loss of a valuable watermelon, her dentistry and transportation to heaven, followed by an exposition of the heavenly land in terms of Israel and Montreal and her return to earth the day Edward the 7th dedicated the London Sewer.

If you're interested:
Films 1 thru 5 I made under the influence of marijuana.
Number 6, schmeck
Number 7, cocaine and ups.
8 thru 12, anything I could get my hands on,
But mostly uhhh
Depravation.
I'm working on uhh
Film #13, a 3-hour meditation on Shamanism
Disguised as an animated adaptation of *The Wizard of Oz* ...
At ten thousand dollars a minute
It's the most expensive animated feature ever made ...
Liz Taylor, Henry Phipps have been most generous ...

ALLEN: Mind blowing stuff, but freaked me out
End of the night
He tries to sell me *Heaven and Earth Magic* for a hundred bucks.
What am I gonna do with a movie? I don't own a projector,
But Harry was living in squalor and I ...
He would do that –
Get you high, mess with your head,
Destroy his stuff, hit you up for 20 bucks ...
I bought it.
Took it to Jonas Mekas at Film-Makers' Cooperative –

JONAS MEKAS (JORGE): Holy fucking shit! Who is this guy? He's a fucking genius...

ALLEN: Mekas starts showing his films ...

JONAS MEKAS: 1980? '81? First screening of *Mahagonny* ...

    Complicated like nothing you've seen ...

    Harry built a special projector,

    Simultaneously projected four images –

    In all kinds of combinations ...

    At the screening?

    Harry goes bat shit,

    Throws the projector out the window.

    First and last screening of *Mahagonny*. Oh, well ...

ALLEN: Harry was always broke. From the time we met to when he lived in my apartment to –

STRANGER EMCEE: Hold up ... he lived in your apartment?

ALLEN: '84? '85? Got himself kicked out some Bowery flophouse. Needed a place for a few days.

Sound of a taxi honking, screeching, hitting something that sounds like bones, coming to a halt.

ALLEN: Harry gets hit by a cab. Compound fracture.

    Few days turns into an eight month ordeal ...

    I took pictures – he hated me taking his picture ...

    There's one – him pouring a glass of milk.

    I call it "Alchemist Transforming Milk Into Milk"

    One day,

    Who comes by the apartment?

Buzzer. Annie plays the piano part of "Like a Rolling Stone" on a toy piano.

ALLEN: Who is it?

VOICE OF BOB DYLAN (JORGE): 's me. Bobby.

ALLEN: Bobby! What a surprise! Come up, come up ...

Allen buzzes him in. Footsteps up stairs, a knock.

ALLEN: Bobby!

BOB DYLAN: Ginzie!

ALLEN: So good to see you ... what brings you here?

BOB DYLAN: Smells like shit in here, Allen ...

ALLEN: Oh, yeah

BOB DYLAN: Shit and piss! Wait: that semen?
　Place smells like the men's toilet in Washington Square ... What's going on, you
　depressed again?

ALLEN: No, no no ... just a
　Houseguest ... You'll want to meet him

BOB DYLAN: If he smells like shit, I don't –

ALLEN: It's Harry Smith.

BOB DYLAN: *The* Harry Smith? *Anthology* Harry Smith?

ALLEN: One and only.

BOB DYLAN: He smells like shit?

ALLEN: No no no no ... I mean, yes. He's
　Living in the room off the kitchen, he's doing paintings
　Using his own shit and dead butterflies

BOB DYLAN: He pissin on em too?

ALLEN: Oh, no, no ...
　He pees in milk cartons, saving the stuff for some alchemical ...

BOB DYLAN: Can I meet him?

ALLEN: Sure! I'll get him –
　Bob Dylan, Harry Smith, same room, Holy shit.
　HARRY!

Sound of Allen excitedly pounding on the door.

HARRY: *(Inaudible noises)*

ALLEN: Harry? You okay? You drunk?

HARRY: *(Inaudible noises)*

ALLEN: Harry ... Bobby Dylan's here. He wants to meet you.

HARRY: *(Inaudible noises)*

BOB DYLAN: Tell him I owe him ...

ALLEN: Hear that, Harry? Bob Dylan wants to tell you he *owes* you ...

BOB DYLAN: Tell him ... He invented me.

ALLEN: Bobby wants to tell you you *invented* him ...

HARRY: *(Inaudible noises)*

ALLEN: HARRY!!!! Bob. Fucking. *Dylan*. Is *here*. He wants to pay *tribute*.

HARRY: TELL HIM HE CAN GO PISS UP A TREE!!!!

The band starts up — playing a tune reminiscent of something that might have been an outtake from Ginsberg's "First Blues" recordings. Ginsberg plays the harmonium.

CURATOR: Combing through another index —
> *The Letters of Allen Ginsberg*
> (Bill Morgan, editor, DaCapo, 2008) ...
> September 1988:

ALLEN: *(sings)* Dear Harry it was best for us to get off the telephone
> Dear Harry it was best for me to hang up the telephone
> We dug ourselves into a hole, sorry but you're on your own

CURATOR: He follows this with an accounting of financial outlays to Harry:

ALLEN: *(sings)* Stay away from New York City it costs money to live here
> Four seventy a week adds up to 20 grand a year
> Can't afford this subsidy, to pay for your rent and beer

CURATOR: Ginsberg arranged a Shaman-in-Residence for Harry at Naropa —
> Things got out of hand ...

ALLEN: *(sings)* I won't pay for your ticket to come back to New York City

    Saying this to you my friend makes me feel real shitty

    If you find your way back here, you sure as hell can't stay with me

CURATOR: One can't help but wonder – if he read it at all – what Harry thought reading:

ALLEN: *(sings)* You indulge in magic thinking, you talk evasive yak

    You depend on me for everything, you never pay me back

    I hate to lose my patience but you're giving me a heart attack

CURATOR: Yet Ginsberg can't help closing on a warm note:

ALLEN: *(sings)* I wish you well dear Harry, don't forget your medicine

    Stay away from Kefflex, you're allergic to Penicillin

    Signing off with reverence, your humble friend Allen …

Applause light.

ALLEN: Harry came to town again in '91 …

    To get his Grammy.

    I was so happy for him, finally being recognized …

    He gave a beautiful speech.

HARRY: "I'm glad to say my dreams came true …

    That I saw America change through music"

ALLEN: Brief. But beautiful.

    What it said:

    That the homeless, the minority, the impoverished, the poet –

    which he himself was –

    The forgotten of America –

    Altered the country's consciousness …

STRANGER EMCEE: Did he stay with you that time?

ALLEN: No …

    Ended up back at the Chelsea … Few weeks later, he was dead.

His memorial service — St. Mark's Church ...

You could see all the different people he touched —

the film people, musicians, anthropologists,

poets, brain scientists, the Ordo Templi Orientis guys ... I'm still paying his back
rent at the Chelsea,

But when he died ... I wept for him.

There will never be anyone else like Harry Smith.

STRANGER EMCEE: Thank you, Allen ...

For the visit ...

ALLEN: Sure thing. If you ever make it here ... look me up.

Take care, everybody!

He waves. Applause light. The band kicks into a Rockabilly instrumental.

STRANGER EMCEE: Ladies and gennelmen ...

Don't know if you heard the sound but I sure did ... Call of nature and the sweet
come hither of a lonely urinal ... Good time to hit the rest stop, folks —

So, stretch your legs, grab a cocktail, smoke outside,

And excuse us while we ... powder our noses ...

Music continues. Button.

End of Part One.

PART TWO

The audience returns. Blank Marlowe and The Red Herrings take the stage and begin a song, playing up its naughty humor.

SONG: "THE BIBLE SALESMAN'S DAUGHTER" OR "NO SIR!" (BASED ON "THE SPANISH MERCHANT'S DAUGHTER")

MARLOWE: *(singing)* Tell me girl, please tell me truly

> Tell me why you scorn me so?
> When I ask, you always hurt me
> Cause you always tell me No.

ANNIE: *(singing)* No sir, no sir, no sir, no sir

> Daddy was a bible salesman
> As he walked out the front door
> Made me promise I would say No
> To everything you did implore

MARLOWE: I know your father he despised me

> But should he not return to thee
> I know that you don't have a mother
> Will you still say no to me?

ANNIE: No sir, no sir, no sir, no sir

> Yes it's true I have no mother
> And if my pop abandons me
> I'll have you know, I've got a brother
> Who will kill to protect me

MARLOWE: When you walk into the garden

> To pluck roses wet with dew
> Girl would you be offended
> If I walked and talked to you?

ANNIE: No sir, no sir, no sir, no sir

> My big brother got a letter
> To the Army he must go
> He told me that I had better
> Keep my promise to say No.

MARLOWE: If while sitting in the garden

> My fingertips and yours did brush
> Tell me would you feel offended
> If my lips and yours did touch?

ANNIE: No sir, no sir, no sir, no sir

MARLOWE: If my hand slips under your dress

> Would you pull away from me?
> If to my room I did invite you
> Would you refuse to lie with me?

ANNIE: No sir, no sir, no sir, no sir

ANNIE & MARLOWE: No sir, no sir, no sir, no sir

A change in the tenor of the song — what began as buoyant, jaunty, tongue in cheek, shifts. The song becomes an honest expression of the unrequited love between Marlowe and Annie — perhaps these verses are sung a cappella.

ANNIE: The empty rooms have grown so quiet

> Looks like Daddy's gone for good
> My dear brother fell in battle
> He came home in a box of wood.

MARLOWE: Will you tell me you don't want me

> After all that we've been through?
> Will you say "No" to my sad brown eyes
> When I say that I love you?

ANNIE: No sir, no sir, no sir, no sir ...

MARLOWE & ANNIE: No sir, no sir, no sir, no sir

Applause light. The Stranger Emcee returns.

STRANGER EMCEE: Big round of applause for Blank Marlowe and The Red Herrings!
Every time you do that number just warms the cockles of my lederhosen ...

MARLOWE: Thank you, sir

STRANGER EMCEE: And Annie?

ANNIE: Yeah, darlin?

STRANGER EMCEE: I know a version of that song. What say you and me do it
together some time ...

ANNIE: Oh yeah? What version is that?

STRANGER EMCEE: Little version I call: "Yes miss, Yes miss, Yes miss, Yessss misssss"

Rim shot.

Ladies and gentlemen
Welcome back for the second half ... Normally this point in the show,
I'd introduce the
Albuquerque Youth Ballet and their
Dance adaptation of the
classic Harry Smith film *Heaven and Earth Magic*
Received word backstage that uhhh
They won't be joining us tonight ...
Something bout a run in with Border Patrol? Area 51?
Truly a shame cause
You ever seen the film? No doubt you'd ask —
"How they gonna pull *that* off?"

Shit. Anyway ... uhhhh
Let's move on, shall we? To uhh
nother installment of *Shadow of the Shining City:*
Chronicles of the American Underground ...

*Applause light — real and recorded applause. Theme music begins ... something stately, grand,
a little self-important like certain documentaries you see on PBS.*

SHADOW OF THE SHINING CITY: CHRONICLES OF THE AMERICAN UN-DERGROUND, PART TWO

KEN BURNS-ESQUE DOCUMENTARY ANNOUNCER VOICE (MARTIN):
> Washington, D.C. Summer. 1973.
> A long national nightmare in progress.
> The U.S. Constitution dangles precariously
> Over the grinding teeth of an overstuffed document shredder.
> The cancer has grown malignant on the White House.
>
> Yet in the midst of national crisis,
> In the White House basement,
> A few steps from the new bowling alley,
> The White House Library, for the first time in history
> Adds sound recordings to its collection.
>
> Among the first obtained by the Library:
> Harry Smith's *Anthology of American Folk Music* ...
>
> Join us for tonight's episode of
> *Shadow of the Shining City: Chronicles of the American Underground* ...
> Part Two: "Patriotic Acts of Treason"

Applause light goes on — real and recorded applause. The band begins a song.

SONG: "WHITE HOUSE BLUES"

JORGE: *(singing)* Old Nixon was bothered, old Nixon he did bawl
> As his chopper flew over the National Mall
> From Washington to San Clement
>
> Gerald in the White House, he's doin' his best
> Prayin' he'll wake up from dreamin' this mess
> We'll pardon him, for pardoning you
>
> Quiet down little Checkers, now don't you yelp
> Ain't nothing for Nixon you can do will help
> '74 ain't '52

You went on the TV, said "I ain't no crook"
Time to go home now and write yourself a book
From Washington to San Clement

Ain't but two things that grieve my mind
Boys in Vietnam, the wives they left behind
They're long gone, won't ever come home

You shook hands with Brezhnev, you broke bread with Mao
Yorba Linda poor boy, hey look at you now
From Moscow to Beijing-town

Eighteen long minutes the tape went blank
One by one your cronies, walked down the plank
It's hard times, it's hard times

Yonder comes Woodstein, with their headline
Effective noon tomorrow Dick Nixon will resign
Won't have you to kick around no more

Some cheered "Good riddance," some wept real tears
As you waved bye bye to your White House years
From Washington to San Clement

F. Scott Fitzgerald says "Ain't no second act"
If he knew your story that saying he'd retract
You may be down, but you'll come back
From Washington to San Clement

Applause light.

STRANGER EMCEE: Ladies and gentlemen, please welcome Pop culture historian, rock critic, novelist, painter, documentarian and authority on all sorts of obscure stuff, Dr. Alger Crimus ...

Applause light.

ALGER CRIMUS (MARTIN): The symmetry is almost *novelistic*
   '73: White House acquires the *Anthology* –
Beginning of the end for Nixon –

Who, of course is elected Eisenhower's Vice President
In '52. The year the *Anthology*'s first *released* ...
Perfect bookends to an era that begins and ends in crisis for Nixon –
Checkers and Watergate, but in '73
Tricky Dick can't go on TV, pimp the family dog, no –
Dylan's prophecy in '64 had come true:
The Times Had Indeed A-Changed.
Which shows that the *Anthology*
Functioned as a kind of alchemic social engineering
Not from the top *down* but from underground *up* ...

STRANGER EMCEE: Say what?

ALGER CRIMUS: Imagine:
Nixon, battered by Watergate,
Prowling the White House basement late at night
After his fourth Mai Tai
Grumbling to himself ...

NIXON (JORGE): JesusHHaldErlichmanHuntslushlushhushfundBernwardWoodstein-
JEdgarLiddyWashingtonPostsonsabitchesIamNotACrook*CHRIST*

ALGER CRIMUS: Picture him: troubled,
Pulling the *Anthology* off the shelf ...

NIXON: Uhh, Pat? Pat? Where are you?

PAT (ANNIE): Right here, Dick.
I was just feeding King Timahoe ...

NIXON: Erm ... have any idea what this is?

PAT: Why, Dick,
That's the *Anthology of American Folk Music* ...
One of the records in the new collection ...

NIXON: I see uhhh
Folk music, you say. Why is the cover so ...
Peculiar ...

PAT: Why Dick, that's the hand of God reaching down from the heavens to pluck a Celestial Monochord ...

CURATOR: Etching by Theodore de Bry, 1618. From *De Musica Mundana* by Robert Fludd. English physician, astrologer, Paracelisian ...

NIXON: Parasaywhat?

ALGER CRIMUS: The White House copy is the original 1952 issue ...
With Harry's original artwork. See:
Reissues replaced Harry's design with
Sentimental photos of hard-luck Depression hobos ...
Which appealed to the Romanticism of folkies who
Held the *Anthology* as a kind of *bible* –
But in actuality missed the point – the
Alchemical purpose of Harry's design –
They misread the *Anthology* as a nostalgia trip, rather than what it was:
A peephole to the *past* as a way of engineering the *future* ...
Of American music
Of a desegregated society
Of challenging post-war consumerist America
Of Bob Dylan dispensing with the Newport Folkies,
Creating an explosively NEW American folk music
Of America *itself* ...

PAT: Shall we give it a listen, Dick?
Get your mind off that impeachable offenses business.

NIXON: Erm ... sure, Pat. Care for a Mai Tai?

Sound of a record player stylus landing on vinyl. First notes of "Henry Lee."

ALGER CRIMUS: What the Nixons would have heard is what America sounded like before it became a Republic of Amnesia and Homogeny ...

NIXON: Pat ... this music isn't easing my mind. It's giving me the heebee-jeebees.

PAT: Peculiar ...

NIXON: What is it Plum?

PAT: Booklet that comes with the set ... listen: "A few quotations that have been useful to the editor in preparing this handbook."

HARRY: "Civilized Man Thinks Out His Difficulties, At Least He Thinks He Does. Primitive Man Dances Out His Difficulties."

CURATOR: "R.R. Marret"

NIXON: Hmph.

PAT: And this one ... my word ...

HARRY: "Do What Thou Wilt Shall Be The Whole Of the Law."

CURATOR: "Aleister Crowley"

NIXON: What in God's name is that supposed to mean?

ALGER CRIMUS: I have this fantasy?
   That while they listen?
   A perverse, narcotic fueled *Mr. Smith Goes to Washington* plays out ...
   Harry himself appears like the Wizard of Oz from behind the curtains ...

HARRY: Evening Mister President ...

NIXON: JESUSCHRISTGODDAMNIT! Who the hell are you?

HARRY: I'm Harry Smith.

NIXON: What in God's name is that supposed to // mean??

PAT: Dick, calm down ...

NIXON: How the hell am I supposed to calm down with derelicts breaking into // the White

PAT: Dick: it's okay ... This is Harry Smith. He edited the *Anthology* ...

NIXON: I see, uhhh

PAT: Welcome to the White House, Mr. Smith.
   Care for a drink?

HARRY: Milk.

ALGER CRIMUS: Imagine them:
    In the darkness,
    Under the watchful gazes of
    Gilbert Stuart's portrait of Washington
    And Charles Bird King's Native Americans
    Listening to the *Anthology* ...
    What strange terrain would their conversation cross?

PAT: Here you are boys ... Enjoy!
    Oooh! This one's is catchy ... what's it called?

HARRY: "White House Blues"

PAT: Oh ...

HARRY: North Carolina Ramblers
    1926, original issue Columbia Records Number 15099D ...

NIXON: Mr. Smith has an encyclopedic knowledge of these records ...

HARRY: Shellac's an amazingly versatile product ...
    Used in everything from furniture finish,
    Rifle butts, flak helmets, your // uhhh –

NIXON: Basic war material ...

HARRY: Not to mention its use in the uhhh
    Manufacture of 78 records ...

NIXON: Wasn't aware of that –
    Didn't have 78s back in Whittier ...
    We were Quakers ...

HARRY: It's the records interested me
    Which is why some people accuse me of treason ...

NIXON: You too?

NEWSREEL INTRO VOICE (MARTIN): Grandma Beware! A Public Service Announcement from the Department of War!

Patriotic sounding marching band music – the kind you would hear on a wartime newsreel. Sound of dozens of cats meowing.

OCTOGENARIAN WIDOW (ANNIE): Down, Frisky ... Muffin, leave Binky alone.

Sound of knocking at the door.

OCTOGENARIAN WIDOW: Who is it?

VOICE OF THE WAR DEPARTMENT MAN (MARTIN): War Department ...

OCTOGENARIAN WIDOW: Just a minute ...

Sounds of an old lady's footsteps crossing to a door – stepping on cat tails every now and then, eliciting pained meows. She hums. Sound of a creaky old door opening.

OCTOGENARIAN WIDOW: Can I help you?

WAR DEPARTMENT MAN: Ma'am: we come to you for assistance with a National
    Emergency...

OCTOGENARIAN WIDOW: Yes ...?

WAR DEPARTMENT MAN: Records, ma'am.
    We're collecting 78s for the War effort ...
    Widows like you are known to horde stashes long after your husbands die.
    Do your patriotic duty and fork 'em over ...

OCTOGENARIAN WIDOW: But you already took Walter's records –

WAR DEPARTMENT MAN: Excuse me, ma'am?

OCTOGENARIAN WIDOW: Just yesterday skinny kid came by ... said the country
    needed records for Shellac ... I may be 82,
    But I'll do my part, even if it means giving away Walter's –

WAR DEPARTMENT MAN: What did this man look like?

OCTOGENARIAN WIDOW: Kind of elfish. Wore sunglasses ... chain smoked Lucky
    Strikes ... Rumpelstiltskin comes to mind. Now that I think about it ... oh, no ...

WAR DEPARTMENT MAN: Goddamnit! Beat us to it again! We need to find this
    record thieving treasonous bastard, hang him by his pinkies!!!

Harry back with Nixon.

HARRY: Not treason, exactly, I ...

    Hoarded 78s during the uhhh

    What was the movie called?

    War to End All Wars: The Sequel?

    Guv-mint declared shellac a // strategic necessity

NIXON: Strategic necess//ity —

HARRY: Right — coming as it does from only one place on earth — the // uhhh

NIXON: Indian subcontinent. Before the War, Pat and I worked for the OPA.

HARRY: Cultivation process is a bitch, shellac —

    "lac" being a derivation of the Sanskrit word "lakh"

    Referring to swarms of larvae known as *laccifer lacca* —

    make a pound of the stuff takes six months, 15,000 lac beetles ...

    War machine can't get a fix cause Indiauhhh —

    World's dope dealer for the stuff — is cut off by the

    Bombing killing maiming —

    Guvmint figured why not?

    Melt down all those 78s

    Recorded when American music uhhh

    Still retained distinct regional qualities,

    Before NPR, *Good Morning America* erased local types

    Into one homogenous Voice of America ...

ALGER CRIMUS: In that moment

    Nixon becomes Pentheus, backed by his Silent Majority,

    To Smith's Dionysus backed by the Bohemian throngs.

    There's an

    Inversion of power,

    An inversion of the

    Very idea of America *itself* ...

HARRY: Me against the War Department.

    You might call it treason,

    I call treason the Levitt house, electric toaster, self-cleaning oven. ...

ALGER CRIMUS: For Harry, witnessing Nixon undergo this transformation,

> Sees his vision manifest in reality — that the work of an underground denizen
>
> Will emerge into the *light,* reshape how we think of ourselves
>
> As a nation. As a culture. As a *people.*

Nixon snores. He startles awake.

NIXON: Sorry, Mr. Smith ... I uhh

> Dozed off for a moment ...
>
> You were saying?

ALGER CRIMUS: You might be thinking:

> "What the *fuck* is this guy talking about?"
>
> Well ... Had I been in Nixon's shoes?
>
> I'd have given Harry the Medal of Freedom
>
> for his Patriotic Acts of Treason.

Theme music swells. Applause light. The Stranger Emcee appears.

DARKEST HEART OF AMERICA: THE NEVER ENDING TOUR OF BLANK MARLOWE AND HIS BAND THE RED HERRINGS, PART THREE

STRANGER EMCEE: I hear crickets and campfire a-cracklin' ...

>   From the White House basement

>   To the streets of Mahagonny ...

MARTIN: Marlowe...? You okay ... ?

MARLOWE: Huh? What?

MARTIN: You drifted ...

>   Merry Andrew ...? Mahagonny...? You followed him...?

MARLOWE: The town. Worse than closed. Dead.

>   Like a neutron bomb'd been dropped on it.

>   Andrew told me stories of the place ...

>   We passed an abandoned well –

MERRY ANDREW: Fella named Henry Lee lies bottom of that well ...

>   *(sings – variation on "Henry Lee")*

>   She pressed him up against a well
>   To steal a kiss or two
>   He did not see the blade in her hand
>   She cut him through and through

>   She said, "Lie there dirty Henry Lee
>   Til your flesh drips from your bones
>   That girl of yours in merry Ireland
>   Still waits for your return ..."

MARLOWE: We pass an abandoned house, dead flowers in the garden

MERRY ANDREW: Every kid in town knows the Gypsy woman lives there –

>   *(sings – variation of "Fatal Flower Garden")*

>   Out came a Gypsy lady
>   Dressed up in yellow and green

"Come in, come in you pretty little boy
To fetch your ball again"

She took him by his lily white hand
Led him down the hall
She locked him in a basement room
Where no one could hear him call ...

MARLOWE: Another house:

MERRY ANDREW: See that window up there?

MARLOWE: Silhouette of girl in the attic window.

MERRY ANDREW: Railroad boy had his way with her, never looked back ...

(sings — variation of "The Butcher Boy")

Her father he came home from work
Heard his daughter weeping so hurt
He went upstairs to give her hope
Found her hanging from a rope

He took his knife and cut her down
In her hand this note he found
"Shape my grave as a marble dove,
To warn this world I died for love."

MARLOWE: He takes me inside an abandoned factory ...

MERRY ANDREW: Used to make shoes here by hand ...

(sings — variation on "Peg and Awl")

They've invented a new machine, peg and awl
They've invented a new machine, peg and awl
They've invented a new machine, prettiest thing I ever seen
Throw away my peg, my peg, my peg, my awl

Make one hundred pair to my one, peg and awl
Make one hundred pair to my one, peg and awl

> Make one hundred pair to my one, peggin shoes it ain't no fun
>
> Throw away my peg, my peg, my peg, my —

MARLOWE: Suddenly he stops.

Pulls out a bottle of pills —

MERRY ANDREW: Want one?

Jorge starts playing the theremin.

MARLOWE: What is it?

MERRY ANDREW: "Dr. Smith's American Balsam."

Cures everything from your high blood pressure to your unending heartache.

Make you happier than a dog with two dicks.

MARTIN: Did you take one?

ANNIE: That's like asking Tennessee Williams if he'd like another mint julep.

MARLOWE: Yeah, I took one.

That's when shit got real weird ...

MERRY ANDREW: Here we are ...

MARLOWE: Rickety sign: Red Herring's Bar, Grill

MERRY ANDREW: and Happy Bottom Riding Club

MARLOWE: If Death was all there was outside ... inside?

If Desolation Row was a real place? Red's would be it ...

Harmonica sounds end the segment, cross fading into the sounds of Jewish Orthodox liturgical music.

STRANGER EMCEE: Ladies and gennelmen,

Let's take a walk.

Down to Manhattan's Lower East Side.

Four Flights up to a tenement apartment on East Broadway.

Tiny hold out of a forgotten Lower East Side of

immigrants, pushcart vendors, rag pickers,

Long before the real estate Pharaoh's figured out

Hipsters'll pay top dollar for the luxury of squalor ...

Please give it up for our last installment of
Shadow of the Shining City: Chronicles of the American Underground.
Part Three: "The Lonesome Burden of Lionel Z."

Applause light.

SHADOW OF THE SHINING CITY: CHRONICLES OF THE AMERICAN UNDERGROUND, PART THREE

The Curator appears with a box.

CURATOR: I am carrying a box.

> In this box. Is one.
>
> Of Harry's. Greatest achievements.
>
> The complete recordings.
>
> Of Rabbi Nuftali Zvi Margolies Abulafia.
>
> *This ...* my friends,
>
> Will be one of, if not *the,* most significant artifact
>
> In the Harry Smith Museum and Interpretive Center.
>
> Allow me to show you —

She opens the box. It's filled with packing peanuts. She digs through, first excited, then baf-fled. Other than peanuts, the box is empty. She looks up in panic when LIONEL Z. rolls on in a wheelchair. He's ancient. Breathes with the assistance of an oxygen tank. Chain smokes Viceroy 100s.

LIONEL (JORGE): Fifty years from now?

> The recordings by Harry Smith
>
> Of my grandfather ... Rabbi
>
> Nuftali
>
> Zvi
>
> Margolies
>
> Abulafia ...
>
> Will be regarded as a
>
> Musicological event of cosmic significance ...
>
> But I'm getting ahead of myself ...

Sound of a door knocking.

> 7am. Door knocks. This is what? '51, '52?
>
> Morning after Joanne and I married ...
>
> I'm thinking: who knocks? 7am? On the door of newlyweds?
>
> I open the door, see this creature ...

At this point he's 28?

Looks older than when he died.

HARRY: I'm Harry Smith.

LIONEL: Who sent you?

HARRY: George Andrews.

LIONEL: Andrews. One of the leading UFO guys ...

CURATOR: Wrote *Extraterrestrials Among Us* (St. Paul: Llewellyn Press, Minnesota, 1986)

HARRY: He says if I want to learn Kabala,

You're the man to see ...

LIONEL: He'd come from Berkeley.

On a Guggenheim Fellowship.

Joanne, also came from there

So it was Berkeley, Berkeley all the time.

Next five years? He practically moves in ...

Every night. Birdland. Miles Davis, Dizzy ...

Harry ropes Joanne to work on the *Oz* picture ...

Million dollar budget.

Liz Taylor, other guy – that died ...

All put money in ...

First time Harry's flush

Hands out hundred dollar bills to bums. ...

Sound of an Orthodox cantor singing.

LIONEL: In Meron, in Israel

Thousands of pilgrims –

On the anniversary of his death,

come to the grave of

Shimon

Bar

Yochai.

CURATOR: Mystic.

>Wrote the *Zohar,*
>Most important book of the Kabbalah.

LIONEL Z.: They come because

>In tradition
>Day he died he
>Revealed the deepest secrets of the Torah ...
>They dance, sing
>All night.

>In New York
>They celebrate at Home of the Sages
>My grandfather does the singing ...

>I think:
>Something Harry'd be interested in,
>An anthropo-musicological happening of the first order right here on East Broadway.
>He goes. With his recording equipment.
>There for hours ... at the end?
>Harry corners my grandfather.
>Harry doesn't talk Yiddish
>My grandfather doesn't speak a word of English
>Yet they're *immersed* ...
>My grandfather, doesn't know from tapes,
>"What's my voice doing in the box?"

>Harry convinces my grandfather to record –
>Thousands of songs he knows by heart ...
>Understand this music is ancient – none of it written down,
>Let alone on record ...

>Three years
>Harry turns my grandfather's tiny room into a recording studio ...
>One day, my grandfather tells me:

RABBI (MARTIN): Lionel, this recording business …

> Can go on til the end of time,
> *Enough!*

LIONEL Z.: They stop, press 18 LPs

> Thousand copies each.
> They sit there,
> In my grandfather's room for years …
>
> On his deathbed …
> My grandfather tells me

RABBI: Lionel, if it's the last thing you do,

> Promise me, you'll distribute the records …

He dies.

LIONEL: Fifty years I carry this burden …

> My uncle. Wanted nothing to do with the records
> Doesn't want his father's voice
> Playing in some record store on 14th Street.
> Records end up in a basement. Housing project in the Bronx.
>
> Twenty years go by,
> Sprinklers go bust, turns the basement into a lake …
> I salvage what I could.
>
> One set. All I have left.
> You have to understand the importance …
> Not like the *Anthology* … those records already existed
> Put em together presto …
> Harry made these recordings from scratch …
> Fifty years from now, this will be regarded as Harry's greatest achievement …
> What do I have now…?
> Handful of records?
> With scratches and dirt?
> They can do it with computers –

What do they call it? Digitizing ... ?

Costs money I don't have

I have to save the sound ...

The liturgical music crescendos. Applause light.

DARKEST HEART OF AMERICA: THE NEVER ENDING TOUR OF BLANK MARLOWE AND HIS BAND THE RED HERRINGS, PART THREE

STRANGER EMCEE: Speaking of sound ...

It's back to Mahagonny, USA

Where Blank Marlowe and Merry Andrew are about to cross the uhhh

Limn

Into

Red Herring's Bar and Grill

The Darkest Heart of America ...

MARLOWE: If Desolation Row was a real place? Red's would be it ...

The band creates the interior environment of Red's. A wild room of desperadoes drinking, fornicating, speculating like it's the end of the world. The band plays an apocalyptic, proto-punk rendition of "I Couldn't Get High" by the Fugs.

SONG: "I COULDN'T GET HIGH"

MARTIN: *(singing)* I went to a party the other night

I wanted to fill my brain with light

I grabbed myself a bottle

I started drinking wine

I thought pretty soon I'd be feeling fine

But I couldn't get high, no no no

Couldn't get high, no no no

So I threw down the bottle

I whipped out my pipe

I stuffed it full of grass

I gave myself a light

I huffed, puffed, smoked and I toked

After awhile my heart was nearly broke

Cause I couldn't get high, no no no

Couldn't get high, no no no

So I threw down my pipe

Mad as I could be

I gobbled up a cube of LSD

Waited 30 minutes for my body to sing

I waited and I waited but I couldn't feel a thing

No I couldn't get high no no no

I couldn't get high no no no

Couldn't get high, don't know why

I thought I would die ... Die die dieeee!

The song falls apart. Applause light goes on — real and recorded applause.

MARLOWE: Like the town motto said:

HARRY: "Do what thou wilt shall be the whole of the Law."

MERRY ANDREW: Girl tending bar?

That's Frankie ...

She'll put you up for the night.

Be careful: One minute?

She'll love you like it's the last night on earth

Next: she'll put three bullets in your back.

MARLOWE: Who are all these people ...?

MERRY ANDREW: Crazy, right? Let's see ... big table?

Black dude with the dark glasses? Blind Lemon Jefferson. Pretty lady's Sarah Carter. Found Christ, gave up singing, but she stops in time to time. Old guy with the banjo – Clarence Ashley. Other two black dudes: Reverend J.M. Gates, Mississippi John Hurt. Locals call it "Resurrection Table" –

MARLOWE: Who's the old man?

MERRY ANDREW: Ha! Which one?

MARLOWE: Wheelchair. Oxygen tank. Smoking Viceroy 100s.

MERRY ANDREW: Lionel Z. Master of the Kabala. Unfulfilled death bed promise keeps him breathing. And worried.

MARLOWE: Guys on stage?

MERRY ANDREW: House band. The Fugs. Harry produced their first record.

MARLOWE: Midget at the bar?

MERRY ANDREW: Bad news Hungarian. Slumlord.

MARLOWE: Man next to him in the expensive suit?

MERRY ANDREW: Phipps. Trust fund kid. Spends all his time druggin with the poets in town. They love him cause he's a High Fashion Goodwill Shop, closet full of Italian suits he wears once, then gives away. Balding dude over there? That's Ginsberg. He's got a mad crush on Phipps ...

MARLOWE: Wait: is that ... ?

MERRY ANDREW: Richard Milhous Nixon. 37th President of the United States ...

MARLOWE: Shit ...

MERRY ANDREW: I know, right? Check out Pat, doin the twist with Thelonious Monk ...

Sound of groaning and nasty, squishy footsteps stumbling.

MARLOWE: What the hell is that ... thing ... stumbling around?

MERRY ANDREW: Oh, that's Harry's Zombie.

MARLOWE: What?

MERRY ANDREW: While back Harry went down to Haiti to learn voodoo,
Came home, found some kid to be his Guinea pig

MARLOWE: Whoa ...

MERRY ANDREW: Yeah ... hasn't figured out how to snap him out of it.
Think the kid's name was Oscar

MARLOWE: Lady over there? Drinking alone?

MERRY ANDREW: Museum Curator. Comes every night to drink, comb through index-es. Museum's going up soon ...

MARLOWE: Old man in the corner ... Drinking milk ...

Merry Andrew is gone.

MARLOWE: Andrew? Old man in the ... ?

> I look up. Andrew's gone.

> I head to the bar,
> Squeeze between Phipps and the Hungarian midget. Hungarian flips.

HUNGARIAN MIDGET (JORGE): I don know vat happened to thet psi-koteek's sheet.
> Don aks. You aks, I knife your gut. Tell zat mutterfukker pay hees rent!

MARLOWE: Bartender ... how to describe her ... Can't be older than 21, still's got acne ...

FRANKIE (ANNIE): Don't mind him, baby. He's just trippin.
> What can I getcha?

MARLOWE: She's
> *Appealing* ... Ripped jeans, camisole ... Siamese cat eyes ...

FRANKIE: You're not from around here ...

MARLOWE: No, miss.

FRANKIE: Call me Frankie ...
> We don't get a lot of foreigners in here ...

MARLOWE: I'm not a foreigner. I'm American.

FRANKIE: Sweetie, anyone from outside Mahagonny –

MARLOWE: Pronounced like the wood

FRANKIE: Is a foreigner ...

MARLOWE: Fellow I came with –
> One in the
> Outfit...?

FRANKIE: Andrew? Aww ... sweetie-boy.

MARLOWE: Mentioned there might be a room ... ?

FRANKIE: I'll get you a room. Long as you're a good boy.
> Whatcha havin?

MARLOWE: Whiskey.

FRANKIE: So what brings you to our quaint little town?

MARLOWE: Car broke down.

Man over in the corner. Drinking milk. What's his story?

FRANKIE: Harry?

HUNGARIAN MIDGET: I tell you already! I don know vat happened to thet psi-koteek's sheet! Aks again, I knife your heart *and* your gut. Tell that mutterfukker pay
// hees rent!

FRANKIE: Oh, shut up, will you?

MARLOWE: You were sayin ... ?

FRANKIE: That's Harry Smith.

MARLOWE: Don't know why but ... Rumpelstiltskin crossed my mind.

On the table: glass of milk, roaches crawling in and out,

Tape recorder, ashtray piled with dead butts, notebooks he's jotting stuff in ...

All the while his hands move wildly making string figures –

FRANKIE: Harry's magic. Touched by the hand of god knows what.

Like his brain's wired to some supercomputer on Neptune ...

Stick around, cause: later tonight? if we're good? He'll take us down to The Palace...

MARLOWE: Palace?

FRANKIE: Movie house on 4th and Desolation.

Rumor round town Harry's screening *Oz* tonight ...

MARLOWE: *Wizard of Oz?*

FRANKIE: *Harry's* Oz ...

Any truth to it, you're in for more treats tonite than you're already imagining.

MARLOWE: Pardon?

FRANKIE: He's got this philosophy?

Reality's one big monster fantasy.

>You pick what fantasy you wanna be in ...
>Like you pick clothes out your closet

MARLOWE: I'm not sure I ...

FRANKIE: When you look at me, what's your fantasy?

MARLOWE: I dunno ...

FRANKIE: Liar.

>You desire me.
>You think my broken wing needs mending,
>I'm a little girl lost that's seen too many people die young.
>You wanna fill my head with fantasies about the
>Big, beautiful world outside Mahagonny?

>That's all well and good mister.
>Cause three o'clock this afternoon?
>Woke up? Sized up the costumes in my closet.
>Picked these jeans, this camisole – ?
>And neglected to put on anything between them and my *parts*
>Cause
>I knew your fantasy before your car broke down ...

MARLOWE: What about your man?

>Frankie's face went cold as the barrel of an unfired pistol.

FRANKIE: How'd you know about Albert?

MARLOWE: Sense I get

FRANKIE: Upstairs. Got his own fantasy, and another woman to convince him it's reality.

>I'll tell you a secret though:
>Every night? I go up there? Shoot em both.
>And every time, the judge is ... well ...
>*Sympathetic*

>What brings you to Mahagonny again?

MARLOWE: At that point the band struck up a song ...

FRANKIE: Excuse me ... boys want me on stage.

SONG: "FRANKIE" (BASED ON MISSISSIPPI JOHN HURT'S "FRANKIE")

FRANKIE: *(singing)* Frankie is a good girl, everybody knows,
  Paid one hundred dollars for Albert's suit of clothes
  He's my man, but he's doin me wrong.

  Frankie went to Red's saloon, ordered a whiskey straight,
  asked the barkeeper, "Why's my Albert always late?"
  "He was here, but he's gone again."

  He said:

JORGE: "Ain't gonna feed you no story, ain't gonna feed you no lie
  Albert was here an hour ago, with that little girl Alice Frye
  He's your man, he's doin' you wrong."

FRANKIE: Frankie went upstairs, clutching her lucky charm
  Spied through the keyhole Alice in Albert's arm
  You're my man, you're doin' me wrong.

  Frankie pointed at Albert, shot him thirteen times,
  says, "Stand back, I'm smokin' my gun, let me see that bastard dyin'
  He's my man, and he did me wrong."

  Judge took Frankie to chambers, patted her behind
  Said, "Don't you worry little girl, you're gonna be justified,
  killin' a man, cause he did you wrong."

  Frankie is a good girl, everybody knows,
  Paid one hundred dollars for my Albert's suit of clothes
  He's my man, but he did me wrong.

MARLOWE: Song ends, place went wild ...
  Hootin hollerin pistol shots to the ceiling ...
  Frankie takes her time coming back
  Inhaling every hug, kiss, pat to her beautiful behind,

CURATOR: Little murderess likes to take her sweet ass time, I WANT MY GOD-DAMN DRINK!

MARLOWE: You uhhh

The Museum keeper?

CURATOR: Who told you that?

MARLOWE: Guy I came in with

CURATOR: Andrew? Awww ... sweetie boy ...

MARLOWE: What kinda museum is it?

CURATOR: Ha! If I could answer *that* question ...

Why do you wanna know?

MARLOWE: *Curiosity* ...

CURATOR: *"Curiosity"* ... You know what they say about curiosity ...

MARLOWE: "Five dollar hooker always wins in the end, dudn't she?"

CURATOR: Excuse me?

MARLOWE: Never mind ... You were saying? Museum...?

CURATOR: See the man sitting in the corner? Drinking // milk

MARLOWE: Harry Smith.

CURATOR: You know Harry?

MARLOWE: Yeah ... I mean no. Not til I ended up here.

CURATOR: Hm.

Kid has no idea how in over his head he is.

MARLOWE: Who?

CURATOR: Interviewing Harry. Writes for some rock rag. Don't know how *he* got in.

MARLOWE: Kid can't be older than 25 – got that look about him – like he'll stay a college sophomore well into his 40s ...

HARRY: Sure you know how to work that thing, Mr. Rock n Roll Journalist?

Things happen – backwards Satanic messages, eighteen minute // gaps,

JOURNALIST: Yeah – um ... I've read interviews? Half of what you say's a pack of lies, SO: I'll try again: what were you like as a child?

HARRY: Information's classified Mr. // FBI Man

JOURNALIST: Okay ...

HARRY: I was born in – check my birth certificate. It's entombed in Fresh Kills Landfill on Staten Island thanks to a no-goodnik, ex-Communist Hungarian midget. Next question.

JOURNALIST: Okay ... ummm. When did you start collecting 78 // records?

HARRY: In truth I should be the Czar of Russia cause my mother was Anastasia –

JOURNALIST: You're serious

HARRY: Serious as the testicular cancer that'll take your life at 43.

My grandfather was the First Guv'ner of Illinois,
First Grand Master of the Illinois Freemasons –
Received my Bachelors, Masters, PhD in mother's womb,
Lived in a treehouse between theeeee
Identical separate houses my parents built
Played with Indians, followed Madame Blavatsky, dabbled in acting –
Played multiple roles in an expressionist reimagining of *You Can't Take It With You* ...
Turned 13, my father built me a blacksmith's shop, said:
"Son: spin straw into gold" – I've been alchemically inclined since ...

JOURNALIST: Pete Seeger, Jerry Garcia, Dylan all cite the *Anthology* as a // major influence.

HARRY: When you're puking blood in a flophouse packed with dying derelicts last thing you wanna hear is someone yodeling "Hey Mister Tambourine Man" –

JOURNALIST: Look, can // we ...?

HARRY: Day my mother died, my father set fire to
A trunk of her erotic correspondence with Aleister Crowley

JOURNALIST: She knew Crowley?

HARRY: Knew him? Crowley's my Daddy!

    She met him riding a grey stallion, naked, bareback on a beach in Oregon

    Don't believe rumors he was sissified – according to my mother

    He's quite the masculine specimen –

    Many nights she'd sneak in my tree house to uhhhh

    Re-enact the encounter in question ...

JOURNALIST: That's just nast –

CURATOR: Kid's falling down the rabbit hole ...

    What about you. What's your story?

MARLOWE: Musician.

CURATOR: Good luck with that.

MARLOWE: Right.

CURATOR: You wanna see it?

MARLOWE: Pardon?

CURATOR: Museum ...

    It's next door. In the abandoned Victor Dealership ...

    It's far from being finished, but ...

    Free booze there.

    Still gonna be awhile before Harry takes us to The Palace to screen *Oz* ...

MARTIN: Did you go?

MARLOWE: Curiosity's pulling me two ways – on the one hand

    Frankie's making eyes at me from Blind Lemon's lap

    On the other, there's this *museum*

ANNIE: Lemme guess which you chose, Marlowe

MARLOWE: Yeah, you'd like to think that, wouldn't you, // Annie

ANNIE: What's the saying? "If she's got a pulse and at least one functioning leg?"

MARLOWE: I went to the museum.

CURATOR: First question you ask yourself: What should a Harry Smith Museum look like?

MARLOWE: She flips a switch. Flourescent light ... mice skitter.

Cobwebs. Boxes and boxes of ...

Stuff.

Middle of the room?

Merry Andrew's Victor Talking Machine ...

CURATOR: Wanna drink?

MARLOWE: No thanks ...

She pours one for herself, slips on a record ...

Mesmerizing banjo sound ...

What's that?

CURATOR: "Coo-Coo Bird." Clarence Ashley. From Harry's *Anthology.*

Did you know Harry's also an expert on Indians?

Take a look at this ... *American Magazine,* 1943

MARLOWE: Faded picture of Harry. He's just a kid, surrounded by Indians –

'40s SOUNDING NEWSREEL VOICE (MARTIN): "INJUN-EER! Fifteen-year-old anthropologist Harry Smith makes expeditions by bike from his home to visit the Indian tribes of Washington. He knows things about them no other white man has learned, is preserving their languages, lore, wild dances. In our picture he's recording the Lummi's annual potlatch. Harry's found Indians friendly except when drunk or suspicious he's a German spy. Eighteen now, Harry hopes to study anthropology under U Washington professors. They hope to study anthropology under *him.*"

MARLOWE: Far out ...

CURATOR: I could kill that sonofabitch ...

MARLOWE: Harry?

CURATOR: Not Harry – I could kill him too, but no

The Hungarian

MARLOWE: Midget guy?

CURATOR: Landlord ...

    Harry goes to Oklahoma?

    Gets arrested, meets these Kiowa Indians in jail?

    Stays months to record their peyote rituals ...

    But he forgot to pay his rent ...

HUNGARIAN MIDGET: Tell zat endomorphic mutterfukker to pay his rent!

CURATOR: Hungarian tossed out all his things ...

    Harry's life's work to that point? Gone ... for good.

MARLOWE: You okay?

CURATOR: Shall I give you the grand tour?

MARLOWE: She told me about his films —

CURATOR: Painted by hand, frame by frame —

MARLOWE: She showed me a faded reproduction of a painting —

CURATOR: *Tree of Life in the Four Worlds*, 1954 —

MARLOWE: She showed me boxes

CURATOR: Plastic mechanical bank shaped like Uncle // Sam —

MARLOWE: Tarot cards —

CURATOR: Golden Dawn Tarot

    Tarot of the // Cat People

MARLOWE: She told me about lost things —

CURATOR: 78s, paper airplanes, Easter // eggs

MARLOWE: She showed me secrets in indexes —

CURATOR: Smith, Harry, 278, // 384

MARLOWE: More she showed me, more I needed to know, more I —

CURATOR: You seeing *Oz* tonight?

MARLOWE: Yeah ...

CURATOR: Take a look:

MARLOWE: She hands me a yellowed *New York Times* obituary

CURATOR: 12 April 1962
  "Henry Phipps, 31,
  Heir to the Phipps fortune,
  Found dead
  At the Hamilton Hotel, West 73rd Street.
  Police say cause of death is
  Quote
  Under investigation..."
  It goes on:
  "Mr. Phipps lived at 101 Central Park West."
  If you've got digs on Central Park West,
  What are you doing dead in a hotel four blocks away?

MARLOWE: I don't // know –

CURATOR: Mentions his "friend" from *Queens*.
  Discovered his body – doesn't explain what
  Mr. Heir-to-the-Phipps-Fortune was doing
  With a "friend" from *Queens* in his room ...

MARLOWE: Okay ...

CURATOR: Mentions his marriage to a Countess' daughter
  Their four year old child ...

MARLOWE: Okay ...

CURATOR: What it doesn't mention:
  Phipp's association with unsavory poets.
  His drug use.
  His forbidden sexual desires.
  His paranoia about a band of black magicians
  Squeezing him of his inheritance ...

And most significant to me:

His financial interest in a highly experimental

3½ hour animated version of *The Wizard of Oz* ...

MARLOWE: She sighed, deep – looked like she was about to cry ...

CURATOR: Is there rhyme...?

Is there reason...?

To all this...?

MARLOWE: Yeah ...

CURATOR: Excuse me?

MARLOWE: The white spaces.

On your Rand McNally ...

CURATOR: Pardon?

MARLOWE: I keep a pile of old Rand McNallys in my car

Look at em all the time, on the road, when I'm lost,

Can't sleep, when I'm empty,

and I'm tryin to remember ...

Web of blue and pink lines

Connecting one place to another –

Make it seem like they

keep the map from tearing itself apart ...

CURATOR: I'm not sure I –

MARLOWE: But you got all that white space

Bypassed by those lines ...

I keep looking for what's in the white spaces ...

Never seen a Rand McNally show what's in them ...

Stuff you throw away. Stuff you lose. Stuff you

Don't want to look at, think about ... Stuff you wanna forget.

Maybe that's what keeps the map hanging together ...

Pause.

She smiled. Turned around to look at Harry's things

CURATOR: You think all this...?

MARLOWE: Maybe...?

CURATOR: This place will be something when I'm done ...

MARLOWE: Think people'll ...

CURATOR: Come?
   What was that saying in that baseball picture? "Build it they will come...?"

MARLOWE: She stopped smiling.
   Her eyes got all ...
   Worried
   Like she could see herself
   Twenty years from now
   Stuck in a museum with no visitors.

CURATOR: Will you hold me?

MARLOWE: Her askin that? Caught me a little off guard ...

MARTIN: Did you?

ANNIE: Psssss ...

MARLOWE: I did ... I held her. Leaned in to kiss her ...

CURATOR: That's not what ...

MARLOWE: Sorry.

CURATOR: Look at the clock ... movie time.
   Shall we head to The Palace?

MARLOWE: We turn to go ...
   Who's standing there?

Toy piano Merry Andrew Theme.

   Merry Andrew ...
   Looking mean, like the first time I laid eyes on him ...

MERRY ANDREW: He wants to see you.

CURATOR: What does he —

MERRY ANDREW: Not you. *Him.*

MARLOWE: Who wants to see me?

MERRY ANDREW: Harry. Be a good boy, come quietly ...

MARLOWE: Out to the street. Desolate. Andrew points his finger west —

MERRY ANDREW: Walk.

MARLOW: Where you taking me?

MERRY ANDREW: Movies.

MARLOWE: We walked ... pitch black except for a movie marquee in the distance ...

MERRY ANDREW: Uhcourse there's the time Harry went a-bowilin in Times Square—

MARLOWE: Huh?

The band strikes up the melody of "Engine One-Forty-Three" by The Carter Family.

MERRY ANDREW: Might make my own movie bout it someday ...

    Got it all in my head, just takes me getting up off my butt ...

    What's that ole saying? Bout the tree falling in the forest?

    Makes you think about all your own trees ...

    Ones in the forest of your heart

Merry Andrew sings, Harry mimes the acts described:

SONG: "GOODBYE TIN WOODMAN'S DREAM" (BASED ON "ENGINE 143")

MERRY ANDREW: *(singing)* Henry Phipps, they found him dead, he lies in a lonesome grave

    Regret to tell you Harry, your film we cannot save

    You labored years to make it, spent Henry's every last dime

    Many a man has lost his way trying to make up lost time.

    Harry stood on a concrete isle, 42nd and Broadway

    Lost among speed freaks, failed comics, preachers gone astray

Harry went a-bowling with the reel of Film Thirteen
A Times Square night in '62, goodbye *Tin Woodman's Dream*.

HARRY: Whoosh ...

MERRY ANDREW: Of all that vanished celluloid, nine short minutes remain
If old Walt Disney could see them now, he'd hang his head in shame
Mama said don't waste your time wonderin what could have been
Life's too short and fleeting, a frame on a movie screen.

The song abruptly ends. Silence. Merry Andrew and Marlowe contemplate the enormity of the loss.

MERRY ANDREW: Whole thing went bust ...

HARRY'S VOICE: When a major investor
Was found dead under
Embarrassing circumstances ...

MERRY ANDREW: Nine minutes ... is there more? Somewhere?

MARLOWE: We get to 4th and Desolation ...

Sound of buzzing marquee neon. Crickets. Leaves and paper bags blowing in the wind against the pavement.

MARLOWE: Line of folks under the marquee
That reads:

HARRY: *Film Number 13 – Oz or Tin Woodman's Dream or Fragments of a Faith Forgotten*

MARLOWE: Underneath

HARRY: Restored version – never before seen footage. One night only ...

MERRY ANDREW: Where do you think you're going?

MARLOWE: Getting in line?

MERRY ANDREW: Uh-uh. Side entrance ...

MARLOWE: Andrew leads me to an unmarked door,
Flanked by two unconscious winos.

Teenage girl in a white wedding dress

Gives them sips of wine, kisses their lips ...

Angel blessing the dying.

MERRY ANDREW: Upstairs ...

Sound of footsteps climbing metal stairs. Ominous music reminiscent of a Hitchcock thriller.

MARLOWE: Takes me to the empty balcony ...

Curtain to the projection booth is open ...

Inside: Harry loads the projector –

Strange machine like nothing I ever seen ...

Frankie's with him ...

Harry pays no mind to Andrew and me,

But Frankie ...

Jungle stare that says –

FRANKIE: Think you're alone now

Wait'll we're done with you ...

MERRY ANDREW: Down front.

MARLOWE: Andrew sits me down.

Below:

Rowdy anticipation.

MERRY ANDREW: *SHHHHHHHHHH!* Show's about to start ...

FRANKIE: Evening Ladies and Gentlemen

Welcome to tonight's screening of *Film Number 13* ...

Before we begin, please give a warm welcome to Harry's good friend

The legendary neurosurgeon once called "The Greatest Living Canadian"

Dr. Wilder Penfield ...

Applause light.

MARLOWE: Medical technicians roll out a dentist's chair ...

Woman on it,

Weird smile on her face,

Back of her skull's open, brain exposed

Attached to wires and needles ...
It's the Curator ...

On the screen, strange diagram – kind of a
Medieval looking cartoon ...

DR. PENFIELD (JORGE): The cartoon-like image you see is called the Motor Homunculus – it maps the cortices of the human brain. Like all maps, this one distorts reality. It renders the body in proportions that relate to the complexity of movement of each body part. Note the head, mouth, hands appear gigantic, monstrous – they possess the most complex range of movement.

This map stems from my work with epileptics. I discovered, by stimulating the temporal lobe I could trigger patients' forgotten memories, which they recall with an intensity absent in ordinary memory.

Allow me to demonstrate.

He moves to the Curator and begins stimulating her exposed brain.

CURATOR: Ooooh.

DOCTOR: Feel anything?

CURATOR: It's cold. I'm in the snow. Making snow angels ...

DOCTOR: Now?

CURATOR: Daddy holds my hand ...
Through the glass the ghostly shape of a beluga whale swims towards us ...

DOCTOR: Now...?

CURATOR: I feel empty space next to me
where I should feel the warmth of my big brother ...

The Doctor ceases probing.

DOCTOR: Discovering the physical basis of memory
Led me to the question
I asked til the day I died:

Is it possible to locate,

    thus prove scientifically,

    The existence of the human soul? Thankyouverymuch.

Applause light. Merry Andrew, deeply moved, eyes watery, applauds deeply.

MARLOWE: Lights go down ...

    Audience goes silent

    Only sound the whirring projector ...

    First image appears ...

    Flying towards Emerald City ...

    Breathtaking ...

    Like nothing I ever seen ...

    But it lasts only a second.

Cacophony of a projector devouring and melting celluloid.

MARLOWE: From the projection booth

    Sound of a mechanical monster

    Devouring celluloid ...

A collective gasp. Followed by an unearthly voice raging.

    On screen ... Emerald City boils into brown blotches

    That disappear ... only blinding white on screen ...

    Harry goes nuts,

    Projector smashes through the booth window ...

    Sails over the balcony

    Crashes in a million pieces at the foot of the screen ...

Cacophony of destroyed machinery.

    Theater's silent.

    One by one,

    Folks leave without a word.

    Andrew bites his lip, bows his head.

MERRY ANDREW: Come on.

MARLOWE: He leads me to the booth.

    Curtain's closed.

MERRY ANDREW: Open it.

MARLOWE: I pull it back.

> Frankie,
>
> Fierceness gone from her eyes,
>
> Just red from crying.
>
> And Harry ...
>
> Looks at me with
>
> Gentle eyes,
>
> Wise, yet childlike,
>
> There's a sweetness to him
>
> Yet his look pierces
>
> Like he can see through every layer of me ...
>
> "You asked to see me, sir?"
>
> He reaches to the corner of the booth
>
> Grabs a shovel,
>
> Hands it to me and

The power goes out. The only light on stage is the campfire. Dr. Kurtz enters, stands near the fire, which illuminates him. A long silence. The sound of crickets and embers burning.

DR. KURTZ: Thus, *A Thick Description of Harry Smith*, ends. Mid-sentence. The encounter between Marlowe and Harry, unwritten. Or perhaps written, but lost, like so many of Harry's things. Two possibilities: Javier gave up, unable to unravel the mystery of Harry Smith, and by extension, solve the riddle of America. Or, this is precisely what Javier intended: a tale with no resolution, an America condemned to purgatory. Which, given his own biography, and the loss he suffered, was the truth he lived.

On the tapes, Javier suggests a possible ending in the form of a stage direction:

JAVIER'S VOICE: An ending? Maybe ... "Dawn ... landfill outside of Mahagonny ... mighty – in the light it might be mistaken for the Cahokia Indian mounds in Illinois ... Atop the landfill, Harry, Merry Andrew, Marlowe, silhouetted against the rising sun ...

"Harry wears headphones attached to a beachcomber's metal detector ..."

"Um ..."

"Andrew holds a sieve ... filtering garbage from gold..."

"Marlowe ... what's he doing ...
Shovel in one hand ... In the other
Rand McNally ... ?
He shovels deep into the landfill..."

"They look for Harry's things."

On the tape sound of a little girl calling out "Daddy? Daddy!" in another room. Rustling sound of Javier trying to turn off a recorder. He says to himself: "Shit." He calls out: "Just a second..." A cough. A dog barking down the street. A click. The sound of blank tape.

The campfire flickers out. Silence. Lights come up. The band kicks into a rocking, celebratory/ apocalyptic version of Bob Dylan's "A Hard Rain's A-Gonna Fall."

SONG: "A HARD RAIN'S A-GONNA FALL"

ALL: *(singing)* Oh, where have you been, my blue-eyed son?
        Oh, where have you been, my darling young one?

MARLOWE: *(singing)* I've stumbled on the side of twelve misty mountains
        I've walked and I've crawled on six crooked highways
        I've stepped in the middle of seven sad forests
        I've been out in front of a dozen dead oceans
        I've been ten thousand miles in the mouth of a graveyard

ALL: And it's a hard, and it's a hard, it's a hard, and it's a hard
        And it's a hard rain's a-gonna fall

        Oh, what did you see, my blue-eyed son?
        Oh, what did you see, my darling young one?

MARLOWE: I saw a newborn baby with wild wolves all around it
        I saw a highway of diamonds with nobody on it
        I saw a black branch with blood that kept drippin'
        I saw a room full of men with their hammers a-bleedin'

I saw a white ladder all covered with water
I saw ten thousand talkers whose tongues were all broken
I saw guns and sharp swords in the hands of young children

ALL: And it's a hard, and it's a hard, it's a hard, it's a hard
And it's a hard rain's a-gonna fall

And what did you hear, my blue-eyed son?
And what did you hear, my darling young one?

MARLOWE: I heard the sound of a thunder, it roared out a warnin'
Heard the roar of a wave that could drown the whole world
Heard one hundred drummers whose hands were a-blazin'
Heard ten thousand whisperin' and nobody listenin'
Heard one person starve, I heard many people laughin'
Heard the song of a poet who died in the gutter
Heard the sound of a clown who cried in the alley

ALL: And it's a hard, and it's a hard, it's a hard, it's a hard
And it's a hard rain's a-gonna fall

Oh, who did you meet, my blue-eyed son?
Who did you meet, my darling young one?

MARLOWE: I met a young child beside a dead pony
I met a white man who walked a black dog
I met a young woman whose body was burning
I met a young girl, she gave me a rainbow
I met one man who was wounded in love
I met another man who was wounded with hatred

ALL: And it's a hard, it's a hard, it's a hard, it's a hard
It's a hard rain's a-gonna fall

Oh, what'll you do now, my blue-eyed son?
Oh, what'll you do now, my darling young one?

MARLOWE: I'm a-goin' back out 'fore the rain starts a-fallin'
I'll walk to the depths of the deepest black forest

Where the people are many and their hands are all empty
Where the pellets of poison are flooding their waters
Where the home in the valley meets the damp dirty prison
Where the executioner's face is always well hidden
Where hunger is ugly, where souls are forgotten
Where black is the color, where none is the number
And I'll tell it and think it and speak it and breathe it
And reflect it from the mountain so all souls can see it
Then I'll stand on the ocean until I start sinkin'
But I'll know my song well before I start singin'

ALL: And it's a hard, it's a hard, it's a hard, it's a hard
It's a hard rain's a-gonna fall

End of play

YOUR NAME WILL FOLLOW YOU HOME

MEMORIES OF AN INVISIBLE MUSE:

An Introduction to *Your Name Will Follow You Home*

Alicia Hernández, Professor Emeritus, Rio Hondo College

THE QUEST

In the summer of 2002, I stood on a ridge photographing *Seaward*, the D.L. James manor home designed by Charles Sumner Greene located in the Carmel Highlands. Eighteen years earlier, Danny (the son of D.L. James) invited me for a visit knowing my admiration for Craftsman homes designed by architects Greene & Greene. He remembered my letter written 25 years earlier while I was house hunting. However, the invitation came soon after he found himself at the center of a major literary scandal and

I was still in turmoil from the revelations.

Thus it was that in the spring of 2002, I finally summoned the courage to write to his daughter, Barbara, inquiring whether her late mother had located any of my letters initially requested six months after Danny died in 1988. It was my intention to write a memoir and the letters were crucial to the task. Danny and I corresponded for thirteen years, enough time for me to evolve from classroom critic to friend to muse. Barbara's reply was a very generous invitation

to make use of her guest house for a summer weekend in Carmel Valley. It was an opportunity to sort through Danny's papers, journals, and files in hopes that my numerous letters were among all that were boxed and stored. Additionally, Danny's study overlooked the Pacific and I was interested in seeing where he labored for years editing and revising his book, *Famous All Over Town*, where my letters were likely preserved. Finally, I asked whether a tour of *Seaward* was possible. She replied that it was not, having been sold years earlier.

Arriving in Carmel, Barbara offered directions to *Seaward*. The architect had constructed a viewpoint across the rocky cliffs on a promontory. It was a spectacular view with the Pacific crashing into the bedrock, which served as the foundation. Los Lobos State Reserve surrounded the estate and enhanced the organic beauty of this magnificent dwelling. Majestic conifers facing the south façade sheltered the stone arch replicated from an English manor home — it dripped romantic splendor.

By this time, Danny had been deceased for 14 years, so I found myself alone with *Seaward* in the distance longing for answers to my questions and hoping to locate my letters. A writer friend, knowing of my intense interest in finding the letters, said she was praying to St. Anthony, the patron saint of lost causes. She wrote that despite my being Protestant, he was an "equal opportunity saint." Unfortunately, as I later learned, the saint had also been marginalized and demoted.

My thoughts on that pristine summer day standing on a spot where the house was within sight and yet access was unavailable to me: once again I was relegated to the margins of the life and times of author Dan James or as I knew him, Danny Santiago. Separation and distance were the hallmarks of our lengthy odyssey.

The publication in 1970 of "The Somebody," a short story by promising Chicano author Danny Santiago, corresponded with my first year teaching in the Montebello District, a middle class Los Angeles suburb located east of East Los Angeles, about 15 miles from the City's civic center. I taught five sections of ninth grade English totaling approximately 150 fidgety adolescents. The district at the time was majority Hispanic; however, reflecting Montebello's population, classes included Armenians, Russians, Asians, and a sprinkling of Anglos. Countless hours were spent developing uninspired lesson plans and finding my way.

In the middle of the academic year, the short story "The Somebody" appeared in *Redbook Magazine.* Reading it, I wept with joy because here was literary material with high reading appeal destined to become a classroom hit. The protagonist was Chato de Shamrock, a very cheeky Chicano teen living in East Los Angeles who expresses very keen observations about his Mexican family. There was much similarity in the story to the lives of my students, unlike any other literature they'd read to that point. The story was set in the Boyle Heights area in East Los Angeles where I once attended middle school, so the number of recognizable landmarks were very familiar. Ignoring copyright laws, I typed the story on 10 ditto masters and ran off 30 ten-page sets for the class. It took two surreptitious trips to the ditto machine given the amount of restricted paper required. Danny Santiago, the author, was a unique and talented writer. Who was he and did more published material exist? After I exhausted all the language arts exercises in my repertoire, I wrote to *Redbook* asking how to contact the author.

Two weeks later I received the first letter from Santiago stating how pleased he was that "The Somebody" landed in a classroom and that he was curious about student reaction. I read the letter to the classes and they were intrigued that an author responded. I replied with an eight-page handwritten letter describing my search for literature the students could identify with that met the curriculum criteria. I asked, "Do you have more stories?" Again another letter arrived instructing me to mail all correspondence to an address in Pacific Grove on the Monterey Peninsula and not to his New York agent on Fifth Avenue as first directed. Hallelujah! He was a Californian not an Easterner! Yes, he had plenty of stories and yes, he would mail them to us, and yes, I could transfer them to ditto masters and run off as many as the paper budget permitted. This was the start of our friendly yet mysterious thirteen-year correspondence.

True to his word, more short stories arrived and more letters too. The students waited with bated breath for new Chato adventures. I assigned short written critiques to Danny, describing their reactions to the various chapters. He instructed them to be truthful and not avoid criticism. The short evaluations became valuable feedback to a work in progress. They pointed out when a story seemed incomplete, boring, or funny. In one letter he wrote that he was planning to combine all the short stories as chapters for a book. Some of the students had suggested this and I agreed. My motive, of course, was to use the book in the classroom where dramatic changes in student demeanor ensued from rowdy to cooperative when we discussed the life of the main character, Chato de Shamrock.

Changes

The letters flowed steadily between Northern and Southern California. I wrote more often than he and pressed for answers to personal questions about his life asking, for example, if he had been raised and schooled in Boyle Heights, was he employed, and could he send a photograph? None were answered. My tenure lasted two and half years at the high school before accepting a job offer as an Adult School Counselor in another district. Danny was concerned, questioning who would provide feedback on new chapters. I assured him that nothing would change from my perspective; in fact, my availability for editing would increase.

My letters now contained details of my personal as well as my professional life, plus I spent many hours evaluating chapters mailed to my home. I encouraged him to keep his "eyes on the prize" when his letters arrived weighted with despair instead of the usual repartee. He acknowledged my influence on maintaining his focus while completing the novel. Early in our correspondence he wrote: "You lifted me out of one of the worst periods of my life." The letters characterized me as his anchor and the one most responsible for this book being written. Toward the end of our first year of correspondence he wrote: "And if it hadn't been for you, I doubt that this book would have ever gotten itself written. When it is published, you're in for the killing or whatever."

My task as a teacher, as I interpreted it, was to present literary work with high reader appeal that validated the students' culture, and would lead them into the established canon. Having reviewed the many chapters, I felt that Danny's book held great promise and was destined to be enjoyed by readers of all ages. In addition, the lack of Chicano/a Literature available at the time was intolerable; unlike today when publishers such as Texas-based Arte Público devote their entire catalog to Hispanic literature and major publishers support departments dedicated to this market. Currently, there's an array of exemplary Chicano authors including Lorna Dee Cervantes, Ana Castillo, Michele Serros, Sandra Cisneros, Gary Soto, Jimmy Santiago Baca, Luis Valdez, Denise Chavez, and others who enrich all

Per. III
English 2

To Danny Santiago, you think you're a big cholo, by the way the story was to make up.
Maria J. Mora

I think the story was good I enjoyed it and it made sence. It wasn't like those other kind of stories that don't make sence.
Elizabeth Navarro,

I enjoy your stories very much and I think they sound very real I think this was very good and I wouldn't mind receiving copies of your stories for my self so I could collect them. You see I'm all for the Mexicans and their rights.
Darlene Sloane

Per. III
English 2

I thought that the story was good but it could have been all of your stories our class have read all deal with Mexicans.
Willard Yamaguchi

I liked it a lot, But it left me curious I want to know what happened when his father gets a hold of him. I've only read two of your stories they were good. I would like to read more.
Marta Stywich

IT WAS GREAT
GILBERT LUJON

genres. Scholars in the field maintain that this literature existed in 1971, but those were the early works – chronicles from early settlers, memoirs of journeys north. None were focused on East Los Angeles with a brash adolescent as the protagonist.

As the years passed, Danny's lack of disclosure and mysterious responses caused me much frustration and there were months when I ceased correspondence in protest. All the letters went to the Pacific Grove Post Office, so I surmised that he was free to move around. For years I thought he was a majordomo in the vast agricultural fields around Salinas while living in a tent or garret. Or perhaps he was in jail and allowed outside work privileges. He was very knowledgeable about agricultural matters, offering expert advice for my freshman garden. Instructions arrived suitable for 40 acres. My letter writing resumed when his letters once again appeared. One contained the following:

> *Please don't give up on me yet. You're one of the diminishing few strands of hope that hold me together. I think of you more often than you might guess and when your letters come it's always a big day for me.*

Finally in December 1982, a good news letter arrived. Instead of a date on the right hand corner, he typed 3:45 a.m. "A flock of angels" appeared with a publishing contract for the novel! He wanted me to be one of the first to know that Chato de Shamrock found a publisher. I longed to speak with him to celebrate even if it was over the phone. Would I finally see a photo of my longtime correspondent? Would I be listed in the Acknowledgements? He explained rewrites would take about half a year in 1983, with a publication date early the next year. In the spring of 1984 he wrote that Simon & Schuster was mailing a complimentary copy.

That summer I enrolled in an Art History class at Cambridge University in England. *Famous* arrived the same week as the demanding course reading list. Two weeks prior to my leaving, I received another letter: "What did I think of the book? When would I mail a review?" My answer was that since I had been reviewing the chapters for 13 years, the review would have to wait until I returned from England in a month's time.

Bliss interruptus ...

The Cambridge summer was one of the happiest I'd experienced abroad.

Trinity Hall appeared medieval with modern day conveniences. The view from my dorm window framed the River Cam. In the mornings, the Master's Garden, with its heady array of summer blooms, intoxicated my senses. The class was stimulating and the field trips provided memorable views of the lush English countryside. Again, I mailed

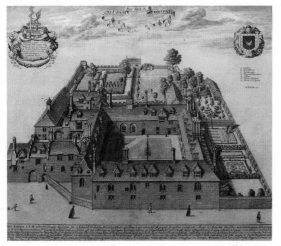

postcards to Danny, fixated on my role as mentor and muse. One explained how the cluster colleges functioned and another featured Kings College Cathedral where my classmates attended Evensong. I also described the gazebo at Trinity College where Byron purportedly wrote poetry. In short, I never allowed a teachable moment to dissipate.

A week before returning home, at breakfast, a classmate passed the *Herald American* to me. At the bottom of page one this headline appeared: "Latino Author Guilty of Deception." Who in Latin America was dishonest? When I reached paragraph three, the name Danny Santiago appeared. I kept reading with disbelief. The young/witty/talented/high school dropout/inmate was in truth Daniel Lewis James, a white 73-year-old Yale graduate in Classics, blacklisted Hollywood screenwriter, and "septuagenarian ex-Stalinist aristocrat" as described by John Gregory Dunne.

At last the answers I sought for thirteen years. In the midst of Cambridgeshire's natural splendor and remarkable history, the sense of betrayal and bewilderment were beyond measure.

On my return to California, I read the many lengthy newspaper articles, interviews, and angry columns by respected literary critics and academics. There was extensive discussion of cultural appropriation and the ethics of assuming a false identity to lend authenticity. Two well-known Chicano writers published newspaper columns defending Danny's right to tell the story of the Medina family. It was difficult to separate the book from the accusations, and a long time passed before I was able to formulate my own position. First, I dealt with no author information and no credit when *Famous* arrived, now I had to support one of two well-articulated opposing points of view. One article ended with a quote from a young female Montebello student who had been assigned a Danny Santiago story in her English class saying, "I like it. Can we have another?" That was the extent of any Montebello links throughout the in-depth article. Not only was I not named, but neither was the editorial role played by the Montebello students acknowledged.

A short letter from Danny awaited me, apologizing for his deceit and asking me to read the long biographical article in the August *New York Review of Books* written by John Gregory Dunne. He added that over the years he had been tempted to park across the street from my home hoping to catch a look at me. He never did considering this a very unfair advantage.

In October we met face to face for the first and only time. After 13 years of exchanging personal correspondence, the evening was electric and memorable. It resembled a line from a Sandra Cisneros poem *"hablamos con ganas, era un alimento."* (Our words were nourishing, spoken with desire and affection.) Did I squander the short time spent with Danny on that autumn night? I was so dazzled by his notoriety and literary affiliations that I failed to ask the two questions most often asked of me: why did Danny privately praise me and ignore me publicly? Did he ever want to end the ruse and confess the truth?

His letter after our first and only meeting reads:

> *It was good to hear from you. I was really afraid that the exposé of the septuagenarian ex-Stalinist aristocrat would put an end to our beautiful, if remote, relationship.*

In the months that followed, our correspondence became sporadic. The letters went into a manila folder and the book in my bookcase. Also filed away was the life lesson of another deceptive man. The sense of betrayal was mitigated by what I considered the most important aspect of this saga: the book was finally available to others. Now many readers would find an honest depiction of a Chicano family, something missing from the literary canon. Danny passed away three years later on May 18, 1988 from a heart condition. I learned about his passing in the obituary section of the *Los Angeles Times*. It was a profound loss of a unique friendship and collaboration.

RESURRECTION

In 1989, after 18 years as an Academic and Personal Counselor at Rio Hondo College in Whittier, my request for reassignment to my first discipline, teaching English, was granted. I spent a sabbatical year pursuing a Master's in English. Much had changed since my undergraduate days 25 years earlier. Included in the curriculum were novels and poetry authored by women, and assignments on Native American writers. In the Women in Fiction seminar, I introduced Chicana authors, new to the professor and other Master's candidates. For the Adolescent Literature course my presentation on novels of initiation focused on *Famous All Over Town*, sans the correspondence. During my first year in the English Department, I developed the first Chicano/a Literature course taught at the college and assigned *Famous* as one of the required texts. (This was a bittersweet moment knowing Danny missed my teaching the book by a mere two years.) My students struggled with the issue of authenticity after reading and discussing *Famous*.

Professional opportunities resulted from my correspondence with Danny. In 1996 I was selected as a participant for a Seminar on Literary Biography held in New York City under the auspices of the National Endowment for the Humanities. My purpose was to continue my professional emphasis on Chicano Literature, focusing on biographical research of what was now a fully accepted genre of American Literature. During my introductory remarks, I mentioned the Santiago correspondence to the group almost as an afterthought. It caused an excited explosion. They insisted that I disregard my research focus and concentrate on compiling material for a memoir based on the correspondence. The participants also stressed that I should contact the James family inquiring if my letters were saved. I estimate that I wrote over two hundred during the thirteen-year period. The group also convinced me that Danny's letters were safer in a bank vault than a manila folder. Danny's agent and editor were both New York City-based, and I arranged for us to meet. They too had been duped by Danny but nonetheless considered him a diligent working author with enormous talent. This memoir would address ongoing issues in the humanities: what categories do we impose on literature – British, American, Chicano, Asian, Black, and so forth? Who has the right to write about a culture? We ended our study of literary biography by submitting research summaries/approaches in a book of essays published by Krieger.

In 2002, during my final sabbatical prior to retirement I contacted Barbara James. My request for my letters in 1988 was first addressed to Lilith, Dan's wife. She said she was still finding it difficult to edit his papers six months after his passing. About four years later, she passed away. My letter to Barbara began, "I was a friend of your father's." I also sent copies of letters as proof of my claim. The first sentence of her reply was:

> *Of course I know who you are. You are the person who provided the one thing that would lift Papa's black fits when he really felt hopeless.*

She described Lilith's progressive dementia. As the illness progressed, Lilith spent much of her time relocating objects in strange and inappropriate places. If she did locate my letters, she most likely moved them to a mysterious place. Another possibility was that the letters were stored in the carriage house where a roof leak turned all the contents to cement. These rock-like bundles were then tossed in the trash. Barbara closed the letter with:

> *I am so glad you got in touch. I've wanted to meet you. Your enthusiasm and support meant much more to him than he probably let you know.*

BALM OF GILEAD

In July 2012, I received a letter from my former employer, Rio Hondo College. Letters from the college are usually tossed in the trash unopened as they are usually requests for donations. For some curious reason I did open this one. It turned out to be an email from a Chicago playwright regarding a play he was writing about Danny. He was familiar with my memoir in the Krieger publication, and asked that I contact him.

A play about Danny? A request for my side of the story? How did this playwright become aware of the controversy surrounding Danny? Over the course of that summer we exchanged emails and telephone calls. I shared a few letters not included in the memoir and sent additional material including interior photographs of Seaward, Dan's graduation photo requested from the Yale Alumni Office, plus a written summary of my Carmel visit in 2002. The playwright mentioned that a character based on my experience was an integral part of the play.

In August 2013, I traveled to Chicago for a reading of *Your Name Will Follow You Home* at the renowned Steppenwolf Theatre, the title based on Danny's original choice for the title of his book. Sitting in the audience, hearing my writing transformed into dialogue, having personal occurrences dramatized, and viewing an unfolding of Dan's life on stage was an overwhelmingly emotional experience. This play was very thoroughly researched, as different acts depicted Dan's life's events: his privileged upbringing in Kansas, the remote relationship to the outlaw Jesse James, his decision to join the Commu-

DANIEL LEWIS JAMES, "Dan," was born on January 14, 1911, in Kansas City, Mo. His father, D. L. James (B.A. Yale 1902, M.A. 1907), is manager of the retail store of the T. M. James & Sons China Company in that city. He has also lived in Carmel, Calif. His mother's maiden name was Lily Hyatt Snider. Dan is a nephew of Thomas M. James, Jr., '98.

His preparatory training was received at the Kansas City Country Day School and at Phillips-Andover. He entered Yale with our Class, but withdrew at the end of Junior year; he expects to return to finish his course with '33. He was a scholar of the second rank in Freshman year and of the third

nist Party and the blacklist that resulted. Also mentioned were the years he spent as a social worker in Boyle Heights and his many successes working with Mexican American families. In the play, one character grows from skeptic to believer as he discovers the many facets of this complex man.

THE FINAL FAREWELL

What did St. Anthony, even with limited powers, help me find at Carmel? He helped me find three of my letters, including the one written after the truth emerged. It reads as if written by a scolding English fishwife. There were chapter galleys with my notes attached and many were merged into the final text. In addition, there was a large envelope labeled "Fan Mail – Eastmont" with the long ago reviews from my five classes. For the students I've located, I made copies of their work; they're always amused to see their writing from forty years ago. Another interesting group of letters was from famous actors and actresses, authors, and screenwriters. Classmates from Andover and Yale were also filed. It was Danny's practice to mark the envelopes "Answered" along with the date and a sentence that captured the response. This was more evidence that he kept my letters as well.

As requested in my letter, Barbara shared photos, anecdotes, and events of Dan's life. As a young girl she also participated in the Boyle Heights family celebrations, sort of an "honorary Mexican." These she remembered with great fondness. She described the various families that were models for the book, close friends of the James'. She showed me a songbook of ballads, corridos, and other songs Dan had compiled.

254

The visit to Carmel reaffirmed my admiration for this very complicated, talented man. It heightened my respect for his creativity and work habits. It is my stance that during Danny's twenty years volunteering in East Los Angeles he came to admire and respect the culture and values of the Mexican-American families. Fictionalizing their lives with such authenticity was a labor of love for him. Further, being Chicano depends not on the color of the skin, but is a matter of the heart.

During my stay in Carmel, Barbara, without hesitatation, acknowledged my contributions to the writing of the novel. When it came time to say goodbye in front of the guesthouse, she asked if there was any remembrance I wanted of Danny's, a gift from him. There were so many tempting artifacts, but instead I asked for the return of my students' comments. Everything else, I proposed, should be left for biographers to peruse. Because I kept my three letters found in his papers, there remains no written evidence of my relationship with Danny.

I still hope to publish Danny's letters along with my reconstructed letters to offer readers some insight into this relationship. When speaking to classes they're always surprised that despite the betrayal, I nevertheless value the friendship we shared. My hopes are that this memoir will be unique to the study of literature and to the canon of Chicano Literature. Above all, it's a tribute to an uncommon friendship between two strangers who became confidants.

Saying goodbye to Barbara and little Olive, her dog, cemented the last link to him. It's been a threefold loss: first when I found out there was no Danny Santiago, then when I read Dan James' obituary, and finally when I organized and packed all his papers.

I'm no longer standing alone on that ridge. Over the years others have joined me in support of my role. *Your Name Will Follow You Home* binds us both on the same page for the first time. Instead of finding what I was searching for in that shimmering Carmel sea light, I bid farewell, cloaked with an embracing peace.

Whittier, California

255

NOTES ON IMAGES, BY PAGE

243   *Sjøtobellet (The Sea Troll), 1887 by Theodor Kittelsen (1857-1914).* Photo in public domain.

244   *Entry portal to Seaward, the home of DL James, designed by Charles Sumner Greene in 1918. Photo by William Current.* Greene and Greene Archives, Gamble House USC, Huntington Library.

245   *Interior sitting room is Seaward overlooking the Pacific.* Greene and Greene Archives, Gamble House USC, Huntington Library.

   Seaward as seen from a nearby overlook on the Pacific Coast Highway. Greene and Greene Archives, Gamble House USC, Huntington Library.

246   *Polaroids of students in Alicia Hernandez's 9th grade English class in Montebello.* Photo by Alicia Hernandez

247   *Exterior of Pacific Grove Post Office in Monterey County, California.* Photo by Alicia Hernandez

248   *Students notes written to Danny Santiago in response to reading unpublished chapters of what would become the novel* Famous All Over Town. Photos by Alicia Hernandez

250   *Bird's eye view of Trinity Hall, Cambridge by David Loggan, Cantabrigia Illustrata, 1690.* Photo in public domain – Wikimedia Commons

251   *Assemblage of articles about the Danny Santiago controversy.* Photo by Carlos Murillo.

254   *Daniel James' entry in the Yale College History of the Class of 1932.* Yale University archives.

255   *Alicia Hernandez's first edition copy of* Famous All Over Town *with a note from Danny Santiago.* Photo by Alicia Hernandez

YOUR NAME WILL FOLLOW YOU HOME

Characters

Alvaro, writer. US born Puerto Rican/Colombian/Jewish. Early 30s.

Herman, adjunct professor. US born of German-Jewish descent. Mid 30s.

Valerie, designer. Caucasian. Early 30s.

Javier, writer. Born in Colombia, immigrated as a child to NYC. Early 30s.

Nero, actor. Caucasian. Likely grew up in the Midwest. Early 30s.

Lina, actor. Mixed race — Asian-Latina or possibly Filipino. Mid 20s.

Emiliano Kurtz, university professor. White, though origins uncertain. Mid 40s.

Alex Tanner, graduate student. White. Mid 20s.

Setting

Act One takes place in a shabby tenement apartment in Hell's Kitchen, New York City and a seminar classroom at an unnamed university somewhere in the United States.

Act Two takes place in the courtyard of a shabby motel in Puerto Angel — a tiny fishing village on the Pacific coast of Oaxaca, Mexico.

Time

The scenes in Hell's Kitchen and Puerto Angel take place in 1988.
The scenes in the seminar room and Kurtz's apartment take place in 2012.

ACT ONE. Hell's Kitchen

1. AUTHENTICITY, 1988

Cramped kitchen/living room of a tenement apartment in Hell's Kitchen. It's overcrowded with second hand furniture, tons of books, musical instruments and children's toys. Off the living room, a closed door that leads to a bedroom.

Alvaro, Herman and Valerie sit around the kitchen table. On the table: take-out containers, empty wine and beer bottles, a full ashtray. Valerie sits closer to Herman. Perhaps a little too close – if you were a stranger passing, you might think they were "together."

Also in the kitchen, Nero and Lina. They awkwardly share a chair, Nero slightly behind Lina, rubbing her shoulders. They half listen to the conversation – Nero seems more fixed on getting Lina enticed enough to lure her to some place more private.

Javier is quiet, strums a guitar. He sits on a child's chair in the living room. He seems "checked out" of the proceedings, in his own world.

ALVARO: *New York Times* crowns the kid
    calls him a "new," "distinct," "streetwise,"
    "authentic" voice from "*el barrio,*"
    captures the people, rituals,
    language, violence, the *passion*,
    "urban grit," I'm like "Yeah, I can dig that."
    But when I look at the critic's name?
    I'm like,
    huh.
    How much time has *he* spent
    in East LA? That a frequent stop for him?
    Yeah, America anything's possible, right?
    Maybe he's hooked in
    minored in Chicano Studies or
    is a secret card carrying member of *La Raza*
    got some
    lost branch a the family

wrinkled little abuelita
boils him up
magical realist tamales
that cast spells on you so
butterflies fly out your asshole
when you're making love?
Just like in Azteca times.
So yeah, *maybe*
Critic's got something to back up
his assertion
that the goods are "authentic."

HERMAN: Okay, but —

ALVARO: *But*

the *other* critics …
all say the same thing —
"authenticity this," "gritty realism that" —
there really that many secret Chicanos
infiltrating the mainstream press?

HERMAN: Um. No.

ALVARO: So why do *we* take their word for it?
Authentic?
Fuck do they know?
Worst shit? People eat that shit up!

VALERIE: Alvaro! Keep it down. You'll wake Pablo and Lila.

HERMAN: Did you actually read the book?

ALVARO: Yeah, I read the book.

HERMAN: And?

ALVARO: And what?

HERMAN: Did it seem … authentic?

ALVARO: You're really asking me that?

HERMAN: Yeah …

ALVARO: You're *really* asking me that / / shit.

HERMAN: Did I say something off / / ensive

ALVARO: Yeah, *Herman,* I read it and I'm like
    "I guess critic's right
    sounds authentic Chicano to me."

HERMAN: So what's the problem

ALVARO: Problem is
    Mr. "Did-I-Say-Something-Offensive"
    you automatically assume I'd be some kind of authority

VALERIE: Boys, would you please / / keep it down …

HERMAN: Well aren't you? If anyone in this room —

VALERIE: Well, Javi —   ALVARO: "If anyone"????….

ALVARO: Fuck do *I* know is "authentic Mexican"
    I'm triple breed Puerto Rican Colombian Jew —
    I'm as qualified as Mr. *New York Times*
    to pass that judgment
    Few times I been in LA? I avoid downtown
    Let alone East side,
    My mother? She fucking hated Mexicans.

VALERIE: You're exaggerating —

ALVARO: It's true, God rest her soul?
    She used to say
    all kinds of racist shit —
    I grew up on Long Island …
    Closest I ever got to a Mexican
    before college? Our cleaning lady
    Though now that I think about it
    She was Salvadoran …

HERMAN: Wait a minute. *You* grew up on Long Island?

ALVARO: Yeah, what about it?

HERMAN: What town?

ALVARO: Great Neck.

HERMAN: Ooooh. *West Egg.*

ALVARO: Hilarious –

VALERIE: I'm sorry – I'm missing the reference – ?

HERMAN: *Great Gatsby*? Surely you read it in high school?

VALERIE: Asshat –

She playfully swats Herman. Javier notices this.

HERMAN: West Egg? Where Gatsby lives?

VALERIE: Right // right

HERMAN: modeled after Alvaro's home // town –

ALVARO: What//ever

HERMAN: Nouveau Riche? As opposed to *East* // Egg?

VALERIE: Old money. Got//cha …

HERMAN: Then why do you talk like that?

ALVARO: Like what?

HERMAN: All … "street"

ALVARO: Fuck you, why do *you* talk like that?

HERMAN: How do I talk?

ALVARO: Like a smug son of a bitch.

HERMAN: It sounds like this whole thing is making you *mad*.

ALVARO: Yeah, it's making me mad.

HERMAN: *What's* making you mad

    Are you mad at the *critic*?

    Or the people who "eat that shit up"?

ALVARO: *Both.*

    Critic's selling me on "authenticity" –

VALERIE: Which he has no authority to do –

ALVARO: *Exactly* –

HERMAN: Of course he has the authority, he writes for *The New York Times.*

Valerie cracks up at this.

ALVARO: Yeah, / /

    Whatever –

VALERIE: I think what Alvaro is trying to say, / / Herman is –

ALVARO: Valerie, I don't need a translator, thankyou / / verymuch?

VALERIE: Okay, / /

    Asshole.

ALVARO: Critic says the book's "authentic" … Why?

    Cause the shit affirms every worn out cliché

    he picked up reading comic books.

    But *New York Times* says "Bitch roll over, play dead"

    All you bitches roll over and play dead.

    Everyone – critic? Public?

    Keep on wearing the saaaame old straitjacket.

HERMAN: *Strait / / jacket*

ALVARO: So yeah, shit makes me mad. But most of all? I'm mad at *you*

HERMAN: What did I do?

ALVARO: For bringing it to us

    thinking we'd even consider –

VALERIE: Volume …

HERMAN: We? I don't recall you ever being appointed // spokesperson for

ALVARO: I ain't touching that shit with a 200-foot pole.

Javier abruptly stops strumming his guitar. Doing so silences everyone. They all look at him. Even Nero and Lina. Pause.

VALERIE: You were gonna say something, Javi?

JAVIER: Yeah. What about the writer?

ALVARO: What *about* him?

JAVIER: You mad at him?

ALVARO: Bitch is a fraud.

JAVIER: What makes him a fraud?

HERMAN: Good question, Javi.

ALVARO & JAVIER: Eat me Herman.

JAVIER: What makes him a fraud, Alvaro?

ALVARO: Uhhh …
     He's a liar?

JAVIER: How's he a liar?

ALVARO: Uhhh … let me count the ways?
     One: it's not his real name

HERMAN: There's countless examples throughout history of writers using pseudonyms—

ALVARO: Not the same —

JAVIER: How is it different —

ALVARO: You siding with him?

JAVIER: I'm not siding with anyone,
     I want to understand
     Why this is different?

ALVARO: He didn't he use his own name

cause he wants you to *believe*

he's a 14-year-old Mexican kid

HERMAN: He's clearly not 14, he's an adult *writing* about a kid that's // 14.

ALVARO: In the *first person*

HERMAN: So?

Javier's hands tense up, as if he's restraining the fantasy of strangling Herman. He tunes out, resumes strumming on his guitar.

ALVARO: He's obviously trying to pass it off like it's an autobiography –

HERMAN: It's clearly labeled a work of fiction,

Nowhere does it say it's autobio//graphical

ALVARO: It's *implied*

VALERIE: *Guys … Volume.*

HERMAN: All his bio says

Is that he grew up in Los Angeles –

ALVARO: Which is *another* lie –

HERMAN: Yeah, but how do you get auto//biography

ALVARO: A lie to trick the reader into confusing

Danny Santiago the writer with Chato Medina the character

When in fact the *real* author is // about as far from

VALERIE: What was his name again?

HERMAN: Daniel James

ALVARO: When the *REAL* author is about as far from being Chicano from East L.A.

As is humanly possible –

HERMAN: Which proves my point: it's a work of *fiction*

ALVARO: If he signed it "Daniel James, 80 year old rich white fuck"

I might buy it's fiction, *but*

He wrote in the first person, signed it Danny. Santiago.

HERMAN: Then why did he name the protagonist Rudy Medina?

VALERIE: I thought it was Chato de Shamrock

HERMAN: Chato's his gang name

VALERIE: But why Shamrock — what is he half Irish?

HERMAN: Huh? No. Shamrock's the name of the street he grew up on — Did you even // read

ALVARO: He's fucking around with names,
    shit's intentional obfuscation
    so, yes, Herman, bitch wanted us to believe
    it was autobiographical.

HERMAN: That's just your imagination.

ALVARO: Oh, you motherfucker,
    don't make me crack this bottle // over your head

VALERIE: Whoa! // Whoa! Whoa!

HERMAN: Whoa! See that? You see that?
    He gets violent

ALVARO: You condescending puto, "my imagination"
    I'll show you my imagination cause I got like six hundred ways
    I imagine cracking open your skull!

Nero, sticking his fingers in his mouth, loudly whistles, stopping the room.

VALERIE: Nero! For Christ's sake, you'll wake the goddamn kids!

NERO: What the fuck are you guys talking about?

VALERIE: Haven't you been listening?

ALVARO: (To his pi pi may//be)

NERO: I've been listening but I have no idea // what you're

HERMAN: The book, Nero.
    Famous All Over Town?
    One that I asked you all read?
    Did you read it?

NERO: No.

HERMAN: Why not? I went out of my way to —

NERO: I don't have time to read shit —

HERMAN: We have a *deadline* Nero — we have a *commission?* To write a *play?*

NERO: I know.

HERMAN: Not just any commission? The Public Theater?
    That little place down on Lafay//ette?

NERO: I know.

HERMAN: Yeah, well Joe Papp? He only calls once
    We're already months late
    I keep coming up // with

NERO: I don't have time to read shit
    Unless it's a hundred percent sure we're doing it.

HERMAN: Did anyone read the book?

Alvaro and Lina raise their hands. Valerie waves hers as if to say "skimmed it." Nero and Javier keep their hands down.

HERMAN: That's just great —
    someone finally commissions us to write something,
    we're all supposed to come with ideas,
    zip from all // of you —

NERO: Whatever … you lost me.

HERMAN: Where did we lose you, Nero?

NERO: All these names you're throwing around —
    Just tell me. Who wrote the book?

HERMAN: Okay. Nero. There's a book.

NERO: Yeah.

HERMAN: It's called *Famous All Over Town*.

NERO: Yeah —

HERMAN: Simon & Schuster, 1983

NERO: I don't need all the details

HERMAN: Fine. It's a classic bildungsroman with —

NERO: Build a what what?

HERMAN: Bildungsroman — coming of age story?
About a Mexican kid growing up in East Los Angeles.
His family's coming apart, while his neighborhood's — the *barrio's* —
being torn down to make way for the railroad —
Following?

NERO: Following.

HERMAN: Book's author is a young unknown // writer—

ALVARO: *Purported* auth//or

HERMAN: *Purported* author is a young, unknown writer // named

ALVARO: *Chicano* writ//er

HERMAN: *Chicano* writer named Danny Santiago ...

NERO: Why'd they purport him?

HERMAN: Huh?

NERO: Was he like
an illegal alien?

ALVARO: Jesus mother // of Christ

HERMAN: That's *de*ported // not

NERO: You use these words
what the fuck does "purported" mean, anyway

LINA: To have the false appearance of being

Nero licks the back of her neck.

NERO: So he's like fake …

HERMAN: He's "like fake"

NERO: So someone else wrote it.

HERMAN: Precisely. A gentleman by the name of // Daniel James.

ALVARO: Oooohhh, so he's a *gentleman*

HERMAN: Who, as Alvaro has pointed out, is not Chicano, but a white man.

ALVARO: A ninety-eight year old *filthy rich* white // man

HERMAN: Seventy-two. He's *seventy-//two*

NERO: Okay … so what's like … the big deal?

HERMAN: That's what we're trying to establish here.

Alvaro picks up an empty can of beer and tries to eat it in frustration.

JAVIER: Alvaro. Calmate.

Everyone quiets. They look at Javi. There's a long pause.

VALERIE: Did you … wanna say something … Javi?

Long pause. Javier picks on his guitar. They wait. When Javier speaks, there's an eerie calm in his voice.

JAVIER: Yes. I was gonna say something.
> But
> Herman
> wanted a turn.
> I didn't get to finish.

HERMAN: Sorry, Javi …

JAVIER: It's all good.
> Alvaro …
> My friend …
> You used the word
> "straitjacket" …

Pause. They wait to see if he'll continue. He doesn't.

ALVARO: Yeah.

JAVIER: Cause if I understand what you mean by // straitjacket

HERMAN: What he means is

Valerie places her hand on Herman's forearm to shut him up. Pause.

JAVIER: Sounds to me
    of all people you're mad at? —
    Critic ...
    Reader ...
    Writer ...
    Herman ...

Only one not wearing the straitjacket is the writer.

Long pause.

JAVIER: Isn't that what we need? You and me?
    To not get stuck in a straitjacket?

Long silence. Suddenly a toddler's cry from behind the closed door. Valerie lets out a sigh.

VALERIE: Goddamnit! See what you knuckleheads did? You woke Lila.

JAVIER: Want me to go in?

VALERIE: I got it. I'm gonna kill her if she wakes up Pablo ...

Valerie downs her wine glass. Goes to the door, making gentle hushing noises. She shuts the door behind her. Silence. Herman looks at his watch.

HERMAN: Shit. Look at the time. 2:30.

No response.

Well. Illuminating as always. But ... adjuncting first thing in the morning ...

He gets up. Waits for a spell. Javier and Alvaro say nothing.

Take care, gentlemen.

He gets to the door. Turns around.

Please tell Valerie I said goodnight.

JAVIER: Take it easy, Herman.

HERMAN: You too.

>And Alvaro … ?

>Didn't mean to let the uh …

>*sparring*

>get out of hand.

ALVARO: I'm good.

HERMAN: Nothing personal —

ALVARO: I'm good.

Herman leaves.

ALVARO: Dude's an asshole.

During the previous exchange, Nero and Lina have gotten their coats. They leave quietly, thinking they're being discreet.

JAVIER: Alvaro …

>can I borrow your copy of the book?

ALVARO: Here …

Alvaro hands him the book. Silence. Javier strums, lost in his thoughts.

ALVARO: You okay, man?

JAVIER: I'm fine. Look, uh …

>I'm gotta hit the sack soon.

ALVARO: A'ight.

Alvaro rises, sips the last of the wine, picks up his notebook. He watches Javier. Alvaro goes to him, kisses him on top of the head. It's a deep kiss — like he harbors a great love and longing for him. Javier doesn't respond, just continues playing. Valerie re-enters, just as it's ending — enough for her to see it. Alvaro sees her, clears his throat.

ALVARO: Night Valerie.

VALERIE: Night.

He exits. Valerie and Javier alone. She watches him play. He doesn't notice her. Lights fade as we hear a Godzilla-like monster growl from a '50s B monster movie, transitioning us to:

2. MONSTER MOVIE SEMINAR
OR THE MYSTIQUE OF FAILURE, 2013

Graduate Seminar: "The Mystique of Failure." The seminar room is empty, except for Emilia-no Kurtz, the instructor, and a single female student, Alex Tanner. Kurtz is in his 50s, somewhat cocky and slick. He's not conventionally handsome, but looked at through a par-ticular lens, he does have a certain sex appeal. He speaks in an unidentifiable accent – could be Eastern European, Latin America, a hybrid of both, or could be fake. Alex is in her 20s. She's driven, whip-smart and attractive in a librarian's assistant sort of way. Kurtz talks as if the classroom is full. Behind him is a screen, on which is projected a black and white photograph of an elderly Daniel James.

KURTZ: Search of the Internet Movie Database for the films of Daniel James
Reveals a spectacularly unremarkable career trajectory.

His introduction to the profession suggests great promise –
First job in Hollywood:
Second Unit Director of Charlie Chaplin's
The Great Dictator.
Accounts of his contribution to the film vary:
Some suggest he co-authored the screenplay,
Others describe James as Chaplin's errand boy ...

In an article by John Gregory Dunne
published in *The New York Review of Books* in 1984,
James describes his contribution as follows, quote:
"Chaplin felt the Nazis could capture me, pull out my fingernails,
I would never turn against him."

He laughs. Alex doesn't think much of the joke.

Remember those words – they will resonate later.

This auspicious start was followed in 1943
With a screenwriting credit for *Three Russian Girls* –
Regret to inform you,
Not an early Hollywood attempt to Americanize *Chekhov* ...
Story is set in the Soviet Union during the Nazi invasion.

An American pilot, downed by the Nazis, lies in a hospital

Nursed by a sweet young thing named Natasha (played by Anna Sten).

They fall in love, but resist the

bourgeois temptation to *consumate*

As they have pressing, world-historical matters at hand,

Namely, resisting the Nazi advance into Soviet territory.

Questions?

No? Good.

Ten years pass before James resurfaces.

From 1953 to 1961, he scripts four films:

Slide reproductions of posters and stills from each film appear on the screen.

1953 *Beast from 20,000 Fathoms*

"Ferocious dinosaur awakened by Arctic atomic test terrorizes New York City."

1958 *Revolt in the Big House* — starring a young Robert Blake —

A film whose title accurately summarizes its plot —

1959 *The Giant Behemoth*

"Marine atomic test resurrects undersea dinosaur that proceeds to destroy London."

Last but not least:

Gorgo. 1961.

"Greedy sailors capture giant lizard off Irish coast.

 Sell it to London Circus.

Then its mother shows up."

Daniel James' name appears on none of these films.

Screenplays are attributed to one Daniel Hyatt.

For ten thousand dollars and an all expenses paid weekend with me at the hotel of your choice, can anyone explain to me … *WHY?*

Silence. Alex raises her hand.

KURTZ: Yes, Ms. … *(He studies his class roster.)*

ALEX: Tanner.

KURTZ: Ms. Tanner.

ALEX: You do realize I'm the only one enrolled in this seminar.

KURTZ: Your powers of perception stagger.
  Do you have an answer to the question?

ALEX: I might.

KURTZ: What I said —
  All expense paid weekend … ?
  Joke.

ALEX: Ha ha.

KURTZ: Shall I continue —

ALEX: He must have been blacklisted.

KURTZ: Very good.
  In 1951.
  Which is odd – don't you think?

ALEX: How so?

KURTZ: Being blacklisted seems to
  have had the paradoxical effect of
  reviving a film career that died in 1943,
  eight. years. before HUAC blacklisted him.

ALEX: Okay …

KURTZ: Does it trouble you? Me suggesting he did better *after* the blacklist
  Than he did *before?*

ALEX: Why would it trouble me …

KURTZ: One of those episodes …
  In your American history … ?
  Subterranean Monster beneath the Shining City on the Hill surfaces … ?
  Still raises hackles …
  You're probably too young to remember, but when Kazan —

ALEX: Won the lifetime achievement Oscar

    half the audience sat on their hands cause he named names.

KURTZ: Where do you stand on such matters?

ALEX: You want to know my political persuasion ... ?

KURTZ: Well —

ALEX: I'll take the Fifth.

KURTZ: Touché.

ALEX: I've actually seen the films — the monster ones.

KURTZ: Really.

ALEX: Yeah. When I was a kid, my dad, he —

Pause.

KURTZ: He ... ?

ALEX: Never mind.

Pause. Supreme awkwardness. Kurtz looks at his watch.

KURTZ: Oh! Look at that!

    5:10. Where did all the time go?

ALEX: Professor Kurtz? Is it safe to assume this course will be cancelled?

KURTZ: Why would you assume such a thing?

ALEX: Um ... low enrollment?

KURTZ: Even if the swimming pool is empty, one must never cease throwing rose petals into it.

Alex starts gathering her things.

KURTZ: Next session,

    triple creature feature: *20,000 Fathoms, Giant Behemoth and Gorgo.*

ALEX: Can't wait ...

KURTZ: Drink?

ALEX: Um. No thank you.

KURTZ: See you next week.

ALEX: Yeah.

Alex leaves. Kurtz is left alone.

3. LATE NIGHT PHONE CALL

In the darkness a telephone rings. Once. Twice. Three. Four. Five.

Out of the darkness Alvaro appears — stirred from sleep, he's a wreck — hair mussed up, dressed in underwear and a t-shirt. Phone keeps ringing. He picks it up.

ALVARO: Allo?

JAVIER: You need to come over.

ALVARO: Javi?

Lights up slowly on Javier in the kitchen. He's wired.

JAVIER: You need to come over —

ALVARO: I ain't comin over, I'm asleep

JAVIER: You talking to me from your sleep?

ALVARO: No, man, I'm awake now, you woke me up

JAVIER: Then come over I gotta talk to you

ALVARO: No man, I'm hanging up this motherfuckin phone and going back to sleep

JAVIER: No. Nononononono, NO. What are you asleep for anyway?

ALVARO: It's 3:30 in the morning —

JAVIER: Oh …

ALVARO: Are you high?

JAVIER: Fukken soaring man,
    I'm like the space shuttle,
    burning through the atmosphere

ALVARO: What'd you take?

JAVIER: Nothing, bro.

ALVARO: Call me in the morning …

JAVIER: I finished reading it.

ALVARO: What?

JAVIER: *Famous All Over Town?*

ALVARO: What'd you think of it?

JAVIER: It was a'ight.
  Not Dostoevsky but I dug it. ...

ALVARO: You read his obituary?

JAVIER: Yea, I read it.

ALVARO: Did it bother you // that –

JAVIER: Bother me? Yeah
  I'm always bothered but
  it bothered me
  in a way
  that it like
  bothered me? that it bothered me?

ALVARO: Huh?

JAVIER: Cause
  eating the book,

ALVARO: *Ay Dios // Mio* ...

JAVIER: Eating the book, his obituary,
  thinking about what you said last night
  about straitjackets, thinking about straitjackets

ALVARO: Okay ...

JAVIER: Thinking about my *mother* –
  I ever tell you she took me to see *Macbeth* when I was a kid?

ALVARO: *Mier//da*

JAVIER: Shit was like someone exploded a pipe bomb in my cranium –
  All that killing – who woulda thought murder could be so beautiful –
  But my mother, ohhhh my mother –

She was disgusted.

She had Solon's objection.

ALVARO: Reference check –

JAVIER: Solon. Greek cat. One of the Seven Wiseguys.

We should do something with that –

GreekPhilosopherMafiososSayHellotoMyLeetel//Frieng –

ALVARO: *Solon.*

JAVIER: Rightrightright

Saw Thespis act in the first Greek Tragedy

in like 80,000 BC, went up to him

at the stage door afterwards? said

"What the fuck?"

"LIES, ALL LIES! Aren't you ashamed?

Telling a big pack a lies to all those subscribers?"

It's in Plutarch – I'll check the reference later –

ALVARO: *Coño madre!*

JAVIER: *Thespis* said:

"What's the harm, it's make-believe … "

Pissed Solon off so much

he threw down his walking stick –

which in those days was like a Jet

whipping out his switchblade on an unsuspecting Shark

"I like to leeeve een Amerrrrr//ika"

ALVARO: I can't deal with you when you're // like this –

JAVIER: Papi, papi, papi … Listen, please, it's relevant I promise you:

Solon whipped out his AK was like

"WELL. FUCKHEAD.

If we commend make-believe like this,

everything will be make-believe,

Capitol Hill, Wall Street, New York Times, *marriage* … "

My mother, know what she said?

After *Macbeth*?

ALVARO: Jav—

JAVIER: (cause I saw the poster on the 7 train
  I kicked, screamed, sat on the pavement,
  on a steaming pile a dog shit
  til she promised she would take me)
  Know what she said?

ALVARO: No.

JAVIER: "Que asqueroso ... all those people clapping
  For a bunch of cold blooded murderers ... "

ALVARO: Javi: remember that tea I gave you?
  One that's supposed to *calm* your nerves?

JAVIER: Yeah, I drank like eight cups of it.

ALVARO: I'm tired man, let's talk // tomorrow

JAVIER: Thespis busted outta the *straitjacket,* see what I'm saying?

Pause.

JAVIER: Alvaro? You there?

ALVARO: I'm listening ...

JAVIER: *Thespis.* Busted. Outta the *straitjacket.*

  Solon, my mother, me, YOU ... ALL happy to walk through life wearing the straitjacket —

ALVARO: I'm not wearin no straight // jacket.

JAVIER: What do you and I hear time and time again
  When some bitch producer reads our shit?
  "Too intellectual. Too universal. Not street enough, not ghetto enough,
  not enough 'grit,' not poetic enough, not *magical* enough."

ALVARO: Javi —

JAVIER: When it is, they say the exact opposite –

> "Too *raw*, too *specific*,
>
> too poetic – no one talks like *that*
>
> *too* street, *too* ghetto, too gritty, grit like that?
>
> Subscribers won't stand for it, and how do you think
>
> they're gonna put all that magic on stage?"

> I hear it all the time,
>
> you hear it all the time,
>
> enough's enough, right compa?

ALVARO: Okay, but what's that got to do // with

JAVIER: The book?

> Like *I said* – not so much the book,
>
> but the *writer* ... *writer*. busted. through his own straitjacket ...

ALVARO: I'm hanging up, I can't take it when you're like // this ...

JAVIER: Papi, papi, papi, papi, don't hang up on me.

> Just one more thing.
>
> I promise ...

ALVARO: *One* thing.

JAVIER: Promise.

ALVARO: Take a breath ...

Javier takes a loud, audible, deep breath for Alvaro's benefit.

ALVARO: Okay ...

JAVIER: O. Kaaaay.

Silence.

> I finished reading the book.

Breath.

> Read the obituary.

Breath.

Saw his picture.

Breath.

Thought. Book. Obituary. Picture.
What the fuck.

Then a thing happened.

ALVARO: What … thing …

JAVIER: That feeling?

When you're alone at night?

Startle you feel when a stranger looks at you through the window?

Alvaro closes his eyes tight, restrains himself from responding. Breath.

I got that startle.
Stranger. Looking at me.
Through the kitchen window.

ALVARO: Javi. You're on the *fifth. floor.*

Window in your kitchen
looks out to the airshaft.
There's no stranger looking at you.

JAVIER: I felt that *startle.*

I look up, expect to see a stranger.

Stranger's me.
In the glass — hazy, distorted reflection. Me.

Then BOOM!
Glass shatters.

ALVARO: What?

JAVIER: Not literally, but I see something on the other side of the glass …

ALVARO: What'd you see?

JAVIER: Ruined street. From the end of the book.

After the railroad tears down the neighborhood?

ALVARO: Okay …

JAVIER: Outside the Aztec Club. Boarded up –

    Street looks like a bomb exploded

    Houses obliterated …

    Mounds of garbage –

    People left behind –

    Book of Bones, comic books, crumpled red dress

    Crayons like little flecks of color in the …

ALVARO: I get the picture …

JAVIER: Who shows up. Old Man. Daniel James …

    He's tall, 6' 6"

    Grey hair, dressed like a 1940s longshoreman …

    Old man takes a red crayon from the pile,

    Goes to the boarded window –

    Writes in big, curvy, sexy letters –

ALVARO & JAVIER: "Chato de Shamrock"

JAVIER: Old man's tagging the boarded up window,

    Who shows up? Kid …

ALVARO: Danny.

JAVIER: You and me, we're grooving now.

ALVARO: Go on, baby.

JAVIER: Kid sees the old man …

    Old man finds a picture of Chato's family,

    Sister, mother, baby

ALVARO: *Father*

JAVIER: Old man?

    He goes to hang the picture up, next to his tag

    Kid extends his arm,

    Makes the shape of a gun with his finger and

ALVARO: BANG!

Silence.

ALVARO: What happens next.

JAVIER: I don't know.

   Why I need you, bro.

   Come over?

ALVARO: No, man … it's late

JAVIER: We're rolling

ALVARO: I don't wanna go down that road.

JAVIER: You don't need to be scared – I'll hold your hand

ALVARO: I ain't scared of shit, bro.

JAVIER: Know what I think?

   You like living inside your straitjacket.

ALVARO: Hilarious coming from you.

JAVIER: So comfortable in there …

   You wouldn't know what to do with your hands if they were set free.

ALVARO: Punch you in the mouth, maybe …

   Only straitjacket I'm wearing is you.

Pause.

JAVIER: We got a deadine. You know what that means?

ALVARO: I know // what that

JAVIER: Years, you and me

   On our own

   in the trenches getting nowhere

   Finally big theater steps up? Throws us a bone?

   Joe Papp only calls once, my friend.

ALVARO: I *know*

JAVIER: *You* need this. // *We need*

ALVARO: I don't need this — I don't know // why you

JAVIER: *I need this.* I got two little monsters
  They're asleep, but when they wake?
  They're gonna need to eat, need clothes, toys
  Fuckin' trips to the ice cream parlor …
  They want and want and need and need …
  I got NOTHING to give them.

  No one ever gave us a commission before.
  Might be the only chance we ever get.
  I need this.

ALVARO: We'll come up with some other material …

JAVIER: We got nothing, we been running round in circles.
  We could do some cool shit with this …
  Come over. Papi? Por fa?

ALVARO: Javi … I don't know —

JAVIER: When the glass shatters … you gotta listen …
  Besides … means you and me get to spend more time …

  Alvo?

ALVARO: *(Deep sigh)*

JAVIER: You comin'?

ALVARO: I'll think about it.

He hangs up. Javier hangs up. He smiles. He thinks he might have him. Lights fade as we hear a Godzilla-like monster growl from a '50s B monster movie, transitioning us to:

4. GORGO

Kurtz and Alex watch the final moments of Gorgo when Gorgo's 200-foot-tall mother rips through the Battersea Amusement Park to rescue her son. We hear Mama Gorgo's roar, accompanied by sounds of urban destruction and a melodramatic film score.

BBC REPORTER FROM FILM: *(Absurd English accent, like a mental patient pretending to be a cricket announcer.)* "Maybe our prayers have been answered.

> The Great City,
>
> overwhelmed, exhausted,
>
> lies helpless under the immeasurable power and ferocity
>
> of this towering apparition from before the dawn of history.
>
> Yet,
>
> As though disdaining the pygmies under her feet,
>
> she turns back,
>
> turns with her young,
>
> leaving the prostrate city,
>
> and leaving Man himself
>
> to ponder the proud boast
>
> that he alone is Lord of all Creation"

LITTLE BOY FROM FILM: "You're going back now … back to the sea … "

Music swells. Kurtz switches off the projector. He and Alex sit in silence in the dark.

KURTZ: Lights, please!

Alex rolls her eyes, gets up, switches on the light. Kurtz wipes tears from his eyes.

ALEX: You're kidding me, right?

KURTZ: You're not moved? Mother?

> Rescuing her son from being made a public spectacle?

ALEX: Um, no. She's a 200-foot-tall monster. She destroyed half of London.

KURTZ: Watch it again someday if you ever have kids.

Silence.

ALEX: You have kids?

KURTZ: Two.

ALEX: How old?

KURTZ: 17 and 14.

ALEX: Are they —

KURTZ: They live with their mother in Seattle.
    Look we're not here to talk about trivialities,
    we're here to talk about *Gorgo*.

ALEX: Movie seems pretty trivial to me …

KURTZ: Does it? How so?

ALEX: Run of the mill '50s monster movie —
    Bad special effects?
    Inept dialogue,
    Zero character development,
    Plot threads that go nowhere …
    Moral universe that's about as
    Black and white // as —

KURTZ: That's one, very narrow, way of looking at it.

ALEX: And I'm missing … ?

KURTZ: Hell, I don't know — are there political dimensions you can ex//tract—

ALEX: Only the most obvious ones …

KURTZ: Enlighten me.

ALEX: Greedy American shipwreck pillagers, *bad*.
    Salt-of-the-earth-Irish-villagers-who-subsist-on-no-more-than-what-they-need-from-the-sea, *good*.
    Toss in some soft boiled Marxism,
    Between the images of urban apocalypse you *really* want to see —
    It's like porno, only with monsters.

Kurtz laughs.

KURTZ: That's // good.

ALEX: What would compel the guy

    to write the same movie

    three. times?

KURTZ: You see them as the same.

ALEX: Essentially ...

KURTZ: Interesting.

    I'll answer your question with a question.

    Why write the same movie three times?

ALEX: Box office?

    Big market for that kind of thing in the '50s, // '60s ... ?

KURTZ: Perhaps ... but a bit too easy?

ALEX: Simple explanation's usually the right one.

KURTZ: What things do you return to?

    What things do you repeat?

ALEX Excuse me?

KURTZ: Surely you repeat things in your life,

    You know the outcome

    Yet you repeat, repeat, repeat ...

ALEX: That's none of your business ...

KURTZ: As if someone has already written your life

    And you're just playing the script they handed you.

ALEX: That's depressing.

KURTZ: You ask: why make the movie three times.

    You answer, glibly, "box office," "fashion of the times."

    Yes, inside all glib answers lies a kernel of truth,

    like when you tell yourself

    "I dumped him because he doesn't see the *real* me" time and time again —

But you know,
in the darkest,
shakiest corners of your soul —
there's another *reason*
for all that *repetition*.

ALEX: You can decide to break the pattern …

KURTZ: You arrive at this conclusion from personal experience?
Or is trolling the self-help section of Barnes & Noble your guilty pleasure …

ALEX: Again, none of your business …

KURTZ: Yes, you might say Daniel James is making the same damn film over and over again, OR

ALEX: Or … ?

KURTZ: You can identify which patterns he's *breaking* in *Gorgo*,
And perhaps reveal something …

ALEX: Like … ?

KURTZ: Actual profundity underneath its cheapness.

Pause.

ALEX: Okay … ending's different …

KURTZ: That's a start …

ALEX: Monster doesn't get killed like in the first two.
Gets to escape back to the sea …

KURTZ: Happy for the monster, not so happy for humanity.

I think that little variation is key to
answering your question. What else?

ALEX: There's no nuclear testing theme in *Gorgo*.
It's the inciting incident for awakening the monster in the first two.

KURTZ: Good.

What *does* incite Gorgo?

ALEX: Greedy American shipwreck hunters.

    No moral quandary that

    they're essentially grave robbers.

KURTZ: Bingo. Other pattern breaking?

ALEX: In *20,000 Fathoms* and *Behemoth*

    The human ingenuity that unleashes the monster,

    Is used also to destroy it. Whereas *Gorgo*

    Human ingenuity is useless … Gorgo's mother destroys everything.

KURTZ: Now you're getting somewhere …

ALEX: But: once she rescues *Gorgo*,

    Neither mother nor son has any interest in continuing their destruction.

    They retreat to the sea …

Pause.

KURTZ: Did I just see a light bulb?

ALEX: Daniel James is angry.

KURTZ: Whatever for?

ALEX: The blacklist?

KURTZ: Lots to be angry about. Destroyed careers, broken friendships, shattered families.

ALEX: He's had to hide

KURTZ: They steal his name. Has to make up a new one … Daniel Hyatt …

ALEX: He wants revenge …

KURTZ: Not so sure it's that –

ALEX: He wants to show – at least in the first two

    that human beings do idiotic things like nuclear testing

    and in doing so unleash monsters, but

    in the face of annihilation

    can correct themselves …

    redeem their humanity …

KURTZ: Go on …

ALEX: He's saying that if HUAC recognized the destruction they unleashed
   They could fix their errors, redeem their humanity, put the monster back into its box

KURTZ: A possible reading …

ALEX: But in *Gorgo*, it's too late … Ten years later
   no one's in the mood to fix the past …
   it's as if he's saying
   the monster is more *human* than *humans* …
   She's a destroyer, but only because
   she wants to protect her child above all else …

Pause.

KURTZ: Hm.
   Last film he ever made … his farewell —
   As if to say, "I'm tired of hiding behind false names,
   I'm retreating to the sea … Goodbye."

Silence.

ALEX: What happened to him … ?

KURTZ: He slummed it for awhile.

ALEX: Pardon?

KURTZ: Nothing. He uhhh …
   Doesn't resurface again
   For twenty-two years.

   And not because he wanted to.

Pause.

ALEX: Are you going to tell me what happened?

KURTZ: Look at the time. 5:10.
   How about we blow this popsicle stand and get dinner …

Alex considers this.

ALEX: Maybe some other night ...

She gathers her things. Before she leaves, she turns.

ALEX: Professor Kurtz?

KURTZ: Yes?

ALEX: Thank you.

She turns to exit.

KURTZ: Ms. Tanner ...

I don't presume it would be of interest to you, but

At present I am at work on a major project of a highly sensitive nature.

ALEX: Okay ...

KURTZ: I'm in need of someone –

Someone trustworthy.

An assistant

Who can

Assist me.

ALEX: What kind of project is it?

KURTZ: An excavation.

ALEX: That's all you're going to give me?

KURTZ: Were you to express interest I might allow you a peek at the cat inside
the proverbial bag.

ALEX: And if I don't?

KURTZ: Sorry. Cat stays in the bag.

Would you be interested in seeing the cat?

ALEX: Perhaps.

KURTZ: Good. We'll discuss it next time.

*Kurtz smiles. Alex, uncertain whether a deal has been made, hesitates, moves to the door,
turns around, opens her mouth as if about to say something. Thinks better of it. Smiles.
Exits.*

5. THREE DAYS

The apartment. Evening. Valerie on the rampage trying to organize the place — it's a mess. Papers, books, empty coffee cups, bottles on the kitchen table. Toys scattered throughout the living room. Alvaro stands by the door, just arrived.

ALVARO: What do you mean "asleep"?

VALERIE: Asleep. As in sleeping // unless there's

ALVARO: For three days?

VALERIE: Wired three days, Crash! Three days down.

ALVARO: What was he doing?

VALERIE: Obsessing over that stupid novel —

ALVARO: Shit …

VALERIE: Yes, and I'm doing fantastically well — thanks for asking.

ALVARO: Sorry, Valerie … everything okay?

VALERIE: I'm *managing.*

ALVARO: Where're the kids?

VALERIE: *Just* now got Lila to sleep.

ALVARO: Pablo?

VALERIE: Don't get me started about Pablo … little monster.

ALVARO: What'd he do this time?

VALERIE: Other night? After you idiots finally left? We go to sleep.
    4:45 in the morning Lila wakes up. Great.
    I go in to feed her and who's not in his bed?

ALVARO: Oh, shit …

VALERIE: Wandered off. Again.
    I comb through the apartment — nowhere.

ALVARO: Oh, shit …

VALERIE: Out into the hall, up and down the stairs …

Nowhere. I'm thinking fine – good riddance, kid,

Wanna see the world? Be my guest …

ALVARO: Valerie –

VALERIE: I'm joking, Alvaro.

What kind of person do you think I am?

I'm practically shitting my pants –

I keep thinking – what's his name? the milk carton kid?

ALVARO: Etan Patz.

VALERIE: I actually *exit* the building. *In my nightgown.*

It's freezing, Lila's hanging off my nipple.

He's not out in the street.

I'm thinking I've got to call the cops –

Great, child services will take Lila.

Javi and I'll get thrown in jail for neglect.

Before I go up to call, I think "basement"

"laundry room," and there he is

curled up inside the dryer looking at a *National Geographic.*

"Hi mommy!"

ALVARO: Jesus …

VALERIE: I'm at the end of my rope. I'm really // at the

ALVARO: Where's he now?

VALERIE: Dropped him off at my sister's in Jersey yesterday.

He's safe there until I can get things under control here.

ALVARO: Thought you didn't talk to her.

VALERIE: Sometimes you gotta swallow your pride, pick up the phone after three years.

ALVARO: Maybe you should have sent *Javi* there …

His attempt at humor falls flat.

VALERIE: Do something with this.

She hands him a child's rocking horse. He slips it under the kitchen table.

VALERIE: Not there.

He opens the front door and leaves it out in the hall.

VALERIE: I'll tell him you stopped by.

ALVARO: Want me to ... ?

VALERIE: ... ?

ALVARO: I could try to rouse him?

VALERIE: HA!

ALVARO: What?

VALERIE: Be my guest, Alvaro ... *Rouse* him.

Unsure if she's really seeking his help or implying something else, he moves to the door.

VALERIE: Cause that would be. *great*. That would be a *fucking* miracle.

ALVARO: What ...

VALERIE: Three days of me. "Go to bed, Javi! You're gonna regret it." "I'm working, baby." *Working*. Followed by three days of me pounding at the door, *"get. up."* Three days of Pablo begging him to come out and play, me up all hours to feed Lila, who refuses to sleep through the night – NOTHING. So go ahead, slither on in, work your *magic* ...

ALVARO: Valerie ...

VALERIE: Like *I* don't have work to do ... like I don't have my *own* deadlines on top of all this crap. All *him. Him, him, him.* Just sickening ...

The door to Javi's room flings open. He's a mess. Boxers, soiled t-shirt. Hair a mess. By Alvaro's reaction, he stinks, as well.

JAVIER: Yo, whassup, baby?

He embraces Alvaro, who squirms – stench. Javier kisses his cheek. He notices Valerie.

JAVIER: We got any eggs?

Valerie stares at him, arms burdened with things — books, kids' toys. She drops them where she stands. Big crash. She puts her coat on, exits.

JAVIER: What's the matter with her?

ALVARO: Heard you had a long nap.

JAVIER: Come here, I gotta show you something.

He goes to the kitchen table. It's clear, except for the newspaper.

JAVIER: What happened to my shit?

He starts tearing apart the newspaper, as if whatever he's looking for might be found in it.

JAVIER: Where did she put my shit?!?!?!

Alvaro goes to a bookcase, where a stack of books and papers is wedged in a space between the volumes. He brings it to the kitchen table, while Javi looks in ridiculous places like the knife drawer.

JAVIER: Fucking kill that bitch! Always moving my shit!

Alvaro calmly deposits the books and papers on the table.

ALVARO: Looking for this?

JAVIER: Where'd you find that?

ALVARO: Bookshelf.

Javier tears through the pile, burying the kitchen table in the process. He finds what he's looking for.

JAVIER: Check this out …

He hands Alvaro a page ripped from an architectural magazine.

ALVARO: What am I supposed to be looking at …

JAVIER: *Seaward*

ALVARO: C-word?

JAVIER: Huh? No, no, bro – not the C-word, *Seaward* – like in the direction of el mar.

ALVARO: *Sea* … // gotcha

JAVIER: Know who lived in this house?

ALVARO: Looks more like a castle than a house—

JAVIER: Know who lived in this *castle?*
   Our Chicano impersonator …

ALVARO: Motherfucker lived *here?*

JAVIER: Carmel-by-the-Sea

ALVARO: And he's running around pretending he's some
   dirt poor brown kid?

JAVIER: I know … Isn't that cool?

ALVARO: No, man, NOT cool …

The apartment buzzer goes off.

JAVIER: It's cool he could live in a place like that
   Come up with a book like *this.*

ALVARO: No. No. No. // No.

Buzzer rings again.

   You gonna get that?

Javier goes to the buzzer.

JAVIER: Can I help you?

HERMAN ON INTERCOM: Herman.

JAVIER: What are you doing here?

HERMAN ON INTERCOM: Ummm … thought we were having a meeting?
   I'm a little early … but …

Javier looks at Alvaro, confused.

ALVARO: It's Tuesday night, bro

Javier buzzes him in, unlocks the front door.

ALVARO: Where'd you find this?

JAVIER: Library. Copy of some architecture magazine …

ALVARO: You just rip it out like that?

JAVIER: Who's gonna miss it?

ALVARO: There's a spiritual emptiness inside you, Javi, that needs // filling –

JAVIER: Whatever …

ALVARO: You seriously still thinking about this imposter bullshit

JAVIER: No, I'm thinking about the straitjacket bullshit …

ALVARO: You keep saying that – straitjacket –
    it's starting to bug // me out

JAVIER: Yooooouuuuu know what I mean …

Herman appears at the door's threshhold. A leather shoulder bag slung over his shoulder. He eats pistachios from a small brown sack.

HERMAN: *(In his most self-conscious, piss poor Spanish accent.)* O-la, cumpadrayce …

ALVARO: *(Agonized groan.)*   JAVIER: Whassup Herman!

HERMAN: Were uh … you two in the middle of something?

JAVIER: Nah, man.

HERMAN: I just ran into Valerie? On Ninth?

JAVIER: Yeah?

HERMAN: Is she … ?
    Nevermind.
    Pistachio?

JAVIER: No thanks …

HERMAN: Alvaro?

ALVARO: I'm good …

Herman looks at the magazine tear out.

HERMAN: Oh! Charles Sumner Greene.

ALVARO: Huh?

HERMAN: House in the photo? By Charles Sumner Greene.

ALVARO: How do you know that?

HERMAN: My *degree?*

    Art History?

    U Chicago?

    Summa Cum Laude?

    They teach you how to look at things?

    Recognize who made them?

JAVIER: You know this house?

HERMAN: It's pretty well-known.

    Client kept making changes. Drove Greene nuts ...

    House is unique cause Greene was known for his use of glass and wood –

    Only example in his *oeuvre* where stone's the primary medium

ALVARO: How do you remember shit like that?

Herman shrugs.

HERMAN: It's on a rocky bluff overlooking the Pacific Ocean – hence the
    use of native stone.

Pops a pistachio in his mouth.

    He was an acolyte of the Prairie School.

    You know, Chicago?

Another pistachio.

    Louis Sullivan?

    Frank Lloyd Wright?

Pistachio.

    Organic relationship between a building and its site?

Pistachio.

    No?

Silence. They stare at him.

HERMAN: Why are you cumpadrayce looking at it?

ALVARO: Cut it with the "cumpadrayce"?

HERMAN: What – ?

Buzzer. No one moves.

HERMAN: Someone gonna get that?

No one moves. Herman goes to the buzzer.

ALVARO: Not me   JAVIER: Ohhhhh yessss …

HERMAN: Who is it?

NERO ON INTERCOM: Nero.

Herman buzzes him in.

JAVIER: Know who lived in that house?

HERMAN: No …

JAVIER: Daniel James.

HERMAN: Ooooohh. Interesting … hm.
    That would make sense.

JAVIER: Why?

HERMAN: Sometimes it's referred to as the D.L. James House.

Nero enters with Lina. Nero has a twelve-pack of beer.

NERO: Yo.

JAVIER: Yo.

During the next conversation, Nero puts the beer in the fridge, takes one. Lina goes to the couch, picks up a magazine and reads. Nero joins the men looking at the picture.

ALVARO: Who, pray tell, is D.L. James, Mr. I-Majored-in-Art-History?

HERMAN: Probably his father.
    If I remember correctly, made his fortune importing fine china.
    Something also about him being related to Frank and Jesse James.

This gets Nero's attention.

NERO: *The* Frank and Jesse James?

Javier goes to the window, stares out, wheels turning. Hint of his reflection in it.

HERMAN: That's right.

NERO: You're saying Daniel James was related to Jesse James.

HERMAN: Yep. What I said.

NERO: Whoa ... cool.

He goes to the couch, sits next to Lina. She reads the magazine while he plays with her hair. As the scene progresses, Nero loses interest in his surroundings and becomes obsessively focused on Lina. The rest of the group pretends not to notice, but there is an unspoken annoyance.

HERMAN: This mean you cump — *gentlemen* — are still noodling // on this

ALVARO: I'm outta here —

    Call me when you come up with something else —

JAVIER: Sit your ass down — we don't got anything else ...

Valerie enters carrying a plastic shopping bag. She sees the mess on the table. She glares at Javi, removes a carton of eggs from the bag. She opens it, holds it out for Javi to see. She flips the carton over, smashes it on Javi's research. She smiles, exits into the bedroom.

JAVIER: I'm calling the meeting to order.

ALVARO: You gonna at least clean up, get dressed?

JAVIER: What for?

ALVARO: Cause you smell like — never mind.

JAVIER: So I been thinking ...

ALVARO: You been *sleep//ing*

JAVIER: I been thinking about Daniel James/Danny Santiago

HERMAN: Great, can't wait to // hear

JAVIER: I been thinking we could do something with it, like —

Valerie enters the room, hair is up in a bun. She wears glasses. She carries a stack of notes and books, places them on the coffee table. She sits.

JAVIER: I been thinking we could do something with it, like —

VALERIE: He wasn't pulling stuff out of thin air.

ALVARO: Huh?

VALERIE: Daniel James. He wasn't pulling stuff out of thin air.
I've been doing a little research. On my *own*.

JAVIER: Oh, you have, have you?

VALERIE: Somebody had to get off their ass and do something.
Listen: from an article about him by John Gregory Dunne
In the *New York Review of Books*. Daniel James is quoted as saying:
"We moved into East L.A. and started making a new life for ourselves there."

ALVARO: So?

VALERIE: "For the next fifteen years the James' activities were concentrated on three
square blocks in Lincoln Heights."

ALVARO: Okay …

VALERIE: He'd been blacklisted —

NERO: He was black//listed?

VALERIE: He couldn't work in film, so he and his wife
spent the '60s volunteering there.
organized youth clubs, helped get kids off the street, out of gangs

ALVARO: He was "down"

VALERIE: Stood at weddings, funerals, baptisms —
He was even godfather to a bunch of kids

ALVARO: He was *really* "down"

HERMAN: They gave him a community service award …

*Valerie gives Herman a look. Herman shuts his mouth. Javier notices this exchange. Stares
at Valerie. Herman and Valerie have evidently talked about this privately.*

ALVARO: Maybe we should call him Daniel "Saint" James

HERMAN: Isn't that what "Santiago" translates to?

ALVARO: Doesn't make him one of them, doesn't mean he's got the // right to –

VALERIE: I never said he was "one of them"

  I'm only saying he had *access*

  More access than you have –

  What did you say the other night?

  about avoiding?

ALVARO: Avoiding?

VALERIE: Going there. When you are in L.A.

ALVARO: Never had reason to go there – I'm not looking for "access"

VALERIE: Well there you go.

ALVARO: Point being … ?

VALERIE: You aren't lacking in the *opinion* // department

ALVARO: I'm entitled to my opinion –

VALERIE: By your own admission –

  you know *less* than him about what's // authen

ALVARO: Thank you Valerie for telling me what // I know and don't

HERMAN: All we're saying is

  He served the community.

  They respected him enough to invite him into their world.

  They didn't seem to have any trouble with the fact he wrote about it.

ALVARO: Okay … I dig that.

  But if I wake up one day, and I'm like,

  "Hm. I got an *urge* …

  Do some community service,

  but where?

  East L.A.,

  been done.

  South Bronx? *Done.*

CARMEL-BY-THE-SEA
Yeeeaaaah,
I would love to do me some community service
in Carmel-by-the-Sea …
Where do I sign up?
I'd be one happy half Puerto Rican
Sit there, lookin at the Pacific,
talk to you about your problems
over mint juleps …

HERMAN: You could mow the lawn.

ALVARO: Eat me Herman.

VALERIE: You're so negative …

ALVARO: What's negative? I'm asking a question.

VALERIE: You poke holes … your whole MO
Poke holes in everything. You know why?

ALVARO: Enlighten me, mamacita

VALERIE: Cause you're like a walking hunk
of human Swiss cheese
Can't plug the holes in your own soul
So you gotta poke, poke, poke holes in everyone and everything else …
It's *exhausting*

HERMAN: You know … all this talk about Daniel James, Danny Santiago … it's gotten
me thinking about Ben Franklin.

They all look at him – what the fuck?

HERMAN: That's right. Ben Franklin.
Cause that's where it all started.

ALVARO: Ben Franklin pretended he was Mexican?

HERMAN: No, jackass.
I'm talking about the concept of self-improvement.

ALVARO: Why do I got the feeling

    I'm gonna LOVE the next pile a dog shit // that's

NERO: ALVARO! Would you shut up, let the man SPEAK?!?!

Lina touches his arm to calm him.

HERMAN: Why thank you, Nero.

    Ben Franklin made a list.

    Thirteen virtues — *which*

    If you lived by them,

    You'd walk the path to self-improvement …

ALVARO: Okay …

HERMAN: Now: with all this *speculation*

    about our little impersonator friend

    I've taken it upon myself to do a little

    preliminary dramaturgy

Collective groan. He takes from his bag a stack of packets.

    I xeroxed these packets // for you —

Groans as he hands out packets.

HERMAN: What? This is my *role*

    You *assigned* me this role —

VALERIE: *(Reading from the packet.)* "Thirteen Virtues. One: temperance. Eat not to dullness, drink not to elevation."

NERO: *(Raising his beer.)* Here, here!

VALERIE: Shhhh! You'll wake up Lila.

ALVARO: "Two: silence. Speak not but what may benefit others or yourself, avoid *trifling* conversation."

HERMAN: Very good, Lina?

LINA: "Three: order. Let all your things have their places, let each part of your business have its time."

NERO: Dude, we can read these on our own?

Look, I have two auditions first thing in the morning – just cut to the chase?

Herman gets flustered. Goes around the room snatching packets from everyone.

HERMAN: Fine! Read em on your own!

VALERIE: Just explain what you're getting at –

HERMAN: He's saying that as Americans
we have the power to *will* ourselves
to be *different. Better.*
We can invent ourselves – not like Europeans
where self is pre-determined, Founding Fathers
cleaned the slate – individual Americans can clean // the slate

ALVARO: You vote for Ronnie Ray-Gun?

HERMAN: What happens in the voting booth is between me and my // ballot

ALVARO: Whatever – "clean slate"? That's just caca –

JAVIER: Yeah – but inside every piece of caca's
A kernel of truth …

Room stops. Intense focus on Javier. Silence.

JAVIER: Okay …
Ben Franklin's this dude.
Accomplished ridiculous amounts of shit in his life.
People wonder: how'd he do that?
Here he's telling you – follow these rules,
make a whole new self –
if I can do it, you can too.

ALVARO: So if Nero quits drinking, chasing little hotties fresh outta NYU – he'll get
his face on the cover of *Variety*?

VALERIE: Alvaro!   NERO: You dick …

Everyone laughs.

LINA: If you'll excuse me.

Lina exits to the bathroom. Nero crumples a napkin and throws it at Alvaro.

HERMAN: Like Javi says, we're all trapped in straitjackets …

> Only reason anyone writes? Reads? Autobiography?
>
> They need an instruction manual,
>
> on how to be Harry Houdini
>
> slip *out* of the straitjacket, free themselves

ALVARO: You yourself said it wasn't an autobiography …

HERMAN: Yes, it's fiction that has the contours of autobiography …

ALVARO: Whatever …

HERMAN: And who in this society needs that more than anyone else?

> Anyone … ?

VALERIE: The um … "marginalized"?

HERMAN: Bingo …

ALVARO: You mean to tell me

> Simon & Schuster
>
> published the motherfuckin' thing
>
> cause they saw it as a "self-improvement"
>
> manual? – tap that untapped Chicano market?
>
> Cause all East LA is waiting for that *New York Times* approved novel to
>
> teach them how to "free" themselves?

HERMAN: Not exactly, I –

ALVARO: What then?

HERMAN: If you'd let me finish –

ALVARO: By all means, Herman, I can't wait to hear this // shit …

VALERIE: Shhhhh …

HERMAN: Okay. Historically. Speaking.

> The uhhh
>
> *Ethnic*

Autobiography

Served a

Two conflicting purposes …

ALVARO: Yeah? What purposes …

HERMAN: I'll use the example of the slave narrative.

On the one hand,

slave, former slave might read it,

see how the writer *overcame* …

situation … enslavement … But …

who *else*

was it for?

VALERIE: White Americans.

HERMAN: Very good –

VALERIE: Remember that course, Javi? At Oberlin?

About slave narratives?

JAVIER: Huh?

VALERIE: Professor told a story …

Abolitionist asked Frederick Douglass

before a speech to

"tone down the high falutin' rhetoric,"

be "more plantation"

so people would believe he'd actually been a slave.

JAVIER: You gotta play to your audience …

HERMAN: Point I'm making, Alvaro,

Autobiographer –

especially a

"marginalized" autobiographer

is trapped in a Catch-22.

On the one hand they're writing

An instruction manual, how to get out of the straitjacket
for their own kind —

ALVARO: "Own // kind" …

HERMAN: On the other hand …
they have to "represent"
to the folks they perceive as holding the key
to the straitjacket —

VALERIE: White Americans …

HERMAN: Most cases, yes,
that they need to *be seen* as human.

ALVARO: Which is why this country // is —

HERMAN: Exactly. Why should anyone have to prove they're human?
But they can't just tell their own story,
they have to be spokespeople for a whole group …
which is dangerous …

VALERIE: Cause it puts you back in the straitjacket you were trying to escape —

ALVARO: None of this applies to Daniel James.

HERMAN: Why not?!?

Herman buries his head on Valerie's shoulder in frustration.

ALVARO: *He's not writing for "his own kind"*
He can't "represent" for a group he's not part of
You can't say you're in a straitjacket
When the whole time you got the key hidden in your back pocket

VALERIE: Hush!

JAVIER: I think I know what Alvaro's trying to say.

Room stops. Attention on Javier. Silence.

JAVIER: And you're right. To a degree. *But*
if we're to believe what Herman

and Valerie, my *wife*
are saying …

Valerie and Herman shift so as not to seem so close.

JAVIER: He did his homework.

HERMAN: Levi-Strauss of the Urban Beast.

JAVIER: Shut up.

He went in.
Got the key to their modest kingdom –
had access …
He wasn't "making shit up" –
Insider could read it, say yeah,
he was there, witnessed, got it right.

But if we're gonna do *this* …

ALVARO: Do // what?

JAVIER: Our problem, ladies and gentlemen
We ain't got no access …

ALVARO: Do *what* Javi?

JAVIER: No access, no details …
No details, no authenticity.

HERMAN: What do you mean "do this"

JAVIER: Huh?

HERMAN: You said, "If we're going to do *this* … "

Pause.

JAVIER: Okay …
Dude's old, blacklisted, can't write, can't get a gig. He's –

ALVARO: Rich

VALERIE: Relevance?

JAVIER: *Filthy* rich —

ALVARO: *Blanco*

JAVIER: *Blanco* … right. More important he's washed up.
   He's a has-been who never really *was*.

HERMAN: In all fairness, he did write that play —

NERO: Which play?

HERMAN: *Winter Soldiers. Best Plays 1942.*

JAVIER: I read that shit, only proves my point.
   Dude's gotta find something to do with his time.
   Pulls up in Lincoln Heights
   In his convertible Caddy …
   Meets a bunch of Chicanos
   Feels an affinity,
   Feels like he's *home*
   Picks up the language,
   Mannerisms, stories …
   Over the years they crystallize
   Into this kid — Chato

   Chato starts talking

   You've felt it, Alvaro
   Voice in your head?
   That keeps talking, talking, talking?
   You don't ignore it
   You write down what it *says* …

   If you're Daniel James?
   Masochist who's been making dents in his forehead
   Getting nowhere at a typewriter for *fifty. years?*
   and suddenly? A *real* voice pops in your head?
   You write down what it says, no matter
   how big a price you'll pay …
   Especially if you've been *silenced*.

311

HERMAN: Exactly what Valerie and I are trying to say.

JAVIER: Just shut up, will you?

So this voice, this monster comes out

voice more real than anything he wrote for fifty years.

are you gonna get tangled in some useless ethical dilemma,

cause the voice is a barely literate kid, while you studied classics at Yale?

NO … You justify, you say, I put my time in,

helped those people, broke bread in their homes, loaned them money

got drunk with the men, played stickball with the kids, prayed at their funerals …

I *earned* the right to write about it — who cares if real Chicanos get escorted out the

lobby of Simon & Schuster … I tapped *my* inner Chicano, I don't owe them shit …

HERMAN: Exactly what I am trying to say —

JAVIER: NO, you fucking knucklehead, I'm not DONE.

Silence.

JAVIER: Key is … if we're gonna do this …

We have no access.

HERMAN: *Do. what?*

VALERIE: Yeah, do what?

JAVIER: *Be* him.

ALVARO: Huh?

JAVIER: *Be* him.

VALERIE: You mean …

JAVIER: *Be. Him.*

Silence.

ALVARO: I have no idea what you mean?

But I can tell you, my brother,

I have

ZERO interest

in *"Being"*

that vampire-mother//fucker.

HERMAN: Why not?

ALVARO: I don't have to explain it to you.

HERMAN: I think you do.

ALVARO: Do *you* know what he means by "being" him

HERMAN: No, but …

ALVARO: Then you can't be ask//ing me —

HERMAN: Just your

Vehemence —

NO, your total inflexibility

to even consider what Javi's propos//ing

ALVARO: Well, *Herman*

I'm a little skeptical of you and *Valerie's* willingness

to accept whatever he's say//ing

HERMAN: I'm not accepting any//thing —

ALVARO: You are // you are

HERMAN: No no no // NO

VALERIE: *Boys.*

The room stops.

VALERIE: Javi: Do you mean a forgery.

JAVIER: Huh?

A pause. Valerie stares at Javier.

VALERIE: A forgery. That's what you mean, isn't it? Javi?

Silence.

HERMAN: That's brilliant. That's genius.

NERO: What?

ALVARO: What do you mean forgery?

Javier seizes the moment, though it is offset by the fact he's in boxers and t-shirt and unclean.

JAVIER: We're gonna *be* him.
    We're gonna *write like him* —
    we're gonna write *his* story,
    story that ain't ours to tell,
    story we got no *right* to tell
    cause we're not white.
    we're not rich.   NERO: I'm white
    we're not ex-Communists.
    we never been blacklisted
    never hobnobbed with Charlie Chaplin
    broke bread with John Steinbeck.
    We're not seventy-two
    and none of us has ever set foot in a mansion in Carmel.
    But we're gonna tell it.
    Make everyone think he wrote that shit —
    last will and testament.
    Never seen by human eyes.
    Written by *you. Me.*

ALVARO: We could rip that motherfucking straitjacket off once and for all …

JAVIER: Joe Papp only calls once, *muthafukka*

Silence.

NERO: Look, this conversation …
    Call me when you have some material … ?
    I'd be happy to swing by and read —
    I have to go, I've got //aud—

HERMAN: Auditions. First thing. Right …

Nero downs the remainder of his beer.

NERO: LINA! Let's go!

VALERIE: Would you shush?! Lila …

Lina comes out of the bathroom. She's seething. They exit.

ALVARO: Why does she put up with him?

VALERIE: You shouldn't have said – chasing co-eds?

ALVARO: You think she don't know?

VALERIE: She didn't need a reminder. From you. In front of everyone.

ALVARO: Just keeping it real …

The child in the next room begins to cry. Valerie sighs.

VALERIE: Great. See what you jerks did? You woke Lila

Neither she nor Javier move. The child continues to cry.

HERMAN: Anyone um

    going to …
    get that?

No one moves. Alvaro gets up, heads to the room.

VALERIE: No, Alvaro I –

ALVARO: I *got* it.

He disappears into the room. Silence.

HERMAN: This mean we're done for the evening?

No answer.

HERMAN: Okay … I uhhh …

    should head out.

VALERIE: Let me show you to the door.

In the threshold they hug – long enough to make one wonder …

HERMAN: Night, Valerie …

    Javi … ?

Javier responds with a vague nod. Herman exits.

JAVIER: You fucking him?

VALERIE: Don't be ridiculous.

She starts cleaning up the mess. Silence. Javier watches her.

JAVIER: What do you think?
   Should we do this?

VALERIE: Not for me to decide.

JAVIER: I'd like your opinion.

VALERIE: Oh, you would?

JAVIER: Yes.

VALERIE: If you're gonna do it, start writing it already.
   I'm sick of talking about it.

JAVIER: That's not what I –

VALERIE: Any case, seems to me you've already // decided.

JAVIER: Talk to me, please.
   I want to know what you're thinking. Really thinking.

Valerie stops cleaning.

VALERIE: I think you're afraid.

JAVIER: Oh yeah? What am I afraid of?

VALERIE: That bringing this old, sad, empty, *forgotten* man to life –
   a man you think is so far outside of yourself –
   white, patrician, a mediocre writer …
   You might realize? Him? You? No difference.

Javier smiles. She's nailed him.

JAVIER: I fucking love you.

VALERIE: Stop it.

He slowly moves to her.

JAVIER: I fucking *love* you …

VALERIE: Javier ... no ... I'm cleaning

He gets behind her, presses against her, kisses her neck. Doesn't take her long to get into it. They're all over each other. Alvaro re-enters, closing the door to the child's room. He watches as Javier lifts Valerie onto the kitchen counter and hikes up her skirt. They're in their own world. Alvaro gathers his things. He stands in the threshold watching as Javier undoes his belt. He exits. As Javier and Valerie begin having sex, Lila's cries emerge from the next room. They continue, letting the child cry it out. The child's cries intensify as we reach the —

End of Act One

ACT TWO. Puerto Angel

1. JESSE JAMES

Courtyard of a small hotel in Puerto Angel, a small fishing village on the Pacific coast of Mexico.

It's an open space with patio style furnishings, filled with sunlight. The place is a bit shabby, decorated with kitschy tropical motifs. Along the upstage wall a series of numbered doors – guest rooms. Alvaro, Javier, Herman and Valerie arrange the furniture, creating an impromptu rehearsal space. They set up a table, complete with scripts, highlighters, water and a large sketch pad which Valerie will use later. A low table and two chairs serve as a "set." On the table, a large box – perhaps the discarded packaging of a children's toy.

Valerie wears a sarong and a wide-brimmed hat. Alvaro, a tank top and cut-off jeans. Herman sports a pink golf shirt with light khakis. Javier wears a faded Pink Floyd Dark Side of the Moon t-shirt and jeans.

JAVIER: I went down there with Pablo to teach him how to make paper airplanes, and this guy was running around naked, looked like he hadn't showered in a week.

VALERIE: Guidebook said that stretch of beach is crawling with German tourists.

JAVIER: Pablo was like, "Papi? Why's that man running around with his pi pi flapping around?"

HERMAN: Where was this?

JAVIER: Mile up the road –

HERMAN: Is it a town?

JAVIER: Just a stretch of beach with some shacks.
People rent hammocks, stay out in the open air ...
Dude and his crew had dreadlocks, skin all red ...

HERMAN: They were all Germans?

JAVIER: Every last one.
I told him – look, I don't mind you running around butt naked?
But I got my son here? You mind not having sex with your girl out in the open like that?

VALERIE: They were having sex?

JAVIER: Know what he says to me?

"Look meestah ... Ve're in nayychah ...

Ve're ze speereechual descendantz of ze Mayan race."

Alvaro cracks up.

ALVARO: For real? He said that? What'd you say?

JAVIER: I walked away – how do you respond to something like that?

HERMAN: Where are the kids?

VALERIE: The guy who runs this place introduced us to a little old *abuelita*

that lives down the road. They're spending the afternoon there.

ALVARO: And you trust her?

VALERIE: What's not to trust?

A guest room door opens. Lina appears in a bikini. Nero follows, dressed rather bizarrely in Western gear: cowboy boots, tight jeans, wide belt with an enormous ornate buckle, Western shirt, brown leather vest, red scarf around his neck. Only thing missing: cowboy hat. He holds a stack of paper rolled into a scroll. Everyone notices his peculiar appearance. Nero unrolls the pages, reads them, mouths the words to himself. He makes gestures punctuating words we can't hear.

Lina sits on a chair and rubs sunblock on her body.

HERMAN: Warm enough for you, Nero?

Nero stares at him for a beat, goes back to the script. The furniture by this point has been rearranged.

JAVIER: Okay ...

so you know,

I'm not married to any of this –

more a

first stab. Not sure if it comes at the beginning, middle –

VALERIE: Could come at the end –

HERMAN: How so?

VALERIE: A kind of Rosebud moment?

   That puts everything else into perspective?

HERMAN: It's too long for that kind of // thing

JAVIER: It's a first stab —

ALVARO: Let's just do it

NERO: Let's do it!

Points to the toy box.

   That's the present?

VALERIE: Yes.

NERO: Anything inside?

VALERIE: It's a surprise …

ALVARO: Look, we're not staging it, we're just messing a//round

NERO: Alright! Let's do it!

The men get into position. Nero sits in one of the chairs. He covers one eye with his fist as if he's holding an ice pack. Javier hovers over him. While they play the scene, Valerie makes sketches of what she's seeing in a large drawing pad. Alvaro reads the stage directions:

ALVARO: Scene. D.L.'s study at *Seaward*. 1934. D.L., fifty-something stands over Daniel James, 23 who has an ice pack over his eye. The men are dressed casually — but expensively, as if they've just come from the Country Club. A low table sits between them, on top of which rests a large wrapped gift box.

VALERIE: What's Nero wearing?

HERMAN: He's "lobbying."

VALERIE: Lobbying? For what?

LINA: *Shhhhhhhhh.*

The men begin. They are skilled actors, but being a first read, their performances are slightly stilted. Even so, they are very committed to the scene's stakes.

D.L. (JAVIER): *(Hint of an accent — Javier's idea of what a Missourian from the '30s might sound like.)* How's the face?

DANIEL JAMES (NERO): *(Similar accent that doesn't fit quite comfortably yet.)* Aches.

D.L.: Got you good in the eye, huh?

DANIEL: Should have seen the
    Rageful look on that copper's face.

Herman makes a note. Javier senses it, but continues.

DANIEL: Like he wanted it to hurt.

D.L.: Billy club grand slam home run to your head.

DANIEL: Protest started out peaceful, Dad – police came in?
    Turned it into a war zone …

D.L.: Be thankful it wasn't worse, Dan.
    Could've lost an eye …

DANIEL: Plenty of others got it worse than me.

ALVARO: *(Making a note on the script.)* Hm.

D.L.: Anyhow …
    you're here now, safe – take your time to recuperate.

DANIEL: I'm thinking of going up to San Francisco

D.L.: Dan …

DANIEL: Tension's been building for months …
    ILA's gaining the upper hand, Longshoremen
    are gonna strike any day …
    They got the backing of the seamen
    They need support

Valerie whispers something in Herman's ear. He chuckles. Everyone notices, but pretends to ignore.

D.L.: You have no business trucking with them.

Herman makes a note in his script.

DANIEL: It *should* be everyone's business. Should be the whole *world's* business.

D.L.: Dan. No.

DANIEL: (*Pointing to the box on the table.*) What's in the box?

D.L.: All in good time.

>   Son ... you realize there are many ways to
>   make a meaningful contribution to the betterment of this world

DANIEL: Advancing the strikers' cause is one of them

D.L.: Perhaps

DANIEL: Hawking Limo-jes china to –

HERMAN: *Limoges*

DANIEL: *Limoges* – Hawking *Limoges* china to starving Okies is *not*.

D.L.: Wasn't for you – I understand.

>   Dan, I'm proud of you.
>   I've watched you since graduating Yale

Herman makes a note in his script. Sensed by everyone. Javier stops, turns to him.

JAVIER: Something you wanna say?

HERMAN: No ... // no.

JAVIER: I keep hearing that pencil of yours scratching away

HERMAN: Just sounds ...

>   Exposition-y?
>   Continue.

NERO: Where do you want to go from?

D.L.: Dan, I'm proud of you.

>   I've watched you since graduating Yale
>   trying on different suits for size –
>   discarding ones that don't fit,
>   retailoring ones that sort of fit
>   not being satisfied til you find the one that fits you like a glove.

I admire that ... I know your mother may not approve, but

you and me? We're kindred spirits

cut from a more complex cloth

than other members of this family.

You, me, we want more, we *need* more.

DANIEL: We have more than plenty. That's the problem –

D.L.: I don't mean *things,* Dan.

I mean more in the sense of *purpose.*

Hawking Limoges china door to door,

Not your idea of purpose, // I –

DANIEL: I felt like a darn fool, knocking on doors?

Half-starved people with their sallow, hungry faces

Should have seen the *looks* they gave me –

"What is this *boy* doing here?

Does he have any idea we're in the middle of a Depression?

I'm not in the market for *Limoges.*"

D.L.: Awkward times to sell luxury items.

Herman chuckles.

DANIEL: Awkward? It was *horrible.*

Ended up giving them my samples

So *they* could sell them ten cents a pop,

Put some food on their tables.

D.L.: You root for the underdog.

Long history of that in this family, Dan.

Proud you've inherited it.

Pause. Nero breaks character.

NERO: I have a thought ...

HERMAN: Let's hold thoughts for the end?

JAVIER: No, no – I wanna hear what you gotta say.

NERO: I was thinking,

>   This might be the right point to … ?
>   You know
>   *Introduce?* Jesse James?

HERMAN: Huh?

NERO: They're talking about family … inheritance …

VALERIE: May not be a bad // idea –

NERO: His grandfather was Jesse James' first cousin, for // God's sake

JAVIER: Let's just get through it –

NERO: Cool … I'm just saying – from?

ALVARO: "underdog"

D.L.: You root for the underdog –

>   Long history of that *in the James* family,
>   Proud that you inherited it.

>   That said –
>   All that fine china? Built *this*.

He gestures to indicate the surroundings.

DANIEL: I'm aware of that, and I'm not ungrateful.

D.L.: China salesman suit doesn't fit.

>   I understand.
>   You wanted something more,
>   Learn what it feels like to make a living –
>   Fantastic.
>   What do I do?
>   I make some calls. Land you work in the oil fields.

DANIEL: *Dad* –

D.L.: Again, I'm proud of you.

>   While your fellow Elis were off

on their post-graduation Grand Tours of Europe

You busted your rear-end in Oklahoma. Takes balls, Dan.

DANIEL: It was hard work.

D.L.: When I was your age?

Sure as hell wouldn't've got me

Working as a *swamper.*

ALVARO: What's a swamper?

HERMAN: Oil trucker's assistant

ALVARO: Bitch was slummin' it

HERMAN: "trucking" with the "truckers"

LINA: *Shhhhhhh*

D.L.: When I was your age?

Sure as hell wouldn't have gotten me

Working as a *swamper.*

Valerie cracks up.

VALERIE: Sorry …

DANIEL: I learned more in those six months

Than I ever did at Yale.

D.L.: Don't doubt it.

But I'd venture to guess *one* thing you learned:

it's next to impossible for a man to reinvent himself *down.*

DANIEL: What do you mean?

Javier rises as D.L. He seizes the moment for the forthcoming monologue.

D.L.: Whole country's founded on the idea, son

That a man can *reinvent* himself

Start with a pile of straw? Spin it into gold

ALVARO: Psss.

D.L.: Abe Lincoln. Poor kid from the Kentucky backwoods.

Reinvents himself? Becomes President.

Alvaro shakes his head through the rest.

My buddy Chaplin?
Orphan straight out of a Dickensian nightmare.
Crosses the Atlantic? Invents a new self?
He's the most famous man on earth.

Story never goes the opposite direction.
Never hear the likes of Rockefeller
Reinventing himself as a *swamper.*

Once you've got the Yale in you,
Can't ever rub it out.

VALERIE: *(To Herman.)* I love that line …

DANIEL: I know I can't ever *be* one of them.
But I can organize, educate, stand in solidarity –

D.L.: Get your face cracked open by a cop.

DANIEL: This is going nowhere –

He gets up.

D.L.: Dan, you are not excused. Sit down.

I recognize your passion.
But there are lines, Daniel.
Cross them? There's no going back.
Work in an oil field? Carmel's here for you
when you've had enough.

But jail. That's a no-no.

DANIEL: I'm sorry you had to bail me out.

D.L.: Part of me was envious. Takes balls to get yourself arrested.

Herman makes a note in the script. Mouths the words "takes balls" to Valerie, gestures "twice" with his fingers. Valerie cracks up.

D.L.: But you understand …

    Arrest … the implications …

    To this family …

NERO: See here it is again – opportunity …

    Jesse James.

HERMAN: Jesus …

NERO: It's like the whole reason he has to *become* Danny Santiago

    is cause Jesse James.

HERMAN: That's an interesting … *leap.*   ALVARO: Say what?

NERO: What leap? There's no leap.

    Next speech:

    "Half the family's changed their name.

    They would get a transfusion if they could –

    Rid themselves of that TAINTED blood.

    Though some of us, myself included, ARE GLAD TO HAVE THAT BLOOD RUNNINNG

    THROUGH OUR VEINS. I THINK YOU ARE ONE OF US."

    And I love the next part – let's read it:

D.L.: Don't think I didn't notice the games you played when you were a child.

DANIEL: What games?

D.L.: Re-enactments?

    Of certain criminal acts?

    Committed by those Sibling-Relations-Whose-Names-Must-Go-Unspoken?

NERO: Why do those names have to go unspoken?

HERMAN: Because they both know who they're talking about?

    If they say it, it'll sound exposition-y…

NERO: That would be a great opening scene,

    Little Danny – reenacting the Daviess County bank robbery.

ALVARO: I like that –   HERMAN: That was the first one—//

                                       right

Nero's struck by an idea.

NERO: Whoa.

JAVIER: What?

NERO: Did Jesse ever hide out in Mexico?

LINA: They used to do that, right? Outlaws hiding out in Mexico?

NERO: You could have this little kid,
    playing bank robber?
    And like a light could come up …
    There's Jesse
    behind a scrim
    wearing a sombrero –

ALVARO: Yeah, he could be like –
    (In an over the top "Mexican" accent – purposefully offensive.)
    "Oye, muchacho … der r too kines uff pee-pel een dees worl:
    Mejicanos an doz dat weesh
    Dey wer Mejicanos."

Javier cracks up.

HERMAN: Could we just please finish the scene –

NERO: Okay … I'm just saying. Jesse James.

Pause.

D.L.: Don't think I didn't notice the games you played when you were a child.

DANIEL: What games?

D.L.: The re-enactments?
    Certain criminal acts?
    Committed by those *Sibling-Relations-Whose-Names-Must-Go-Unspoken?*
    You were always a rebel.
    For family decorum sake,
    I kept you in check. But in my heart
    I wanted you to doubt.

To question. To see that
every coin?
Has two faces.

You can do more with what you *have*
than what you can do if you
let them take it all away from you.
Because they can. *They will.*

HERMAN: *(Whispering to Valerie.)* Who's they?

Valerie giggles. Alvaro crumples up a piece of paper, throws it at her.

DANIEL: What do you propose I do?

ALVARO: D.L. points to the gift on the table.

Javier does this as Alvaro reads — eye contact: "I'm doing it, why are you reading that?"

D.L.: Open it.

Daniel unwraps the box, revealing a 1934 Remington Noiseless Portable typewriter.

D.L.: She's a beauty, idd't she?

DANIEL: What's this for?

D.L.: Want to be useful?
　　You can go to San Francisco, get your head knocked in.
　　OR
　　you can bring San Francisco to the *world*. With *this*.

DANIEL: You've got to be kidding me.

D.L.: Why do you think I write plays?

DANIEL: Uhhh … to kill time?

Alvaro cracks up.

JAVIER: What?

ALVARO: Line's hilarious

D.L.: To change the world, transform the way people think

Alvaro can't help but crack up. He covers his mouth and tries to make a "serious" face.

DANIEL: Dad, your plays have never seen the light of day —

D.L.: One I'm working on will ... *(whispers)* ... It's about "the brothers"

DANIEL: You serious ...

D.L.: Show the world who they *really* were. Don't tell your Mother ...
> she's sensitive about that ...
> *episode* ...
> in the family's history ...

DANIEL: How close are you to finishing?

D.L.: Got act one sewed up ...
> Just gotta sort out acts two three four and five ...

He smiles. Daniel smiles.

D.L.: It's Shakespearean in scope.

They both laugh. A warm moment between father and son.

D.L.: Look: I'm just a dabbler.
> I love the company I built,
> feel of china on my fingers
> rush you feel when you close a deal ...
> I love knowing I can dream up a house like this,
> build it to my specifications —
> My play's never seen the light of day
> but the hole that leaves in me?
> Iddn't big enough that I need to fill it.

> But you son —
> you got fire,
> sense of mission,
> *resources* —
> *talent* —
> and you've got that thing

most men at the end of their lives realize they've squandered:

Time.

VALERIE: Love that …

DANIEL: I don't know the first thing about writing plays.

D.L.: I'll help you, Dan.

D.L.: You. Me. Twins. Co-writers.

DANIEL: You want to collaborate on a play.

D.L.: Everything that's happening in San Francisco
we'll capture right here — show the world what must be done.

DANIEL: I'm not sure I'm comfortable inheriting —

D.L.: Indulge your old man?
Who bailed you out of jail?

ALVARO: D.L. smiles his most disarming smile. Daniel lets out a deep exhale.

D.L.: That's my boy.

DANIEL: So when do we start?

D.L.: Tomorrow.

DANIEL: Tomorrow …

D.L.: "To-morrow, and to-morrow, and to-morrow,
Creeps in this petty pace from day to day,
To the last syllable of recorded time … "

Tomorrow. We'll start first thing.

Daniel gets up to go.

D.L.: I got us a good title.

DANIEL: Oh yeah?

D.L.: *Pier 17.*
Like the sound of it.
Muscular. Gritty.

DANIEL: Tomorrow.

   Dad?

D.L.: Yes, Dan?

DANIEL: Thanks.

D.L.: You bet, son.

Alvaro can't help himself from groaning. Daniel starts to leave.

D.L.: One more thing ...

   Steinbeck's swinging by for drinks tonight.

   Might be a good idea if you joined us.

ALVARO: Daniel nods, exits. Lights fade. Sounds of the Pacific Ocean crashing against the bluff. Blackout.

Half enthusiastic applause.

VALERIE: Beautiful ... really good start ...

   Right, Herman?

HERMAN: It's something. ...

Javier has curled up into a ball under a table. Nero goes straight to Lina where he gets the approval he needs.

VALERIE: Javi ... you okay, baby?

Dying animal groan from Javier.

ALVARO: Wanna know what I think?

Javier lowers his arms slightly — he wants to pay attention to this.

ALVARO: It's a little Hallmark for my tastes, bro.

NERO: You kidding me? That's primo father-son shit.

Javier sits up, focuses on Alvaro. This is painful for him, but his opinion matters.

VALERIE: Alvaro — why are you so mean —

ALVARO: I seen that a million times.

   Tired, pseudo-Freudian *mierda*.

"Son, I want you to be like me"

"Daddy! I don't want to be like you"

"Look, we're just like each other!"

"Thanks, son!"

"Thank *you,* Dad."

Cue the violins.

Cause the rich also cry, right?

Puro Hallmark.

HERMAN: It might actually make sense … I mean

If it's supposed to be a forgery of a lost Daniel James play

Most of what he wrote *was* crap —

Angry dying animal sound from Javi.

VALERIE: What do you want it to do, Javi?

Javi forces himself off the floor.

JAVIER: It's about inheriting something

That's gonna ruin your life …

ALVARO: Reads like they're gonna go play catch in the backyard

JAVIER: No. NonononononononoNO.

What I'm trying to get across —

He never wanted to be a writer,

But his father laid down this burden —

If he doesn't give in

Would he have inherited the house?

His father's desire to write?

His father's *failure* as a writer?

Would he have written *Famous All Over Town*?

It's like he sees his own future and all he can do

Is sigh … Sigh like he's

sighing out his soul —

NERO: Comes across to me …

ALVARO: Okay, Jesse James …

JAVIER: FUCK!
FUCKFUCKFUCKMEIRDACOÑOFUCKSHITPUTACOÑOMADRE!

The outburst stuns everyone. Silence.

NERO: I really think there's gotta be a scene with Jesse James.

Javier goes up to Alvaro — confrontational, nose to nose. Neither man is used to this.

JAVIER: You got something to show?

ALVARO: You getting up in my face?

JAVIER: You talk shit,
You got something to show?

ALVARO: Yeah, I got something to show.
Step back.

Javier holds his ground for a spell, steps back and sits. Alvaro distributes pages from a folder to everyone except for Javier.

ALVARO: Herman?
Stage directions?

HERMAN: Sure …

ALVARO: Lina?

She looks up from her magazine.

ALVARO: You're Anna Maria.

HERMAN: Who's Anna Maria?

ALVARO: Listen and learn.
Nero?

NERO: Yo.

ALVARO: Daniel James.

VALERIE: Who's playing Danny Santiago?

Alvaro and Javier make eye contact.

ALVARO: Me.

    Ready?

HERMAN: Scene One. 1984. Light up on Anna Maria, a woman in her 30s, surrounded
    by piles and piles of open letters.

*Lina, sits on the ground. Her performance is simple, focused and heartfelt. During the scene,
the visual landscape transforms slowly — as if the courtyard has become a theatre where the
play is being performed. This transformation is not a literal shift in time and space — rather
it's an imaginative leap the characters are taking — what they see in their mind's eye, like
the material is casting a spell on them.*

ANNA MARIA: I woke that Tuesday morning
    Had no idea I'd end the week with a shattered heart.

    Letter came in the mail.

    Familiar envelope

    paper, typeface ...

    Familiar smell of sea salt and pine ...

Javier tilts his head back and closes his eyes.

ANNA MARIA: I'd received dozens of letters from him
    Over thirteen years.

    Each one

    lit up a familiar

    giddiness inside me —

    reawakened a long lost teenage girl

    who finds a note

    from a secret admirer ...

    Heartbeat quickens

    Skin tingles ...

    Each letter

    I re-lived that first moment

    you entertain the thought,

    "maybe I am special ... "

HERMAN: Anna Maria picks up a letter.

ANNA MARIA: The letter that came on Tuesday had its

    familiar envelope,

    paper and typeface …

    sea salt and pine …

    But the familiar music of his voice …

    Absent.

HERMAN: A Young Man appears behind Anna Maria. She senses his presence. It is Danny Santiago. She opens the letter and reads.

Javier sighs. He's not liking this one bit.

DANNY SANTIAGO: Dearest Anna Maria.

    I want you to read this letter

    while the seas are still calm.

    In a few days time

    the surface will roil

    awakening a long dormant monster

ANNA MARIA: Danny always opened his letters with

    a little flirtation –

    He was so *bad.*

    First sentence …

    Something was wrong.

DANNY SANTIAGO: On the 16th, I ask you to purchase

    The New York Review of Books.

    In its pages you'll find an article by John Gregory Dunne –

    a biography. Of me.

    Or at least someone that bears a resemblance.

    Unearths all the secrets I kept from you all these years.

ANNA MARIA: "Unearths"

    Thirteen years

    Danny never used that word.

    "Secrets" – yes, there were secrets –

    Not mine –

When I open my heart?

It's wide open …

But he had secrets:

where he lived, where he was from,

what he did when he wasn't writing …

if he had a girl, a family, a life …

Never bothered me —

every man's got a whole world of secrets inside him,

no one's allowed to see.

DANNY SANTIAGO: Make sure you're sitting when you read it.

It will shock you. Shocks me.

Shock you feel when you sense a stranger

staring at you through a window at night

only to see

it's just a hazy reflection of yourself …

Javier looks up, glares at Alvaro.

JAVIER: Plagiarist …

Everyone is into the scene, so no one pays attention.

ANNA MARIA: For a long time

I figured

he was in jail …

or he was married …

But secrets so big?

They'd write an article in

The New York Review of Books?

Would it be something I couldn't stomach?

Did he kill someone?

Rape someone? Hurt a child?

I prayed to God …

Don't let that be his secret.

HERMAN: Daniel James appears behind Danny. Danny is aware of him, but not Anna Maria.

Nero follows the stage direction. At this point the world of the hotel courtyard has fully transformed into the imagined stage world of the scene.

DANNY SANTIAGO: I hope learning the truth

DANNY SANTIAGO/DANIEL JAMES: About the man typing these words,

DANIEL JAMES: You can still see me as I see you ... as whole ...

ANNA MARIA: Yours, Danny ...

HERMAN: She folds the letter and presses it against her heart.

ANNA MARIA: What do I do with this feeling
that's grown inside me for thirteen years ...
Do I have to hate a man I've grown to love?

HERMAN: Shift in time and place – thirteen years earlier, 1971. An imaginary landscape, somewhere between the world of *Famous All Over Town*, Daniel James' imagination, and bleak reality.

JAVIER: Ha! What does that mean?

VALERIE & HERMAN: Shhhh

HERMAN: Ruined street in East Los Angeles, outside the Aztec Club, a dive bar that's boarded up. Mounds of garbage – detritus from destroyed homes. Prominent in the pile: a red dress and crayons scattered, flecks of color in the dreariness –

JAVIER: You puto thief –

No one pays attention. Nero enacts the following.

HERMAN: An old man, Daniel James, appears, towing a red child's wagon piled with artifacts he's collected from the ruins. He's tall, gangly, dressed like a longshoreman from the '40s –

He finds a red crayon on the pile. On the boarded window he writes in big, curvy letters: Chato de Shamrock.

Nero, finding a marker on the table writes this on the wall.

JAVIER: Thief …

Alvaro stares at him.

HERMAN: Danny Santiago appears in jeans and a clean white t-shirt. Daniel James finds a broken picture frame – a family photo. He's a about to hang it when Danny makes the shape of a gun with his hand, points it at the old man.

DANNY SANTIAGO: BANG!

That's how your ancestor got it, right?

Jesse James?

Nero breaks character for a second and gives thumbs up to Alvaro.

DANIEL JAMES: Yeah, though …

St. Joseph, Missouri's a tad bit more bucolic than this place.

DANNY SANTIAGO: Why you always comin down here to steal shit, old man?

DANIEL JAMES: Can't call it stealing if it's just lying around discarded.

DANNY SANTIAGO: People might come back,

reclaim what they left behind.

DANIEL JAMES: Doubtful.

DANNY SANTIAGO: What are you gonna do with all of it?

DANIEL JAMES: I don't know …

recycle it, turn it into a book …

DANNY SANTIAGO: Know what I did today?

DANIEL JAMES: Lemme guess … jacked a car? Went for a joyride?

DANNY SANTIAGO: Yeah, you'd think that …

No, man … I went down to the PO Box

DANIEL JAMES: More rejection letters?

DANNY SANTIAGO: Fan letter.

DANIEL JAMES: Really …

DANNY SANTIAGO: From a woman

DANIEL JAMES: *Woman*

DANNY SANTIAGO: She musta sprayed perfume all over the pages –
    made me cross-eyed …

DANIEL JAMES: Lemme see it.

DANNY SANTIAGO: No, bro … letter's for my eyes only.

DANIEL JAMES: Who is this fan letter writing woman?

DANNY SANTIAGO: School teacher.
    Teaches ninth grade English at Garfield.
    Crazy shit? She's a sister, man
    from the *barrio*

    Feel sorry for her …

DANIEL JAMES: Why's that?

DANNY SANTIAGO: Freshman English at Garfield?
    Bet they talked in British accents where you went –
    Teachers quoting Shakespeare?
    Garfield? Man, b.s. they make you read,
    room full a kids that don't give a shit.

DANIEL JAMES: Hope she's not good-looking.

DANNY SANTIAGO: Why would you hope that?

DANIEL JAMES: Teenage boys –
    spend the whole class making movies in their heads
    about getting in her pants – so much for David Copperfield

DANNY SANTIAGO: More like David Cop a Feel

Daniel laughs.

DANIEL JAMES: I've seen teachers like that –
    watch too many Hollywood movies
    come in all idealistic, think that just by
    being there they'll make a difference

DANNY SANTIAGO: Cynical … She's gonna be different

DANIEL JAMES: How so?

DANNY SANTIAGO: She's a sister.
    She's got taste.

DANIEL JAMES: How do you know she has taste?

DANNY SANTIAGO: She wrote me.
    She reads that ladies' magazine

DANIEL JAMES: *Redbook?*
    She read the story?

DANNY SANTIAGO: Mmm hmmm …

DANIEL JAMES: Lemme see that letter.

DANNY SANTIAGO: Nah, man. So you could stick it in your wagon with your other
    piles a stolen shit?

DANIEL JAMES: I'm not gonna do that
    Read it to me at least … ?

HERMAN: Danny Santiago is struck by Daniel James's sudden vulnerability. He takes
    the letter from his pocket and opens it.

ANNA MARIA: I came across your story "The Somebody" in *Redbook*.
    I am very impressed by its vivid portrayal
    of *barrio* life through the eyes of a teen. This kind of material is
    painfully absent from the curriculum.

    I copied the story to share with my students – they loved it.
    It's a miracle – like they finally see themselves in what they read.
    Chato's become a hero to them

DANNY SANTIAGO: Think she's blowing smoke up my ass?

DANIEL JAMES: Sounds like the genuine article to me …

ANNA MARIA: For at least a few class sessions, your story rescued me
    from the dreaded non-response

a teacher always fears from her students …

They want more stories.

I want more —

Are there further Chato adventures you'd be willing to share?

Gratefully Yours …

DANNY SANTIAGO: Anna Maria Mayorga
English Department
Garfield High

Danny laughs. He's very proud of this achievement.

Putty. In My. *Hands.*

DANIEL JAMES: That's quite a letter …

DANNY SANTIAGO: Bet you never got one like that …

DANIEL JAMES: It's impolite to gloat.

DANNY SANTIAGO: I rescued her … I can gloat all I want.

DANIEL JAMES: You going to write her back?

DANNY SANTIAGO: Yeah …
I got a classroom full of fans.

DANIEL JAMES: What are you gonna tell her?

DANNY SANTIAGO: My mouth's gonna jump out the envelope,
kiss her right on the lips …

DANIEL JAMES: She'll ask you questions …

DANNY SANTIAGO: She can ask me anything she likes …

DANIEL JAMES: What'll you say if she asks where you live?
Pause.
If she asks for your phone number?
Pause.
What'll you say if she wants to meet you?

DANNY SANTIAGO: Enough, man

> I got answers …
> I got ways of keeping things mysterious …
> Women like that, right?

DANIEL JAMES: What about stories? You have more stories you can send her?

Danny Santiago looks at Daniel James seriously, vaguely threatening.

DANNY SANTIAGO: Yeah, I got stories,

> What? You don't think I got stories?

HERMAN: Daniel James goes to the pile, finds a half busted 1930s typewriter.

DANIEL JAMES: You'll need this.

HERMAN: He blows dust off it. Danny Santiago reaches for it, lights abruptly shift —

The group applauds, except Javier. "Nice work," "Not bad." etc. The world restores to the "normal" courtyard. After the collective congrats, everyone notices Javier's silence. They turn to him and await his reaction.

JAVIER: He wouldn't write like that.

VALERIE: Javi, don't be a prick —

JAVIER: It's confusing …

> Like watching one of those multiple personality movies —
> *Three Faces of Eve? Sybil?*
> Whatchya gonna call it —
> *Three Faces of Daniel James?*

HERMAN: I thought it played pretty good.

JAVIER: Only good stuff in there? You stole from me.

> He wouldn't write it like that.

Javi gets up, kicks over his chair, goes to one of the rooms. Door slam. Silence. Valerie looks at her watch.

VALERIE: Well … guess I should go pick up Pablo and Lila …

2. TESTIMONY

Kurtz's apartment. Kurtz and Alex on the couch. Alex sits with her legs folded under her, shoes off. Kurtz tries to manipulate an iPad he's using as a remote control to operate an unseen television. Take-out food containers, notebooks, library books, two bottles of wine (one empty, one half full). Cozy informality with more than a hint of flirtation.

ALEX: Index cards?

KURTZ: Thousands – I tried to get him to digitize but he was an old school technophobe.

ALEX: And the cards documented the lives of playwrights?

KURTZ: Playwrights no one's ever heard of.
 Slowik called them the "Ugh-Known Vitals."
 You must understand:
 Slowik never doubted the importance
 of O'Neill, Miller, Williams, Albee, Shepard, et cetera –
 But he set out to prove
 they owed their existence to playwrights
 written out of the "official" history

ALEX: Sounds like he was being ironic –

KURTZ: When you are shot down behind enemy lines
 and spend more than half the War in a
 Nazi prison camp … you rarely have time for irony.

 In any case,
 I did his research, dug up lost manuscripts,
 located ruined men, peeled them off bar stools to interview them …
 Most of the plays were garbage, BUT
 every now and then … gold.

ALEX: Like who?

KURTZ: Esther Fox?

ALEX: Never heard of her …

KURTZ: Serena Lowman, August Phelps, Henry Butterfield Ryan

ALEX: They don't ring a bell.

KURTZ: What about Alvaro Mendez? No? Javier C.? You've never heard of *Javier C.?*

Alex shrugs in non-recognition.

KURTZ: So sad …

ALEX: But all that work – that's how you …

KURTZ: Built my formidable reputation?

ALEX: Unearthing gold from the garbage …

KURTZ: In a sense …

ALEX: And he just … gave them to you?

KURTZ: Not exactly. We were preparing a book.
      The accident happened. He didn't make it.
      No one besides me was willing to carry on his work.

ALEX: And Daniel James was …

KURTZ: One of them, yes.
      But the last notation on his card
      was made in Slowik's hand in 1952.
      Just one play to go on:
      Winter Soldiers, Best Plays of 1942.

ALEX: Is it gold or garbage?

KURTZ: Unwashed recycling.

ALEX: Okay, then why the obsession with him?

KURTZ: I have reason to believe Daniel James wrote more –

ALEX: So is this the big, secret, mysterious project you want me to assist you on?

KURTZ: Not exactly.

ALEX: Or did you make that up to get me to come to your apartment?

KURTZ: Do you have any idea how to use this thing?

She takes the iPad away from him. She gets it working.

KURTZ: Ah! Watch:

Sounds from the television set. Low fidelity — a document from the 1950s.

CONGRESSMAN'S RECORDED VOICE: Mr. Daniel James?

Will you raise your right hand and be sworn?

Shift. While Kurtz and Alex watch, the world of the motel courtyard appears. The group reenacts the testimony. They're focused, committed to the material. Javier plays the Congressman, Nero plays Daniel James.

CONGRESSMAN: Do you solemnly swear to tell the truth and nothing but the truth, so help you God?

DANIEL JAMES: I do.

CONGRESSMAN: Mr. James, when and where were you born?

DANIEL JAMES: Kansas City, Missouri. January 1911.

CONGRESSMAN: What is your profession?

DANIEL JAMES: I'm a freelance writer.

CONGRESSMAN: What has been your record of employment?

DANIEL JAMES: First years out of Yale I was a traveling salesman, which I hope isn't too incriminating. I began writing in 1935. '38 I came to Hollywood, was employed in an independent studio as a sort of junior writer-assistant to a producer.

Kurtz laughs, pauses the video.

KURTZ: I love that. "Independent studio/junior writer-assistant to a producer."

ALEX: I don't get it ...

KURTZ: Who refers to United Artists and Charlie Chaplin that way?

He clicks play.

DANIEL JAMES: '42 I wrote a play, *Winter Soldiers*, which was produced in New York. I did a screenplay on it but it was shelved. I then worked with my wife on what turned out to be a Broadway musical. Since that period my
fortunes
have been rather bad.
Wrote a novel, couple of plays ... none were published or produced.

CONGRESSMAN: Mr. James, have you at any time been a member of the Communist Party?

DANIEL JAMES: I would like to answer that by saying

I am not a member of the Communist Party.

However, as to the second part of your question

I will stand on the fifth amendment and refuse to answer.

ALEX: Huh?

KURTZ: Right?

CONGRESSMAN: I asked you only one question, Mr. James.

When did you withdraw from the Communist Party?

DANIEL JAMES: I would have to decline, sir, on the same ground.

CONGRESSMAN: What ground?

DANIEL JAMES: That an American citizen, as I understand it, is not compelled to testify against himself in such a way as to be incriminated, prosecuted in – something. I am not a lawyer, sir. I think that should be sufficient.

ALEX: Awkward …

KURTZ: He's bombing …

CONGRESSMAN: Have you ever been a member of any Communist front organizations –

DANIEL JAMES: To the best of my knowledge, I am not. Nor am I sympathetic to communism. At the same time, I must decline to answer the question on the grounds stated.

CONGRESSMAN: Well, that's a strange answer.

You heard me ask witnesses whether or not they believe this committee serves an important function. What is your answer to that same question?

DANIEL JAMES: I think it is necessary for there to be an investigation of subversive organizations. At the same time, I am not sympathetic to communism nor am I sympathetic to this investigation.

In addition – this takes a considerable amount of courage,

though I expect no applause either from this committee,

nor from *The Daily Worker*.

This is a lonely position.

I assure you:

When I say I am not a Communist,

I am meaning it.

KURTZ: Watch: this is the kicker ...

Daniel James reaches into his pocket, removes an antique, small brown volume. He's hoping to make this a "moment."

DANIEL JAMES: I have in my pocket this little brown book. If you gentlemen would like to see it.

It's in French. First edition.

CONGRESSMAN: May I —

ALEX: What is he doing?

KURTZ: Watch ... Congressman takes the book ...

Looks at it ...

Congressman looks over the book, unmoved by the possibility of what's coming.

KURTZ: Hands it right back

Congressman hands the book back.

CONGRESSMAN: I realize you've come prepared to make a "speech,"

But I want to ask you, again —

ALEX: Wait. Pause that. What was that about?

Kurtz pauses it.

KURTZ: Brought a first edition

of Voltaire's *Candide*.

Borrowed from his father's library ...

ALEX: What? Why?

KURTZ: Voltaire published it under a pseudonym.

"Monsieur Le Docteur Ralph" —

Wanted to show if the Committee got its way

American writers would be forced to hide behind false names ...

James' way of going for the jugular ...

ALEX: What a kick in the gut ...

KURTZ: He was no Dalton Trumbo ...

Alex's phone goes off. Incoming text. She reads it. Frustration.

KURTZ: What is it?

ALEX: I have to go.

KURTZ: So soon?

ALEX: Trish. My roommate. Locked herself out of the apartment.

KURTZ: One more, before you go ... ?

He pours her a glass of wine.

ALEX: Sure.

KURTZ: Watch ... end the evening on a comic note.

He clicks play. As before, what begins as a recording becomes a full blown re-enactment in the motel. Valerie plays Lilith.

CONGRESSMAN'S RECORDED VOICE: Will you state that again?

LILITH'S RECORDED VOICE: Lilith James. –

In the courtyard.

CONGRESSMAN: In what profession are you engaged?

LILITH: I am a writer-housewife.

CONGRESSMAN: How long have you been writing?

LILITH: My first writing was on a Broadway musical, *Bloomer Girl*, in 1944.

CONGRESSMAN: Are there some ...

little Jameses?

LILITH: There is a little James and a big James.

CONGRESSMAN: I take it then you are not writing much now ...

LILITH: I still write.

CONGRESSMAN: Have you ever been a member of the Communist Party?

LILITH: I am not a Communist, but I decline to answer your questions on Fifth Amendment grounds.

CONGRESSMAN: When did you leave the Communist Party?

LILITH: I never said I was a Communist.

CONGRESSMAN: Were you a member of the Communist Party before these hearings began? Say, this past Sunday?

LILITH: I decline on the same grounds.

CONGRESSMAN: On Monday? Tuesday?

LILITH: I decline —

CONGRESSMAN: What about when you entered this room today?

LILITH: No I was not.

CONGRESSMAN: I have no further questions.

Kurtz clicks the recording off. Alex is strangely affected by it.

KURTZ: What's the matter?

ALEX: I really have to go …

She gathers her things. As she moves to exit, Kurtz removes a large cardboard box from behind the couch, puts it on the coffee table. The sound stops Alex. She turns.

ALEX: What's that?

KURTZ: Open it.

ALEX: Does it have to do with the big, mysterious project you keep dangling like a carrot?

Kurtz shrugs. Alex moves to the box. She's about to open it, Kurtz touches her hand.

KURTZ: So it's clear: you open the box, there's no closing it.

She moves his hand away and opens the box. She removes a couple of old manuscripts.

ALEX: *Death of a Liberal* by Javier C.? *The Rich Also Cry.* Javier C.

She looks at him puzzled. She removes another item from the box — a rolled up poster of Charlie Chaplin's The Great Dictator. *Another puzzled look. She removes what appears to be a full head mask of a Godzilla-like creature. More puzzlement. Last, she pulls out an identical typewriter to the one D.L. gifted Daniel James.*

ALEX: What is all this?

KURTZ: Don't you have to go rescue your friend – Trish? Is that her name?

ALEX: Trish can wait …

KURTZ: Will you help me?

They stare at each other for a long time. Kurtz puts on the Godzilla-like mask. Unclear who initiates it, but the two fall into a sexual embrace.

3. MONTAGE

Hotel courtyard. The group is spread out across two tables. Javier, Herman and Alvaro are at one table combing over stacks of paper trying to determine a scene order.

The other table is covered in different colored fabrics, drawings and a sewing machine. Lina stands wearing a Gorgo costume, while Valerie makes adjustments to the fabric.

Nero sits sunbathing in his underwear. Valerie eats a nacho dipped in salsa.

VALERIE: Awesome sauce.

HERMAN: —beginning's always a
    good place to start

VALERIE: You look fantastic.

LINA: I don't look ridiculous?

JAVIER: But what beginning —
    We got like seventy-two years of
    Beginnings—not to mention
    Beginnings, like *deep* beginnings

VALERIE: You look *amazing.* Is it too
tight around the neck?

NERO: What about that massacre?
    What was it? Centralia Massacre?

LINA: No, it's fine.

ALVARO: Enough with Jesse James!

HERMAN: HUAC's as good a place as
    any to start —

Javier throws his pencil down.

Valerie steps back.

JAVIER: NO!

VALERIE: Wave your arms around like
    you're on the rampage.

Lina does so, making Gorgo-like sounds.

HERMAN: Why not? It's inherently dramatic
    We don't even have to write anything
    Type up the transcript
    Presto, a first act

VALERIE: Feel like you can move?

JAVIER: Boring!

LINA: Perfect.

HERMAN: Total destruction of lives? Friendships? Careers? Explain how that's boring ...

JAVIER: Too obvious!

Herman throws a pile of papers in the air.

VALERIE: Fantastic ...

  I'm gonna take some photos

  Maybe you can strike some poses ...

Valerie finds a camera. Lina puts on Gorgo's head and goes to Nero—stalking him like a monster, growling. He laughs. She straddles him. They kiss. Valerie snaps a photo.

Throughout the following "photo shoot," Lina strikes poses for Valerie. Some are "monster-like," while others mock "sexy." The women and Nero enjoy this immensely.

ALVARO: Might give it, you know, a sense of scope? World-historic importance?

JAVIER: Why do you have to say shit like that?

ALVARO: What'd I say? I'm making a // sugg

JAVIER: Like you think I'm some pompous ass who thinks about shit like "world-historical // imp —

ALVARO: You do think about shit like that, and, yeah, Javi, you are a pompous ass

Javier flips. He lunges over the table and physically attacks Alvaro. Neither is a skilled fighter — more elementary school playground fisticuffs than anything. They roll on the ground punching, wrestling each other.

HERMAN: Whoa! Whoa whoa // whoa whoa ...

VALERIE: Javi!   NERO: Jesus.

Lina cracks up, while everyone tries to peel the men apart. Lina pretends she's Gorgo, knocking furniture over, throwing paper, empty drink bottles, fabric around. She roars wildly, having a grand old time. The fight between the men, and the struggle to peel them apart ... well ... just kind of fizzles out. They all notice Lina going nuts as Gorgo — at first they're puzzled, but then they start cracking up. The laughter becomes maniacal — some of them are literally rolling on the floor.

353

Lights shift, and suddenly, as before, we are inside the world of their play. We will stay in this world through the end — as we go deeper into it, the performers become so engrossed in the story that we, the audience, forget we're watching a play-within-a-play.

VALERIE: *(Reading stage direction.)* Sound of ocean waves transitions us to:

> Office of a Theatrical Producer in New York City, 1936. Daniel James, 25, sits across from a no-nonsense man in his 60s.

Nero, as Daniel, and Herman, as producer, perform the scene. Nero/Daniel wears a wool red and black plaid hunting jacket. He wears it through the remaining scenes. They do not have scripts this time — they are fully committed to the performance.

PRODUCER: Who's your father?

DANIEL: D.L. James.

PRODUCER: D.L.? That stand for —? Any//thing?

DANIEL: Funny story actually …

> His parents gave him initials when he was born
> Thinking when he was old enough
> He'd choose his own name
> D.L. just kind of stuck …

PRODUCER: What's he written?

DANIEL: Plays, mostly

> West coast productions, Midwest
> Hasn't really
> *Broken*
> In New York …

> He's working on a play about Jesse James

PRODUCER: You don't say

DANIEL: It's quite the epic.

> Kind of an
> American *Macbeth*
> Grapples with whether Jesse
> Was a sinner or sinned against.

PRODUCER: Man was a racist, cold-blooded killer.

DANIEL JAMES: We're related to him …

Awkward pause.

DANIEL JAMES: So have you … ?

PRODUCER: Yes. *Pier 17.*
   Which you and your father

DANIEL JAMES: Co-authored, yes.
   We wanted to uhhh
   Render *dramatically* the
   Human cost of the labor struggle
   On a *working* family, working *immigrant* family

PRODUCER: Yes, I got that –

DANIEL JAMES: Based on a true story –
   San Francisco longshoremen's strike couple of years back

PRODUCER: Eight-year-old kid got shot by the National Guard?

DANIEL JAMES: Not exactly – uhhh – dramatic license, sharpen the uh
   Impact

PRODUCER: Dead kid's'll do that …

Awkward pause.

PRODUCER: How much of this play is yours, how much your father's?
   Ballpark.

DANIEL JAMES: 70 percent mine? 20 percent his? Other 10 … ?
   We were made to understand you're one of the
   Producers in town who
   Believes in using the stage
   To
   Wrestle
   With the great issues of our time.

PRODUCER: I'm all for "issues."

> But.
>
> Reality is …
>
> A theater is a very large room.
>
> Filled with empty seats.
>
> Facing a big, empty platform.
>
> It's basically a useless piece of architecture
>
> Sitting on squandered real estate –
>
> *Unless* there are human *buttocks*
>
> *in* those seats.
>
> Now: it's more sorcery than science,
>
> But to get butts *in* those seats
>
> You gotta figure out
>
> What to put on that empty platform.
>
> If that something has redeeming social value,
>
> Icing on the cake.
>
> But when you've done this as long as I have –
>
> You know what NOT to put up there.

DANIEL JAMES: Does that mean … ?

PRODUCER: Look:

> You seem like a really nice kid.
>
> But this writing business?
>
> Not for everyone.
>
> You're lucky. You're young.
>
> You have what most men at the end of their lives realize they've squandered …
>
> *Time.*
>
> Do something else with your life …

ALVARO: Shift in time and space: 1948, the Brentwood, Los Angeles home of Daniel James and his wife, Lilith.

Nero as Daniel, and Lilith, played by Valerie.

LILITH: They're coming from New York?

DANIEL JAMES: That's right.

LILITH: They want to do it *here?* In our *house?*
   Tell them NO.

DANIEL JAMES: Can't say no to them.

LILITH: Why not? You want that on your head?
   Watch the Comintern hang Maltz by his toes.
   In our *living room.*

DANIEL JAMES: He's the best writer in the Party.
   They can't afford to hang him.

LILITH: You read *The Daily Worker* rebuttal to his editorial –
   They're out for blood.

DANIEL JAMES: They just want to sit him down, have a conversation –

LILITH: This isn't going to be a conversation, Dan.
   It's going to be a lynching. Make him
   An example to anyone who doesn't toe the Party line –
   We're opening our home to facilitate that?

DANIEL JAMES: That upsets you

LILITH: Of course it upsets me – it doesn't upset you?

DANIEL JAMES: He'll recant, the whole thing'll blow over.

LILITH: Is that what you think he ought to do? Recant?

DANIEL JAMES: It's not what I think, what the Party thinks is what matters

LILITH: You. What do *you*. Think.

DANIEL JAMES: Maltz is a good man.
   But repudiating the idea
   That art is a weapon
   In the cause –

LILITH: That's *not* what he said –

DANIEL JAMES: Lilith –

LILITH: No! No. He said

> We've been straitjacketed into believing
> That serving the cause is art's *sole* purpose.
> With every contradictory directive
> Sent down from the Party heads,
> It's impossible to finish *anything* –
> It's impossible to write anything true …

DANIEL JAMES: I know what he said, Lilith.

LILITH: Then where's your outrage?

> Why won't you stand up, say NO!
> You may not stage a lynching in my home.

DANIEL JAMES: You're saying I'm in a straitjacket –

LILITH: Yes. And you know it's true.

Pause.

DANIEL JAMES: Yes, Lilith. We're all wearing straitjackets.

> BUT. If everyone took Maltz's position …

Pause.

LILITH: I'm waiting, Dan.

DANIEL JAMES: It'd be every man for himself.

> That would be the end of the Party.
> End of the whole movement.

LILITH: You actually believe that horseshit.

DANIEL JAMES: Lilith … I can't not believe it. Without it, what do I have?

> I have NOTHING. I *am* nothing.

LILITH: They didn't put you in a straitjacket.

> Straitjacket *you're* wearing is entirely of your own creation.
> You love it. Because it gives you the perfect excuse to do nothing.

HERMAN: *(Performing text of stage direction.)* Shift … 1971. Danny Santiago replies to
Anna Maria's first letter.

Shift. Danny Santiago. Daniel James hovers behind him.

DANNY SANTIAGO: Dear Anna Maria –

> My agent forwarded me your letter
> Was like an early Christmas present ...

> You'll be happy to know
> I got lots of Chato stories ...
> Even playing with stringing them together
> Some day make a novel out of them ... .
> Knowing I got a school teacher
> Plus a class full of fans
> Might motivate me to put em down.

> I'm sending you skeletons of a few chapters
> Maybe you'll write me back ... ?
> Tell me what you think?
> Maybe share them with the kids
> Tell me what *they think* ... ?

ANNA MARIA: Dear Danny –

> I love the chapters you sent –
> Hope it's not too forward of me, but
> I'm sending you notes –
> Places where we could fix the grammar
> Clarify the storytelling –

DANNY SANTIAGO: Listen to you, Miss English Teacher

ANNA MARIA: Am I crossing a line?

DANNY SANTIAGO: No ... I like having you as my teacher.
> What did the kids think?

ANNA MARIA: They went crazy for them ... said it was like looking in a mirror
> They had lots of ideas, suggestions, which I'm also forwarding ...

DANNY SANTIAGO: How'd I get so lucky to find a little angel like you?

ANNA MARIA: So … you're up in Salinas? You ever get to LA?

My students would get a kick out of meeting a real life author …

So might a certain English teacher –

DANNY SANTIAGO: I'm always on the move, maybe some day

ANNA MARIA: I'm enclosing a few of the "must-read" books I wrote you about

Melville, Virginia Woolf, Steinbeck … inspiration for the inspired.

VALERIE: Sound of ocean waves crashing against a bluff transitions us to: 1983.

HERMAN: Night. *Seaward*. Daniel James' study – the room where many years earlier

Daniel inherited his father's typewriter.

VALERIE: Daniel James, now 73, chats with his friend John Gregory Dunne, 52.

Nero as Daniel James and John Gregory Dunne, played by Javier.

DANIEL JAMES: They need a bio, John.

DUNNE: Who needs a bio?

DANIEL JAMES: The committee.

DUNNE: What committee is that, Dan?

DANIEL JAMES: THE committee. *Pulitzer* committee.

DUNNE: Fuck.

Schuster's submitting it?

DANIEL JAMES: They need a bio and a *photograph*.

Otherwise they won't consider it.

DUNNE: Well there's your answer …

Shame on the one hand, but

Take it as vindication.

DANIEL JAMES: How's Joan?

DUNNE: She's well –

DANIEL JAMES: And Quintana Roo? She must be quite the young lady now …

DUNNE: Dan, you're not thinking …

DANIEL JAMES: Course it's impossible — but amusing isn't it?

>To entertain all kinds of hypotheticals?

>Hypothetically, a bio could ... *surface*

DUNNE: Why do I get the feeling this

>"hypothetical" bio's already been written?

DANIEL JAMES: It's the photograph that's the pain in the ass —

DUNNE: Why don't you get one of your

>Charity youth club kids

>To loan you one?

DANIEL JAMES: Not a bad idea ...

DUNNE: I'm joking. That was a joke, Dan.

DANIEL JAMES: Oh, I'm *teasing* John.

>Indulge a crotchety old man.

>If you lived my history,

>I'd forgive you entertaining multiple "what ifs" ...

>Might make for a nice third act twist to a pretty glum movie.

DUNNE: I'm appalled.

DANIEL JAMES: You weren't appalled when you sent Danny's first story to Carl.

DUNNE: I never thought —

DANIEL JAMES: They were publishable?

DUNNE: I never would have sent them to Carl if I didn't think they were good.

>Look, I told you I was uncomfortable about the pseudonym business *then* —

DANIEL JAMES: Then why'd you do it?

DUNNE: One, I thought the stories had a chance.

>Two? When Joan and me were starting out? You were good to us.

>At that point I was in a position I could return your kindness.

DANIEL JAMES: Hm. But the possibility of a Pulitzer makes you uncomfortable.

>I respect your discomfort, John.

>If I were in your shoes, I might feel a little on edge ...

DUNNE: What are you getting at?

DANIEL JAMES: You wrote under a pseudonym yourself // so you

DUNNE: *Once.*

DANIEL JAMES: Kill a man once, you're always a killer.

DUNNE: Look: you're not gonna win.

DANIEL JAMES: Ouch.

DUNNE: There might exist an alternate universe where you DO win –
　　You realize how fucked you'd be?

DANIEL JAMES: Jack Kennedy won the Pulitzer.

DUNNE: What does that have to do with anything?

DANIEL JAMES: He didn't write a word of that book.

DUNNE: Look: they want to submit it.
　　Isn't that vindication enough?

DANIEL JAMES: I suppose in the way that
　　Seeing your hazy reflection in a window
　　Is vindication that you exist in the world …

DUNNE: Promise me you won't do this –

DANIEL JAMES: Don't worry, Johnny-boy, I won't.
　　Relieved?

Pause.

　　Wouldn't that be something?
　　To have that? Relief?

Silence.

　　Maybe in the next life.

VALERIE: Shift. Danny and Anna Maria, Late 1970s.

HERMAN: A decade into their correspondence. Yet, they have never met in person.
　　However, their intimacy has deepened to the point they inhabit the same space.

Shift. Danny and Anna Maria.

DANNY SANTIAGO: Five, six, seven, eight rejection letters ...

ANNA MARIA: I am *so* sorry Danny

DANNY SANTIAGO: Should have known no one would care –
    Story of my life –

ANNA MARIA: I care. My students care.

DANNY SANTIAGO: I feel like I disappointed you –
    All that time you put in? Helping me finish?

ANNA MARIA: Disappointed?
    Danny: I'm *proud* of you ...
    It's a beautiful book. Some day
    Every publisher will realize the mistake they made
    It's going to happen, Danny.
    You deserve it.

HERMAN: Shift. Outside the Aztec Club – the ruins of Chato's neighborhood. 1983.

VALERIE: Danny Santiago throws rocks at the wall. Daniel James appears reading a
    newspaper.

DANIEL JAMES: Ouch.

DANNY SANTIAGO: What?

DANIEL JAMES: *San Francisco Chronicle*.
    " ... Santiago's novel will seem just a gallery of stereotypical Mexican characters –

DANNY SANTIAGO: Whoa ...

DANIEL JAMES: "The drunken Mexican macho father who beats up
    his wife and abandons his family –

DANNY SANTIAGO: That shit happens.

DANIEL JAMES: "The ever suffering wife who returns to Mexico with her youngest
    child;

DANNY SANTIAGO: Again, known to happen.

363

DANIEL JAMES: "The perplexed son who becomes a gang member to feel wanted … "

DANNY SANTIAGO: We should find him. Beat his ass.

    What does he know …

DANIEL JAMES: Name's worrisome.

    Arturo Islas.

DANNY SANTIAGO: He's probably Cuban.

DANIEL JAMES: He's Chicano.

    Says here in his bio.

    Stanford University. "First Chicano in the US to earn a PhD in English Lit."

DANNY SANTIAGO: He's one of *those* Chicanos.

DANIEL JAMES: What do you mean?

DANNY SANTIAGO: All uppity cause he got fancy degrees.

DANIEL JAMES: All the other reviews have been good –

    Bad review in the *Chronicle* won't do much damage.

DANNY SANTIAGO: It's the principle …

    Where does he get off

    Taking another brother down?

DANIEL JAMES: Best to leave it.

DANNY SANTIAGO: How can you say that?

    That's your problem –

    You let the world walk all over you

    Fifty years a that shit,

    Ain't you sick of it?

Silence.

DANNY SANTIAGO: Fine. Sit there

    Like a dog used to getting his ass beat –

    But not me, nah uh.

Danny finds the typewriter.

DANIEL JAMES: What are you doing?

DANNY SANTIAGO: "Dear Mr. Arturo 'Uppity PhD' Islas –

    I would love for you to come up here

    say the shit you wrote in your so called 'review' to my // face –

DANIEL JAMES: Danny …

DANNY SANTIAGO: What?!?!

DANIEL JAMES: Reason. *Eloquence.*

    Harsh language – will only blow up in your face.

DANNY SANTIAGO: This dude is blowing up in my face.

DANIEL JAMES: Some people's agendas are for

    Things to be "uplifting" at all costs

DANNY SANTIAGO: So if I lied, said his Papa

    Was a CPA instead of a mean drunk?

    Think he'd be cool with that?

DANIEL JAMES: Why don't you ask him?

DANNY SANTIAGO: Alright …

    "Dear Mr. Islas,

    I read your review of my book, and it pissed me off –

DANIEL JAMES: How about …

    "Dear Mr. Islas,

    It was with considerable puzzlement and dismay that I read your review" –

DANNY SANTIAGO: "Puzzlement," "dismay" – I like that

DANIEL JAMES: "Why do I take the trouble to write to you?

    Not because yours is the only truly negative review –

    My beef is against the 'stereotypical' way certain people

    Insist Mexicans should only be shown as

    Dentists and CPAs."

DANNY SANTIAGO: That don't sound like me.

DANIEL JAMES: You gotta show you can match wits with him.

DANNY SANTIAGO: Okay – I got it:

"You will be surprised to see what happens in the sequels."

Daniel turns inward.

DANNY SANTIAGO: "There will be five novels in all –

That's a project no writer would undertake

If he has only a bunch of 'pathetic figures' –

As you say in your review –

To write about."

Danny notices Daniel looking morose.

DANNY SANTIAGO: What's the matter?

We got sequels planned, right? *Right?*

DANIEL JAMES: Right.

DANNY SANTIAGO: *(Typing.)* "Saludos,

Danny Santiago."

Danny takes the paper out of the spool, folds it, and puts it in an envelope.

DANIEL JAMES: May not be the best idea to send that.

DANNY SANTIAGO: I'm sending it.

LINA: Sounds of waves crashing transition us to: Seaward, 1984.

HERMAN: Night. Daniel James' study.

LINA: Daniel James, his wife Lilith and John Gregory Dunne, six months later …

DUNNE: *New York Review of Books* asked me to review it.

DANIEL JAMES: Talk about serendipity. Surprised it got their attention.

DUNNE: After the Rosenthal Prize fiasco

DANIEL JAMES: Wasn't the first time

Writer doesn't show to

Pick up an award.

DUNNE: It's raised ... doubt. In certain circles.

You understand the pickle I'm in ...

DANIEL JAMES: What are you asking

DUNNE: I could turn them down.

I could review it as I'd review any other book ...
Or I could tell the truth.

LILITH: Tell the "truth"

Funny that's an option unto itself.

DUNNE: What are you getting at?

LILITH: Would there be no truth in turning it down?

Reviewing it as you would any other book?

DUNNE: I'm not here to play rhetorical games.

LILITH: Neither am I.

DANIEL JAMES: You're your own man.

You're faced with a crisis.

Decision is yours and only yours to make.

DUNNE: Are you just saying that?

DANIEL JAMES: It's not an abstraction to me, John.

You know, once upon a time
I picked up my daughter
From a friend's house.
Girl's father was also a writer.
Named names. Made some pretty good pictures.
On the way home
She ranted and raved, what an awful man he was.
Called him a rat.
Hearing this sweet kid say that ...
Last person on earth
Who deserved to inherit grudges from the past ...

I pulled the car over,

Told her, "Sweetie …

We have no right to judge someone

Forced into a tougher decision than we had to make."

DUNNE: This is a chance to set the record straight.

Tell the whole story –

LILITH JAMES: Including your participation in it.

DUNNE: Including my participation.

DANIEL JAMES: Why the crisis of conscience now?

DUNNE: The Rosenthal Award bothers me, Dan.

If all this comes out in an uncontrolled way

They're gonna come after you.

You think you've been living in a grave all these years?

They will dig you out of that one, Dan

Just so they can bury you in another one.

They won't give a shit

You got a nice review in the *Times*.

DANIEL JAMES: Nice? I'd say it was a // rave

DUNNE: Look:

Hundreds of novels come out each year

Most collect dust on bookstore shelves

None of those books

Get the attention of

The Academy of Arts and Letters.

It's a *major*. Award.

People that dole out those sorts of things

Live inside very exclusive rooms.

They protect

Who they let in, keep out.

Danny Santiago?

They've gone out on a limb

To admit someone of *dubious* pedigree.

They expect him to *thank* them on his knees.

When he doesn't show?

"How dare a half-literate *cockroach*

snub us."

Daniel laughs.

DANIEL JAMES: I didn't need the five grand —

DUNNE: You didn't show because you're ashamed.

LILITH: How dare you?

We put years of our time serving those people.

They welcomed us, made us part of their community.

Dan had every right to write about it.

Show him the letters.

DANIEL JAMES: Lilith ...

LILITH: Show him, Dan.

Daniel rises and retrieves a thick bundle of letters. He drops it on Dunne's lap.

DUNNE: What's this.

DANIEL JAMES: Letters. Thirteen years of them.

First one? 1971.

Twenty-two-year-old schoolteacher in East L.A.

Writes to *thank* me.

For telling a story her kids could relate to.

Kids that see only three future options —

Getting mowed down on the mean streets,

Getting mowed down in Vietnam,

Getting mowed down in prison.

Kids that have no idea

Their miserable lives are worthy of being chronicled anywhere

Let alone in the pages of a book

That *thing* happens, John.
Interest. Possibility.
For a moment
Class becomes a class,
Teacher *teaches,*
Students *learn.*

DUNNE: She wrote you for thirteen years?

DANIEL JAMES: That's right.

DUNNE: You wrote to her as Danny … ?
Lilith, you knew … ?
Wow. That's fucked.

DANIEL JAMES: Sometimes you have to deceive a little to serve a more essential truth.

DUNNE: "Essential truth … "
Didn't know "truth" needed any adjectives to make it more of what it is.

Silence.

DUNNE: You know what, Dan? Lilith?
I don't give a shit about truth.
If you're honest with yourself, Dan,
Neither do you.

What we *do* care about
Is a good story.
We're the same that way.
Good story trumps everything.
Friends, spouses, family, country.
Mexican women who write you fan letters.
Your own damned *self.*

We're writers.
Not every day a story this good falls in your lap.

I can do it with or without your cooperation.
Either way it's good.

But it could be a knockout if you help me.

Get the whole picture right.

DANIEL JAMES: By "whole picture" you mean …

DUNNE: Everything.

Danny.

East L.A.

Monster movies.

HUAC.

The Party.

Chaplin.

This house.

Your father.

Jesse James.

School teacher groupies —

DANIEL JAMES: You leave her name out of this.

DUNNE: Okay …

This is an American story, Dan.

DANIEL JAMES: Call it *Citizen Santiago*.

LILIITH: It's taken years to put it all behind us.

You want to destroy us all over again?

You want our permission to name our names?

DUNNE: I'm not HUAC, Lilith.

DANIEL JAMES: Fifty years, John.

Couldn't find an honest word.

Danny shows up,

Stranger peering through a window at night.

He gives me honest words.

I'm more *me,* more *free* as him

Than I ever was writing as myself.

DUNNE: Everyone's looking for some whiz kid to throw accolades at

While you're alone up here, in the house your father built?

You can finally get the recognition I know you crave in your heart.

DANIEL JAMES: It's gonna kill him.

DUNNE: You don't have to stop writing as him.

DANIEL JAMES: It's gonna kill him.

DUNNE: He's not real.

DANIEL JAMES: It's gonna kill him.

VALERIE: Shift. 1984. Sounds of a monster from a 1950s B Movie. Danny Santiago, Daniel James, Anna Maria.

DANNY SANTIAGO: I ask that you purchase a copy of *The New York Review of Books.*

ANNA MARIA: Every man's got a whole world of secrets inside him — no one's allowed to see

DANNY SANTIAGO/DANIEL JAMES: It will shock you.

ANNA MARIA: Did he kill someone? Hurt a child?

Don't let that be his secret.

VALEIRE: Shift. 1985. Living room of Anna Maria's modest Los Angeles home.

HERMAN: Daniel James face to face with Anna Maria for the first and only time.

Danny Santiago hovers in the background, silenced.

DANIEL JAMES: Am I anything like you expected?

ANNA MARIA: No. Am I?

DANIEL JAMES: Pictured you different. But now I see you …

Danny was right to feel what he felt for you.

ANNA MARIA: I sent you books by Steinbeck. You broke bread with him.

DANIEL JAMES: Ironic, isn't it.

Can you forgive me?

ANNA MARIA: My mother always told me forgiveness is everything.

I think you belong in my "Men Behaving Badly" file …

VALERIE: Shift. May 18, 1988. The Death of Daniel James.

HERMAN: Ruined Street in East L.A. Old Daniel James writes in crayon on the wall: "Chato de Shamrock". He finds a family photo, tries to hang it on the wall. Danny Santiago appears, carrying a gun. Points it at the Old Man.

JAVIER: Wait …

Nero, can I have a crack at this?

Nero turns, looks at Javier, puzzled.

JAVIER: Just this one time, Nero … I promise.

Nero removes the wool hunting jacket and exchanges it with Javier. Nero steps away, Javier puts on the jacket, assuming the role of Daniel James. He and Alvaro stare at each other.

DANNY SANTIAGO: BANG!

That how it went down? With your famous ancestor?

DANIEL JAMES: Yep. Though St. Joseph, Missouri's

Tad bit more bucolic than this place.

DANNY SANTIAGO: Hear he's got a plaque there.

Think they'll hang a plaque for you on this wall?

DANIEL JAMES: Nah.

Taking a stroll down memory lane?

DANNY SANTIAGO: Not much left to remember

They murdered this place.

DANIEL JAMES: How's your mother?

DANNY SANTIAGO: Back in Mexico. With the baby.

DANIEL JAMES: Your sister?

DANNY SANTIAGO: Married that Mexican Romeo.

She put on the inevitable few pounds.

He's growing the inevitable bald spot.

DANIEL JAMES: Your father?

DANNY SANTIAGO: Who?

DANIEL JAMES: That bad, huh?

DANNY SANTIAGO: Don't care where he is.

> Got stuck in his own straitjacket …

DANIEL JAMES: What about you?

DANNY SANTIAGO: Between places …

> Waiting. For the next chapter.
> Got all this anticipation built up …
> *For the next chapter.*

They stare at each other.

DANIEL JAMES: I know …

DANNY SANTIAGO: That something you gonna help me out with?

DANIEL JAMES: Can't.

DANNY SANTIAGO: But I heard you got *Famous All Over Town*.

DANIEL JAMES: I knew a man once.

> Was accused of a crime.
> He knew it was his right to say nothing.
> Still, judge found him guilty. Sentence?
> Took half the alphabet from him for 20 years

DANNY SANTIAGO: That's cruel and unusual

DANIEL JAMES: Worst part, he only got one vowel. A "u."

> Even the word "I" was off limits to him.
> Twenty years trying to put words together,
> Could only make growling sounds,
> Like some monster under the sea.
>
> Twenty years later,
> He got all his letters back.

DANNY SANTIAGO: What'd he do with them?

DANIEL JAMES: Like you said. He got famous.

> But the price …

> Had to give up the whole alphabet.

DANNY SANTIAGO: Sad story.

DANIEL JAMES: Would you really pull that trigger?

DANNY SANTIAGO: Maybe.

> Would you kill me if you could?

DANIEL JAMES: I'd give up everything to keep you alive.

DANNY SANTIAGO: Yeah?

DANIEL JAMES: That's not up to me anymore.

> Man only gets a finite number of names in his life.

> Once they're used up, poof …

> I don't have any names left.

DANNY SANTIAGO: What about me? Don't I got names left?

Daniel James shrugs, he turns to go.

DANNY SANTIAGO: What about *me?* You listening old man?

> *How many names do I got left?!?!?*

DANIEL JAMES: Take care of yourself, Danny. Was good while it lasted …

Daniel James walks away.

DANNY SANTIAGO: Back to your castle, huh?

> Back to your fortress by the sea?!

> Back to starin out that window?

> At the waves? At your reflection?!?!

Daniel James is gone.

DANNY SANTIAGO: You know there's a monster under that sea!!!!

> BIG MOTHERFUCKING GODZILLA MONSTER!!!!

> UNDER THAT SEA! Waiting to come up …

Danny goes to the "Chato de Shamrock" tag on the wall. He picks up a black crayon, and scribbles thick lines obliterating the name. Slow fade. Just before blackout, the world of the courtyard pops up. It's night. Nero pops open a bottle of champagne. Celebration. The group exchanges hugs, high fives, etc. They cheer, pour drinks — it gets raucous quickly. Herman and Valerie embrace. A kiss to the cheek turns sexual instantly. Nero lifts and spins Lina. They're all over each other. Javier and Alvaro embrace. A brotherly kiss becomes a sensual exchange.

Suddenly one of the motel room doors opens — blast of light and the frightened, terrifying cry of a toddler silences the group. They all freeze in their respective embraces looking at the door. They watch in fear — no one dares to step forward. Alvaro finally moves towards the door. He looks in. By his reaction at the threshold, something has gone dreadfully wrong. He enters the room. No one moves. He returns carrying Lila, who screams.

VALERIE: Alvaro … what is it … ?

ALVARO: Pablo's gone.

Valerie and Javier rush to the threshold to look inside the room. They hold that position through the end of the play —

World shift. Kurtz's apartment. Clothes strewn on the floor, take out food cartons, empty liquor bottles, a beat up video camera on a tripod, stacks of pages, post-its, index cards. Images are pasted to the wall — Daniel James, Chaplin, Seaward, Jesse James, posters for Gorgo, Behemoth, Great Dictator, black and whites of HUAC hearing rooms, etc.

On the coffee table the same typewriter D.L. gave to Daniel James. Kurtz is on the couch furiously typing. He's in his boxers and a dirty t-shirt. Next to the typewriter a neatly stacked manuscript.

Sound of a toilet flushing. Alex appears wearing a green slip. She's a wreck. She stumbles to Kurtz, kisses him. She's drunk and distraught.

ALEX: No. Not Pablo. He's just a little boy, you can't do that to a little boy …

KURTZ: Hush.

ALEX: You can't do that to them!
  They finished their play. They're going to make their deadline —
  it's supposed to be a happy ending.
  You *can't* make Pablo disappear —

KURTZ: They weren't paying attention. They deserve it.

ALEX: No one. No one deserves to lose their child.

You *can't. do* that to them.

Kurtz types a few more strokes. Stops. He removes the page from the scroll, places it on the completed manuscript.

KURTZ: It's done.

End of play

AFTERWORD: THE MYSTIQUE OF FAILURE

by Dr. Alexandra Tanner

The following is an unedited, partial transcript of a talk given by Alexandra Tanner, PhD at the Modern Languages Association conference in Chicago in January 2014. Due to technical difficulties with the recording device, no documentation exists of the complete talk. The transcript marks points in the talk when the recording device ceases to function properly.

"To each eye, perhaps, the outlines of a great civilization present a different picture. In the wide ocean upon which we venture, the possible ways and directions are many; the same studies that have served for my work might easily, in other hands, not only receive a wholly different treatment and application, but lead to essentially different conclusions."

— *Jacob Burckhardt, from* The Civilization of the Renaissance in Italy

A thousand years from now, if the only cultural artifacts to survive an American apocalypse were the output of its dramatists, what picture would future cultural historians paint of the civilization that produced them? Would they deem America a latter day ancient Greece, a Renaissance Italy, an Elizabethan England? Would judgment of its surviving plays relegate America to the pantheon of enigmatic lost civilizations like the Harappa of the Indus Valley, or the pre-Inca Puma Punku in South America, Baalbek hidden beneath the ruins of ancient Heliopolis in Lebanon or Göbekli Tepe in eastern Turkey? Or would America remain as illegible, inscrutable and inaccessible as the Asmat of southwestern New Guinea?

If cultural artifacts, as art historian Jacob Burckhardt posits, provide essential clues to understanding the ethos of a civilization, what do the plays by the Colombian-born, American playwright Javier C. reveal about the late 20th-century landscape of the American theater and, in a larger sense, the America, in which they were written? Further, what will they make of the unlikely resurrection, reconsideration and renaissance (yes, admittedly a minor one at that) of his work in the second decade of the 21st century?

Our internet era has spawned a phenomenon described by the late cultural historian Emiliano Kurtz as "resurrection fever," a term he coined in the introduction of his seminal *The Mystique of Failure: A Reconsideration of Modern American Drama Through its Lost Plays and Playwrights* (Northwestern University Press, 2007). Kurtz argues that the information superhighway has been clogged by a virtual bumper-to-bumper traffic jam of historians, critics, museum curators, documentarians and bloggers bent on digging into the shadowy recesses of the past to resurrect works of artists, writers and musicians that have long languished in obscurity. Their aim is fourfold: 1) to rewrite accepted art-historical trajectories; 2) to create new markets for artifacts that history originally

deemed marginal; 3) to mark their territory as vital contributing authors of the never-ending narrative of cultural development; and 4) to feed the public with the comforting myth that resurrection is not just the stuff of biblical fairy tale, but a fact of contemporary life.

In the visual art world, the trend of resurrecting obscure 20th-century artists (Konrad Lueg, Germaine Richier, Esteban Gutierrez y Palma, Julije Knifer and Richard Van Buren, to name a few) is as much about creating new and lucrative market opportunities as it is about filling gaps in (if not entirely redefining) the trajectory of modern art. A recent example of artistic exhumation and reanimation centers on the work of Vivian Maier, Chicago's reclusive "North Shore nanny-slash-street photographer," chronicled by her "discoverer" John Maloof in the forthcoming film *Finding Vivian Maier* (IFC, 2014).

[Editor's note: The film had an official release date of March 2014 – Dr. Tanner apparently saw an early cut of the film in a private screening she attended in December 2013. For an alternative documentary treatment of the subject, see Jill Nichols' The Vivian Maier Mystery (FilmBuff, 2013).]

Maloof, a former product design student at Columbia College in Chicago and "a top real estate agent for Century 21" ("Accidental Archivist," *Demo: The Alumni Magazine of Columbia College Chicago*, Issue 20) stumbled on a treasure trove of Maier's photographs and personal artifacts at an auction in 2007. Maier, living out her last remaining months penniless in a Rogers Park one-room apartment at the time, had neglected to pay the rent on her storage unit, relegating her personal effects and life's work to the highest bidder, as it were.

Initially unaware of what he stumbled on, Maloof did what any directionless post-collegiate 20-something would do – he uploaded the images to his blog. Only after reading enthusiastic responses in the comments section, and quickly turning a tidy profit on a handful of prints he sold on eBay, did Maloof realize that the mountain of discarded images he was sitting on was a potential money printing machine, initiating his journey from real estate whiz kid to art world mogul. Maloof claims to have attempted locating Maier – eerily, in the two years between the "discovery" in 2007 and the online publication of her obituary in April 2009, Maloof could discern no footprint of Maier's on the Internet. Maloof's unleashing of the deceased Maier's work on the public raises numerous controversies, the most obvious being the fact that thousands of rolls of Maier's film remained undeveloped decades after they were exposed, and that in her lifetime she never sought attention for her work. Would she have consented to having her photographs seen by, let alone sold to, the public, or would she have preferred they disappear into obscurity, mirroring her own destiny? Maier's photographs are indeed striking – at least the ones made available to the public by Maloof, who, as the self-appointed gatekeeper of her estate, deems what is and isn't worthy of public consumption.

All this would be troubling enough. More disturbing, Maloof has fueled "Maier-Fever" through his fixation with uncovering her strange biography, placing a fetishistic

emphasis on her peculiarities, suggesting her eccentricities were a sign of deep mental instability (crazy artists sell, the crazier the better, let's face it), his necrophiliac inclusion of Maier's personal effects alongside prints of Maier's photographs in gallery exhibitions of her work, conflating the personality of the creator with the work itself – a curatorial strategy that on the one hand sells lots of prints, but on the other, poisons any clear-eyed assessment of her work's value on its own terms. In the film, she's described as a missing link between Henri Cartier-Bresson and Diane Arbus. Maier undoubtedly was aware of the output of these giants of photography. Equally certain, these masters knew nothing of the anonymous chronicler of Chicago's gritty street life in the 1950s. Which raises the question: Is it even possible to label an artist a "missing link" when no one on either end of the chain knew of her work or that she even existed? Undoubtedly –

[Ed. note: Here, the technical difficulties in the recording begin. A full 2 minutes and 47 seconds of silence pass before sound resumes.]

– same "resurrection fever" phenomenon perpetuated by the music industry, not coincidentally at a time when the Internet has brought that Goliath industry to its knees. A cursory glance at Elijah Wald's provocative reassessment of 20th-century popular music, *How The Beatles Destroyed Rock 'n' Roll: An Alternative History of American Popular Music* (Oxford University Press, 2011), reveals with high-definition clarity our culture's deep hunger for art-historical revisionism. Also, one only has to consider the recent explosion of documentary films chronicling and reassessing obscure rock musicians that were overlooked in their day: *Big Star: Nothing Can Hurt Me* (Ardent Studios, 2012), *A Band Called Death* (Drafthouse Films, 2012), and my own forthcoming film *This Record Will Kill You: The Life and Times of Gummy Rickett* (Subterranean Films, 2015). Of course, the gold standard of the rock-n-roll-resurrection-fable genre was set by the popular Oscar-winning 2012 documentary-slash-bedtime story *Searching for Sugarman*. In *Sugarman*, our contemporary Lazarus, the "lost" musician Sixto Rodriguez, is depicted as an unheard "voice of his generation" comparable to Bob Dylan.

By summoning an artist of incomparable stature, Dylan, as a point of comparison with the "unknown" Sixto, the filmmaker employs a tried and true narrative deception – similar to Maloof's comparison of Maier with Cartier-Bresson and Arbus. Juxtaposing an unknown with an icon in the context of a film lends such pronouncements an authority that has little basis in objective reality. Context here is everything: if I made

such pronouncements after putting back five Cosmopolitans at a bar, you might forgive my overzealousness as a consequence of my alcohol-fueled state – but if I stare into a camera, sober, with my credentials neatly summarized in a tasteful subtitle, the statement becomes magically endowed with weight and authority. Add to all this the fact that the filmmaker goes out of his way to paint a picture of Sixto's hopeless reclusiveness contrary to conveniently omitted facts – for example, the film omits the minor detail that Sixto Rodriguez staged at least two successful concert tours of Australia at the peak of his "obscurity."

Entombed as a working stiff and activist in inner-city Detroit, Sixto Rodriguez, our Lazarus, is raised from the dead by Jesus-in-the-guise-of-first-time-Swedish-filmmaker Malik Bendjelloul.

[Ed. note: At this point on the recording, we here stirring and muttering in the audience. The first walkout happens here.]

Bendjelloul grants Rodriguez that rare second act in American life, providing audiences with a true-life triumph-of-the-human-spirit narrative that trumps any fictional concoction Hollywood could ever dream up – precisely because it is "real." Contrast Sixto Rodriguez with the protagonist of another, albeit fictional, triumph-of-the-human-spirit film, Rocky Balboa. *Rocky* (and its sequels, though to an exponentially lesser degree) uplifts our spirits, spinning for us the comforting tale that even the most wretched and forgotten figures can earn their 45 minutes in the ring – and find true love in the process. But we know in the darkest corners of our hearts that Rocky is *not* real, and therefore his promise to us must be counterfeit. Whereas, "Sugarman" is "real," so the promise he makes us by being called forth from his tomb in Detroit and thrust into the glaring lights of Hollywood celebrity must be the genuine article.

But is it "real," especially when considering the many well-documented omissions in the film?

Both the Maier and Rodriguez films satisfy all the criteria of the "resurrection fever" phenomenon: 1) history is rewritten by inserting previously marginal figures into an accepted sweeping art-historical narrative; 2) the once bear markets for the work of Maier and Rodriguez become bullish overnight; 3) Maloof and Bendjelloul, stumbling on hidden tombs containing riches, become

latter-day Howard Carters *[Ed. note: Howard Carter, British archaeologist, "discovered" the tomb of King Tut in 1922. Questions remain to this day whether or not Carter stole artifacts from the tomb and smuggled them back to England prior to its "official" opening. See: Crossland, David. "Howard Carter 'stole from the tomb of Tutankhamen.'" The National. January 21, 2010]*; and 4) both tales are ominously successful in casting the resurrection narrative spell on audiences.

It is this fourth impulse — crafting the contemporary resurrection narrative — that is the chief preoccupation of this talk and its aim to illuminate the plays of Javier C. Before addressing the plays in question, it's worth taking a moment to revisit the West's original resurrection narrative — Jesus' restoration of life to the dead Lazarus — as told in Chapter 11 in the Gospel of John.

[Ed. note: At this point in the recording, audible groans and mutterings are heard coming from the audience. More walkouts.]

Jesus arrives to Bethany four days after the death of Lazarus. Mary and Martha, Lazarus' sisters, mourn his death and tell Jesus, "Lord, if you had been here my brother would not have died." Jesus weeps, and asks the women to lead him to Lazarus' burial place. At first Martha resists Jesus' request that they remove the stone ("Lord, by now there will be a stench; he has been dead for four days!") to which Jesus responds: "Did I not tell you that if you believe you will see the glory of God?" After removing the stone, uttering a prayer, and calling out to the dead man, Lazarus emerges confused, bleary eyed, perhaps a little cross from having been stirred from eternal sleep, but alive, nonetheless. This climactic action provides definitive proof that Jesus is Messiah, adding an army of former doubters and haters to the ranks of his small following of true believers. The act also serves as the straw that broke the camel's back: learning of

this deed and the popularity it yielded for Jesus, the Pharisees conclude that the vagabond teacher and rabble rouser must be rubbed out, precipitating –

[Ed. note: Here, the technical difficulties interrupt the recording. A full three minutes and seventeen seconds of silence pass before it resumes.]

– contours and meaning of this narrative in a contemporary context, it is not enough only to consider the story's actual content, it is essential to undertake a rigorous analysis of what is *missing* from it. The central narrative abyss lies in the question: Who is Lazarus? Aside from the fact that Lazarus and his sisters loved Jesus and were devoted acolytes to his mission, why is *he*, of all the Israelites who died that week, chosen for resurrection? Remember: this is not just any run-of-the-mill miracle – it's THE miracle that precipitates the Passion. It is the key to both Jesus' and, paradoxically, Lazarus', attainment of immortality. Lazarus' name resonates through the ages, yet you would be hard pressed to find a more passive protagonist in all of literature – there is no indication that he did anything remarkable to deserve this distinction. For the narrative to have meaning in a contemporary cultural-historical context, this omission must be corrected. In other words, the contemporary Lazarus must possess some cultural worth to justify the act of resurrection. In Vivian Maier's case, her cultural worth lay in the 100,000 plus negatives she left behind. In the case of Sixto Rodriguez, he owes his cultural currency to his two albums, *Cold Fact* (1970) and *After the Fact* (1971). Though largely ignored at the time of their creation, both artists' creative output served as the equivalent of a small sum of money deposited in a long-term, high-interest IRA. But what did Lazarus ever produce?

And what of Jesus? How does the modern cultural historian transpose His through-line as described in John to fit the contemporary resurrection narrative? First, Jesus' motives in John must be scrutinized carefully, and second, those motives must find distinct, convincing and concrete contemporary parallels in order for them to be of any use in this present inquiry. Even the most cursory reading of John begs the question: if Jesus has demonstrated his healing abilities *prior* to the death of Lazarus, why does he show up four days *after* his death, as opposed to appearing sooner? Clearly Jesus had a masterfully intuitive – albeit primitive – understanding of the high-impact, well-timed media event. Yes, he could have shown up in Bethany and healed Lazarus as he writhed in agony on his deathbed. But that would have downgraded the healing to lesser miracle status, when circumstances necessitated a more decisive –

[Ed. note: Here, the technical difficulties interrupt the recording again, this time for 37 seconds.]

– crucifixion became the endgame. To connect this to contemporary manifestations of "resurrection fever" one might scoff – Maloof and Bendjelloul were hardly crucified for resurrecting Vivian Maier and Sixto Rodriguez – it would be the apex of absurdity to equate receiving an Oscar with the physical agony of crucifixion. However, both Oscar victory and crucifixion assure the recipients a measure of immortality, the differ-ence being only with regard to scale. *[Ed. note: This speech was delivered five months prior to Bendjelloul's suicide in May, 2014, and a year prior to Maloof's Oscar nomination for his Maier documentary.]* Filling in the omissions of Lazarus as recounted in John, the contemporary resurrection narrative takes on the contours and simplicity of a folk tale, but promises near endless malleability depending on whose hands the story is in.

The narrative goes something like this:

1. Artist creates remarkable work.

2. Artist launches remarkable work into marketplace.

3. Marketplace responds to remarkable work with indifference.

4. Inconclusive speculation by artist: marketplace indifference stems from a) work being ahead of its time; b) poor marketing strategy on part of those responsible for disseminating work to public; c) ignorance/complacency/conservatism/insider-y-ness of cultural industry and audience it claims to serve; d) plain, old-fashioned rotten luck. Lurking in the shadows, a hidden "e," which artist only entertains during darkest hours, usually under influence of alcohol or narcotics: work was not remarkable to begin with.

5. Artist makes attempt at second go-round believing market will get it right this time. In doing so, not only will they gain recognition for new work, original work will be rediscovered and recognized as remarkable.

6. Repeat steps 2, 3 and 4. Add to step 4: f) God hates them.

7. Artist concludes world conspiracy against them. They either: a) continue to make work which, to inflict punishment to an indifferent world, tends towards aggressive, alienating and/or hostile to public, therefore unmarketable (see my forthcoming documentary film on Gummy Rickett's post-"She's Like Jesus" work); b) abandon art-making activities to join labor force, often pursuing employment some would consider "degrading" or "beneath them"; c) commit suicide (either literally or figuratively).

8. Artist and work languish for years in obscurity.

9. After lengthy period of time – often a generation or two – work rediscovered.

10. Discoverer(s) shocked that work of such quality failed to reach large audience.

11. Discoverer becomes evangelist for work.

12. Discoverer crafts formulation: SRLA=ARA–CPA–UM x MTCWUO. (Translation: Successfully Resurrected Lost Artist equals Accomplished Revered Artist minus Critical and Popular Acclaim minus Units Moved multiplied by Mystique That Comes With Unjust Obscurity.)

13. Acolytes of new church search for creator of work, often forced to untangle myths of artist's death/suicide on stage, and bear witness to artist's unjust relegation to economic situation far beneath perceived worth of artist.

14. Acolytes' plan to exhume artist and work meets with initial reluctance on artist's part (they had a rough time the first go round, they're not keen on reopening old wounds).

15. Acolytes overcome artist's resistance with delivery of concrete evidence of success of work (reviews, unpaid royalties, Google search hits).

16. Artist emerging from private Dark Age into public Renaissance experiences initial trauma – similar to Lazarus' eyes burned by sunlight when emerging from the lightless tomb – that people actually care.

17. Audience clamors for piece of artist.

18. Unspoken question hovers: is newfound interest result of genuine recognition of high quality art that slipped through the cracks? Or does interest stem from resurrection mythology surrounding artist and artist's contemporary discoverer's marketing skill.

19. Artist becomes force in marketplace for period of time. Reputation grows or wanes depending on generosity of time, fickleness of marketplace and ability to create new work matching or superseding quality of original.

20. Time determines whether artist and work earns permanent place in accepted historical trajectory of form.

Which brings us to the curious case of the Colombian-born, American playwright Javier C. *[Ed. note – at this point on the tape we hear a heckler utter "finally" loud enough to be picked up by Dr. Tanner's microphone.]* Who is this would-be Lazarus of the American Theater?

Little is known about Javier C. The first attempt to chronicle his work and life appears in the aforementioned *The Mystique of Failure: A Reconsideration of Modern American Drama Through its Lost Plays and Playwrights* by my mentor, the late Dr. Emiliano Kurtz. For those not familiar with Kurtz's monumental work, it is the outcome of a two-decade study. Having served as Kurtz's graduate assistant during the writing of his magnum opus, I can personally attest to the rigor, intensity and obsessiveness he brought to the project. Most analogous studies of the field measuring the health of the American Theater focus on widely produced, critically acclaimed and otherwise successful plays and playwrights. Kurtz's innovation was to dive head first into the immense body of American dramatic literature that never saw the light of day, believing those neglected works – or what Kurtz called "The Shadow Cannon" or, jokingly, "The Theater That Never Was" – would reveal the true state of American playwriting, and, borrowing from Burckhardt, "lead to essentially different conclusions" than more traditional studies. Kurtz's work was painstaking: from 1985 to his death in 2008, he amassed and catalogued 270,000 plus unproduced manuscripts written by American playwrights, wrote brief but penetrating critical analyses for thousands of works, capsule biographies on as many authors as he could find, and a sobering statistical analysis that concluded that a mere .063% of plays written each year in the period of the study were ever seen by the public on any meaningful scale.

Like most of the dramatists chronicled in *Mystique*, Javier C. left virtually no imprint on the American theater during his lifetime, let alone a footprint on the civilization that spawned him. Having read and re-read the entire body of Javier C.'s extant work over the years, it remains unclear to me why Javier C. became Kurtz's White Whale. Unlocking the source of Kurtz's fixation still escapes me. The entry in the book reads:

"Little is known about the Colombian born, American playwright Javier C. Born in Bogota in 1958, he emigrated with his mother to the United States in 1958 following the murder of his father during the waning days of *La Violencia*, the political civil war in Colombia that claimed 200,000 lives between 1948 and 1958. Settling in Jackson –

[Ed. note: Here, more technical difficulties interrupt the recording. Two minutes and forty nine seconds of silence pass before it resumes.]

– dropped out of NYU, forming a collective with fellow students that staged two of his plays for a total of six performances in 1981 at Club 57 on St. Mark's Place – (where

388

I'm told he frequently attended on Monster Movie Tuesdays and Model World of Glue Nights, when patrons would build plastic model airplanes, set them on fire and get high off the burning glue).

During that time, he married visual artist and theatrical designer Valerie Marcks. According to several people who knew them, they had two children, although others insist they only had one.

"Documentation exists in the archives of The Public Theatre that the collective was commissioned by Joseph Papp in 1988 to write a play. According to the commission contract, the play would 'explore appropriation of Latino culture in the US through the lens of exiles at the margins of the culture.' No evidence exists that they ever completed the commission.

"From 1988 through 2007, details of Javier C.'s life remain sketchy. It can be inferred that he moved around quite a bit, spending stints in NY, Chicago, Chippewa Falls, Wisconsin, Mexico City, and finally Gallup, New Mexico where he spent the final year of his life.

"Body of work includes: 3 full length –

[Ed. note: Technical difficulties. Seven minutes and four seconds of silence pass before it resumes. From here to the end of the recording, the device captures only fragments of the remainder of the talk. Brackets and ellipses ([. . .]) indicate where the recording ceases.]

– it is likely apocryphal."

Of all [....] –rgotten American Dramati [...], why has this man's work [....] been tapped for resurrection? [...] –pecially when none of his work meets [...] the four criteria I outlined before?

[Ed. note: Here the recording goes silent for three minutes and twenty-seven seconds.]

Who owns the legacy [...] of Javier and his work? [...] Despite dubious claims to his discovery by Professor Carlo—

[Ed. note: Here the recording goes silent for two minutes and eleven seconds.]

— so-called "Dramatic Reconstructions," [...] so called [...] really amount to nothing more than forgeries and [...] file cabinet? An intern named "Nicole"? Really? [....] owes his resurrection not to [...] but to [...] painstaking work of the late [...] sexual exploitation [...] which I would categorically de— [...] unfounded accusations [...] devoted the last two [...] of his caree —

[Ed. note: Here the recording goes silent for four minutes and twenty-three seconds.]

Murillo's [...] vampiric, fetishistic [....]

— appropriation and fascists —

[....]

— genuine artistic preoccupations or masturb—

[...]

—that pale in comparison to —

[...]

— grandiosity, delusion —

[...]

— like flogging dead horses —

[...]

— exhume and fuck a corpse because all that he —

[...]

—f can do nothing [...] abou—

[...]

—in the end twice — or perhaps thrice — buried.

[Ed. note: At this point the recording device ceases to function.]

379 Jacob Burckhardt (1818-1897) on his way to a lecture at the University of Basel, 1890. Burckhardt, regarded as a pioneer in the discipline of cultural history, is best known for *The Civilization of the Renaissance in Italy* (1860).

380 Illustration depicting the murder of Ingram Frazer by Elizabethan playwright Christopher Marlowe - a bold example of historical revisionism given Frazer murdered Marlowe. The illustration appears in the 1895 novel *It Was Marlowe* by W.G. Ziegler, which makes the case that Marlowe faked his death in order to write under the pseudonym "William Shakespeare." Image in the Public Domain.

The Temple of Baalbeck in present-day Lebanon. Romans worshipped the Gods Jupiter, Venus and Bacchus at this site. In their own act of revisionism, they superimposed these Romn deities onto existing iconography depicting indigenous deities Hadad and Atargatis.

Asmat ancestor skull from the DeYoung Museum in San Francisco. The Asmat people of southwestern New Guinea preserve and worship the skulls of deceased ancestors, decorating them with feathers, seeds and carved sea shell rings. Image in the Public Domain.

381 April 22, 1955, Central Park, a vintage color transparency of a portrait of Vivian Maier from the Ron Slattery Collection. Pamela Bannos, artist, researcher, Maier scholar and professor at Northwestern University originally shot this image in color, noting, "It's quite extraordinary that Maier, most well known for her black and white work, was shooting this color transparency film at that time." Courtesy Pamela Bannos.

"Finding Vivian Maier: Chicago Street Photographer" exhibition in Chicago, 2011.

382 Apartment building in Rogers Park neighborhood where Vivian Maier lived in the final years of her life. Photo by Carlos Murillo

Park bench in Rogers Park Beach where Vivian Maier was known to sit afternoons. Photo by Carlos Murillo.

383 Sixto Rodriguez live in concert in 2014.

384 Harry Burton's legendary photo of Howard Carter (kneeling), an unknown Egyptian worker and Arthur Callender before the entrance to the burial shrine of Tutankhamen's tomb. The photo, taken on January 24, 1924, is almost definitely a recreation/staging of the actual opening of the shrine which, according to Carter's diary, took place the day before. Public Domain, New York Times Archive.

385 Etching of Christ raising Lazarus from his tomb by Friedrich August Ludy (1823-1866) from a painting by Johann Friedrich Overbeck (1789-1869). From Wellcome Images.

389 A legendary nightclub located on St. Mark's Place in NY City, Club 57 was a hub for performance and visual artists, musicians and punk scenesters from it's origins in the mid-70s to it's demise in 1983. Gary Winter archive.

Valerie Marcks, theatrical designer and sculptor, who was married to Javier C. in 1982 and divorced in 1990. Photo Courtesy Amanda Powell.

ACKNOWLEDGEMENTS AND CREDITS

Over the last eight years, *The Javier Plays* has occupied a significant part, if not the bulk, of my creative life. In that time, I have accumulated significant debts to many family members, friends, collaborators, organizations and funders who helped me along the way. My gratitude runs deep.

First and foremost, I want to express my deepest thanks to my wife, Lisa Portes, and our two children, Eva Rose and Carlitos. Without their love, encouragement, sense of humor and support, these plays would not exist. They've patiently endured numerous periods of absence (and absent mindedness), but embrace me with warmth and kindness when I return. They provide inspiration, respite, reality checks and soft landings when I am in the thick of my work. Scary to imagine what my life would be without them. I love and cherish them dearly.

In 2007, I was granted the gift of a seven-year residency at New Dramatists in New York City – *The Javier Plays* were born and raised there. My residency kicked off with a reading of the ten-page *Fragment of a Paper Airplane* at the Class of 2014 Welcome Celebration, and culminated three months prior to graduation with a weeklong Creativity Fund workshop presentation of the entire 350 page trilogy. In between, the plays were conceived and nurtured, grew up and found their legs through The Creativity Fund, PlayTime, and many conversations with the extraordinary resident playwrights, staff and extended artistic family of the organization. I want to name names: Todd London for keeping true to his mensch-y promise on day one that New Dramatists was our artistic home and that it existed so we could pursue even our wildest ideas; Emily Morse, for her tireless support, dramaturgical insight, genius for connecting artists with the right collaborators and her artistry in creating spaces in which artists can do their best work; John Steber, a true alchemist who innately senses the heartbeat of a character on the page and unfailingly finds the actor whose heartbeat matches that rhythm – even when, astonishingly, the character has yet to be written; Joel Ruark, who always welcomes you home with an embrace, a fantastic story and, from time to time, a glass of the best Kentucky bourbon; and everyone on the New Dramatists staff past and present: Morgan Allen, Tiffany Kleeman Baran, Christie Brown, Erin Detrick, Jennie Greer,

Rachel Hutt, Ron Riley, the Board of Directors and the dozens of interns that cycle in and out – each individual at New Dramatists plays a vital role in making the church a true sanctuary for American playwrights. I also want to thank my peer playwrights in the Class of 2014 – Eugenie Chan, Sarah Hammond, Taylor Mac, Julie Marie Myatt, J.T. Rogers, Deborah Stein, and John Walch – their singular and inspired voices, their generosity and humanity, made me a better person and writer for having walked alongside them over seven years.

I've been blessed to have my friend and agent Antje Oegel in my corner for almost a decade. Our paths crossed at a static point in my professional life – her infectious positive energy, passion for the work, her honesty, collaborative spirit and kindness reenergized me then, and still does to this day. When I approached Antje with the idea of doing a book that wasn't a typical three-play anthology, but a hybrid work containing drama, autobiography, literary criticism, memoir, fiction, and a load of images, she understood it, embraced it and set the wheels in motion to make it happen. The form of this book and its publication stems directly from Antje's out-of-the-box thinking and visionary approach to disseminating her writers' work.

I am extremely grateful for Karinne Keithley Syers, who performed heroic work in editing and designing this volume. Her attention to detail, patience and artistry are evident on every page. It was a long process piecing the world of this book together, and I couldn't have asked for a more generous and tireless collaborator.

My colleagues and students at The Theatre School of DePaul University, especially Dean John Culbert, Associate Dean, Dean Corrin, and Chair of Theatre Studies, Barry Brunetti, have been a strong supporters and champions not only my work within the school, but my creative endeavors outside of it. On numerous occasions, *The Javier Plays* took me away for extended stretches of time from my day-to-day duties at The Theatre School – they've often bent over backwards to accommodate, and always have been nothing but generous and kind about it. I'm grateful for my students, who keep me honest – I feel strongly that if I'm not in the thick of my own writing while guiding them through their own processes, I really have no business being there. They challenge me and I learn as much from them as they learn from me.

I try to impart to my students the idea that each play they write is a unique organism with its own origin story, DNA, life support system, nervous system, chemical and psychological makeup. Being distinct organisms, each play follows a very specific journey through its life cycle. This applies to all three of the plays that make up *The*

Javier Plays — each one had its own unique travelogue from their origins to landing in the pages of this book.

The Goodman Theatre provided instrumental early support when they awarded me The Ofner Commission in 2007 to write *Diagram of a Paper Airplane*. I am especially grateful to Tanya Palmer, the Goodman's Director of New Play Development, who championed my work to Artistic Director Bob Falls. Sarah Jane DeHoff and William DeHoff provided valuable writing time on *Diagram* when they hosted a retreat for New Dramatists Playwrights at their beautiful camp near Lake Placid, NY in 2008. Philip Himberg and Christopher Hibma provided invaluable support when they selected *Diagram* as a project of the Sundance Theatre Lab in 2009. They assembled a remarkable team of collaborators to explore the play in the majestic setting of the Sundance Resort: director Eric Rosen, who wowed me with the razor sharp intelligence he brought to the room, Mame Hunt, a dramaturg of tremendous insight, a fierce cast that included Giancarlo Esposito, Laura Innes, Maximilian Osinski, Larry Pine and Maria Thayer. A number of other institutions supported *Diagram* over the years: The William Inge Theatre Festival, the Playwrights Realm in NYC, Forum Theatre in DC, the Kennedy Center's Page-to-Stage Festival, Chicago Dramatists and the National New Play Network. There's a long list of actors and directors to thank: Raphael Baez, David Greenspan, Elizabeth Morton, Mary Shultz, Liam Torres, Larry Neumann Jr., Lisa Tejero, Henry Godinez, Mando Alvarado, Michael Cumpsty, Teresa Avia Lim, Joyce O'Connor, Janet Ulrich Brooks, Ian Paul Custer, Ricardo Gutierrez, Kay Kron, Rick Foucheux, Juan Villa, T.Ryder Smith, Betty Gilpin, Lou Moreno, Joe Tippett, Lori Wilner, Jerry Ruiz, Shade Murray, Jenny McConnell Frederick and Kip Fagan.

A Thick Description of Harry Smith was originally commissioned by Berkeley Repertory Theatre in 2008 thanks to the advocacy of Madeleine Oldham, their Director of New Play Development. I am deeply indebted to two organizations for subsequent support: New Dramatists, which presented two Creativity Fund workshops of the play in 2009 and again in 2014, and Page 73 Productions, which produced a workshop production at The Culture Project in New York City in July 2012. The folks at P73, Liz Jones, Michael Walkup and Asher Richelli, are fantastic producers, genuine advocates for adventurous new work and kind spirits — I'm grateful for the leap they took to make this project a reality. The brilliant Kip Fagan has been a key collaborator, having helmed all three of these incarnations of the piece. The play is so much better for all his insight, imagination, humor and the effortless way he handles a room full of larger than life personalities. I'm also grateful for the crack design team Kip assembled for the P73 version: Seth Reiser (sets and lights), Jessica Pabst (costumes) and Daniel Kluger (sound) fashioned a rich, immersive world that transformed the basement space at The Culture Project into the Medicine Show-Fantasia that lives inside Harry's mind. The extraordinary actor and musician Lucas Papaelias has been an indispensible force in the life of this play through all its incarnations. He brings his heart and soul into playing the role of Marlowe – to the point where I can't make the distinction between their voices. Lucas crafted explosive arrangements for the music, making old folk songs sound like they were written yesterday, and led the band with ferocity and passion. I'm especially in awe of him for putting 100 percent of himself into the P73 version, when he was simultaneously putting 100 percent into performing *Once* eight times a week on Broadway. The play has been blessed to have amazing actors and musicians breathe life into it from the beginning: David Patrick Kelly, Larry Neumann, Jr., Sean Patrick Reilly, T. Ryder Smith, Birgit Huppuch, Kate Ferber, Joe Jung, Joe Tippett, Chris Sullivan, Paul Whitty, Ray Rizzo, Matthew Stadelmann, Kellie Overbey, Alfredo Narciso, Gabe Ruiz, Andrew Gallant, Stephanie Chavara, Sandra Delgado and Aaron Rustebakke. I also wish to thank Peter Taub, the Director of Performance Programs at Chicago's Museum of Contemporary Art, and Anthony Moseley, artistic director of Chicago's Collaboraction Theatre, for co-presenting a concert version of *Harry Smith* in the summer of 2011, directed by that force of nature, Michael John Garcés. Lastly, many thanks to The Watermill Center and the NYC Summer Play Festival for providing me with a two-week residency in winter 2011 to finish the play.

I thank the brilliant Polly Carl, former Director of New Play Development at Steppenwolf Theatre in Chicago, for bringing my work to the attention of Artistic Director Martha Lavey, which lead to a commission to write *Your Name Will Follow You Home*. In December 2012, I arrived at New Dramatists for their annual Playtime Festival with a thick folder containing the gigantic, incoherent, unfinished mess I'd been making over the previous year. I left the building two weeks later with the complete version of the play thanks to the collaborative brilliance and generosity of Kip Fagan, Raúl Castillo, Christy Escobar, Polly Lee, Greg McFadden, Hanna Moon, Bobby Plasencia and Michael Tisdale. Steppenwolf held two workshops of the play in 2013, culminating in a performance at the First Look Festival of New Work, directed by Dexter Bullard and featuring a superb cast including Cliff Chamberlain, Sandra Delgado, Yasen Peyankov, Adam Poss, Amanda Powell, Sarah Price and Juan Villa. I also want to thank Jaime Castaneda for including the play in Atlantic Theatre Company's Latino Mix Fest in 2013. *Your Name* received the 2013 MetLife Nuestros Voces Award from the legendary Repertorio Español in NYC, Robert Federico, Executive Producer. In November 2014, the play received its Spanish language world premiere off-Broadway at Repertorio, translated by Caridad Svich and directed by Jose Zayas. The excellent cast included

David Crommet, Luis Carlos de La Lombana, Ana Grosse, Gerardo Gudiño, Soraya Padrao, Bobby Plasencia, Thallis Santesteban González and Jerry Soto, with scenic, costume and projection design by Leni Méndez, lights by Eduardo Navas and sound by David Margolin Lawson.

I wish to acknowledge several folks who were instrumental in researching the real life backstory of *Your Name*.

Alicia Hernández, Emeritus Professor of English at Rio Hondo College in California, was immensely helpful in bringing this play to life. I came into contact with her when I stumbled on a riveting short memoir she wrote chronicling her 13 year correspondence with Danny Santiago in a hard-to-find collection of essays, *Life Writing / Writing Lives* (Bette H. Kirschtein, Ed., Malabar, FL: Krieger, 2001.) Alicia provided me with a rich account of their correspondence, as well as examples of letters exchanged, photos, newspaper articles, and a wealth of stories about her life and relationship to Danny. Over time we've developed a rewarding friendship stemming from our own regular correspondence through snail and e-mail. I was deeply moved when she traveled from California to Chicago to see the Steppenwolf reading, and again when she brought a huge contingent of family and friends to a staged reading of the play at Pasadena's Theatre @ Boston Court in November 2014. She is currently writing a book-length memoir of her friendship with Danny Santiago / Daniel James – I can't wait to read it.

I nod to Eric F. James, a family relation of Jesse James, who I met via his blog "Leaves of Gas." Eric is the author of *Jesse James: Soul Liberty*, a multi-volume saga chronicling the James Family. Volume I of the history, *Behind the Family Wall of Stigma & Silence*, includes a highly informative chapter detailing the life and times of Daniel Lewis James. Eric James was generous enough to share his work with me prior to the book's publication, as well as valuable insights into the James family history. In our conversations, we discovered common ground: Eric grew up in the south side of Chicago, a few addresses away on the same street where I live in the Bridgeport neighborhood with my wife and children.

A word of appreciation for journalist Jonah Raskin, who provided me with the raw transcript of an interview he conducted with Daniel James after his "outing" in 1984, as well as a few examples of their correspondence. The resulting article, "The Man Who Would be Danny Santiago" appeared in the *San Francisco Bay Guardian* in 1984. A handwritten postcard he included in the package he sent to me read: "Facts are all well and good, but whatever happened to imagination?" Vital words when I needed them most.

There are a bunch of folks who have, more generally, in both past and present, and in both large and small ways, kept me afloat in my life and work: my father Francisco Murillo, my late mother Minerva Murillo, my siblings Frank Murillo, Mario Murillo and Susan O'Brien, my in-laws Nancy and Doug Kuhnel, Alejandro Portes and Patricia Fernandez-Kelly, Mark Sanders, Andrew Dausch, Brian Lennon, Todd Lauterbach, Robert Steel, Tamsen Wolff, Lisa D'Amour, Jennifer Rudin, Bonnie Metzgar, Stuart Flack, Morgan Jenness, Robert Woodruff, Maria Irene Fornes, Paul Rivadue, Dr. Clayton, Ms. Jural, and David Bowie.

Finally – Robert Panico, a kid I went to middle and high school with and barely knew. I have not seen you since graduation in 1989. I have no idea where you are or who you have become. For reasons unknown to me, you randomly popped in my head summer of 2007, and in doing so you set this whole beast in motion. Thanks, man. I hope it got better.

—Carlos Murillo, Chicago, June 2015

CARLOS MURILLO is the recipient of a 2015 Doris Duke Impact Award in performing arts. His most recent work, *Killing of a Gentleman Defender*, was commissioned by The Goodman Theatre in Chicago, where he was a member of the 2014-15 Playwrights Unit. His work has been seen widely throughout the US and Europe. Plays include: *The Javier Plays, dark play or stories for boys, Augusta and Noble, Mayday Mayday Tuesday, Unfinished American Highwayyscape #9 & 32, Mimesophobia, A Human Interest Story or The Gory Details and All, Offspring of the Cold War, Schadenfreude, The Patron Saint of the Nameless Dead, Near Death Experiences with Leni Riefenstahl, Never Whistle While You're Pissing* and *Subterraneans*. They have been seen at venues throughout the US and in Europe, including Theatre der Stadt Aalen in Germany, the Vigszinhaz in Budapest, Hungary, The State Youth Theatre in Vilnius, Lithuania, Actors Theatre of Louisville, NYC Summer Play Festival, P73, En Garde Arts, Soho Rep, Repertorio Español, Salt Lake Acting Company, Adventure Stage in Chicago, Collaboraction, Walkabout Theatre, Theatre @ Boston Court, Circle X, Son of Semele, the University of Iowa International Writers Program, the Hangar Theatre Lab, The Group in Seattle, Red Eye in Minneapolis, the Sundance Theatre Lab, The Playwrights' Center and others. His plays have been commissioned by The Goodman, The Public, Berkeley Rep, Playwrights Horizons and South Coast Rep, and published by Dramatists Play Service, Playscripts, Smith & Kraus and Broadway Play Publishing. Awards include The Frederick Loewe Award from New Dramatists, the MetLife Nuestros Voces Award from Repetrorio Español, the Ofner Prize from The Goodman Theatre, the Otis Guernsey Award from the William Inge Theatre Festival, two National Latino Playwriting Awards from Arizona Theatre Company and a Jerome Fellowship from The Playwrights' Center. Carlos was a resident playwright at New Dramatists from 2007-14, and currently is an Associate Professor and Head of Playwriting at The Theatre School of DePaul University. He lives in south side of Chicago with his wife, the director Lisa Portes, and their two children Eva Rose and Carlos Pablo.

53rdstatepress.org

THE ANTI-INFLAMMATORY DIET COOKBOOK

THE
ANTI-INFLAMMATORY
DIET COOKBOOK

No Hassle 30-Minute Meals
to Reduce Inflammation

Madeline Given, NC
FOREWORD BY JENNIFER LANG, MD

**ROCKRIDGE
PRESS**

For Sesame. It felt like we created this together.

Photography: © Stockfood/Jonathan Gregson, cover and p. 72; Stockfood/Keller & Keller Photography, p. 2; Stockfood/Oliver Brachat, p. 6; Stockfood/PhotoCuisine/Chris Court Photography, p. 10 and back cover; Stockfood/Eric van Lokven, p. 24; Stockfood/Sarka Babicka, p. 34; Stocksy/Tatjana Ristanic, p. 52; Stockfood/Hein van Tonder, p. 88 and back cover; Stocksy/Natasa Mandic, p. 106; Stockfood/Sarah Coghill, p. 126; Stockfood/People Pictures, p. 144 and back cover; Stockfood/Great Stock!, p. 168; Stocksy/Nadine Greeff, p. 182.

ISBN: Print 978-1-62315-812-5
eBook 978-1-62315-813-2

Contents

Foreword

You might be one of the nearly 40 million Americans suffering from arthritis. Perhaps you have been diagnosed with an autoimmune condition such as lupus, ulcerative colitis or psoriasis. You may be an athlete recovering from injury, or work in a field that involves repetitive hand motion. You might be a parent of a child on the autism spectrum or suffering from food allergies. Regardless of your reason for picking up this book, I understand that inflammation is an issue for you.

We all inherit genes from our parents, and those genes do vary our risk for developing certain diseases, but this is only the beginning of the story. Stimuli from our environment decide which genes get activated, controlling their expression. And what we put into our bodies each day is the prevailing environmental factor that affects the expression of our genes. This means that certain foods and chemicals can trigger our propensities–whether it's to obesity or to inflammation–and other foods and chemicals can keep these at bay.

As an obstetrician, I can tell you that this process begins at the very earliest stages of human life, inside a mother's womb. It continues through infancy, childhood, and our entire lifetime. Among other factors, the food we eat matters.

In this book, Madeline Given explores how today's foods cause and promote inflammation in the body. Add in chemical exposures, a sedentary lifestyle, and chronic stress, and unfortunately, it results in the perfect petri dish for inflammation to grow and thrive. Inflammation is at the root of many ailments; however, we can control so many of these issues through diet.

Here you will find information that inspires impactful life changes, and delicious recipes that are as beneficial as they are satiating. Within days to weeks of instituting an anti-inflammatory diet, most people find some relief from symptoms. And turning this way of eating into a lifestyle can help you prevent inflammation-driven conditions and achieve the optimal health and vibrancy you deserve.

Jennifer Lang, MD
Obstetrician/Gynecologist and Gynecologic Oncologist
Author of *The Whole 9 Months*

Introduction

This book guides you in understanding and following an easy anti-inflammatory diet. This way of eating is not really a diet, but a lifestyle, a way of consuming energy-giving, delicious whole foods in their natural state. It's less about counting calories and more about knowing the nutrients within those calories. There are no empty calories or fluffy fillers here, only real ingredients that benefit the human body.

In my mid-twenties, I began to feel the effects of my standard American diet. I didn't have a diagnosis, but I simply didn't feel well. Thank goodness I had begun to explore holistic nutrition—the belief that our body systems affect each other, for better or worse, and that eating healthy foods as close to their natural states (unprocessed, unrefined, organic, local) can positively influence those systems.

Holistic nutritionists investigate health issues to uncover the root cause, rather than treat the symptoms. When I adopted this approach, I was able to explore and support my health in a more natural way. I discovered that I was indeed suffering: I had adrenal fatigue, anxiety, and gut dysbiosis, to name just a few ailments. My cortisol (stress hormones) levels were out of whack; my body was in full-blown inflammation mode! Even now I still combat these symptoms, because there is no overnight cure. And in addition to food choices, I continue to pursue other ways to reduce inflammation in my body, whether through yoga, massage, detox baths, or essential oil use.

One size does not fit all, however. As a nutritionist, I customize food and nutrition plans that are unique to each of my clients—more than three-fourths of whom, often unknowingly, struggle with some form of autoimmune disease. Whether their symptoms are weight-loss resistance or something more urgent like crippling pain, I always start by aiming to eliminate chronic inflammation.

Proper nutrition is a significant health investment. When you eat poor-quality food, you dip into the nutrient reserves in your bones, soft tissues, organs, glands, skin—even hair! I'm a firm believer that you can teach an old dog new tricks, and that means relearning how to feed ourselves.

Eating in a way that heals inflammation does not have to be a time-consuming ordeal. The principles in this book will help you make shorter trips to the grocery store. You'll quickly choose foods that benefit your body over flashy sweets and treats that leave you depleted. Also, the recipes I provide in this book are easy: Meal prep and cooking times are under 30 minutes, so even your busiest day will allow for healthy eating.

Much nutrition information these days strives to be politically correct. All-encompassing claims demonize entire food groups without well-researched explanations. *The Anti-Inflammatory Diet Cookbook* is different; it includes some previously disparaged foods with information on why preparation and processing are key. For example, many diets kick dairy to the curb, but you'll find it tucked into these pages as an option in its *unprocessed or cultured state*, such as raw cheese or cultured yogurt with natural enzymes and beneficial bacteria that aid digestion and nutrient absorption.

At the top of each recipe I include the following labels so you can identify which ones suit your particular dietary needs:

> **Dairy-free:** includes no dairy products
> **Gluten-free:** includes no gluten-containing ingredients
> **Lactose-free:** includes no diary, but uses ghee
> **Paleo:** appropriate for Paleo diet followers
> **Probiotic:** contains cultured and probiotic-rich dairy, which
>   has a different effect on the body than plain, processed dairy
> **Soy-free:** includes some fermented soy, such as miso
> **Vegan:** includes no animal products
> **Vegetarian:** plant-based recipes that may include eggs,
>   dairy, or honey

This book takes all your meals and snacks—from weeknight comfort foods to special dinners—and pares them down to just the anti-inflammatory ingredients. You can stop searching for new recipes or revising old favorites; this book does the work for you, and the results are healthy, delicious, fast, and easy.

If not actively fighting inflammation and disease, there's a chance you are indirectly encouraging it. Enjoy these recipes knowing each bite provides nourishment that fights inflammation on a molecular level. Do you want to know how a nutritionist feeds her family every day? I show you in this book.

CHAPTER ONE

Healthier Eating Made Easy

An anti-inflammatory diet doesn't have to be restrictive or complicated to follow. Once you understand the basic concepts, you'll quickly and easily reap the benefits. And instead of focusing on what you shouldn't eat, I show you what to eat. Take a minute to flip through these pages to see the satisfying array of easy-to-make, nutrient-dense foods you can enjoy in no time at all.

What Is Inflammation?

Having grown up in California, I've lived through my fair share of wildfires. If contained properly, the flames actually benefit the wildlands and are crucial to the survival of many species. Wildfires clear out old brush, kill off disease, and make room for new generations of plant life to enter the ecosystem.

There are two types of inflammation: Acute inflammation is like a roaring wildfire. While it sounds scary, it cleanses the body of disease and acts as the first phase of healing—working primarily to rid the body of its assailant. On the other side of the spectrum, chronic inflammation is better compared to a never-ending, smoldering fire. If left unaddressed in the body, it will result in an ever-increasing number of immune cells fighting an endless battle, leading to serious disease. Think of acute inflammation as fast acting, high level, and healing, whereas chronic inflammation is lingering, low level, and self-perpetuating.

LIFESTYLE HABITS THAT REDUCE INFLAMMATION

Addressing inflammation with diet is just one piece of the puzzle. A complete solution requires daily lifestyle changes that don't have to be difficult to take on. Here are some basic tips to consider:

Exercise: While a sedentary lifestyle should always be avoided, it is possible to get too much of a good thing when it comes to cardio and high-intensity interval training. Finding the optimal middle ground for your body is key to healing inflammation. Allow plenty of recovery time between workouts, and consume enough nutrients to support tissue repair. Opt for gentler exercises such as yoga, swimming, light weight lifting, and walking.

Manage stress: Both positive and negative stress can have the same detrimental effect on your body. Try restorative or hatha yoga in slow-paced forms that focus on breathing. If you can handle the heat, spend time in an infrared sauna, which may help balance your cortisol levels, or levels of hormones attributed with stress and inflammation regulation.

Get more sleep: Not getting enough sleep will cause inflammation even in the healthiest people. Set a strict bedtime to help your body wind down consistently every night. Incorporate calming supplements, such as magnesium, and teas, such as chamomile tea, into your bedtime routine, and try aromatic lavender and cedarwood essential oils to enhance relaxation.

Our guts house about two-thirds of our bodies' immune cells. These cells work minute by minute to protect us from any intruders we may ingest in the form of food, drink, and other substances such as medicine or supplements. If the gut begins to see too many repeat offenders such as highly reactive foods, allergens, environmental toxins, or medications, the inflammation begins to change from acute to chronic. Inflammation in the gut damages the flora, or good bacteria, that act as neighborhood watchdogs in our intestines. Once damaged, our intricate gut lining can begin to leak foreign matter into the bloodstream, which will be marked as dangerous by our immune systems, inciting even more inflammation. And the vicious cycle will continue.

This inflammation problem is so widespread that just about every disease can be linked to it in some way. Though it may sound overly dramatic, no one is spared when it comes to inflammation. Even if we control our diets to the best of our abilities, we still live in a world where environmental toxins, viruses, bacteria, and yeast run rampant. Some well-known ailments linked closely to chronic inflammation include Alzheimer's disease, carpal tunnel syndrome, Crohn's disease, heart attacks, psoriasis, and strokes. In diseases like anemia, asthma, and rheumatoid arthritis, inflammatory cytokines trigger an immune response that promotes systemic inflammation. This inflammation can lead to everything from heart disease to tissue destruction and cancer.

Even when your inflammation stems from the gut, you may experience symptoms in other parts of your body, such as overall fatigue, brain fog, sore joints, insomnia, depression, anxiety, and muscle pain. If you experience any or all of these symptoms, don't lose heart. Making even small tweaks in your regular diet and including a few more anti-inflammatory foods will begin to alieviate your symptoms.

Following an Anti-Inflammatory Diet

It's important that you don't become overwhelmed when embarking on an anti-inflammatory diet. Here are four easy dietary guidelines to focus on as you begin your journey.

1. *Provide your body with unprocessed, nutrient-dense, healing foods that protect against inflammation.* Choose antioxidant-rich organic produce; wild-caught, cold-water fish high in omega-3 fatty acids; grass-fed,

antibiotic-free meat and animal products; nuts and seeds high in healthy fats, protein, and fiber; and alliums (onions, garlics, leeks) and herbs (basil, oregano, rosemary) packed with unique inflammation-fighting compounds.

2. *Avoid highly reactive foods that cause inflammation.* Not everyone will have the same foods that trigger imbalance in the body, but a few common ones tend to inflame all of us to one degree or another, including wheat gluten, processed dairy, refined sugar, peanuts, processed corn, soy, feedlot animal products, caffeine, and alcohol. Some people are also sensitive to citrus fruits and produce in the nightshade family (such as tomatoes, potatoes, peppers, and eggplant), although these foods are otherwise generally beneficial.

3. *Add supplements and spices that combat inflammation.* When buying supplements, choose natural, food-based ones that will be absorbed by your body more easily. Fermented cod liver oil is the perfect inflammation-fighting supplement. It's one of nature's richest sources of omega-3 fatty acids.

     Anti-inflammatory spices, such as ginger, garlic, cinnamon, and turmeric, are wonderful additions to meals, or you can purchase them in capsule form as a whole food supplement. Each contains unique and powerful compounds. For example, garlic contains high levels of sulfur, which encourages the immune system to fight disease.

4. *Focus on gut healing.* Take a supplemental probiotic—a substance that promotes the health and growth of beneficial intestinal flora (good bacteria naturally present in your intestines). Choose one that contains several strains of bacteria, in several billion CFUs (colony-forming units). Such a supplement is frequently needed because many things we ingest today kill these good bacteria, including NSAIDs (nonsteroidal anti-inflammatory drugs), birth control substances, antibiotics, and many processed foods.

     Sip on bone broth, which contains amino acids that soothe and heal your gut's lining. Enjoy an array of fermented foods (such as sauerkraut, kimchi, traditionally fermented pickles, cultured yogurt, kombucha, and kefir) that deliver healthy gut bacteria straight to your digestive tract.

Foods that Fight Inflammation

Think of starting your anti-inflammatory diet as an act of empowerment. You're taking your health into your own hands and healing your body. The plethora of anti-inflammatory foods far outweighs the list of restricted ones, so take hope: eating through the dishes in this book will be more delicious and nutritious than you think!

HEALTHY FATS

How a fat-containing food is raised or grown and prepared, as well as how many additives it contains, can make a huge difference in the overall healthiness of the fat itself. Trans fats are always harmful; unsaturated fats are widely accepted as good in our culture, in moderation; saturated fats have been controversial but are beginning to shine as necessary in a healthy diet, in moderation, depending on how the food was raised or grown and prepared.

When eating a whole foods diet, fat doesn't have to come just from cooking oil. You can receive the majority of beneficial fats from whole foods such as avocados, nuts, seeds, and some animal products like meat and eggs.

Both avocados and olives are delicious in their whole form or when pressed into a pure oil. They contain high amounts of monounsaturated fats, which support a healthy heart. Avocados also contain a unique group of fats called phytosterols, which supply their own special inflammation-blocking properties.

The primary fatty acids in flaxseed are crucial to protecting against inflammation in blood vessels. The benefits of the fats found in flaxseed, however, go beyond cardiovascular health. They also protect against a wealth of diseases, including type 2 diabetes, obesity, and asthma.

ORGANIC FRUITS AND VEGETABLES

When it comes to organic produce, you definitely want to eat the rainbow! Colorful fruits and vegetables are packed with phytonutrients that fight inflammation and supply your body with enough antioxidants to ward off harmful invaders.

> > Berries—with their high levels of antioxidants and phytonutrients that guard against free radicals—protect against cellular damage while containing only a small amount of natural sugar compared to other fruits. In this way, they minimally affect your blood sugar levels. This is important because insulin resistance is one of the first negative outcomes when unbalanced blood sugar

levels become the norm. Your body produces insulin to help move sugar from the blood to the muscles. If your diet forces this valuable hormone to work overtime too often, your body will eventually stop responding to insulin.

> Dark leafy greens contain two hallmark anti-inflammatory nutrients: vitamin K and omega-3 fatty acids.

> Pineapple contains special enzymes that help our digestive tract break down certain food compounds, resulting in less inflammation overall.

> Root vegetables and squash contain large amounts of vitamins A and C, both highly effective antioxidants that nourish the digestive tract and immune system.

FOOD REACTIONS: SENSITIVITY OR ALLERGY?

Food intolerance and sensitivity typically only disrupt your digestive tract. If your gut feels sensitive to or intolerant of a certain food, it may lack the proper enzymes required to digest that food. Consuming digestive enzymes before large meals can help counter these reactions. Symptoms of sensitivity or intolerance, while never fun, are usually contained within the digestive tract and include bloating, nausea, constipation, or diarrhea.

In contrast to these reactions, allergies arise when your immune system reacts to a specific protein in a food as if it is an invader, and produces antibodies to fight it.

Allergy symptoms can be much more severe, including dizziness, hives, swelling, shortness of breath, and even death.

Your gut could also be reacting to a natural toxin in a food, such as the phytic acid naturally found in nuts that is indigestible to humans.

Soaking grains, legumes, and nuts to remove phytic acid before consumption can make digestion easier.

Food poisoning can also cause digestive distress, making your body react to the toxic bacteria that snuck.

Psychological factors, such as high levels of stress or the sheer dislike of a certain food, can also cause food intolerances to varying degrees.

THE BIG 8 ALLERGENS INCLUDE:

> Dairy
> Wheat
> Fish (e.g., bass, flounder, cod)
> Crustacean shellfish (e.g., crab, lobster, shrimp)
> Tree nuts (e.g., almonds, walnuts, pecans)
> Peanuts
> Eggs
> Soy

Animal products like red meat, eggs, and milk often make it onto the "naughty" list when it comes to a healthy diet and lowering inflammation. However, much of this negativity is related to feedlot animals raised under inhumane conditions and fed poor diets. For example, the food eaten by grass-fed cows is very different from the food eaten by conventionally raised cows. Cows raised 100 percent on grass produce beef and milk that are noticeably higher in healthy omega-3 fatty acids, vitamin E, beta-carotene, and the beneficial fatty acid CLA (conjugated linoleic acid).

Similarly, chickens raised on pastured land instead of in cages are free to eat any grasses, bugs, and legumes they find, allowing them to produce eggs containing 200 percent more vitamin E than caged hens. The omega-3 fatty acids present in egg yolks is also increased when chickens are traditionally pasture-fed rather than crammed into unsanitary cages.

The most widely sought animal-based omega-3s come from wild-caught fatty fish such as salmon. Many nutritionists now recommend a supplement with fish oil, like krill or cod liver oil, to increase your intake of these beneficial inflammation-fighting omega-3s.

HERBS AND SPICES

Cooking with fresh herbs and spices does more than just add good flavors to your food; think of it as sprinkling a dust of antioxidants, vitamins, and minerals every time you shake your spice jar. Spices and herbs found to be significant at quelling inflammation include cinnamon, cloves, ginger, basil, oregano, rosemary, sage, thyme, and turmeric.

Basil is unique because it contains compounds called eugenols that mimic over-the-counter, anti-inflammatory drugs like ibuprofen. Basil's medicinal qualities have been used to help those suffering from inflammation in the form of inflammatory bowel disease and rheumatoid arthritis.

Foods that Worsen Inflammation

Just as you want to be fully informed about foods that will alleviate and reduce inflammation, spend some time becoming familiar with the following inflammation-inducing foods. You'll want to be able to recognize these ingredients quickly to avoid them, especially when they're skillfully hidden by the manufacturer.

If you intentionally avoid these inflammation-worsening foods for a few weeks, you may find your body doesn't crave them as much after all.

GLUTEN

Gluten, a protein in wheat that acts as a glue to help food maintain its shape and texture, seems to be the most talked about food compound in our country. Besides wheat, it's also in other grains like bulgur, farro, semolina, rye, spelt, and any flour made from these grains. For people with celiac disease–a genetic autoimmune disorder–the ingestion of gluten leads to damage in the small intestine. Even if you don't have celiac disease, gluten is still a difficult protein to digest, causing a wide array of symptoms from brain fog to joint pain. Anyone suffering from a chronic autoimmune disease will most likely benefit from eliminating gluten from their diet.

Gluten has been around since the dawn of time, so why has there been so much negativity about it in just this past decade? While ancient grains nourished our

SHOULD I DETOX FIRST?

Strict cleanses and extreme detoxification protocols are not necessary for most people, and can even cause severe die-off reactions (when large amounts of pathogens die at once, releasing metabolic by-products, leaving you feeling ill) if not planned carefully. Instead, try a gentler approach to help your body's intrinsic detoxification pathways.

> Start your day with a glass of warm water, plus a splash each of apple cider vinegar and lemon juice. Filtering your drinking water is an important step toward better health, because even "clean" tap water can be dirtier than it looks after traveling through miles of old pipeline and being laced with disinfectants from water treatment plants. Apple cider vinegar encourages your stomach to start the day by

creating the proper amount of stomach acid, which is necessary for proper nutrient absorption and digestion. Lemon juice stimulates the liver to produce bile, priming your system for digestion.

> Avoid the reactive foods previously mentioned. Replace them with gentle foods easier for your unique body to digest, such as steamed vegetables, broths, and liver-stimulating spices.

> Sip on probiotic tonics like kombucha and kvass, which include probiotic material that help clean out your gut.

> Help your body work out toxins through the lymphatic system via lifestyle activities like massage, yoga, or infrared saunas.

ancestors for thousands of years, it wasn't until this past century that modernized wheat varieties were created. One theory behind modern gluten intolerance stems from the use of new chemical pesticides while growing them.

Gluten can be hidden in everything from soy sauce to deli meat, so read the nutrition label for anything relating to wheat protein or gluten. Rather than replacing glutenous products like breads or pastas with gluten-free versions, simply add more nourishing anti-inflammatory foods to your plate (suggested in the pages of this book). Most gluten-free products contain lots of extra sugar and simple carbohydrates that aren't necessarily healthy for you either.

DAIRY

While modern milk ads feature everyone from schoolteachers to Olympic athletes, dairy may not be as healthy as we've been led to believe. It's not milk's fault, however, but rather that of modernization and conventional processes thrust upon it.

Conventional dairy products often have added sugar and preservatives. They're also pasteurized at high heat, which means they're devoid of the natural enzymes that help the digestive tract properly break down milk's proteins. Pasteurized milk is a processed food. The healthier alternative for some people is organic, raw, cultured dairy, which is a whole and unadulterated food. Raw milk contains lactase, the enzyme required to digest lactose. Cultured dairy, like kefir and yogurt, contains beneficial bacteria that have partially digested the complete proteins found in the dairy, making it easier for humans to digest.

If you know you're sensitive to dairy, and because most conventional dairy sold today is pasteurized, consider trying cultured or raw dairy from a trusted organic source.

SOY

This controversial legume is a common allergen in the United States, yet it's widely enjoyed in many other countries. Part of the reason behind this controversy is that the majority of soy grown in the United States has been genetically modified, causing a wide variety of digestive problems in both animals and humans.

Soy contains high levels of an anti-nutrient called phytic acid, which prevents our bodies from absorbing other nutrients. The phytoestrogens found in soy have been linked to thyroid diseases like autoimmune disorders and cancer.

Fermenting soy can help neutralize some of the toxins found in it today, which is the way many other countries enjoy soy. Traditionally fermented soy sauce, miso, and tempeh are examples.

CORN

Like soy, corn is not inherently bad for you, but it's been treated in such a way over the past several decades that its chemical makeup has changed into a food that poses potentially serious health risks for consumers. Again, the majority of corn in the United States is genetically modified and not organic, leading to compromised immune systems and the promotion of inflammation in our bodies.

If you were raised on a standard American diet, you've probably consumed lots of processed corn constituents like high fructose corn syrup and corn oil. When choosing to eat this grain, always choose a non-GMO organic from a trusted source.

ANTI-INFLAMMATORY PANTRY CHECKLIST

Keeping a good supply of anti-inflammatory pantry staples provides a solid foundation for creating quick, healthy meals. Following is a list of kitchen staples for an anti-inflammatory diet that are used in many recipes in this book.

Grains
> Flour: almond
> Oats, rolled
> Quinoa
> Rice: brown, white, wild

Legumes
> Dried and canned beans: black, cannellini, garbanzo (chickpeas), kidney, navy
> Lentils: brown and red
> Peas

Nuts and Seeds (preferably raw)
> Almonds and almond butter
> Cashews
> Hazelnuts
> Pistachios
> Seeds: chia, flax, hemp, sesame, sunflower
> Tahini (sesame paste)

Fats
> Ghee, pasture-raised
> Oil: avocado, coconut, flaxseed, olive (extra-virgin), sesame seed (expeller-pressed)

Sweeteners
> Coconut sugar
> Honey, raw
> Medjool dates
> Stevia, liquid extract
> Syrup, maple (100 percent pure)

Miscellaneous
> Coconut: aminos (bottled soy-free seasoning sauce made from coconut tree sap), cream, milk
> Collagen peptides (protein powder)
> Fish sauce
> Matcha powder
> Mayonnaise, Paleo
> Miso paste
> Salt, unrefined
> Spices, organic
> Vinegar, apple cider, balsamic

Healthy in a Hurry

If you're feeling even the littlest bit overwhelmed at this point, don't lose heart! This new anti-inflammatory adventure doesn't need to create stress. Follow these quick tips to save time and energy in both the grocery store and kitchen.

1. *Plan ahead.* While just about every healthy cookbook will tell you this, I really mean it. A few minutes organizing ingredients the night before can make the entire next day of cooking so much smoother. For example, pour some dried beans in a bowl of filtered water to soak overnight or place your smoothie ingredients in a freezer bag before heading to bed.

2. *Make a detailed shopping list.* Walk through the grocery store in your head, picturing where each category of ingredients is displayed. Group the items by area or aisle to make your next shopping trip a confident speed-walk rather than a frustrated search.

3. *Leftovers are your new best friend.* Cut the number of meals you make each week in half by doubling the recipes, or being mindful of portions and refrigerating or freezing any extras for another day.

4. *Batch cook.* Plan to make extras of a few basic dishes over the weekend that you will add to different meals throughout the week. Plain quinoa, versatile dressings, cooked beans, and grilled chicken can all be worked into various meals in many ways. Do this on a larger scale and freeze quantities of already prepared ingredients. Just remember to move them to the refrigerator to thaw well in advance of when you need them.

MAKING HEALTHY FOOD CHOICES

WHAT TO ENJOY (FOODS THAT FIGHT INFLAMMATION)

Dark Leafy Greens
- Collard greens
- Mixed lettuces
- Mustard greens
- Romaine lettuce
- Spinach
- Swiss chard

Root Vegetables
- Beets
- Carrots
- Celery root
- Parsnips
- Squash: butternut, Hubbard, kabocha, pumpkin, spaghetti, zucchini
- Sweet potatoes
- Yams

Alliums
- Garlic
- Onions
- Scallions
- Shallots

Cruciferous Vegetables
- Arugula
- Bok choy
- Broccoli
- Brussels sprouts
- Cabbage
- Cauliflower
- Kale
- Radishes

Fruit
- Apples
- Bananas
- Blackberries
- Blueberries
- Cherries
- Lemons
- Limes
- Pineapple
- Raspberries
- Stone fruits
- Strawberries

Nuts and Seeds
- Almonds
- Brazil nuts
- Cashews
- Hazelnuts
- Pistachios
- Seeds: chia, flax, hemp, pumpkin, sesame
- Walnuts

Beans and Legumes
- Beans: black, cannellini, garbanzo (chickpeas), kidney, navy
- Lentils
- Split peas

Grains
- Buckwheat
- Millet
- Quinoa
- Rice: brown, white, wild
- Teff
- Sprouted flours like spelt

Herbs and Spices
- Basil
- Cinnamon
- Cloves
- Cumin
- Dill
- Fennel
- Ginger
- Oregano
- Rosemary
- Sage
- Turmeric

Animal Products

- Anchovies
- Beef, grass-fed
- Bone broth
- Chicken, pasture-raised
- Halibut
- Lamb
- Salmon
- Shrimp
- Trout
- Tuna
- Turkey

Fats and Oils

- Butter, pastured
- Ghee, pastured
- Oil: avocado, coconut, flaxseed, olive (extra-virgin), sesame seed (expeller-pressed), as well as the whole foods themselves

Sweeteners

- Coconut sugar
- Honey, raw
- Medjool dates and date paste
- Molasses
- Stevia leaf and extract
- Syrup: brown rice, maple (100 percent pure)

WHAT TO AVOID (FOODS THAT WORSEN INFLAMMATION)

Fats and Oils

- Margarine
- Oils: canola, corn, peanut, rapeseed, soybean, vegetable
- Trans fats (often called hydrogenated or partially hydrogenated oils on the ingredients label)

Nuts and Seeds

- Peanuts

Grains

- Corn, genetically modified (i.e., not organic per the USDA's National Organic Standards, or verified non-GMO by a third-party organization like the Non-GMO Project)
- Refined wheat flours
- Wheat and other gluten-containing grains: barley, bulgur, farro
- Wheat pastas

Unfermented Soy Products

- Soy: beans, milk, protein, sauce
- Vegetable protein, textured

Citrus Fruits (in excess)

- All

Nightshade Vegetables (if sensitive to them)

- Eggplant
- Peppers
- Potatoes, white
- Tomatoes

Feedlot Meat and Animal Products

- Dairy products, processed
- Eggs, factory-farmed

Sweeteners

- Agave nectar
- Sugar: brown or white, refined
- Syrup: corn, high fructose corn syrup

CHAPTER TWO

Kitchen Staples

BEANS

DAIRY-FREE, GLUTEN-FREE, SOY-FREE, VEGAN

MAKES 2 ½ CUPS COOKED BEANS / PREP TIME: 5 MINUTES,
PLUS OVERNIGHT SOAKING TIME / COOK TIME: 1 HOUR

I am a huge fan of making all kinds of beans from scratch. It's the cheapest way to do it, and it's the healthiest. Canned beans are often high in salt, and can introduce toxic BPA (bisphenol A) from the plastic lining in the can. When you're in charge of the process from start to finish, you can soak the dried beans before cooking them, which cuts down on cooking time and removes the gut-harming phytic acid. Plus, they're a versatile ingredient in all kinds of recipes and they freeze well.

8 ounces dried beans

Filtered water, for soaking and cooking

Pinch salt

Seasonings, such as bay leaves, garlic, onion, cumin (optional)

PER SERVING (½ cup)
Calories: 153; Total Fat: 1g; Saturated Fat: 0g;
Cholesterol: 0mg; Carbohydrates: 28g; Fiber: 7g;
Protein: 10g

1. In a large glass bowl, cover the beans with water. Add the salt and let soak on the counter, covered, overnight.

2. Drain the beans and rinse well. Transfer to a large pot and add any seasonings you like (if using).

3. Cover the beans with 1 to 2 inches of water, place the pot over high heat, and bring to a boil. Reduce heat to low and simmer for 1 hour.

4. Check the beans for doneness; some varieties require longer cooking times. Continue to simmer, if needed, and check every 10 minutes until done. Use immediately in soups or chilis, or refrigerate in an airtight container for up to 1 week. Cooked beans can also be frozen for up to 3 months.

COOKING TIP: One cup of dried beans will expand two or three times in size when cooked. Measure with this in mind.

ALMOND-HAZELNUT MILK

DAIRY-FREE, GLUTEN-FREE, PALEO, SOY-FREE, VEGETARIAN

MAKES ABOUT 4 CUPS / PREP TIME: 15 MINUTES

Nut milk is a popular alternative to dairy milk. It is anti-inflammatory, low calorie, and easy to make. Mix and match different types of nuts, as I've done here, until you find a flavor profile you prefer. If you're using nut milk as a dairy replacement in savory recipes, omit the honey and vanilla.

½ cup soaked raw hazelnuts, drained (See Preparation Tip)

½ cup soaked raw almonds, drained (See Preparation Tip)

4 cups filtered water

1 teaspoon raw honey (optional)

¼ teaspoon vanilla extract (optional)

PER SERVING (1 cup) Calories: 85; Total Fat: 5g; Saturated Fat: 0g; Cholesterol: 0mg; Carbohydrates: 10g; Fiber: 1g; Protein: 2g

1. In a colander, combine the hazelnuts and almonds and give them a good rinse. Transfer to a blender and add the water. Blend at high speed for 30 seconds.

2. Place a nut milk bag (see Equipment Tip) or other meshlike material over a large bowl and carefully pour the nut mixture into it.

3. Pick up the top of the bag and strain the liquid into the bowl, squeezing the pulp to remove as much liquid as possible.

4. Using a funnel, transfer the nut milk to a sealable bottle. Add the honey (if using) and vanilla (if using). Seal the bottle and shake well. Refrigerate for up to 4 days.

EQUIPMENT TIP: There is nothing special about a nut milk bag, it just needs to be made from a meshlike material. If you don't have one, use cheesecloth or even an old pair of clean tights.

PREPARATION TIP: The raw nuts can be soaked together, for at least seven hours, with 1 tablespoon of sea salt (this will get rinsed off so it doesn't affect sodium levels).

LEMON-DIJON MUSTARD DRESSING

DAIRY-FREE, GLUTEN-FREE, PALEO, SOY-FREE, VEGETARIAN

MAKES ABOUT 6 TABLESPOONS / PREP TIME: 5 MINUTES

Using high-quality extra-virgin olive oil makes all the difference in this dressing—and for your health. This oil contains a compound similar to aspirin that inhibits inflammation, and even has similar benefits used topically; those suffering from arthritis in the hands can rub it on like lotion for added relief. Poor-quality olive oil tastes bland, whereas cold-pressed extra-virgin olive oil is a deeper green and adds bright olive under-tones to your dish.

¼ cup extra-virgin olive oil

2 tablespoons freshly squeezed lemon juice

1 teaspoon Dijon mustard

½ teaspoon raw honey

1 garlic clove, minced

¼ teaspoon dried basil

¼ teaspoon salt

PER SERVING (1½ tablespoons) Calories: 128; Total Fat: 13.5g; Saturated Fat: 1.8g; Cholesterol: 0mg; Carbohydrates: 1.8g; Fiber: 0.1g; Protein: 0.1g

In a glass jar with a lid, combine the olive oil, lemon juice, mustard, honey, garlic, basil, and salt. Cover and shake vigorously until the ingredients are well combined and emulsified. Refrigerate for up to 1 week.

INGREDIENT TIP: I use whole-grain Dijon mustard because it adds texture. If you prefer a creamier dressing, use a smoother Dijon.

TAHINI-LIME DRESSING

DAIRY-FREE, GLUTEN-FREE, PALEO, SOY-FREE, VEGETARIAN

MAKES ABOUT ¾ CUP / PREP TIME: 5 MINUTES

Tahini comes to us from several Middle Eastern countries and stems from the Arabic word "to grind." It's a smooth paste made from ground, hulled sesame seeds. Sesame is extremely high in copper, known for lowering the inflammation that causes rheumatoid arthritis. Purchase tahini or make your own by toasting sesame seeds and grinding them to a paste in a food processor. This dressing is rather nutty, with a splash of zesty citrus that tickles your taste buds.

⅓ cup tahini (sesame paste)

3 tablespoons filtered water

2 tablespoons freshly squeezed lime juice

1 tablespoon apple cider vinegar

1 teaspoon lime zest

1½ teaspoons raw honey

¼ teaspoon garlic powder

¼ teaspoon salt

PER SERVING (1½ tablespoons) Calories: 157; Total Fat: 12.6g; Saturated Fat: 2.1g; Cholesterol: 0mg; Carbohydrates: 5.1g; Fiber: 0g; Protein: 6.2g

In a glass jar with a lid, combine the tahini, water, lime juice, vinegar, lime zest, honey, garlic powder, and salt. Cover and shake vigorously until the ingredients are well combined and emulsified. Refrigerate for up to 1 week.

PREPARATION TIP: Tahini can differ in consistency and thickness. If yours becomes too thick to shake in a jar, whisk in a bit more water.

PALEO CAESAR DRESSING

DAIRY-FREE, GLUTEN-FREE, PALEO, SOY-FREE

MAKES ABOUT ½ CUP / PREP TIME: 10 MINUTES

Traditional Caesar dressing includes anchovies. Since these are not a staple in the typical American pantry, I keep a small tube of anchovy paste in the refrigerator. It lasts a long time, and you still get the flavor and omega-3 benefits. If you can't find anchovy paste, substitute miso paste or fish sauce, or omit it altogether for a slightly less rich taste.

¼ cup Paleo mayonnaise

2 tablespoons extra-virgin olive oil

2 tablespoons freshly squeezed lemon juice

½ teaspoon lemon zest

2 garlic cloves, minced

1 tablespoon white wine vinegar

½ teaspoon anchovy paste

¼ teaspoon salt

Freshly ground black pepper

PER SERVING (2 tablespoons)
Calories: 167; Total Fat: 18.9g; Saturated Fat: 2.4g;
Cholesterol: 22.3mg; Carbohydrates: 1.3g;
Fiber: 0.3g; Protein: 0.2g

In a small bowl, whisk the mayonnaise, olive oil, lemon juice, lemon zest, garlic, vinegar, anchovy paste, and salt until well combined and emulsified. Season with pepper. Cover and refrigerate for up to 1 week.

INGREDIENT TIP: I use Primal Kitchen brand mayonnaise, made with avocado oil and organic, cage-free eggs. You can also make your own Paleo mayonnaise using recipes found on the Internet.

THE EVERYTHING AIOLI

GLUTEN-FREE, PROBIOTIC, SOY-FREE

MAKES ABOUT ½ CUP / PREP TIME: 5 MINUTES

This aioli is a lighter spin on the traditional dip made with mayonnaise and garlic. Use plain yogurt without added sweeteners or flavors. I prefer full-fat, cultured dairy because it's typically easier to digest than conventional dairy that had its fat processed and reduced. Serve this with a rainbow plate of crudités for healthy snacking, or alongside Baked Zucchini Fries (page 71), plantain chips, or any of the burgers in this book.

½ cup plain whole-milk yogurt

2 teaspoons Dijon mustard

½ teaspoon hot sauce

¼ teaspoon raw honey

Pinch salt

PER SERVING (2 tablespoons)
Calories: 43; Total Fat: 2.4g; Saturated Fat: 1.5g; Cholesterol: 10mg; Carbohydrates: 3.2g; Fiber: 0g; Protein: 2g

In a small bowl, stir together the yogurt, mustard, hot sauce, honey, and salt. Serve immediately, or cover and refrigerate for up to 3 days.

INGREDIENT TIP: I prefer a hot sauce with no added sugar and only natural ingredients, such as Cholula brand.

PREPARATION TIP: For a vegetarian version, substitute plain coconut yogurt for the whole-milk yogurt, although the taste will be slightly different.

PISTACHIO PESTO

GLUTEN-FREE, SOY-FREE, VEGETARIAN

MAKES 4 CUPS / PREP TIME: 10 MINUTES

Pistachios, while a bit pesky to open, promote heart-healthy blood lipid profiles, meaning you'll have lower risk of heart disease and inflammation. The compound that gives pistachios their green color is lutein, which wards off oxidative stress in the retina and promotes eye health. Basil includes a compound that works to block an inflammation-causing enzyme in the body in ways similar to medications like aspirin or ibuprofen. What's not to love?

2 cups tightly packed fresh basil leaves

1 cup raw pistachios

½ cup extra-virgin olive oil, divided

½ cup shredded raw Parmesan cheese

2 teaspoons freshly squeezed lemon juice

½ teaspoon garlic powder

¼ teaspoon salt

Freshly ground black pepper

PER SERVING (4 ounces) Calories: 229;
Total Fat: 22.3g; Saturated Fat: 3.6g; Cholesterol: 4.8mg;
Carbohydrates: 3.8g; Fiber: 1.7g; Protein: 5.5g

1. In a food processor (or blender), combine the basil, pistachios, and ¼ cup of olive oil. Blend for 15 seconds.

2. Add the cheese, lemon juice, garlic powder, and salt, and season with pepper.

3. With the processor running, slowly pour in the remaining ¼ cup of olive oil until all ingredients are well combined. Serve immediately, cover and refrigerate for up to 5 days, or freeze for 3 to 4 months.

TIME-SAVING TIP: Look for Parmesan cheese sold in small tubs already shaved or shredded.

ALMOND ROMESCO SAUCE

DAIRY-FREE, GLUTEN-FREE, PALEO, SOY-FREE, VEGAN

MAKES 2 CUPS / PREP TIME: 10 MINUTES / COOK TIME: 10 MINUTES

The heart of traditional Spanish romesco sauce is a blend of nuts and red bell peppers. Usually bits of stale bread or bread crumbs are added as a thickener, but this anti-inflammatory option is full of flavor and texture without them. This versatile sauce can be served warm or cold. Try it with the Grilled Salmon Packets with Asparagus (page 140), or the Baked Chicken Breast with Lemon and Garlic (page 152).

2 red bell peppers, roughly chopped

5 or 6 cherry tomatoes, roughly chopped

3 garlic cloves, roughly chopped

½ white onion, roughly chopped

1 tablespoon avocado oil

1 cup blanched raw almonds

¼ cup extra-virgin olive oil

2 tablespoons apple cider vinegar

¼ teaspoon salt

Freshly ground black pepper

PER SERVING (4 ounces) Calories: 358;
Total Fat: 32.2g; Saturated Fat: 3.2g; Cholesterol: 0mg;
Carbohydrates: 13.7g; Fiber: 6.4g; Protein: 7.3g

1. Preheat the broiler to high.

2. Line a baking sheet with aluminum foil. Spread the bell peppers, tomatoes, garlic, and onion on the prepared sheet and drizzle with the avocado oil. Broil for 10 minutes.

3. In a food processor (or blender), pulse the almonds until they resemble bread crumbs.

4. Add the broiled vegetables, olive oil, vinegar, and salt, and season with pepper. Process until smooth. Serve immediately. Cover and refrigerate for up to 5 days, or freeze for 3 to 4 months.

COOKING TIP: Blanched almonds–almonds with their skins removed–are used here because the skins detract from the creaminess of the sauce. Blanch your own almonds in a pot of boiling filtered water for 45 seconds. Promptly rinse them in cool water. Lightly rub the almonds between your fingers and they will burst easily from their skins.

SWEET FIG SMOOTHIE (PAGE 37)

CHAPTER THREE

Smoothies, Beverages & Breakfast

TURMERIC LASSI

Nourishing and quick, smoothies and lassis can be similar in texture and flavor, but differ in their main ingredients: Smoothies are fruit-based, while lassis are yogurt- or kefir-based drinks with roots in India. Turmeric, featured here, is a bright orange-yellow root that contains powerful bioactive compounds called curcuminoids, which target inflammation in the body at a molecular level, similar in many ways to anti-inflammatory drugs.

2 cups plain whole-milk yogurt, or milk kefir

1 banana

1 tablespoon freshly squeezed lemon juice

2 teaspoons raw honey

1 teaspoon ground turmeric

½ teaspoon ground cinnamon

¼ teaspoon ground ginger

PER SERVING Calories: 234; Total Fat: 8.2g; Saturated Fat: 5.2g; Cholesterol: 31.9mg; Carbohydrates: 33.5g; Fiber: 2.2g; Protein: 9.3g

In a blender, blend the yogurt, banana, lemon juice, honey, turmeric, cinnamon, and ginger until smooth. Pour into two tall glasses and serve immediately.

INGREDIENT TIP: Both yogurt and milk kefir are probiotic dairy beverages that can be used interchangeably in many recipes. They are made differently and end up containing different strains of beneficial bacteria, but both typically taste tart.

SWEET FIG SMOOTHIE

GLUTEN-FREE, SOY-FREE, PROBIOTIC, VEGETARIAN

SERVES 2 / PREP TIME: 5 MINUTES

Not only are figs deliciously and naturally sweet, but they are also rich in three very important minerals: potassium, magnesium, and calcium. In addition, their high fiber content helps counter their natural sugar to balance blood sugar levels when consumed.

7 whole figs, fresh or frozen, halved

1 banana

1 cup plain whole-milk yogurt

1 cup almond milk

1 tablespoon almond butter

1 teaspoon ground flaxseed

1 teaspoon raw honey

Ice (optional)

PER SERVING Calories: 362; Total Fat: 12g; Saturated Fat: 3g; Cholesterol: 16mg; Carbohydrates: 60g; Fiber: 9g; Protein: 9g

In a blender, combine the figs, banana, yogurt, almond milk, almond butter, flaxseed, and honey. Blend until smooth. Add ice (if using) and blend again to thicken. Pour into two tall glasses and serve immediately.

PREPARATION TIP: If you need a dairy-free version, substitute a dairy-free yogurt for the whole-milk yogurt.

MATCHA BERRY SMOOTHIE

DAIRY-FREE, GLUTEN-FREE, PALEO, SOY-FREE

SERVES 2 / PREP TIME: 5 MINUTES

This easy smoothie contains matcha, a nutrient-packed green tea powder from Japan that supports healthy blood pressure. Its small amount of natural caffeine is paired with L-theanine, which slows and sustains the effects of caffeine on the body, keeping the jitters and other negative side effects at bay while promoting mental clarity.

2 cups nut milk of choice

2 cups frozen blueberries

1 banana

2 tablespoons neutral-flavored protein powder (optional)

1 tablespoon matcha powder

1 tablespoon chia seeds

¼ teaspoon ground cinnamon

¼ teaspoon ground ginger

Pinch salt

PER SERVING (without protein powder)
Calories: 208; Total Fat: 5.7g; Saturated Fat: 0.3g;
Cholesterol: 0mg; Carbohydrates: 31g;
Fiber: 8.3g; Protein: 8.7g

In a blender, blend the nut milk, blueberries, banana, protein powder (if using), matcha, chia seeds, cinnamon, ginger, and salt until smooth. Pour into two glasses and serve immediately.

INGREDIENT TIP: Collagen peptides are my neutral-flavored protein powder of choice. They are short chain amino acids naturally derived from collagen protein from pasture-raised, grass-fed cattle.

YEAR-ROUND PUMPKIN PIE SMOOTHIE

DAIRY-FREE, GLUTEN-FREE, PALEO, SOY-FREE, VEGAN

SERVES 2 / PREP TIME: 5 MINUTES

Why wait all year for that fall-only pumpkin spice craze? Whip up this smoothie any time. While pumpkin, like most squash, is mostly starches, these starches are unique in that they provide special antioxidant, anti-inflammatory, and anti-diabetic properties. Vitamin A heals inflamed, damaged skin while boosting immunity. And pumpkin's rich serving of fiber keeps blood sugar balanced while supporting healthy digestion.

1 banana

½ cup unsweetened canned pumpkin

1 cup nut milk of choice

2 or 3 ice cubes

2 heaping tablespoons almond butter

1 teaspoon ground cinnamon

1 teaspoon ground nutmeg

1 teaspoon pure maple syrup

1 teaspoon vanilla extract

In a blender, combine the banana, pumpkin, nut milk, ice, almond butter, cinnamon, nutmeg, maple syrup, and vanilla until smooth. Pour into two tall glasses and serve immediately.

INGREDIENT TIP: The nut butter adds that pie crust taste. If you have cashew butter on hand, try that instead for a different flavor profile.

PER SERVING Calories: 235; Total Fat: 11g; Saturated Fat: 0.6g; Cholesterol: 0mg; Carbohydrates: 27.8g; Fiber: 6.9g; Protein: 5.6g

PINEAPPLE-CARROT-GINGER JUICE

DAIRY-FREE, GLUTEN-FREE, SOY-FREE, VEGAN

SERVES 2 / PREP TIME: 10 MINUTES

Pineapple contains an enzyme called bromelain, known as a powerful digestive aid and inflammation-reducing properties. Including more pineapple in your diet is a sweet way to naturally improve digestion. Carrots contain a unique blend of powerful antioxidants that have an anti-inflammatory effect on the cardiovascular system when they are present together, another reason for eating whole foods in their natural state.

3 cups chopped fresh pineapple

8 carrots, roughly chopped

¼ cup filtered water

1 (1-inch) piece peeled fresh ginger

Ice, for serving

PER SERVING Calories: 135; Total Fat: 0.7g; Saturated Fat: 0.1g; Cholesterol: 0mg; Carbohydrates: 40g; Fiber: 1g; Protein: 2.6g

1. In a blender, blend the pineapple, carrots, water, and ginger until smooth.

2. Place a nut milk bag or piece of cheesecloth over the top of a medium bowl. Pour the juice into the mesh material (see Preparation Tip). Squeeze the juice through the material until all the liquid has drained into the bowl. Discard the solids. In two tall glasses, add ice and serve immediately.

PREPARATION TIP: If you own a juicer, an appliance made for extracting juice from fruits and vegetables, omit the water in this recipe and proceed with the other ingredients per your juicer's instructions. If you don't own a juicer or a nut milk bag or cheesecloth, use a fine-mesh sieve or strainer placed over a bowl. Push the liquid through with a rubber spatula, and allow the mixture to sit for 5 to 10 minutes as it drains slowly into the bowl beneath it.

TART CHERRY SPARKLING LEMONADE

DAIRY-FREE, GLUTEN-FREE, SOY-FREE, VEGETARIAN

SERVES 1 / PREP TIME: 5 MINUTES

According to a 2013 study by the National Center for Biotechnology Information, tart cherries contain antioxidants that reduce the pain and inflammation associated with osteoarthritis. They are also high in anthocyanins, as indicated by their deep red pigment, which improve the body's ability to reduce oxidative damage. Cheers!

8 ounces sparkling mineral water

4 ounces tart cherry juice

2 tablespoons freshly squeezed lemon juice

Few drops raw honey (optional)

Ice, for serving

PER SERVING Calories: 137; Total Fat: 0.1g; Saturated Fat: 0g; Cholesterol: 0mg; Carbohydrates: 34.1g; Fiber: 0.1g; Protein: 1.1g

In a tall glass, gently stir together the mineral water, cherry juice, lemon juice, and honey (if using). Add ice and serve.

INGREDIENT TIP: Tart cherry juice can be found in most grocery stores in the bottled juice section.

PREPARATION TIP: Omit the honey for a vegan option.

CIDER SPRITZER

DAIRY-FREE, GLUTEN-FREE, SOY-FREE, VEGETARIAN

SERVES 1 / PREP TIME: 5 MINUTES

This icy beverage has a tartness that refreshes and cleanses the palate. The acetic acid and high mineral content in the apple cider vinegar have been shown to reduce swelling and inflammation in the body.

8 ounces sparkling water

1 tablespoon apple cider vinegar

1 tablespoon freshly squeezed lemon juice

Few drops raw honey

Ice, for serving

PER SERVING Calories: 6; Total Fat: 0g; Saturated Fat: 0g; Cholesterol: 0mg; Carbohydrates: 1.8g; Fiber: 0g; Protein: 0.1g

In a tall glass, gently stir together the sparkling water, vinegar, lemon juice, and honey. Pour over ice and serve immediately.

INGREDIENT TIP: When buying apple cider vinegar, choose raw, unfiltered, and organic when possible.

PREPARATION TIP: Omit the honey for a vegan version.

SANTA BARBARA MIGAS

DAIRY-FREE, GLUTEN-FREE, PALEO, SOY-FREE, VEGETARIAN

SERVES 4 / PREP TIME: 10 MINUTES / COOK TIME: 10 MINUTES

Traditionally, migas, a dish from Spain and Portugal, includes day-old bread soaked in oil and spices, and possibly heated with some leftover meat. The type of migas typically found on menus in the United States is more in line with Tex-Mex culture–full of eggs and strips of fried corn tortillas (an anti-inflammatory no-no). Plantain chips create the perfect anti-inflammatory substitute.

1 tablespoon avocado oil

½ onion, diced

8 eggs

¾ teaspoon salt

½ teaspoon garlic powder

½ teaspoon freshly ground black pepper

½ cup plantain chips, crushed

½ cup salsa

2 avocados, sliced

Splash of freshly squeezed lime juice

Fresh cilantro leaves, for garnish (optional)

PER SERVING Calories: 374; Total Fat: 27g; Saturated Fat: 6g; Cholesterol: 370mg; Carbohydrates: 22g; Fiber: 6g; Protein: 14g

1. In a small skillet over medium heat, add the avocado oil and sauté the onion until translucent, about 5 minutes

2. In a medium bowl, whisk the eggs, salt, garlic powder, and pepper. Add to the skillet, and stir until cooked to your desired doneness, 2 to 3 minutes.

3. Add the plantain chips to the egg mixture. Stir well and remove the skillet from the heat.

4. Top with the salsa and avocado. Sprinkle with the lime juice. Garnish with cilantro (if using) and serve immediately.

INGREDIENT TIP: Plantains (a member of the banana family) are usually cooked, whereas sweet bananas are mostly eaten raw. Due to their starchier qualities and higher beta-carotene concentration, plantains are treated more like a vegetable than a fruit in modern cuisine.

SPINACH & LEEK FRITTATA

DAIRY-FREE, GLUTEN-FREE, PALEO, SOY-FREE, VEGETARIAN

SERVES 4 / PREP TIME: 5 MINUTES / COOK TIME: 20 MINUTES

A frittata is the Italian version of an open-faced omelet or a little like a crustless quiche. This easy egg dish allows for plenty of creativity when it comes to the vegetables you include. For added protein, if you eat meat, add some small chunks of homemade Turkey-Maple Breakfast Sausage (page 48).

2 leeks (white and pale green parts only), thoroughly washed and finely chopped

2 tablespoons avocado oil

8 eggs

¾ teaspoon salt

½ teaspoon garlic powder

½ teaspoon dried basil

1 cup packed fresh baby spinach leaves, thoroughly washed and dried

1 cup sliced cremini mushrooms

Freshly ground black pepper

PER SERVING Calories: 276; Total Fat: 17g; Saturated Fat: 4g; Cholesterol: 372mg; Carbohydrates: 15g; Fiber: 3g; Protein: 19g

1. Preheat the oven to 400°F.

2. In a large ovenproof skillet over medium-high heat, sauté the leeks in the avocado oil for about 5 minutes until soft.

3. In a medium bowl, whisk the eggs, salt, garlic powder, and basil. Add to the skillet with the leeks. Cook for 5 minutes, stirring frequently.

4. Stir in the spinach and mushrooms. Season with pepper. Transfer the skillet to the oven. Bake for 10 minutes, or until the eggs are firmly set.

INGREDIENT TIP: Baby spinach leaves are the best option for this recipe, but if you have larger spinach, simply cut the leaves into bite-size ribbons.

BREAKFAST "FRIED RICE"

DAIRY-FREE, GLUTEN-FREE, PALEO, SOY-FREE, VEGETARIAN

SERVES 2 / PREP TIME: 10 MINUTES / COOK TIME: 15 MINUTES

Day-old rice makes for a better consistency in this dish than moist, freshly steamed rice. Using leftover rice from dinner the night before is the perfect way to whisk this breakfast dish up in a matter of minutes.

½ white onion, diced

2 garlic cloves, minced

1 tablespoon avocado oil

¼ cup non-GMO organic sweet corn kernels

¼ cup peas

¼ cup shredded carrots

2 cups cooked rice

1 tablespoon sesame oil

2 eggs, whisked

Dash red pepper flakes

¼ teaspoon salt

Freshly ground black pepper

PER SERVING Calories: 453; Total Fat: 19g; Saturated Fat: 43; Cholesterol: 186mg; Carbohydrates: 59g; Fiber: 3g; Protein: 13g

1. In a medium skillet over medium heat, sauté the onion and garlic in the avocado oil until translucent, about 5 minutes.

2. Stir in the corn, peas, and carrots. Cook for 5 minutes more, stirring occasionally.

3. Add the rice and sesame oil, breaking the rice up with a spoon. As the rice begins to soften, add the eggs. Cook, stirring occasionally, until thoroughly cooked, about 5 minutes.

4. Sprinkle with the red pepper flakes and salt, and season with pepper. Serve immediately.

PREPARATION TIP: Most grocery stores sell bags of preshredded carrots, saving lots of prep time in the kitchen. If you can't find any, grab a large carrot and shred it on a box grater or shave off sections with a vegetable peeler.

ALLERGEN-FREE BREAKFAST COOKIES

DAIRY-FREE, GLUTEN-FREE, SOY-FREE, VEGETARIAN

MAKES 10 COOKIES / PREP TIME: 10 MINUTES / COOK TIME: 12 MINUTES

If you avoid the top food allergens like wheat, soy, peanuts, eggs, and dairy, breakfast can be limited and smoothies are often the easiest solution. If you crave something chewier, keep a batch of these nutrient-packed breakfast cookies on hand for an easy to-go option.

3 very ripe bananas

½ cup almond butter

2 tablespoons raw honey

1 tablespoon coconut oil, melted

2 teaspoons vanilla extract

1 teaspoon baking powder

1 teaspoon ground cinnamon

½ teaspoon salt

2½ cups rolled oats

¾ cup dairy-free semi-sweet chocolate chips (optional)

PER SERVING Calories: 306; Total Fat: 16g; Saturated Fat: 5g; Cholesterol: 0mg; Carbohydrates: 39g; Fiber: 5g; Protein: 7g

1. Preheat the oven to 350°F.

2. Line a large baking sheet with parchment paper.

3. In a large bowl, mash the bananas with a potato masher or a fork.

4. Stir in the almond butter, honey, coconut oil, and vanilla until well mixed.

5. Sprinkle in the baking powder, cinnamon, and salt. Add the oats and chocolate chips (if using) in batches, stirring after each addition until all ingredients are incorporated.

6. Place heaping tablespoons of dough onto the prepared sheet, leaving at least 1 inch between dough balls. Bake for 10 to 12 minutes.

7. Let the cookies rest in the pan for 5 minutes, and then transfer to a cooling rack. These cookies will keep refrigerated in a sealed container for several days.

INGREDIENT TIP: Not all chocolate is created equal. Choose a darker chocolate, which generally means less added sugar and milk products, and watch for added fillers or emulsifiers (like soy lecithin). If you can, buy organic and fair trade from a trusted brand. I love the Enjoy Life brand, which offers a line of chocolate that is soy-, dairy-, and nut-free.

TURKEY-MAPLE BREAKFAST SAUSAGES

GLUTEN-FREE, LACTOSE-FREE, SOY-FREE

MAKES 8 SAUSAGES / PREP TIME: 10 MINUTES / COOK TIME: 12 MINUTES

If you're craving animal protein, homemade breakfast sausages are the perfect way to get some at the start of the day. If ground turkey is hard to find, or you simply prefer another option, choose ground chicken.

1 pound ground turkey

1½ tablespoons pure maple syrup

1 teaspoon salt

½ teaspoon freshly ground black pepper

½ teaspoon garlic powder

½ teaspoon dried oregano

¼ teaspoon red pepper flakes

2 tablespoons ghee

PER SERVING Calories: 159; Total Fat: 10g; Saturated Fat: 4g; Cholesterol: 60mg; Carbohydrates: 3g; Fiber: 0g; Protein: 16g

1. In a large bowl, mix the turkey, maple syrup, salt, black pepper, garlic powder, oregano, and red pepper flakes until well combined and the spices are incorporated. With your hands, form the mixture into 8 small patties about ½ inch thick.

2. Place a large skillet over medium heat. Add the ghee.

3. Add the turkey patties, working in batches if necessary. Cook for about 3 minutes per side until done. Serve immediately or refrigerate in a sealed container for up to 3 days.

STORAGE TIP: You can also freeze these patties in a sealed container for up to 2 weeks. Prevent them from sticking together by putting squares of parchment paper between the patties before freezing.

CHIA-CHERRY OATS

Chia seeds are a tiny superfood high in omega-3 fatty acids. Because of this healthy fat content, they help stabilize blood sugar and boost energy. They gel when added to liquid, giving this breakfast dish a thick, puddinglike texture.

1¼ cups nut milk of choice

¼ cup plain whole-milk yogurt

1 cup quick cook oats

2 tablespoons chia seeds

8 fresh cherries, pitted and halved

2 tablespoons nut butter of choice

¼ teaspoon vanilla extract

PER SERVING Calories: 564; Total Fat: 32g; Saturated Fat: 3g; Cholesterol: 4mg; Carbohydrates: 27g; Fiber: 13g; Protein: 22g

1. In a large bowl, stir together the milk, yogurt, oats, chia seeds, cherries, nut butter, and vanilla until well combined.

2. Divide the mixture between 2 lidded jars. Seal and refrigerate for about 25 minutes.

SUBSTITUTION TIP: If you avoid dairy altogether, use a coconut-based yogurt.

GRANOLA CUPS WITH YOGURT

GLUTEN-FREE, PROBIOTIC, SOY-FREE, VEGETARIAN

MAKES 12 / PREP TIME: 10 MINUTES / COOK TIME: 10 MINUTES

These granola cups make a tasty anytime treat. Compared to most other fruit, berries are low on the glycemic index so they have less effect on your blood sugar. This factor is extra important when consuming dried fruit since it's much more compact than its fresh counterpart, making it easier to eat more in one sitting. If you avoid dairy altogether, choose a coconut-based yogurt, or fill these cups with homemade whipped coconut cream (see Blueberry Parfait with Lemon-Coconut Cream, page 174).

1 cup rolled oats

½ cup almond flour

2 tablespoons coconut sugar

½ teaspoon baking soda

½ cup dried cranberries, blueberries, or goji berries

¼ cup pecans, chopped

¼ cup sliced almonds

2 tablespoons unsweetened dried coconut

4 tablespoons coconut oil, divided

3 tablespoons pure maple syrup

1 teaspoon vanilla extract

2 cups plain whole-milk yogurt

PER SERVING Calories: 183; Total Fat: 12g; Saturated Fat: 6g; Cholesterol: 5mg; Carbohydrates: 12g; Fiber: 3g; Protein: 4g

1. Preheat the oven to 325°F.

2. In a medium bowl, mix the oats, almond flour, coconut sugar, baking soda, dried berries, pecans, almonds, and coconut.

3. In a microwave-safe bowl, melt 3 tablespoons of coconut oil. Stir in the maple syrup and vanilla. Add the coconut oil-maple syrup to the oat mixture and stir well to combine.

4. Using the remaining 1 tablespoon of coconut oil, lightly coat the cups of a standard muffin tin.

5. Evenly divide the granola mixture among the cups, pressing it in to create a bowl shape in each cup. Bake for 10 minutes. Cool completely before carefully removing the cups.

6. Fill each cup with some of the yogurt and serve.

BANANA OAT PANCAKES

DAIRY-FREE, GLUTEN-FREE, SOY-FREE, VEGETARIAN

SERVES 2 / PREP TIME: 5 MINUTES / COOK TIME: 10 MINUTES

You don't need heavy milks and gluten-containing flours to make the perfect pancake! Serve these with a drizzle of pure maple syrup and some grass-fed ghee (if eating dairy-free is not a concern for you), or top with your favorite warmed berries.

1 cup rolled oats

1 ripe banana

2 eggs

1 egg white

2 teaspoons ground cinnamon

1 teaspoon vanilla extract

½ teaspoon salt

1 tablespoon coconut oil, divided

PER SERVING Calories: 360; Total Fat: 15g; Saturated Fat: 8g; Cholesterol: 186mg; Carbohydrates: 17g; Fiber: 7g; Protein: 15g

1. In a food processor (or blender), grind the oats into a coarse flour. Add the banana, eggs, egg white, cinnamon, vanilla, and salt. Blend until a smooth batter forms.

2. In a small skillet over medium heat, heat ½ tablespoon of coconut oil. Spoon the batter into the pan to create pancakes of the desired size; cook in batches if necessary to avoid crowding. Cook for about 2 minutes until small bubbles form on the top. Flip and cook the other side for 1 to 2 minutes. Repeat with the remaining coconut oil and batter. Serve hot.

INGREDIENT TIP: Sneak in a handful of spinach as you blend the batter to make an even more nutritious and colorful pancake.

TANGY BRUSSELS SPROUT, ONION & APPLE KEBABS (PAGE 67)

Snacks & Sides

SIMPLEST GUACAMOLE

DAIRY-FREE, GLUTEN-FREE, PALEO, SOY-FREE, VEGAN

MAKES ABOUT 3 CUPS / PREP TIME: 10 MINUTES

There is nothing flashy about this guacamole, but it allows the flavor of the avocado to shine. Avocados, while high in fat, contain mostly heart-healthy, monounsaturated fat. Their anti-inflammatory compounds and antioxidant-rich phytonutrients are most concentrated in the avocado's outermost, dark green flesh nearest to the skin. So scoop out every last bit! Enjoy this dip with baby carrots, mini peppers, or other crudités. For a crunchy treat, plantain chips make a great tortilla chip alternative.

4 medium, ripe avocados, halved and pitted

1 teaspoon garlic powder

½ teaspoon salt

PER SERVING (3 ounces) Calories: 358;
Total Fat: 32.2g; Saturated Fat: 3.2g; Cholesterol: 0mg;
Carbohydrates: 13.7g; Fiber: 6.4g; Protein: 7.3g

1. Scoop out the avocado flesh and put it in a medium bowl.

2. Add the garlic powder and the salt. With a fork, mash the avocados until creamy.

3. Serve immediately, or cover and refrigerate for up to 2 days.

PREPARATION TIP: Play around with the ratio of garlic powder to salt until you find the right balance for you.

SPICY TWO-BEAN DIP

DAIRY-FREE, GLUTEN-FREE, SOY-FREE, VEGETARIAN

MAKES ABOUT 3½ CUPS / PREP TIME: 10 MINUTES

Both black beans and kidney beans are very low on the glycemic index, a system that ranks food based on how it affects blood sugar when consumed, in turn affecting inflammation. This low ranking is primarily based on beans' high fiber content, which is not absorbed by the body but provides roughage to keep the bowels healthy. Foods with a lower glycemic load release their carbohydrates into the bloodstream slowly, so they don't spike blood sugar. Both types of beans also boast high amounts of folate and molybdenum, a lesser known mineral that is key to enzyme function.

1 (14-ounce) can black beans, drained and rinsed well

1 (14-ounce) can kidney beans, drained and rinsed well

2 garlic cloves

2 cherry tomatoes

2 tablespoons filtered water

1 tablespoon apple cider vinegar

2 teaspoons raw honey

1 teaspoon freshly squeezed lime juice

¼ teaspoon ground cumin

¼ teaspoon salt

Pinch cayenne pepper

Freshly ground black pepper

PER SERVING (½ cup) Calories: 166;
Total Fat: 0.6g; Saturated Fat: 0.1g; Cholesterol: 0mg;
Carbohydrates: 34.2g; Fiber: 8.6g; Protein: 9.4g

In a food processor (or blender), combine the black beans, kidney beans, garlic, tomatoes, water, vinegar, honey, lime juice, cumin, salt, and cayenne pepper, and season with black pepper. Blend until smooth. Use a silicone spatula to scrape the sides of the processor bowl as needed. Cover and refrigerate before serving, if desired, or refrigerate for up to 5 days.

INGREDIENT TIP: If you have time and prefer to start with dried beans, use ½ cup of dried kidney beans and ½ cup of dried black beans. After soaking and cooking them, the beans will expand to more than double their dried size (see Beans, page 26).

CASHEW "HUMMUS" DIP

This dip is similar to traditional chickpea (garbanzo bean) hummus in both consistency and mild flavor. It acts as a great base to highlight other ingredients, such as sun-dried tomatoes, curry powder, or a few dashes of your favorite hot sauce. For added flair, drizzle extra-virgin olive oil over the top and add another dash of cayenne pepper for color. Cashews are antioxidant- and mineral-rich, and full of heart-healthy fats.

1 cup raw cashews, soaked in filtered water for 15 minutes and drained

2 garlic cloves

¼ cup filtered water

1 tablespoon extra-virgin olive oil

2 teaspoons coconut aminos

1 teaspoon freshly squeezed lemon juice

½ teaspoon ground ginger

¼ teaspoon salt

Pinch cayenne pepper

PER SERVING (2½ tablespoons) Calories: 112; Total Fat: 8.8g; Saturated Fat: 1.4g; Cholesterol: 0mg; Carbohydrates: 5.3g; Fiber: 0.6g; Protein: 2.9g

1. In a food processor (or blender), combine the cashews, garlic, water, olive oil, aminos, lemon juice, ginger, salt, and cayenne pepper. Blend until smooth. Use a silicone spatula to scrape down the sides of the processor bowl as needed.

2. Cover and refrigerate before serving, if desired, or refrigerate for up to 5 days.

TIME-SAVING TIP: Soak and drain the cashews ahead of time and refrigerate them in a jar for up to 3 days.

AVOCADO-APPLE-PROSCIUTTO WRAPS

DAIRY-FREE, GLUTEN-FREE, PALEO, SOY-FREE

MAKES 12 / PREP TIME: 15 MINUTES

These wraps make the perfect afternoon snack, or they can be an impressive plate of hors d'oeuvres to bring to a party. The honey is optional, but adds a touch of sweetness.

12 slices prosciutto

2 large avocados, halved, pitted, and each half cut into 3 pieces

2 apples, each cut into 6 pieces (see Ingredient Tip)

Raw honey, for drizzling (optional)

PER SERVING (2 pieces) Calories: 245; Total Fat: 17g; Saturated Fat: 4g; Cholesterol: 50mg; Carbohydrates: 11g; Fiber: 5g; Protein: 17g

1. Lay 1 slice of prosciutto on a plate with the short end closest to you. Place 1 avocado slice and 1 apple slice together at the short end of the prosciutto and roll it up, into a cigar shape. Repeat with the remaining ingredients.

2. Drizzle each wrap with honey (if using).

INGREDIENT TIP: If you prefer a tart apple, choose a variety like Granny Smith. For a sweeter apple, go with Gala, Fuji, or Honeycrisp.

GARLICKY ROASTED CHICKPEAS

DAIRY-FREE, GLUTEN-FREE, SOY-FREE, VEGAN

MAKES 4 CUPS / PREP TIME: 5 MINUTES / COOK TIME: 20 MINUTES

Make a double batch to keep some handy for those snack attacks. The interior layer of chickpeas is packed with phytonutrients that possess powerful anti-inflammatory nutrients. To keep this recipe in regular rotation, try different spices, such as cumin, chili powder, or paprika for variety.

4 cups cooked (or canned) chickpeas, rinsed, drained, and thoroughly dried with paper towels (be careful not to crush them)

2 tablespoons extra-virgin olive oil

1 teaspoon salt

1 teaspoon garlic powder

Freshly ground black pepper

PER SERVING (¾ cup) Calories: 150; Total Fat: 5g; Saturated Fat: 0g; Cholesterol: 0mg; Carbohydrates: 21g; Fiber: 6g; Protein: 6g

1. Preheat the oven to 400°F.

2. Spread the chickpeas evenly on a rimmed baking sheet and coat them with the olive oil.

3. Bake for 20 minutes, stirring halfway through.

4. Transfer the hot chickpeas to a large bowl. Toss with the salt and garlic powder; season with pepper. Store leftovers in a sealed container or bag at room temperature; they'll remain crispy for 1 to 2 days.

COOKING TIP: To avoid burning the spices, always season the chickpeas after they've been roasted.

SALT & VINEGAR KALE CHIPS

DAIRY-FREE, GLUTEN-FREE, SOY-FREE, PALEO, VEGAN

MAKES 2 CUPS / PREP TIME: 5 MINUTES / COOK TIME: 20 TO 25 MINUTES

Don't be intimidated by the concept—kale chips are one of the quickest vegetable chips to make at home due to kale's low moisture content and thin structure. They contain far more anti-inflammatory phytonutrients than the average potato chip, so enjoy these guilt free!

4 cups kale, stemmed, thoroughly washed, and dried, leaves torn into 2-inch pieces

2 tablespoons apple cider vinegar

2 tablespoons extra-virgin olive oil

1 teaspoon salt

PER SERVING (1 cup) Calories: 135; Total Fat: 14g; Saturated Fat: 2g; Cholesterol: 0mg; Carbohydrates: 3g; Fiber: 1g; Protein: 1g

1. Preheat the oven to 350°F.

2. In a large bowl, combine the kale, vinegar, olive oil, and salt. With your hands, massage the ingredients into the kale leaves.

3. Spread the kale evenly on a baking sheet. Bake for 20 to 25 minutes, tossing halfway through.

4. Store leftovers in a sealed container or bag at room temperature; they'll remain crispy for 1 to 2 days.

INGREDIENT TIP: Try swapping the apple cider vinegar for a different vinegar, such as balsamic or red wine.

BLUEBERRY-BANANA FROZEN YOGURT BITES

GLUTEN-FREE, PROBIOTIC, SOY-FREE, VEGETARIAN

MAKES ABOUT 50 BITES / PREP TIME: 10 MINUTES, PLUS 20 MINUTES FREEZING TIME

Purchased frozen yogurt typically contains added sugar, flavorings, and preservatives. By creating your own in easy-to-eat snack bites, you control the sweetener and the flavor all at once.

2 cups plain whole-milk yogurt

1 banana

½ cup fresh blueberries

1 tablespoon raw honey

PER SERVING (8 bites) Calories: 90;
Total Fat: 3g; Saturated Fat: 2g; Cholesterol: 13mg;
Carbohydrates: 13g; Fiber: 1g; Protein: 3g

1. Line a baking sheet or plate with a piece of wax paper.

2. In a blender, combine the yogurt, banana, blueberries, and honey. Blend until smooth.

3. Transfer the mixture to a large resealable plastic bag. Trim off one bottom corner of the bag. Squeeze the yogurt mixture into quarter-size dots on the wax paper.

4. Freeze until solid.

STORAGE TIP: Once the bites are frozen, remove them from the wax paper and pop them into a resealable freezer bag. Store in the freezer for up to 1 month.

SPICY AVOCADO DEVILED EGGS

GLUTEN-FREE, PALEO, SOY-FREE, VEGETARIAN

MAKES 12 PIECES / PREP TIME: 10 MINUTES, PLUS CHILLING TIME

In small doses, pure, cultured sour cream can be a great source of probiotics and healthy fats. Remember: The less processed, the better when it comes to dairy products!

6 hard-boiled eggs, peeled and halved
    lengthwise

1 ripe avocado, halved and pitted

1 tablespoon Dijon mustard

1 tablespoon sour cream

1½ teaspoons freshly squeezed lemon juice

½ teaspoon garlic powder

½ teaspoon salt

¼ teaspoon red pepper flakes

PER SERVING (2 pieces) Calories: 124;
Total Fat: 9g; Saturated Fat: 3g; Cholesterol: 189mg;
Carbohydrates: 3g; Fiber: 2g; Protein: 7g

1. Scoop the egg yolks into a small bowl.

2. Scoop the avocado flesh into the bowl with the yolks.

3. Add the mustard, sour cream, lemon juice, garlic powder, salt, and red pepper flakes. With a fork, mash the mixture until thoroughly combined and creamy.

4. Arrange the eggs on a plate. Spoon equal amounts of the yolk-avocado mixture into each egg. Refrigerate before serving, if desired.

STORAGE TIP: With the avocado in this recipe, storing this dish will cause the top of the filling to turn brown over time. Plan to eat them in one sitting!

SWEET POTATO OAT MUFFINS

DAIRY-FREE, GLUTEN-FREE, SOY-FREE, VEGETARIAN

MAKES 12 MUFFINS / PREP TIME: 5 TO 10 MINUTES / COOK TIME: 20 TO 25 MINUTES

While you may not keep a pantry stocked with various gluten-free flours, plain rolled oats are easy to find and affordable. In this recipe, you quickly create a coarse oat flour from the same oats used to make oatmeal. While oats do not contain gluten, if you strictly avoid gluten, choose certified gluten-free oats to avoid any cross-contamination.

1½ cups rolled oats

1 cup cooked sweet potato chunks or purée

1 cup nut milk of choice

⅓ cup coconut sugar

¼ cup almond butter

1 egg

2 tablespoons extra-virgin olive oil

1 teaspoon vanilla extract

1 teaspoon ground cinnamon

1 teaspoon baking powder

½ teaspoon baking soda

¼ teaspoon salt

PER SERVING (1 muffin) Calories: 143; Total Fat: 7g; Saturated Fat: 1g; Cholesterol: 16mg; Carbohydrates: 12g; Fiber: 2g; Protein: 4g

1. Preheat the oven to 375°F.

2. Line a muffin tin with cupcake liners.

3. In a food processor (or blender), pulse the oats until a coarse flour is formed. Transfer the flour to a small bowl and set aside.

4. To the food processor (or blender), add the sweet potato, nut milk, coconut sugar, almond butter, egg, olive oil, vanilla, cinnamon, baking powder, baking soda, and salt. Pulse until smooth.

5. Slowly add the oat flour, pulsing until all ingredients are well incorporated.

6. Divide the batter among the 12 cupcake liners.

7. Bake for 20 to 25 minutes. Cool for 5 minutes.

COOKING TIP: If you want to reduce waste, purchase silicone muffin molds, which are nonstick, washable, and reusable.

BERRY GUMMIES

DAIRY-FREE, GLUTEN-FREE, PALEO, SOY-FREE

MAKES ABOUT 24 GUMMIES / PREP TIME: 5 MINUTES
COOK TIME: 10 MINUTES, PLUS 15 MINUTES FREEZING TIME

Animal bones and tendons, when simmered to make broth, release gelatin, vitamins, and minerals. This gelatin provides collagen our bodies need for healthy nails, skin, hair, and joints. Because collagen is the main protein found in connective tissues, we should not skimp on consuming it—especially as we age. This recipe provides a simple, fruity way to treat your taste buds and your body.

1 cup fresh or frozen berries of choice

½ cup freshly squeezed lemon juice

¼ cup filtered water

3 tablespoons raw honey

¼ cup gelatin powder

PER SERVING (4 gummies) Calories: 68;
Total Fat: 0g; Saturated Fat: 0g; Cholesterol: 0mg;
Carbohydrates: 13g; Fiber: 1g; Protein: 4g

1. In a blender, combine together the berries, lemon juice, water, and honey. Pour the purée into a small saucepan and place it over medium heat.

2. When warm, whisk in the gelatin powder. Continue to whisk for 5 minutes until all ingredients are well incorporated.

3. Pour the mixture into small silicone candy molds or a mini muffin tin. Freeze for 15 minutes until the mixture gels.

4. Transfer the gummies to an airtight container, and store in the refrigerator for up to 1 week.

COOKING TIP: If you don't have silicone molds or a mini muffin tin, pour the mixture into a brownie pan or baking dish coated with coconut oil, and cut the gummies into small shapes after the mixture has set.

ROOT MASH

GLUTEN-FREE, LACTOSE-FREE, PALEO, SOY-FREE, VEGETARIAN

SERVES 4 / PREP TIME: 5 MINUTES / COOK TIME: 25 MINUTES

Celery root, also called celeriac, is a unique root vegetable with a rough exterior. The inside looks similar to a white potato, and, when heated and mashed, closely resembles the texture as well. Use it as a more nutritious substitute for white potatoes. It is lower in carbohydrates and higher in fiber, with a slightly nuttier taste.

2 cups chopped sweet potatoes

2 cups chopped celery root, scrubbed, trimmed, and peeled

2 tablespoons ghee

1 teaspoon freshly squeezed lemon juice

½ teaspoon salt

Pinch cayenne pepper

PER SERVING Calories: 270; Total Fat: 10g; Saturated Fat: 5g; Cholesterol: 0mg; Carbohydrates: 23g; Fiber: 4g; Protein: 2g

1. In a steamer basket over boiling filtered water, put the sweet potatoes and celery root. Cover and steam over medium heat for 25 minutes, or until completely tender. Transfer to a food processor (or blender).

2. Add the ghee, lemon juice, salt, and cayenne pepper. Pulse until smooth and fully puréed.

COOKING TIP: Steamer baskets are made from different materials, and most will work fine here. Find them in kitchen supply stores or on the Internet made from bamboo or stainless steel.

LIME-CHILI ROASTED CAULIFLOWER

GLUTEN-FREE, LACTOSE-FREE, PALEO, SOY-FREE, VEGETARIAN

SERVES 4 / PREP TIME: 10 MINUTES / COOK TIME: 15 MINUTES

Cauliflower is less popular in the United States than in other parts of the world such as China and India, which together produce almost three-fourths of the world's cauliflower. Cauliflower is a cruciferous vegetable bursting with nutrients: it's a powerhouse of vitamin C, which is an important anti-inflammatory antioxidant. Here, the zesty zip of lime and chili powder tingle your palate. Eat up for good health.

1½ teaspoons ground cumin

1 teaspoon salt

½ teaspoon chili powder

½ teaspoon freshly ground black pepper

½ teaspoon garlic powder

1 head cauliflower, roughly chopped
   into bite-size pieces

3 tablespoons freshly squeezed lime juice

3 tablespoons ghee, melted

PER SERVING Calories: 138; Total Fat: 11g;
Saturated Fat: 7g; Cholesterol: 23mg;
Carbohydrates: 9g; Fiber: 3g; Protein: 3g

1. Preheat the oven to 450°F.

2. In a small bowl, mix the cumin, salt, chili powder, pepper, and garlic powder.

3. Spread the cauliflower in a baking pan. Drizzle with the lime juice and ghee. Sprinkle with the spice mixture and toss to coat.

4. Bake for 15 minutes.

COOKING TIP: For a quick way to melt the ghee, place it in the baking pan in the oven as it preheats.

CIDER-BAKED BEETS

DAIRY-FREE, GLUTEN-FREE, PALEO, SOY-FREE, VEGAN

SERVES 6 / PREP TIME: 5 MINUTES / COOK TIME: 25 MINUTES

Centuries ago, beet greens, not the sweet, colorful beetroot, were commonly consumed. Today we know the many nutritional qualities of beetroot, and many consume beetroot far more than beet greens. Beets are a unique source of betaine, a compound that protects cells from environmental stress that causes inflammation. This simple nutrition-packed side dish will add plenty of color and a sweet-tangy taste to your meal.

4 medium golden beets, peeled and diced into 1-inch pieces

4 medium red beets, peeled and diced into 1-inch pieces

½ yellow onion, diced into 1-inch pieces

½ cup apple cider vinegar

½ cup extra-virgin olive oil

2 tablespoons coconut sugar (see Ingredient Tip)

¼ teaspoon salt

Freshly ground black pepper

PER SERVING Calories: 233; Total Fat: 19g; Saturated Fat: 2g; Cholesterol: 0mg; Carbohydrates: 18g; Fiber: 2g; Protein: 2g

1. Preheat the oven to 450°F.

2. Line a baking sheet with aluminum foil.

3. Spread the beets and onion into the prepared pan and drizzle with the vinegar and olive oil.

4. Sprinkle the coconut sugar and the salt onto the vegetables. Season with pepper and toss to coat.

5. Bake for 25 minutes, or until the beets caramelize around the edges and are fork-tender.

INGREDIENT TIP: Beets are naturally sweet, and their sweetness deepens with cooking. If you prefer your veggies less sweet, reduce the amount of coconut sugar so you taste the beets' natural sweetness.

66 The Anti-Inflammatory Diet Cookbook

TANGY BRUSSELS SPROUT, ONION & APPLE KEBABS

DAIRY-FREE, GLUTEN-FREE, PALEO, SOY-FREE

MAKES 12 KEBABS / PREP TIME: 10 MINUTES / COOK TIME: 20 MINUTES

Kebabs make eating vegetables fun for the whole family. Brussels sprouts provide detoxification, antioxidant, and anti-inflammatory support for several body systems. They are also very high in vitamin K, a direct regulator of inflammatory responses.

1 pound Brussels sprouts, discolored exterior leaves removed and discarded

2 apples, diced into 1-inch pieces

2 small red onions, diced into 1-inch pieces

1 tablespoon avocado oil

⅓ cup fish sauce

¼ cup filtered water

3 tablespoons rice vinegar

2 tablespoons freshly squeezed lime juice

2 roughly chopped pitted dates

2 garlic cloves, minced

Dash red pepper flakes

Dash ground ginger

PER SERVING (2 kebabs) Calories: 132;
Total Fat: 3g; Saturated Fat: 0g; Cholesterol: 0mg;
Carbohydrates: 25g; Fiber: 5g; Protein: 3g

1. Preheat the oven to 400°F.

2. Carefully press a skewer through 1 Brussels sprout, 1 apple piece, and 1 onion piece, leaving ½ inch between each piece. Repeat until 12 skewers are evenly filled. Place the kebabs on a rimmed baking sheet. Roast for 20 minutes, or until thoroughly roasted, turning the skewers halfway through

3. While the vegetables roast, in a blender, combine the fish sauce, water, vinegar, lime juice, dates, garlic, red pepper flakes, and ginger. Pulse until smooth.

4. Remove the kebabs from the oven and drizzle with half the sauce. Serve immediately, with the remaining sauce as a dip.

COOKING TIP: If using bamboo or wooden skewers, soak them in warm water for 10 to 30 minutes before adding the vegetables so they don't burn in the oven.

EASY ROASTED VEGETABLES

DAIRY-FREE, GLUTEN-FREE, PALEO, SOY-FREE, VEGAN

SERVES 4 / PREP TIME: 5 MINUTES / COOK TIME: 25 MINUTES

While grilling over an open flame is full of summer romance, it's possible to get the same amazing flavors by roasting vegetables in the oven. This recipe is versatile—you can mix and match your favorite vegetables—but pay attention to varying cooking times. Serve these phytonutrient-rich veggies as a side, or make a delicious vegan plateful for dinner.

2 zucchini, diced into 1-inch pieces

1 red bell pepper, diced into 1-inch pieces

1 yellow bell pepper, diced into 1-inch pieces

1 red onion, diced into 1-inch pieces

1 sweet potato, diced into 1-inch pieces

4 garlic cloves

¼ cup extra-virgin olive oil

1 teaspoon salt

PER SERVING Calories: 184; Total Fat: 14g; Saturated Fat: 2g; Cholesterol: 0mg; Carbohydrates: 15g; Fiber: 2g; Protein: 2g

1. Preheat the oven to 450°F.

2. Line a baking sheet with aluminum foil.

3. In a large bowl, toss together the zucchini, red bell pepper, yellow bell pepper, onion, sweet potato, garlic, olive oil, and salt. Spread the vegetables evenly on the prepared sheet.

4. Bake for 25 minutes, stirring halfway through.

COOKING TIP: Even if the pile of raw veggies looks larger than needed, keep dicing because each piece will shrink once it loses much of its water content in the roasting process.

BURST CHERRY TOMATOES WITH GARLIC

DAIRY-FREE, GLUTEN-FREE, SOY-FREE, VEGAN

SERVES 6 / PREP TIME: 5 MINUTES / COOK TIME: 20 MINUTES

Tomatoes have a reputation for being cancer-preventive, because they protect against the oxidative stress and chronic inflammation that often lead to cancer risk. These bite-size roasted tomatoes, bursting with flavor, work beautifully as an Italian-inspired side, snack, or topping for your favorite meat or pasta dish.

1 pound cherry tomatoes, halved

4 garlic cloves, minced

1 teaspoon dried basil (optional)

2 tablespoons extra-virgin olive oil

Salt

PER SERVING Calories: 46; Total Fat: 0g; Saturated Fat: 0g; Cholesterol: 0mg; Carbohydrates: 10g; Fiber: 3g; Protein: 2g

1. Preheat the oven to 400°F.

2. Line a baking sheet with aluminum foil.

3. In a large bowl, mix the tomatoes, garlic, and basil (if using). Drizzle with the olive oil and toss to coat. Season generously with salt. Transfer to the prepared pan.

4. Bake for 15 to 20 minutes, or until the tomatoes collapse.

INGREDIENT TIP: Using garlic powder instead of fresh garlic cloves is an easy way to distribute the flavor a bit more.

HUMMUS-STUFFED MINI PEPPERS

DAIRY-FREE, GLUTEN-FREE, SOY-FREE, VEGAN

MAKES 12 / PREP TIME: 5 MINUTES / COOK TIME: 10 MINUTES

Crunchy and creamy combine here for bites of fresh flavor. If you have extra time, make the Cashew "Hummus" Dip (page 56) to replace the hummus in this recipe for an extra homemade touch.

2 cups purchased hummus

2 tablespoons chopped fresh basil leaves (optional)

12 mini bell peppers, stemmed

PER SERVING (2 peppers) Calories: 168; Total Fat: 9g; Saturated Fat: 0g; Cholesterol: 0mg; Carbohydrates: 18g; Fiber: 9g; Protein: 6g

1. In a small bowl, mix the hummus and basil (if using). Transfer to a small plastic bag, squeezing it down into one of the bottom corners.

2. Trim off the same bottom corner of the bag and squeeze the hummus into each pepper, filling it to the top.

PREPARATION TIP: For even more flavor, add a few ingredients to the hummus, such as chopped sun-dried or fresh tomatoes, parsley, or radish.

BAKED ZUCCHINI FRIES

DAIRY-FREE, GLUTEN-FREE, PALEO, SOY-FREE

MAKES ABOUT 12 FRIES / PREP TIME: 10 MINUTES / COOK TIME: 20 MINUTES

Believe it or not, there are omega-3 fatty acids in the seeds of summer squashes, such as zucchini. This nutrient, combined with other naturally present antioxidants, makes zucchini a great choice for fighting inflammation.

½ cup almond flour

½ teaspoon salt

½ teaspoon garlic powder

½ teaspoon freshly ground black pepper

1 medium zucchini, trimmed and
  halved widthwise

1 tablespoon avocado oil

PER SERVING (6 fries) Calories: 230;
Total Fat: 21g; Saturated Fat: 2g; Cholesterol: 0mg;
Carbohydrates: 7g; Fiber: 4g; Protein: 6g

1. Preheat the oven to 425°F.

2. Line a baking sheet with aluminum foil.

3. In a small bowl, mix the almond flour, salt, garlic powder, and pepper.

4. Cut each zucchini half into about 6 strips that resemble fries. Brush the strips with the avocado oil, and roll in the almond flour mixture until well coated. Evenly space the fries on the prepared pan.

5. Bake for 20 minutes, or until crispy.

COOKING TIP: These zucchini fries do not save well and lose their crunch when refrigerated. You can cut the zucchini strips and prepare the almond flour mixture ahead of time, but coating the zucchini strips and baking them should be done just before serving.

COCONUT CASHEW SOUP WITH BUTTERNUT SQUASH (PAGE 83)

Soups & Stews

GUT-HEALING BONE BROTH

DAIRY-FREE, GLUTEN-FREE, PALEO, SOY-FREE

MAKES ABOUT 4 QUARTS / PREP TIME: 15 MINUTES / COOK TIME: 8 TO 24 HOURS

Stocks and broths like this are used in countries like France, Italy, China, and Japan, yet they've all but disappeared from the American culinary tradition. We've opted to let food-industry leaders cut corners in food preparation, in turn cutting corners with our health. While this broth needs to simmer for hours, the prep is well under 30 minutes. Making a batch and using it all week or freezing it for later use means you have a nourishing broth to sip and soothe, or to use in soups or sauces at a moment's notice. If you have extra time, roasting the bones beforehand greatly enhances the flavor of the finished broth. Place the bones in a roasting pan, and roast in a 400°F oven for 40 to 60 minutes. Drain off the fat and proceed with the recipe.

2 pounds beef marrow bones

4 garlic cloves

3 medium carrots, chopped

2 celery stalks, chopped

1 medium onion, chopped

2 bay leaves

1 tablespoon apple cider vinegar

Filtered water, to cover

PER SERVING (1 cup) Calories: 40; Total Fat: 0g; Saturated Fat: 0g; Cholesterol: 0mg; Carbohydrates: 5g; Fiber: 0g; Protein: 6g

1. In a 6-quart slow cooker, combine the bones, garlic, carrots, celery, onion, bay leaves, and vinegar. Cover with filtered water. Set the cooker on low and simmer for at least 8 hours and up to 24 hours.

2. Skim off and discard any foam that forms on the surface. Ladle the broth through a fine-mesh sieve or cheesecloth to strain out the solids. Pour into airtight glass containers. The broth can be kept refrigerated for up to 1 week; just reboil it before use. To freeze, allow the broth to completely cool and then fill jars up to 1 inch below the top to allow for expansion, and keep for 4 to 5 months.

SPICY RAMEN NOODLE SOUP

DAIRY-FREE, GLUTEN-FREE, SOY-FREE, VEGETARIAN

SERVES 4 / PREP TIME: 15 MINUTES / COOK TIME: 0 MINUTES

This recipe is a modern take on packaged and processed instant ramen noodles that became popular in the Unites States in the 1970s. Using rice noodles provides a gluten-free base, and the fresh ingredients in the sauce give it a boost of flavor while adding anti-inflammatory elements.

8 ounces buckwheat noodles or rice noodles, cooked

2 tablespoons sesame seeds

¼ cup thinly sliced cucumber

¼ cup sliced scallion

¼ cup chopped fresh cilantro

2 tablespoons sesame oil

2 tablespoons rice vinegar

1 tablespoon grated peeled fresh ginger

1 tablespoon coconut aminos

1 tablespoon raw honey

1 tablespoon freshly squeezed lime juice

1 teaspoon chili powder

In a large serving bowl, thoroughly mix the noodles, sesame seeds, cucumber, scallion, cilantro, sesame oil, vinegar, ginger, coconut aminos, honey, lime juice, and chili powder. Divide among 4 soup bowls and serve at room temperature.

INGREDIENT TIP: Despite its name, buckwheat does not include any wheat or gluten. Rather, it is a fruit seed that is often ground to make a flour that is very high in both fiber and protein.

PER SERVING Calories: 663; Total Fat: 28g; Saturated Fat: 4g; Cholesterol: 0mg; Carbohydrates: 115g; Fiber: 39g; Protein: 21g

QUICK MISO SOUP WITH WILTED GREENS

DAIRY-FREE, GLUTEN-FREE

SERVES 4 / PREP TIME: 10 MINUTES / COOK TIME: 5 MINUTES

Traditional miso soup is made with *dashi*, a broth made with water, dried seaweed, and dried fish flakes. I've simplified it to a broth with a little fish sauce for a touch of savory umami flavor. Miso paste, made from fermented soybeans, makes it a more desirable choice than other processed soy products. Hearty mushrooms take the place of tofu here.

3 cups filtered water

3 cups vegetable broth

1 cup sliced mushrooms

½ teaspoon fish sauce

3 tablespoons miso paste

1 cup fresh baby spinach, thoroughly washed

4 scallions, sliced

PER SERVING Calories: 44; Total Fat: 0g; Saturated Fat: 0g; Cholesterol: 0mg; Carbohydrates: 8g; Fiber: 1g; Protein: 2g

1. In a large soup pot over high heat, add the water, broth, mushrooms, and fish sauce, and bring to a boil. Remove from the heat.

2. In a small bowl, mix the miso paste with ½ cup of heated broth mixture to dissolve the miso. Stir the miso mixture back into the soup.

3. Stir in the spinach and scallions. Serve immediately.

INGREDIENT TIP: If you find strips of kelp (*kombu*) seaweed at the grocery store, add pieces to the broth for a more traditional flavor.

MINESTRONE SOUP WITH QUINOA

GLUTEN-FREE, LACTOSE-FREE, SOY-FREE, VEGETARIAN

SERVES 6 / PREP TIME: 10 MINUTES / COOK TIME: 20 MINUTES

Minestrone soup is a thick, traditional Italian soup made with vegetables and, usually, pasta. Here I've removed the pro-inflammatory wheat pasta and replaced it with protein-rich quinoa, which thickens the soup in a flavorful and hearty way.

1 tablespoon ghee

2 garlic cloves, minced

1 medium white onion, diced

2 carrots, chopped

2 celery stalks, diced

1 small zucchini, diced

½ red bell pepper, diced

5 cups vegetable broth

1 (14-ounce) can diced tomatoes
  with their juice

1 (14-ounce) can cannellini beans,
  drained and rinsed well

1 cup packed kale, stemmed and
  thoroughly washed

½ cup quinoa, rinsed well

1 tablespoon freshly squeezed lemon juice

2 teaspoons dried rosemary

2 teaspoons dried thyme

1 bay leaf

½ teaspoon salt

Freshly ground black pepper

PER SERVING Calories: 319; Total Fat: 5g;
Saturated Fat: 2g; Cholesterol: 0mg;
Carbohydrates: 42g; Fiber: 9g; Protein: 18g

1. In a large soup pot over medium heat, add the ghee, garlic, onion, carrots, and celery, and sauté for 3 minutes.

2. Add the zucchini and red bell pepper, and sauté for 2 minutes.

3. Stir in the broth, tomatoes, beans, kale, quinoa, lemon juice, rosemary, thyme, bay leaf, and salt, and season with black pepper. Bring to a simmer, reduce the heat to low, cover, and cook for 15 minutes, or until the quinoa is cooked. Remove the bay leaf and discard. Serve hot.

COOKING TIP: Always rinse quinoa before cooking to remove its bitter surface compound called saponin. When cooking quinoa, the best ratio is 1 cup quinoa to 2 cups liquid. Bring to a boil and immediately reduce the heat to low. Simmer, covered, for 15 to 20 minutes until the liquid is absorbed. Fluff before serving. If you already have cooked quinoa on hand, add it at the end of the recipe and reduce the broth by 1 cup.

ZESTY BROCCOLI SOUP

GLUTEN-FREE, LACTOSE-FREE, PALEO, SOY-FREE, VEGETARIAN

SERVES 4 / PREP TIME: 10 MINUTES / COOK TIME: 20 MINUTES

For this recipe, try to purchase the broccoli fresh because as soon as broccoli is cut from the main plant, its vitamin C content begins to degrade. If you need to store it for a day or two, place it in a plastic bag without washing it, remove as much air as possible, and store in the refrigerator's crisper drawer.

1 tablespoon ghee
1 medium white onion, diced
3 garlic cloves, minced
1 head broccoli, roughly chopped
1 carrot, chopped
1 celery stalk, diced
3 cups vegetable broth
½ teaspoon salt
½ teaspoon freshly squeezed lemon juice
½ teaspoon lemon zest
Freshly ground black pepper

PER SERVING Calories: 80; Total Fat: 4g;
Saturated Fat: 2g; Cholesterol: 0mg;
Carbohydrates: 10g; Fiber: 3g; Protein: 2g

1. In a large soup pot over medium heat, melt the ghee.

2. Add the onion and garlic, and sauté for 5 minutes.

3. Add the broccoli, carrot, and celery, and sauté for 2 minutes.

4. Stir in the broth, salt, lemon juice, and lemon zest, and season with pepper. Bring to a simmer, and cook for about 10 minutes. Serve immediately.

PREPARATION TIP: This soup can be served chunky, or puréed with an immersion blender (or standard blender) for a smoother consistency.

CREAMY & CULTURED TOMATO SOUP

GLUTEN-FREE, PROBIOTIC, SOY-FREE, VEGETARIAN

SERVES 6 / PREP TIME: 10 MINUTES / COOK TIME: 15 TO 20 MINUTES

Creamy comfort foods don't have to be heavy. The small amount of cultured yogurt in this recipe gives this soup just the depth of flavor and creaminess it needs. If you don't have an immersion blender, you can make the soup in a standard blender (see Cooking Tip, White Velvet Cauliflower Soup, page 80) for the same consistency. This soup makes a great companion to Baked Zucchini Fries (page 71) or Shaved Brussels Sprout Salad (page 91).

1 tablespoon ghee

1 small onion, chopped

3 garlic cloves, chopped

1 teaspoon dried basil

1 teaspoon dried oregano

½ teaspoon salt

¼ teaspoon chili powder

⅛ teaspoon freshly ground black pepper

⅛ teaspoon dried thyme

2 (14-ounce) cans diced tomatoes with their juice

2 cups vegetable broth

¼ cup tomato paste

½ cup plain whole-milk yogurt

PER SERVING Calories: 157; Total Fat: 6g; Saturated Fat: 3g; Cholesterol: 3mg; Carbohydrates: 25g; Fiber: 13g; Protein: 8g

1. In a large soup pot over medium heat, melt the ghee.

2. Add the onion and garlic, and sauté for 5 minutes.

3. Stir in the basil, oregano, salt, chili powder, pepper, and thyme.

4. Add the tomatoes, broth, and tomato paste, and stir to combine. Bring to a simmer, turn the heat to low, and cook for 5 to 10 minutes. Remove the pot from the heat. With an immersion blender (or in batches in a standard blender), purée the mixture in the pot until you have the desired consistency.

5. Add the yogurt. Blend for 1 minute more. Serve immediately.

INGREDIENT TIP: To experiment with different flavor profiles, try fire-roasted diced tomatoes or tomatoes seasoned with Italian spices.

WHITE VELVET CAULIFLOWER SOUP

GLUTEN-FREE, LACTOSE-FREE, PALEO, VEGETARIAN

SERVES 6 / PREP TIME: 10 MINUTES / COOK TIME: 20 MINUTES

If you're eating a more healthy diet, lots of vegetables, like cauliflower, should fill your plate—or bowl. And while cauliflower is perfectly healthy to eat raw, consuming it in a cooked soup like this can be gentler on the stomach. Cooking breaks down the hard-to-digest sugars called raffinose in cruciferous vegetables (such as cabbage, cauliflower, and Brussels sprouts) that can cause gas or stomach discomfort. This recipe makes a velvety-smooth, delicious soup.

1 tablespoon avocado oil

1 small white onion, diced

3 garlic cloves, minced

1 small celery root, trimmed, peeled, and cut into 1-inch pieces

1 head cauliflower, roughly chopped into 1-inch pieces

4 cups vegetable broth

2 tablespoons ghee

2 scallions, sliced

PER SERVING Calories: 183; Total Fat: 8g; Saturated Fat: 3g; Cholesterol: 0mg; Carbohydrates: 10g; Fiber: 3g; Protein: 9g

1. In a large soup pot over medium heat, heat the avocado oil.

2. Add the onion and garlic, and sauté for 5 minutes.

3. Add the celery root and cauliflower. Increase the heat to medium-high and continue to sauté for 5 minutes, or until the cauliflower begins to brown and caramelize on the edges.

4. Stir in the broth and ghee and bring to a boil. Reduce the heat to medium-low and simmer for 10 minutes. Remove the pot from the heat.

5. With an immersion blender, or in batches in a standard blender, purée the soup until creamy. Serve immediately, sprinkled with the scallions.

COOKING TIP: If you use a regular blender, process the hot soup in small batches. Remove the plug in the blender lid and place a clean kitchen towel over the top to allow steam to escape but prevent the ingredients from splashing out.

RUSSIAN CABBAGE SOUP (SHCHI)

GLUTEN-FREE, LACTOSE-FREE, SOY-FREE, VEGETARIAN

SERVES 6 / PREP TIME: 10 MINUTES / COOK TIME: 20 MINUTES

Shchi is a traditional Russian soup that dates back to the ninth century. Light yet nourishing, it remains a popular soup in Eastern Europe to this day. Many studies, such as one conducted by the George Mateljan Institute in 2016, have shown the benefits of cabbage consumption on the digestive tract, specifically for healing the gut lining from ulcers. If you have time or a batch on hand, using Gut-Healing Bone Broth (page 74) adds even more healing properties to this healthy bowlful.

6 cups vegetable broth

1 bay leaf

1 large potato, peeled and diced

1 tablespoon ghee

1 medium white onion, diced

3 garlic cloves, minced

2 carrots, shredded

1 celery stalk, diced

½ large head cabbage, shredded

1 (14-ounce) can diced tomatoes
with their juice

½ teaspoon salt

Freshly ground black pepper

PER SERVING Calories: 180; Total Fat: 3g;
Saturated Fat: 2g; Cholesterol: 7mg;
Carbohydrates: 20g; Fiber: 5g; Protein: 12g

1. In a large soup pot over high heat, combine the broth, bay leaf, and potato, and bring to a boil. Reduce the heat to low and simmer for 15 minutes.

2. Meanwhile, in a medium saucepan over medium heat, heat the ghee. Add the onion and garlic, and sauté for 5 minutes.

3. Add the carrots, celery, and cabbage, and cook for 2 minutes, stirring often. Transfer to the soup pot.

4. Stir in the tomatoes and salt, and season with pepper. Mix well and continue to simmer until all ingredients have softened and cooked, about 5 minutes. Remove and discard the bay leaf, and serve immediately.

INGREDIENT TIP: Sauerkraut (fermented cabbage) can be used in place of the fresh cabbage in this recipe. When the soup is prepared in this manner, it is traditionally called sour *shchi.*

RED LENTIL DAL

DAIRY-FREE, GLUTEN-FREE, SOY-FREE, VEGETARIAN

SERVES 6 / PREP TIME: 10 MINUTES / COOK TIME: 20 MINUTES

Rustic and hearty, *dal* is a common weeknight meal in many Indian households. The word *dal* actually means "lentil," but it also means a thick stew that is prepared with lentils. This stew is a ready source of vegetarian protein. Incorporating lentils in place of meat in your diet is a fantastic source of amino acids—more than 50 percent of the suggested daily value.

3 cups vegetable broth

1 cup red dried lentils, sorted and rinsed well

1 bay leaf

1 medium white onion, diced

2 garlic cloves, minced

1 tablespoon coconut oil

1 medium tomato, diced

1 teaspoon sesame seeds

1 teaspoon ground ginger

1 teaspoon ground cumin

1 teaspoon ground turmeric

1 teaspoon mustard seeds

½ teaspoon salt

Dash ground cinnamon

1 (14-ounce) can unsweetened coconut milk

2 tablespoons chopped fresh cilantro leaves

PER SERVING Calories: 283; Total Fat: 6g; Saturated Fat: 5g; Cholesterol: 0mg; Carbohydrates: 32g; Fiber: 7g; Protein: 14g

1. In a large soup pot over high heat, mix the broth, lentils, and bay leaf, and bring to a boil. Reduce the heat to medium-low and simmer for 20 minutes, or until the lentils are cooked.

2. Meanwhile, in a medium saucepan over medium heat, sauté the onion and garlic in the coconut oil for 2 minutes.

3. Add the tomato, sesame seeds, ginger, cumin, turmeric, mustard seeds, salt, and cinnamon. Cook, stirring frequently, for 5 minutes.

4. Stir in the coconut milk and bring to a simmer.

5. Remove and discard the bay leaf. Add the coconut milk mixture to the lentils along with the cilantro, and stir to combine. Serve alone or over rice if desired.

INGREDIENT TIP: For more flavor and nutrient variation, add strips of wilted greens to the dal toward the end of the cooking time. Kale, spinach, or chard work well.

COCONUT CASHEW SOUP WITH BUTTERNUT SQUASH

DAIRY-FREE, GLUTEN-FREE, PALEO, SOY-FREE, VEGETARIAN

SERVES 6 / PREP TIME: 10 MINUTES / COOK TIME: 20 MINUTES

Don't you love it when something delicious is good for you? Modern studies have shown that fresh ginger contains an active constituent called *gingerol* that can inhibit inflammatory compounds, among numerous other therapeutic properties.

2 tablespoons coconut oil

¾ cup toasted cashews

2 red chili peppers, seeded and diced

3 garlic cloves, peeled and minced

1 white onion, diced

1½ tablespoons fresh ginger, peeled and minced

2 carrots, peeled and chopped

1 small butternut squash, halved, peeled and diced

1 small Napa cabbage, roughly shredded

2 cups green beans, trimmed

3 cups vegetable broth

1 (14-ounce) can full-fat coconut milk

½ teaspoon salt

Freshly ground black pepper

1 cup mung bean sprouts

4 tablespoons toasted coconut shavings

PER SERVING Calories: 340; Total Fat: 25g; Saturated Fat: 20g; Cholesterol: 0mg; Carbohydrates: 23g; Fiber: 5g; Protein: 7g

1. In a large soup pot over medium heat, melt the coconut oil. Add the cashews and sauté for 2 minutes. Remove them from the pan and set aside.

2. Add the peppers, garlic, and onion, and sauté for 6 minutes. Then add the ginger and carrots, and sauté for about 3 minutes, or until the carrots and squash begin to soften.

3. Stir in the cabbage, green beans, broth, coconut milk, and salt, season with pepper. Simmer for 15 minutes. Turn off the heat and stir in the bean sprouts and coconut shavings.

4. Pour into soup bowls and serve immediately.

INGREDIENT TIP: Coconut contains a specific type of saturated fat called medium-chain triglycerides. These fatty acids are associated with lowering inflammation that causes joint pain, muscle aches, and arthritis.

TURKEY MEATBALL SOUP

DAIRY-FREE, GLUTEN-FREE, PALEO, SOY-FREE

SERVES 6 / PREP TIME: 15 MINUTES / COOK TIME: 15 MINUTES

Often when meatballs and vegetables share a soup pot, it's in Italian Wedding Soup. Here I use low-calorie, high-fiber, vitamin- and nutrient-loaded kale, but spinach will work, too.

FOR THE MEATBALLS
1 pound ground turkey
1 tablespoon Dijon mustard
1 teaspoon dried basil
1 teaspoon garlic powder
½ teaspoon dried oregano
½ teaspoon salt
¼ teaspoon red pepper flakes
Freshly ground black pepper
1 tablespoon ghee

FOR THE SOUP
1 medium white onion, diced
2 carrots, diced
2 garlic cloves, minced
½ teaspoon dried thyme
6 cups vegetable broth
2 cups shredded kale leaves,
    stemmed and thoroughly washed
1 bay leaf

PER SERVING Calories: 259; Total Fat: 14g; Saturated Fat: 5g; Cholesterol: 88mg; Carbohydrates: 9g; Fiber: 2g; Protein: 26g

TO MAKE THE MEATBALLS

1. In a medium bowl, put the turkey, mustard, basil, garlic power, oregano, salt, and red pepper flakes, and season with pepper. With your hands, mix the ingredients until they are well combined.

2. Add the ghee to a stockpot over medium-high heat. Roll the meat mixture into 1-inch balls and layer across the bottom of the pot. Cook for about 2 minutes per side, until almost cooked through. Transfer the meatballs to a plate.

TO MAKE THE SOUP

1. To the stockpot, add the onion, carrots, garlic, and thyme. Cook for about 2 minutes, gently stirring, until the onions are translucent.

2. Add the broth, kale, bay leaf, and meatballs. Bring to a simmer, reduce the heat to medium-low, and simmer for about 15 minutes until the meatballs are cooked through and the kale has softened. Remove and discard the bay leaf. Serve hot.

SPICY LIME–CHICKEN "TORTILLA-LESS" SOUP

DAIRY-FREE, GLUTEN-FREE, PALEO, SOY-FREE

SERVES 6 / PREP TIME: 10 MINUTES / COOK TIME: 20 MINUTES

Enjoy this robust Mexican dish without any guilt since we're omitting the tortilla strips. No flavor will be lost amidst the spicy jalapeño, green chiles, and traditional spices in this warming soup, but you will lose the health-sapping fried, processed corn!

1 tablespoon avocado oil

3 garlic cloves, minced

1 medium white onion, diced

1 jalapeño pepper, seeded and minced

6 cups chicken broth or vegetable broth

1 pound shredded cooked chicken

1 (14-ounce) can diced tomatoes
  with their juice

1 (4-ounce) can diced green chiles

3 tablespoons freshly squeezed lime juice

1 teaspoon chili powder

1 teaspoon ground cumin

½ teaspoon salt

¼ teaspoon cayenne pepper

Freshly ground black pepper

1 avocado, sliced

Fresh cilantro, for garnishing

PER SERVING Calories: 283; Total Fat: 7g; Saturated Fat: 1g; Cholesterol: 47mg; Carbohydrates: 12g; Fiber: 3g; Protein: 29g

1. In a large soup pot over medium heat, heat the avocado oil.

2. Add the garlic, onion, and jalapeño pepper, and sauté for 5 minutes.

3. Stir in the broth, chicken, tomatoes, green chiles, lime juice, chili powder, cumin, salt, and cayenne pepper, and season with black pepper. Bring to a simmer, and cook for 10 minutes.

4. Serve hot, topped with slices of avocado and garnished with cilantro.

INGREDIENT TIP: If you miss the texture of tortilla strips in traditional tortilla soup, break up some plantain chips and add to the broth for added crunch. Plantain chips in packages are available at many supermarkets, usually near the dried fruit or other chips.

SWEET POTATO & BLACK BEAN CHILI

DAIRY-FREE, GLUTEN-FREE, SOY-FREE, VEGAN

SERVES 8 / PREP TIME: 10 MINUTES / COOK TIME: 20 MINUTES

When autumn arrives and you crave a warming bowl of soup, this recipe satisfies. This chunky chili is full of protein and fiber, proving that this vegan take on a classic can still be hearty and sustaining. Enjoy the subtle hints of cocoa and cinnamon that deepen the flavor of this dish. Don't be deterred by the long list of ingredients; this chili comes together quickly.

2 tablespoons avocado oil

1 red onion, diced

5 garlic cloves, minced

1 red bell pepper, diced

1 green bell pepper, diced

3 cups cooked sweet potato cubes

3 cups cooked black beans, drained
    and rinsed well

2 cups vegetable broth

1 (28-ounce) can diced tomatoes
    with their juice

1 tablespoon freshly squeezed lime juice

1 tablespoon chili powder

1 teaspoon cocoa powder

1 teaspoon ground cumin

1 teaspoon salt

½ teaspoon ground cinnamon

¼ teaspoon cayenne pepper

¼ teaspoon dried oregano

PER SERVING Calories: 160; Total Fat: 4g;
Saturated Fat: 0g; Cholesterol: 0mg;
Carbohydrates: 29g; Fiber: 6g; Protein: 8g

1. In a large soup pot over medium heat, warm the avocado oil.

2. Add the onion and garlic, and sauté for 2 minutes.

3. Stir in the red bell pepper and the green bell pepper, and sauté for about 3 minutes until soft.

4. Add the sweet potato, beans, broth, tomatoes, lime juice, chili powder, cocoa powder, cumin, salt, cinnamon, cayenne pepper, and oregano, and stir to combine. Bring to a simmer, and cook for 15 minutes. Serve immediately.

TIME-SAVING TIP: Look for bags of organic sweet potato chunks in the frozen food section of your grocery store to save time chopping and cooking.

CHICKEN CHILI BLANCO

GLUTEN-FREE, LACTOSE-FREE, PALEO

SERVES 4 / PREP TIME: 10 MINUTES / COOK TIME: 20 MINUTES

This dish is a crowd pleaser. The dietary fiber found in beans does an excellent job of balancing blood sugar while providing stabilizing, slow-burning energy throughout the day. The high fiber also helps lower cholesterol levels. Experiment with different types of beans in this light chili recipe.

1 tablespoon ghee

2 small onions, chopped

6 garlic cloves, minced

2 (4-ounce) cans diced mild green chiles with their liquid

4 cups cooked white beans, drained and rinsed well

4 cups chicken broth or vegetable broth

4 teaspoons ground cumin

2 teaspoons dried oregano

1 teaspoon chili powder

¼ teaspoon cayenne pepper

4 cups shredded cooked chicken

2 scallions, sliced

PER SERVING Calories: 304; Total Fat: 4g; Saturated Fat: 2g; Cholesterol: 0mg; Carbohydrates: 46g; Fiber: 12g; Protein: 21g

1. In a large soup pot over medium heat, melt the ghee.

2. Add the onions and garlic, and sauté for 5 minutes.

3. Add the chiles, and cook for 2 minutes, stirring.

4. Stir in the beans, broth, cumin, oregano, chili powder, and cayenne pepper. Bring to a simmer.

5. Add the chicken, bring to a simmer, reduce the heat to medium-low, and cook for 10 minutes. Serve immediately, sprinkled with the scallions.

INGREDIENT TIP: Cannellini beans, navy beans, and Great Northern beans are all options when choosing a white bean to use in this chili. Cannellini are a popular choice because the beans hold their shape well when cooked.

BEET SALAD WITH PEAS & GREENS (PAGE 101)

CHAPTER SIX

Salads

MASSAGED KALE SALAD

DAIRY-FREE, GLUTEN-FREE, PALEO SOY-FREE, VEGAN

SERVES 4 / PREP TIME: 15 MINUTES

Thanks to its high fiber content, kale is a great vegetable choice for digestive wellness and intestinal cleansing. Massaging kale helps to tenderize it. Kale also offers more calcium per serving than a cup of milk! Avocado adds healthy fat, and pomegranate seeds, with their anti-inflammatory flavanols, act as a natural arthritis treatment in the body.

2 bunches Lacinato kale, stemmed and torn into bite-size pieces

3 scallions, sliced

1 avocado, diced

¼ cup shelled sunflower seeds

2 tablespoons freshly squeezed lemon juice

3 tablespoons extra-virgin olive oil

½ teaspoon salt

Freshly ground black pepper

¼ cup pomegranate seeds

PER SERVING Calories: 249; Total Fat: 21g; Saturated Fat: 3g; Cholesterol: 0mg; Carbohydrates: 14g; Fiber: 6g; Protein: 6g

1. In a large bowl, combine the kale, scallions, avocado, sunflower seeds, lemon juice, olive oil, and salt, and season with pepper.

2. With your hands, massage the salad ingredients for about 5 minutes until the kale begins to soften and the avocado is creamed into the other ingredients.

3. Mix the pomegranate seeds into the salad and serve immediately.

INGREDIENT TIP: Look for packaged pomegranate seeds (arils) at the grocery store to save the time and mess of separating them from a whole pomegranate.

SHAVED BRUSSELS SPROUT SALAD

DAIRY-FREE, GLUTEN-FREE, PALEO, SOY-FREE, VEGETARIAN

SERVES 4 / PREP TIME: 15 MINUTES

Brussels sprouts are full of beneficial sulfur-containing compounds that activate body systems necessary for proper detoxification. While not typically eaten raw, that doesn't mean they aren't as equally delicious that way. If your body prefers them softer and easier to digest, sauté the shaved sprouts and create a warm salad.

1 pound Brussels sprouts, trimmed and thinly sliced into ribbons from top to stem (discard the stems)

2 hard-boiled eggs, peeled and roughly chopped

¼ cup pine nuts

3 tablespoons freshly squeezed lemon juice

3 tablespoons extra-virgin olive oil

1 tablespoon minced shallot

Pinch salt

Freshly ground black pepper

In a large bowl, toss together the Brussels sprouts, eggs, pine nuts, lemon juice, olive oil, and shallot. Sprinkle with the salt and season with pepper.

PREPARATION TIP: If you own a mandoline and safety gloves, use them when shaving the Brussels sprouts to save some prep time.

PER SERVING Calories: 213; Total Fat: 17.3g; Saturated Fat: 2.2g; Cholesterol: 54.6mg; Carbohydrates: 10.7g; Fiber: 4.7g; Protein: 7.1g

SPICY BROCCOLI SLAW

GLUTEN-FREE, PROBIOTIC, SOY-FREE, VEGETARIAN

SERVES 4 / PREP TIME: 10 MINUTES

Broccoli contains a special flavonoid shown to reduce the impact of allergy-related compounds in our bodies, making it a great choice for an anti-inflammatory, hypoallergenic diet. This recipe makes a great party side or a fun dish to brighten a weekday meal.

1 head broccoli, roughly chopped into bite-size pieces

2 scallions, sliced

¼ cup sliced almonds

¼ cup dried cranberries

2 tablespoons plain whole-milk yogurt

1 tablespoon Paleo mayonnaise

1 tablespoon freshly squeezed lemon juice

1 teaspoon raw honey

½ teaspoon ground cumin

Dash hot sauce

Pinch salt

Freshly ground black pepper

PER SERVING Calories: 110; Total Fat: 7g; Saturated Fat: 1g; Cholesterol: 6mg; Carbohydrates: 12g; Fiber: 2g; Protein: 2g

1. In a large bowl, combine the broccoli, scallions, almonds, and cranberries.

2. In a small bowl, whisk the yogurt, mayonnaise, lemon juice, honey, cumin, hot sauce, and salt, and season with pepper. Pour this dressing over the broccoli mixture and stir well to combine.

INGREDIENT TIP: For a slightly different onion flavor, use minced shallot or red onion instead of the scallions. Also, look for dried cranberries that are sweetened with fruit juice, to reduce some of the sugar content in this dish.

RAINBOW BEAN SALAD

DAIRY-FREE, GLUTEN-FREE, SOY-FREE, VEGAN

SERVES 4 / PREP TIME: 10 MINUTES / COOK TIME: 0 MINUTES

This flavorful, hearty lunchtime salad can last throughout the week. Simply keep the salad ingredients and the dressing in separate containers in the refrigerator so the contents of the salad don't become mushy.

FOR THE DRESSING

½ cup extra-virgin olive oil

¼ cup red wine vinegar

1 tablespoon freshly squeezed lime juice

½ teaspoon garlic powder

½ teaspoon chili powder

½ teaspoon salt

¼ teaspoon red pepper flakes

¼ teaspoon freshly ground black pepper

FOR THE SALAD

3 cups cooked wild rice

2 cups cooked black beans, drained and rinsed well

1 cup non-GMO organic sweet corn kernels

1 red bell pepper, diced

4 scallions, sliced

¼ cup chopped fresh cilantro

PER SERVING Calories: 423; Total Fat: 24g; Saturated Fat: 3g; Cholesterol: 0mg; Carbohydrates: 47g; Fiber: 17g; Protein: 13g

TO MAKE THE DRESSING

In a small bowl, whisk the olive oil, vinegar, lime juice, garlic powder, chili powder, salt, red pepper flakes, and black pepper. Set aside.

TO MAKE THE SALAD

1. In a medium bowl, stir together the rice, beans, corn, red bell pepper, scallions, and cilantro.

2. Pour the dressing over the vegetables and toss to coat evenly. Serve chilled, if desired.

INGREDIENT TIP: For an easy solution to cutting fresh corn kernels off the cob, buy a bag of organic frozen corn kernels. When mixed with the other ingredients, the frozen corn will help chill the salad.

CRISPY KALE SALAD

DAIRY-FREE, GLUTEN-FREE, SOY-FREE, VEGAN

SERVES 6 / PREP TIME: 10 MINUTES / COOK TIME: 20 MINUTES

This salad is full of different textures and tastes that give kale a fresh face full of traditional fall flavors. The moisture from the sautéed leek and apples blends with the spices on the crispy kale so no extra dressing is necessary.

15 ounces kale, stemmed, thoroughly washed and dried, and chopped into bite-size pieces

3 tablespoons extra-virgin olive oil

2 tablespoons apple cider vinegar

1 teaspoon salt

½ teaspoon red pepper flakes

¼ teaspoon freshly ground black pepper

1 small leek, white and pale green parts, thoroughly washed (see Ingredient Tip)

2 small sweet potatoes, peeled

1 apple, peeled

1 tablespoon avocado oil

¼ cup pine nuts

PER SERVING Calories: 213; Total Fat: 14g; Saturated Fat: 2g; Cholesterol: 0mg; Carbohydrates: 22g; Fiber: 5g; Protein: 5g

1. Preheat the oven to 350°F.

2. Line a backing sheet with parchment paper.

3. In a large bowl, combine the kale, olive oil, vinegar, salt, and red pepper flakes, and season with black pepper. With your hands, knead the oil and spices into the kale for 1 minute. Transfer three-fourths of the kale to the prepared pan and spread it evenly. Bake for 20 minutes, tossing halfway through. Set aside the bowl with the rest of the kale.

4. While the kale cooks, chop the leek, sweet potatoes, and apple into bite-size pieces. Add with the avocado oil to a large skillet over medium heat, and sauté for about 10 minutes, until the sweet potatoes soften.

5. Remove the crispy kale from the oven and add it to the reserved uncooked kale.

6. Top with the sweet potato mixture and the pine nuts, and mix well.

7. Serve warm.

PREPARATION TIP: To wash leeks properly, slice them once or twice lengthwise, and slice them from the root up. Discard the roots and the tougher dark green tops. Add the sliced pieces to a large bowl of water. Swish the leeks around with your hands so any dirt particles hiding in the layers wash out and sink to the bottom. With a slotted spoon, remove the leeks from the water.

STONE FRUIT SALAD

DAIRY-FREE, GLUTEN-FREE, SOY-FREE, VEGETARIAN

SERVES 6 / PREP TIME: 15 MINUTES

Summer stone fruit season comes and goes quickly, spanning from May to September in parts of the United States. Making use of these delectable fruits at every meal is well worth the effort. You'll be rewarded with a sweet, juicy nutritional punch including plenty of vitamins A, C, and E that work together to promote healthy nerves and muscles as well as fight infection. If fresh stone fruits are not in season, you can often find frozen peaches and cherries in the freezer section of the supermarket.

4 cups mixed chopped greens

1 cup sliced fresh peaches

1 cup fresh cherries, pitted and halved

1 cup sliced fresh nectarines

½ cup pecans, chopped

¼ cup thinly sliced red onion

¼ cup fresh basil leaves

⅓ cup extra-virgin olive oil

¼ cup balsamic vinegar

1 tablespoon freshly squeezed lemon juice

½ tablespoon raw honey

Dash salt

Freshly ground black pepper

PER SERVING Calories: 235; Total Fat: 19g; Saturated Fat: 2g; Cholesterol: 0mg; Carbohydrates: 16g; Fiber: 3g; Protein: 2g

1. In a large bowl, gently combine the greens, peaches, cherries, nectarines, pecans, red onion, and basil.

2. In a small bowl, add the olive oil, vinegar, lemon juice, honey, and salt, season with pepper, and whisk to combine.

3. Pour the dressing over the salad and gently toss to combine. Serve immediately.

PREPARATION TIP: While stone fruits are delicious when eaten ripe and fresh, grill them and use them in this salad for an even deeper sweetness.

WARM FIG & SWEET POTATO SALAD

DAIRY-FREE, GLUTEN-FREE, SOY-FREE, VEGETARIAN

SERVES 6 / PREP TIME: 10 MINUTES / COOK TIME: 20 MINUTES

This sweet, earthy, slightly spicy potato salad veers far from the standard picnic dish of white potatoes and mayonnaise. The dressing is light, the ingredients unique, and the taste bursts with summer flavor. Figs are a good source of potassium, a mineral needed for blood pressure control and the reduction of hypertension.

4 sweet potatoes, cubed

6 tablespoons extra-virgin olive oil, divided

1 teaspoon salt

6 ripe fresh figs, quartered

2 tablespoons balsamic vinegar

1 teaspoon Dijon mustard

1 teaspoon raw honey

3 scallions, sliced

1 red chile pepper, such as serrano, seeded and thinly sliced

Freshly ground black pepper

Crumbled goat cheese, for garnishing (optional)

PER SERVING Calories: 253; Total Fat: 14g; Saturated Fat: 2g; Cholesterol: 0mg; Carbohydrates: 32g; Fiber: 5g; Protein: 2g

1. Preheat the oven to 475°F.

2. Line a baking sheet with aluminum foil.

3. In a large bowl, toss the sweet potato cubes in 3 tablespoons of olive oil and the salt. Spread on the prepared pan and roast for 20 minutes. Halfway through, flip the potatoes and add the figs.

4. Meanwhile, in a small bowl, whisk 2 tablespoons of olive oil with the vinegar, mustard, and honey. Set the dressing aside.

5. In a small skillet over medium heat, sauté the scallions and red chile in the remaining 1 tablespoon of olive oil for 2 minutes.

6. In a large bowl, combine the roasted sweet potatoes and figs with the scallions and the red chile. Pour the dressing over and gently stir to combine. Season with pepper and sprinkle with goat cheese (if using). Serve warm.

PREPARATION TIP: For a dairy-free meal, omit the optional goat cheese.

CHOPPED THAI SALAD

DAIRY-FREE, GLUTEN-FREE, SOY-FREE, VEGETARIAN

SERVES 6 / PREP TIME: 20 MINUTES

The humble cabbage bursts with anti-inflammatory richness. The pigments in red cabbage, called anthocyanins, do double duty as anti-inflammatory compounds and antioxidants, providing anticancer benefits as they work to lower oxidative stress in the body. While this recipe does require a little chopping, there's no cooking or other fussy prep to slow you down.

FOR THE DRESSING

½ cup extra-virgin olive oil

3 tablespoons filtered water

2 tablespoons coconut aminos

1 tablespoon apple cider vinegar

1 tablespoon freshly squeezed lime juice

1 tablespoon raw honey

1 teaspoon sesame oil

1 teaspoon garlic powder

Dash ground ginger

FOR THE SALAD

2 cups shredded kale, stemmed and thoroughly washed

2 cups shredded napa cabbage

2 cups shredded red cabbage

4 scallions, sliced

1 cup shredded carrots

1 red bell pepper, julienned

1 yellow bell pepper, julienned

1 cucumber, julienned (see Preparation Tip)

½ cup fresh cilantro leaves, roughly chopped

½ cup cashews, roughly chopped

PER SERVING Calories: 515; Total Fat: 24g; Saturated Fat: 4g; Cholesterol: 0mg; Carbohydrates: 67g; Fiber: 9g; Protein: 15g

TO MAKE THE DRESSING

In a medium bowl, whisk the olive oil, water, coconut aminos, vinegar, lime juice, honey, sesame oil, garlic powder, and ginger until combined. Set aside.

TO MAKE THE SALAD

1. In a large bowl, mix the kale, napa cabbage, red cabbage, scallions, carrots, red bell pepper, yellow bell pepper, and cucumber.

2. Top with the cilantro and cashews.

3. Pour the dressing over the salad, toss well, and serve immediately.

PREPARATION TIP: Julienne is a style of cutting food into very thin, matchstick-sized pieces. It can be done with a sharp chef's knife or a simple kitchen tool called a julienne peeler, which makes the process easy and fast, and can be purchased for under $10.

HEARTS OF ROMAINE CAESAR SALAD

DAIRY-FREE, GLUTEN-FREE, PALEO, SOY-FREE, VEGETARIAN

SERVES 6 / PREP TIME: 5 MINUTES

This classic salad is ready in a snap. It's packed with protein from the eggs and healthy fats from the homemade dressing, and the romaine lettuce provides a satisfying crunch in every delicious bite.

3 romaine lettuce hearts, cut into strips

2 hard-boiled eggs, peeled and roughly chopped

¼ cup raw shaved Parmesan cheese (optional)

¼ cup Paleo Caesar Dressing (page 30)

PER SERVING Calories: 49; Total Fat: 3g; Saturated Fat: 1g; Cholesterol: 62mg; Carbohydrates: 3g; Fiber: 2g; Protein: 4g

1. In a large bowl, combine the romaine lettuce and the eggs.

2. Sprinkle with the Parmesan cheese (if using).

3. Pour the dressing over the salad and toss to combine. Serve immediately.

INGREDIENT TIP: Cheeses from other countries are often less processed and pasteurized than those made in the United States. Look for a sheep's milk Parmesan cheese from Europe that's made raw and contains no filler ingredients.

PREPARATION TIP: For a dairy-free salad, omit the optional cheese.

SAUTÉED GINGER & BOK CHOY

DAIRY-FREE, GLUTEN-FREE, SOY-FREE, VEGAN

SERVES 4 / PREP TIME: 5 MINUTES / COOK TIME: 10 TO 15 MINUTES

This grilled Asian salad is simple to prepare yet delivers sophisticated flavors, and it's full of nutritious elements. In the case of bok choy, sautéing actually increases the availability of certain nutrients like lutein—the eye vitamin—to our bodies.

1 tablespoon sesame oil

2 garlic cloves, minced

1 teaspoon minced peeled fresh ginger

3 tablespoons filtered water

2 tablespoons coconut aminos

1 teaspoon rice vinegar

¼ teaspoon red pepper flakes

4 heads bok choy, halved lengthwise

PER SERVING Calories: 143; Total Fat: 5g; Saturated Fat: 0g; Cholesterol: 0mg; Carbohydrates: 21g; Fiber: 8g; Protein: 12g

1. In a large saucepan over medium heat, warm the sesame oil.

2. Add the garlic and ginger, and sauté for 2 minutes.

3. Stir in the water, coconut aminos, vinegar, and red pepper flakes.

4. Add the bok choy, cut-sides down, to the pan and cover. Lower the heat to low and let steam for 5 to 10 minutes. Once tender, remove from the heat and serve.

INGREDIENT TIP: Use fresh ginger for the best nutrient value and flavor here. If you don't avoid soy completely, you can use tamari sauce, which is a gluten-free fermented soy sauce, instead of the coconut aminos in equal amounts.

BEET SALAD WITH PEAS & GREENS

DAIRY-FREE, GLUTEN-FREE, SOY-FREE, VEGETARIAN

SERVES 6 / PREP TIME: 5 MINUTES

Chioggia beets, when raw, have pink and white stripes through their interior flesh which tend to disappear when roasted. Using them raw, as in this salad, not only lets their beauty shine but also preserves their unique phytonutrients, called betalains, which lose much of their power and become damaged when cooked. Enjoy the full antioxidant benefits of raw beets in this salad.

6 cups mixed greens

3 small Chioggia beets, thinly sliced (see Ingredient Tip)

1 cup shelled English peas, or frozen peas, thawed

1 small red onion, sliced

1 large avocado, sliced

¼ cup Lemon–Dijon Mustard Dressing (page 28)

PER SERVING Calories: 107; Total Fat: 4g; Saturated Fat: 1g; Cholesterol: 0mg; Carbohydrates: 15g; Fiber: 6g; Protein: 4g

1. In a large bowl, mix the greens, beets, peas, red onion, and avocado.

2. Pour the dressing over the salad and toss to combine. Serve immediately.

INGREDIENT TIP: English peas are typically shelled and only the peas are eaten. You can use snap peas or snow peas in this recipe if you wish. Those peas are a bit smaller, but their shells are edible so you can use the entire pod, chopped. Substitute red or golden beets for the Chioggias, if you can't find them.

MEDITERRANEAN CARROT SALAD

DAIRY-FREE, GLUTEN-FREE, SOY-FREE, VEGETARIAN

SERVES 6 / PREP TIME: 10 MINUTES

This salad is full of textures and flavors, from the crunch of the pistachios to the soft sweetness of the dates. For a simpler way to dress this dish, use extra-virgin olive oil, lemon juice, and sprinkle with salt.

4 cups grated or shredded carrots

½ cup fresh cilantro leaves, finely chopped

⅓ cup shelled pistachios, roughly chopped

4 Medjool dates, pitted and chopped

3 scallions, sliced

¼ teaspoon red pepper flakes

½ cup Tahini-Lime Dressing (page 29)

PER SERVING Calories: 101; Total Fat: 2g; Saturated Fat: 0g; Cholesterol: 0mg; Carbohydrates: 22g; Fiber: 4g; Protein: 2g

1. In a large bowl, mix together the carrots, cilantro, pistachios, dates, scallions, and red pepper flakes.

2. Pour the dressing over the salad and toss to mix well. Serve immediately.

INGREDIENT TIP: If grating 4 cups of carrots sounds tedious, look for bags of shredded carrots in the grocery store near the bagged and boxed salad greens.

QUINOA & ARUGULA TABBOULEH

DAIRY-FREE, GLUTEN-FREE, SOY-FREE, VEGAN

SERVES 6 / PREP TIME: 10 MINUTES / COOK TIME: 0 MINUTES

Full of fresh flavor, tabbouleh is a Middle Eastern vegetarian salad traditionally made with tomatoes, finely chopped parsley, mint, bulgur, and onion, and seasoned with olive oil, lemon juice, and salt. Since bulgur is a wheat berry, this recipe replaces the gluten-containing grain with protein-rich quinoa. (To cook quinoa or use already cooked quinoa, see Cooking Tip, Minestrone Soup with Quinoa, page 77).

3 cups cooked quinoa

1 cup packed arugula

4 scallions, sliced

½ cup diced tomato

½ cup fresh flat-leaf parsley, chopped

½ cup fresh mint leaves, minced

⅓ cup extra-virgin olive oil

2 tablespoons freshly squeezed lemon juice

½ teaspoon garlic powder

½ teaspoon salt

Freshly ground black pepper

PER SERVING Calories: 235; Total Fat: 14g; Saturated Fat: 2g; Cholesterol: 0mg; Carbohydrates: 24g; Fiber: 3g; Protein: 5g

1. In a large bowl, mix together the quinoa, arugula, scallions, tomato, parsley, and mint.

2. In a small bowl, whisk together the olive oil, lemon juice, garlic powder, and salt, and season with pepper.

3. Add the dressing to the salad and toss to mix well. Serve immediately.

INGREDIENT TIP: These days, you can often find packaged prewashed baby arugula in the produce department of the supermarket. This product saves time, and the tender, smaller leaves are perfect for this salad.

WILD RICE SALAD WITH MUSHROOMS

GLUTEN-FREE, LACTOSE-FREE, SOY-FREE, VEGETARIAN

SERVES 8 / PREP TIME: 10 MINUTES / COOK TIME: 15 MINUTES

Button mushrooms such as creminis are at the top of the mushroom list when it comes to reducing inflammation in the body. They contain compounds that block the production of pro-inflammatory molecules. They can be a bit tricky to clean though—the less water used, the better. Wipe with a damp paper towel before cooking to protect their delicate texture as much as possible.

3 cups cooked wild rice

2 tablespoons ghee

1 small sweet onion, diced

3 garlic cloves, minced

2 cups cremini mushrooms, sliced

½ cup vegetable broth

½ teaspoon dried thyme

½ teaspoon salt

PER SERVING Calories: 143; Total Fat: 4g; Saturated Fat: 2g; Cholesterol: 0mg; Carbohydrates: 22g; Fiber: 2g; Protein: 5g

1. Place the rice in a large bowl and set aside.

2. In a medium saucepan over medium heat, melt the ghee. Add the onion and garlic, and cook for 5 minutes, stirring frequently.

3. Stir in the mushrooms, broth, thyme, and salt. Continue cooking for 7 to 10 minutes until the mushrooms are tender and the broth has reduced by about half.

4. Add the mushroom mixture to the rice and stir well. Serve immediately.

INGREDIENT TIP: Use other mushroom varieties in this dish. Shiitake mushrooms have a meaty texture when cooked, whereas creminis are more similar in taste and texture to other capped white mushroom varieties.

WARM CHICKEN SALAD WITH PEARS & SWISS CHARD

DAIRY-FREE, GLUTEN-FREE, PALEO, SOY-FREE

SERVES 6 / PREP TIME: 10 MINUTES / COOK TIME: 10 MINUTES

Swiss chard is immensely popular in Mediterranean cuisine. It's also one of the most nutritious greens on the planet. Similar to beet greens, chard is high in the unique phytonutrient group called betalains, which provide antioxidant, anti-inflammatory, and detoxification support. Swiss chard is extremely versatile, so look for ways to incorporate it into your meals.

2 cups shredded cooked chicken

6 cups chopped Swiss chard

4 mini bell peppers, sliced

1 pear, sliced

¼ cup toasted pine nuts

1 shallot, minced

½ cup extra-virgin olive oil

2 tablespoons freshly squeezed lemon juice

2 tablespoons apple cider vinegar

1 tablespoon Dijon mustard

¼ teaspoon salt

PER SERVING Calories: 356; Total Fat: 29g; Saturated Fat: 4g; Cholesterol: 34mg; Carbohydrates: 9g; Fiber: 2g; Protein: 14g

1. Preheat the oven to 350°F.

2. Wrap the chicken in a piece of aluminum foil and place it in the oven for 10 minutes.

3. In a large bowl, combine the chard, bell peppers, pear, and pine nuts.

4. In a small bowl, whisk together the shallot, olive oil, lemon juice, vinegar, mustard, and salt.

5. Add the dressing to the salad. Remove the chicken from the oven and add to the salad. Toss the salad well and serve immediately.

INGREDIENT TIP: If you prefer not to include the chard stems chopped up in your salad, you can save them in a resealable freezer bag for later use in a homemade broth. You can even include them for some extra flavor in our Gut-Healing Bone Broth (page 74).

BUCKWHEAT PASTA WITH ZUCCHINI PESTO & SUNFLOWER SEEDS (PAGE 112)

CHAPTER SEVEN

Vegan & Vegetarian

VEGGIE SPRING ROLLS WITH ALMOND DIPPING SAUCE

DAIRY-FREE, GLUTEN-FREE, PALEO, SOY-FREE, VEGAN

MAKES 10 ROLLS / PREP TIME: 20 MINUTES

A lighter take on the traditional fried spring roll, these fresh rolls are made with rice paper wrappers (see Ingredient Tip). Get the kids involved in wrapping—these rolls are fun to make and dip, and work beautifully as a vegetarian anti-inflammatory appetizer or light main dish. If you have a mandoline slicer, it makes prep even easier.

FOR THE SAUCE

½ cup almond butter

1 tablespoon coconut aminos

1 tablespoon coconut sugar

1 tablespoon freshly squeezed lime juice

¼ teaspoon garlic powder

¼ teaspoon red pepper flakes

Dash ground ginger

Filtered water, to thin

FOR THE ROLLS

10 rice paper wrappers

1 large avocado, thinly sliced

1 red bell pepper, very thinly sliced

½ cup shredded carrots

½ cup julienned cucumber

½ cup shredded cabbage

¼ cup sliced scallion

¼ cup fresh cilantro leaves

TO MAKE THE SAUCE

In a small bowl, whisk the almond butter, coconut aminos, coconut sugar, lime juice, garlic powder, red pepper flakes, and ginger. If needed, add a little of the water to thin.

TO MAKE THE ROLLS

1. Prepare the rice paper wrappers according to the package instructions.

2. In a large bowl, gently combine the avocado, red bell pepper, carrots, cucumber, cabbage, scallion, and cilantro. On a clean work surface, divide the vegetables into 10 portions.

PER SERVING Calories: 176; Total Fat: 10g; Saturated Fat: 1g; Cholesterol: 0mg; Carbohydrates: 21g; Fiber: 3g; Protein: 5g

3. On a large plastic cutting board, lay out one wrapper and smooth any wrinkles.

4. Place 1 portion of veggies on the bottom third of the wrapper. Beginning at the bottom edge, roll it like a burrito until about three-fourths of the way to the top. Fold the side edges in, and continue to roll toward the top of the wrapper.

5. Repeat steps 3 and 4 with the remaining ingredients.

6. Serve the rolls with the dipping sauce alongside.

INGREDIENT TIP: Rice paper wrappers are edible and typically made from rice flour, tapioca flour, water, and salt. To become pliable, they require dipping in warm water for a small amount of time, depending on the brand.

SWEET KOREAN LENTILS

DAIRY-FREE, GLUTEN-FREE, SOY-FREE, VEGAN

SERVES 4 / PREP TIME: 10 MINUTES / COOK TIME: 20 MINUTES

This succulent dish is a vegan spin-off of the classic Korean dish *bulgogi*, which is typically made from beef marinated in soy sauce, sugar, sesame oil, and garlic. By replacing a few ingredients with lighter, anti-inflammatory substitutes, this flavorful dish can be enjoyed without any health qualms. It is best served over rice.

1 tablespoon avocado oil

1 small white onion, diced

2 garlic cloves, minced

2 cups vegetable broth

1 cup dried lentils, sorted and rinsed

3 tablespoons coconut aminos

2 tablespoons coconut sugar

1 tablespoon rice vinegar

1 teaspoon sesame oil

½ teaspoon ground ginger

¼ teaspoon red pepper flakes

1 tablespoon sesame seeds (optional)

2 scallions, sliced (optional)

PER SERVING Calories: 281; Total Fat: 5g;
Saturated Fat: 1; Cholesterol: 0mg;
Carbohydrates: 45g; Fiber: 10g; Protein: 14g

1. To a stockpot over medium heat, add the avocado oil, onion, and garlic. Sauté for 5 minutes, or until the onion is translucent.

2. Stir in the broth, lentils, coconut aminos, coconut sugar, vinegar, sesame oil, ginger, and red pepper flakes. Increase the heat to medium-high and bring to a simmer. Reduce the heat to low, cover, and cook for 15 minutes, or until the lentils are cooked.

3. Garnish with the sesame seeds and scallions (if using).

COOKING TIP: If you're in a rush and able to purchase precooked lentils, replace the dried lentils and broth with 2½ cups cooked lentils. Add broth as needed to soften the mixture. Simmer until all ingredients are heated through and combined.

CAULIFLOWER "FRIED RICE"

DAIRY-FREE, GLUTEN-FREE, PALEO, SOY-FREE, VEGETARIAN

SERVES 4 / PREP TIME: 10 MINUTES / COOK TIME: 20 MINUTES

If you avoid grains but crave fried rice, make this cauliflower rice your go-to version! It's surprising how similar the texture of the pulverized cauliflower is to traditional rice. You'll find lots of ways to use this satisfying side dish.

1 head cauliflower, cored, florets
    broken into chunks

1 tablespoon sesame oil

½ cup diced onion

2 garlic cloves, minced

2 scallions, sliced

1 carrot, minced

¼ cup peas

2 eggs, whisked

¼ teaspoon red pepper flakes

Coconut aminos (optional)

PER SERVING Calories: 128; Total Fat: 6g; Saturated Fat: 1g; Cholesterol: 93mg; Carbohydrates: 13g; Fiber: 4g; Protein: 7g

1. In a food processor (or blender), cautiously pulse the cauliflower until it breaks down into small pieces the size of rice grains.

2. In a large skillet or sauté pan over medium heat, heat the sesame oil.

3. Add the onion and garlic. Cook for 2 to 3 minutes until the onion is translucent.

4. Stir in the scallions, carrot, and peas, and cook for 5 minutes, stirring frequently.

5. Add the cauliflower rice and cook for 5 to 7 minutes, stirring, until the cauliflower is crispy on the outside but cooked on the inside.

6. With the back of a spoon, make a well in the middle of the vegetable mixture. Add the eggs in the well, and stir slowly for about 4 minutes until softly cooked.

7. Incorporate the cooked eggs into the vegetable mixture. Stir in the red pepper flakes. Serve immediately, sprinkled with coconut aminos (if using).

BUCKWHEAT PASTA WITH ZUCCHINI PESTO & SUNFLOWER SEEDS

GLUTEN-FREE, SOY-FREE, VEGETARIAN

SERVES 4 / PREP TIME: 5 MINUTES / COOK TIME: 10 MINUTES

Traditionally, Italian pesto is made from basil, olive oil, garlic, salt, pine nuts, and Parmesan cheese. Outside of Italy, you'll find pestos made from a variety of ingredients with different greens added. Feel free to mix and match based on your tastes or the contents of your refrigerator. Buckwheat adds complex carbohydrates, protein, and dietary fiber—a triple win for blood sugar and energy levels since they burn slower throughout the day for sustained energy.

FOR THE PESTO

1 cup tightly packed fresh basil leaves

1 cup chopped zucchini (see Preparation Tip)

¼ cup shelled sunflower seeds, plus more for garnishing

2 garlic cloves

½ cup extra-virgin olive oil, divided

¼ cup shredded raw Parmesan cheese

1 teaspoon freshly squeezed lemon juice

¼ teaspoon salt

Freshly ground black pepper

FOR THE PASTA

8 ounces buckwheat pasta

Filtered water, for cooking the pasta

PER SERVING Calories: 548; Total Fat: 35g; Saturated Fat: 6g; Cholesterol: 5mg; Carbohydrates: 45g; Fiber: 3g; Protein: 10g

TO MAKE THE PESTO

1. In a food processor (or blender), combine the basil, zucchini, sunflower seeds, garlic, and ¼ cup of olive oil. Blend for 15 seconds.

2. Add the Parmesan cheese, lemon juice, and salt, and season with pepper. Pulse to combine.

3. With the food processor (or blender) running, slowly pour in the remaining ¼ cup of olive oil until all ingredients are well combined.

TO MAKE THE PASTA

1. Cook the pasta according to the package instructions.

2. Pour the desired amount of pesto over the pasta, garnish with sunflower seeds, and serve.

PREPARATION TIP: Squeezing out any water from the chopped zucchini can keep the pesto from getting mushy.

ZUCCHINI NOODLES WITH BURST CHERRY TOMATOES & GARLIC

DAIRY-FREE, GLUTEN-FREE, SOY-FREE, VEGAN

SERVES 6 / PREP TIME: 10 MINUTES / COOK TIME: 5 MINUTES

Zucchini noodles, often called "zoodles," are a great alternative to wheat noodles and other pasta made from simple carbohydrates. They're high in the antioxidant vitamin C, and even though they are high in starch, recent studies, such as one conducted by The George Mateljan Foundation in 2016, have shown they contain a unique and beneficial type of starch with properties that help regulate insulin.

2 tablespoons avocado oil

2 medium zucchini, shaved into long strands with a vegetable peeler, or spiralized (see Cooking Tip)

¼ teaspoon salt

Freshly ground black pepper

Burst Cherry Tomatoes with Garlic (page 69)

PER SERVING Calories: 93; Total Fat: 5g; Saturated Fat: 1g; Cholesterol: 0mg; Carbohydrates: 11g; Fiber: 3g; Protein: 2g

1. In a large skillet or sauté pan over medium heat, heat the avocado oil.

2. Add the zucchini and salt, season with pepper, and cook, stirring, for 1 to 2 minutes. Turn off the heat.

3. Top with the tomatoes and garlic, and serve.

COOKING TIP: Do not overcook the zucchini noodles! They have a tendency to become extremely soggy and fall apart if left on the heat for too long.

CHICKPEA CURRY IN A HURRY

GLUTEN-FREE, SOY-FREE, VEGETARIAN

SERVES 4 / PREP TIME: 15 MINUTES / COOK TIME: 15 MINUTES

For this quick and easy vegetarian curry, combine almost any vegetables you have on hand to create a dish unique to your kitchen. Try cauliflower, sweet potatoes, celery, or mushrooms.

2 small white onions, diced

2 garlic cloves, minced

2 tablespoons avocado oil

1 red bell pepper, chopped

1½ cups vegetable broth

1 tablespoon curry powder

½ teaspoon salt

2 cups cooked chickpeas, rinsed and drained

1 medium apple, diced

½ cup golden raisins

½ cup cashews, roughly chopped

½ cup plain whole-milk yogurt (optional)

PER SERVING Calories: 422; Total Fat: 18g; Saturated Fat: 3g; Cholesterol: 6mg; Carbohydrates: 55g; Fiber: 11g; Protein: 11g

1. In a large skillet over medium heat, sauté the onions and garlic in the avocado oil for 2 to 3 minutes until translucent.

2. Add the red bell pepper, and sauté for 5 minutes.

3. Stir in the broth, curry powder, and salt, and bring to a simmer.

4. Add the chickpeas, apple, and raisins, and cook for 5 minutes.

5. Just before turning off the heat, stir in the cashews. Serve hot, topped with yogurt (if using) to soften the heat of the spices.

INGREDIENT TIP: Look for raisins sweetened with natural fruit juice as opposed to processed sugar.

PREPARATION TIP: For a vegan version, omit the optional yogurt.

CHICKPEA & TAHINI LETTUCE WRAPS

DAIRY-FREE, GLUTEN-FREE, PALEO, SOY-FREE, VEGETARIAN

SERVES 2 / PREP TIME: 15 MINUTES

Chickpeas, or garbanzo beans, can be a great vegetarian source of protein and fiber. Their hearty consistency can replace white meat easily in many recipes. Wrapping them in lettuce creates the perfect, crunchy, gluten-free, vegetarian taco substitute.

1 (15-ounce) can chickpeas, drained and rinsed well

1 celery stalk, diced

½ shallot, minced

1 green apple, cored and diced

3 tablespoons tahini (sesame paste)

2 teaspoons freshly squeezed lemon juice

1 teaspoon raw honey

1 teaspoon Dijon mustard

Dash salt

Filtered water, to thin

4 romaine lettuce leaves

PER SERVING Calories: 396; Total Fat: 15g; Saturated Fat: 2g; Cholesterol: 0mg; Carbohydrates: 53g; Fiber: 16g; Protein: 15g

1. In a medium bowl, stir together the chickpeas, celery, shallot, apple, tahini, lemon juice, honey, mustard, and salt. If needed, add some water to thin the mixture.

2. Place the romaine lettuce leaves on a plate. Fill each with the chickpea filling, using it all. Wrap the leaves around the filling. Serve immediately.

INGREDIENT TIP: Shallots have a sweet, mild flavor compared to other members of the *Allium* genus, such as the white or yellow onion, which come with a strong bite.

POACHED EGGS VERDES

DAIRY-FREE, GLUTEN-FREE, SOY-FREE, VEGETARIAN

SERVES 2 / PREP TIME: 10 MINUTES / COOK TIME: 16 TO 20 MINUTES

"Breakfast for dinner" doesn't have to be the usual scrambled eggs or pancakes. Try this light and sophisticated dish for any meal of the day and you'll soon have egg poaching down to an art.

FOR THE DRESSING

¼ cup extra-virgin olive oil

2 tablespoons white wine vinegar

1 teaspoon Dijon mustard

¼ teaspoon freshly ground black pepper

¼ teaspoon salt

¼ teaspoon dried basil

Few drops raw honey

FOR THE EGGS VERDES

2 cups packed baby arugula

½ cup non-GMO organic whole corn kernels

6 cherry tomatoes, halved

Filtered water, for cooking the asparagus and eggs

6 asparagus spears, tough ends trimmed

1 tablespoon distilled white vinegar

4 eggs

PER SERVING Calories: 515; Total Fat: 38g; Saturated Fat: 7g; Cholesterol: 372mg; Carbohydrates: 28g; Fiber: 6g; Protein: 18g

TO MAKE THE DRESSING

In a small bowl, whisk the olive oil, vinegar, mustard, pepper, salt, basil, and honey until emulsified. Set aside.

TO MAKE THE EGGS VERDES

1. Place 1 cup of arugula on each of the two plates. Top each with ¼ cup of corn and 6 of the cherry tomato halves.

2. Bring a medium saucepan two-thirds full of water to a boil. Add the asparagus and cook for 2 minutes. With a slotted spoon, remove the asparagus and run it under cool water to stop the cooking. Divide the asparagus between the plates.

3. Lower the heat under the saucepan so the water barely simmers (only small bubbles coming to the surface). Add the vinegar.

4. Crack 1 egg into a measuring cup with a handle to ease the transfer. Carefully lower the cup into the water and slowly tip it until the egg is submerged in the water. Set a timer to 4 minutes for a runny yolk, or longer to suit your preference.

5. With a slotted spoon, remove the egg and place it on the arugula on one plate. Repeat with the remaining eggs, serving two to a plate.

6. Drizzle with the dressing and serve immediately.

COOKING TIP: To make the poaching process even easier, you can purchase a single egg poacher for under $10 online or at most kitchen stores. An egg poacher holds the egg together while it's in the hot water.

BROWN RICE BIBIMBAP

DAIRY-FREE, GLUTEN-FREE, SOY-FREE, VEGETARIAN

SERVES 2 / PREP TIME: 10 MINUTES / COOK TIME: 15 TO 20 MINUTES

Bibimbap is a Korean dish that in English means "mixed rice." The rice is topped with seasoned and cooked vegetables, sauces and meats, and finished with a fried egg. Traditionally, it is served with *gochujang*, a Korean red chile pepper paste.

2 cups cooked brown rice, divided

1 head baby bok choy, shredded

2 teaspoons sesame oil, divided

2 garlic cloves, minced

1 cup packed fresh baby spinach, thoroughly washed

2 teaspoons avocado oil, divided

½ cup shredded carrots

1 cup sliced mushrooms

1 cup cooked chickpeas, drained and rinsed well

2 eggs

1 tablespoon toasted sesame seeds

Dash salt

PER SERVING Calories: 593; Total Fat: 21g; Saturated Fat: 4g; Cholesterol: 185mg; Carbohydrates: 76g; Fiber: 12g; Protein: 22g

1. Divide the 2 cups of rice evenly between two bowls, with 1 cup in each.

2. In a large skillet or sauté pan over medium heat, sauté the bok choy with 1 teaspoon of sesame oil for 1 to 2 minutes until it begins to wilt. Remove from the heat. Top the rice in each bowl with half of the bok choy.

3. Add the remaining 1 teaspoon of sesame oil to the skillet along with the garlic and spinach, and sauté for 1 to 2 minutes until wilted. Remove from the heat and arrange half in each bowl over the bok choy.

4. Add 1 teaspoon of avocado oil to the skillet along with the carrots, and sauté for 5 minutes, or until tender. Remove from the heat and arrange half in each bowl over the spinach.

5. Add the remaining 1 teaspoon of avocado oil to the skillet along with the mushrooms, and sauté for 5 minutes, or until their liquid has evaporated. Remove from the heat and arrange half in each bowl over the carrots.

6. Divide the chickpeas between the two bowls.

7. Crack the eggs one at a time into the skillet and fry for 1 to 2 minutes, depending on how runny you prefer the yolk. Add 1 egg to each bowl. Sprinkle with the sesame seeds and the salt.

PREPARATION TIP: For an extra nutrient boost, top your bibimbap with kimchi, a spicy pickled cabbage. It's the national dish of Korea.

OVERSTUFFED BAKED SWEET POTATOES

DAIRY-FREE, GLUTEN-FREE, PALEO, SOY-FREE, VEGAN

SERVES 4 / PREP TIME: 5 MINUTES WHILE THE SWEET POTATOES BAKE / COOK TIME: 25 MINUTES

Everyone loves stuffed baked potatoes. In contrast to the plain white potato, the sweet potatoes used here actually help heal inflammation in the body through their many nutrients, such as beta-carotene, manganese, and vitamins B6 and C, as well as their high fiber and complex carbohydrate count. Eat up.

4 medium sweet potatoes

1 tablespoon avocado oil

1 small white onion, thinly sliced

2 garlic cloves, minced

1 (14-ounce) can black beans, drained
  and rinsed well

12 cherry tomatoes, chopped

½ teaspoon chili powder

¼ teaspoon red pepper flakes

¼ teaspoon salt

1 large avocado, sliced

Juice of 1 lime

PER SERVING Calories: 326; Total Fat: 10g; Saturated Fat: 1g; Cholesterol: 0mg; Carbohydrates: 51g; Fiber: 13g; Protein: 10g

1. Preheat the oven to 400°F.

2. With a fork, poke holes 5 to 6 times into each sweet potato. Loosely wrap each sweet potato in aluminum foil, place them on a baking sheet, and bake for 25 minutes, or until cooked (see Cooking Tip).

3. Meanwhile, in a large skillet or sauté pan over medium heat, heat the avocado oil. Add the onion and garlic, and sauté for 5 minutes.

4. Stir in the beans, tomatoes, chili powder, red pepper flakes, and salt. Cook for about 7 minutes. Remove from the heat.

5. When the sweet potatoes are cooked, remove them from the oven and carefully unwrap the foil. Slice each potato lengthwise, almost through to the bottom. Open the potatoes to create room for the filling, and spoon equal amounts of filling into each.

6. Top with avocado slices and a drizzle of lime juice.

COOKING TIP: To speed the sweet potato cooking time, microwave them first before wrapping with foil. With a fork, poke holes in the skin 5 to 6 times. Microwave for about 8 minutes on high temperature, rotating halfway through. Then wrap with foil and bake.

LENTIL SLOPPY JOES

DAIRY-FREE, GLUTEN-FREE, SOY-FREE, VEGAN

SERVES 4 / PREP TIME: 10 MINUTES / COOK TIME: 20 MINUTES

When sloppy joes get a health boost made with ground turkey, they're often called sloppy janes. Here I take it a step further, creating a vegan version with hearty lentils. Use jalapeño chile peppers, other natural sweeteners, and an assortment of spices to make this recipe yours.

2 tablespoons avocado oil, divided

1 small white onion, chopped

1 celery stalk, finely chopped

1 carrot, minced

2 garlic cloves, minced

1 pound cooked lentils

½ red bell pepper, finely chopped

7 tablespoons tomato paste

2 tablespoons apple cider vinegar

1 tablespoon pure maple syrup

1 teaspoon Dijon mustard

1 teaspoon chili powder

½ teaspoon dried oregano

PER SERVING Calories: 277; Total Fat: 7g; Saturated Fat: 1g; Cholesterol: 0mg; Carbohydrates: 29g; Fiber: 12g; Protein: 14g

1. In a large pan over medium-high heat, heat 1 tablespoon of avocado oil.

2. Add the onion, celery, carrot, and garlic, and sauté for about 3 minutes, or until the onion is translucent.

3. Add the lentils and the remaining 1 tablespoon of avocado oil, and sauté for about 5 minutes.

4. Add the red bell pepper, and sauté for 2 minutes.

5. Stir in the tomato paste, vinegar, maple syrup, mustard, chili powder, and oregano. Reduce the heat to medium-low and cook for about 10 minutes, stirring occasionally.

6. Serve over rice or on gluten-free bread, if desired.

COOKING TIP: When cooking with vinegar, it's important to use non-reactive cookware made from materials such as stainless steel or porcelain enamel, which won't react with acidic ingredients.

LENTIL COLLARD WRAPS

GLUTEN-FREE, SOY-FREE, VEGETARIAN

SERVES 4 / PREP TIME: 15 MINUTES / COOK TIME: 0 MINUTES

These no-cook wraps deliver dinner in a dash. Collard greens are related to kale, cabbage, and broccoli, but not many studies have been done on their nutritional content or health benefits. For the cruciferous vegetable group as a whole, cancer prevention tends to be its main point of pride. And of all the green leafy vegetables, collard greens work best as a wrap to replace gluten-filled bread.

2 cups cooked lentils

5 Roma tomatoes, diced

½ cup crumbled feta cheese

¼ cup extra-virgin olive oil

10 large fresh basil leaves, thinly sliced

2 garlic cloves, minced

1 tablespoon balsamic vinegar

½ teaspoon raw honey

½ teaspoon salt

¼ teaspoon freshly ground black pepper

4 large collard leaves, stems removed
    (see Preparation Tip)

PER SERVING Calories: 319; Total Fat: 18g; Saturated Fat: 5g; Cholesterol: 17mg; Carbohydrates: 28g; Fiber: 10g; Protein: 13g

1. In a large bowl, stir together the lentils, tomatoes, feta cheese, olive oil, basil, garlic, vinegar, honey, salt, and pepper.

2. Place the collard leaves on a flat surface. Scoop an equal amount of the lentil mixture onto the edge of each leaf, and roll up as you would a burrito. Cut each wrap in half and serve.

PREPARATION TIP: To make the collard leaves more pliable, steam them for 1 to 2 minutes before wrapping up the lentil filling.

STUFFED PORTOBELLO MUSHROOMS

DAIRY-FREE, GLUTEN-FREE, SOY-FREE, VEGAN

SERVES 4 / PREP TIME: 10 MINUTES / COOK TIME: 10 MINUTES

Portobello mushrooms contain the antioxidant selenium, which protects cells from damage stemming from heart disease, cancer, and other age-related diseases. Mushrooms are one of the only plant-based sources of this valuable element. And they are delicious.

8 portobello mushrooms, stems removed
and gently cleaned
2 tablespoons avocado oil, divided
1 small white onion, diced
2 garlic cloves, minced
½ teaspoon salt
¼ teaspoon freshly ground black pepper
1 teaspoon dried basil
1 small zucchini, diced
1 red bell pepper, diced

PER SERVING Calories: 131; Total Fat: 7g;
Saturated Fat: 1g; Cholesterol: 0mg;
Carbohydrates: 13g; Fiber: 5g; Protein: 5g

1. Preheat the broiler.

2. Line a baking sheet with aluminum foil.

3. Pat each mushroom cap dry and rub them with 1 tablespoon of avocado oil. Place them in the prepared pan and broil for 6 minutes, turning them halfway through so both sides cook evenly.

4. Meanwhile, in a large skillet over medium heat, heat the remaining 1 tablespoon of avocado oil.

5. Add the onion, garlic, salt, pepper, and basil, and sauté for 5 minutes.

6. Stir in the zucchini and red bell pepper, and sauté for about 5 minutes until everything is cooked.

7. Scoop equal portions of the vegetable mixture into each mushroom cap and serve warm.

SERVING TIP: Enjoy these stuffed mushroom caps as a vegetarian entrée, or keep them refrigerated for a quick, cold, low-calorie snack on the go the next day.

BLACK BEANS ON SPROUTED CORN TOSTADAS

DAIRY-FREE, GLUTEN-FREE, SOY-FREE, VEGAN

SERVES 6 / PREP TIME: 10 MINUTES / COOK TIME: 10 MINUTES

Sprouting seeds and grains can increase their protein, vitamin, and fiber content. It also increases their enzyme activity, making the seeds and grains easier to digest and therefore less inflammatory in the body.

1 (15-ounce) can black beans, drained and rinsed well

½ teaspoon ground cumin

½ teaspoon salt

½ teaspoon garlic powder

¼ teaspoon red pepper flakes

Dash freshly ground black pepper

1 tablespoon avocado oil

6 sprouted corn tortillas

1 red bell pepper, thinly sliced

½ red onion, thinly sliced

1 large avocado, sliced

½ cup sliced radishes

Lime wedges, for garnish

PER SERVING Calories: 196; Total Fat: 7g; Saturated Fat: 1g; Cholesterol: 0mg; Carbohydrates: 28g; Fiber: 7g; Protein: 6g

1. In a small saucepan over medium heat, warm the black beans, lightly mashing some of them to make them more spreadable.

2. Stir in the cumin, salt, garlic powder, red pepper flakes, and black pepper.

3. In a large skillet over medium heat, heat the avocado oil. One at a time, add the tortillas and cook on both sides until warmed through and as crispy as you like. Transfer to a work surface.

4. Spread some of the bean mixture over each tortilla. Top each with slices of red bell pepper, onion, avocado, and radish.

5. Sprinkle with lime juice and serve.

INGREDIENT TIP: If you can't find sprouted corn tortillas, look for brown rice tortillas, which may be a bit larger. Since corn is one of the most genetically modified crops in the United States, always choose organic.

FISH STICKS WITH AVOCADO
DIPPING SAUCE (PAGE 130)

CHAPTER EIGHT

Seafood Dishes

LEMON-CAPER TROUT WITH CARAMELIZED SHALLOTS

GLUTEN-FREE, LACTOSE-FREE, PALEO, SOY-FREE

SERVES 2 / PREP TIME: 10 MINUTES / COOK TIME: 20 MINUTES

Caramelized shallots add a beautiful flavor burst to this dish, and are easy to make while the rest of the meal is prepared. The lemon (bitter), capers (savory), and caramelized shallots (sweet) combine to make the perfect trifecta for your taste buds.

FOR THE SHALLOTS

2 shallots, thinly sliced

1 teaspoon ghee

Dash salt

FOR THE TROUT

1 tablespoon plus 1 teaspoon ghee, divided

2 (4-ounce) trout fillets

¼ cup freshly squeezed lemon juice

3 tablespoons capers

¼ teaspoon salt

Dash freshly ground black pepper

1 lemon, thinly sliced

PER SERVING Calories: 399; Total Fat: 22g; Saturated Fat: 10g; Cholesterol: 46mg; Carbohydrates: 17g; Fiber: 2g; Protein: 21g

TO MAKE THE SHALLOTS

In a large skillet over medium heat, cook the shallots, ghee, and salt for 20 minutes, stirring every 5 minutes, until the shallots have fully wilted and caramelized.

TO MAKE THE TROUT

1. While the shallots cook, in another large skillet over medium heat, heat 1 teaspoon of ghee.

2. Add the trout fillets. Cook for 3 minutes per side, or until the center is flaky. Transfer to a plate and set aside.

3. In the skillet used for the trout, add the lemon juice, capers, salt, and pepper. Bring to a simmer. Whisk in the remaining 1 tablespoon of ghee. Spoon the sauce over the fish.

4. Garnish the fish with the lemon slices and caramelized shallots before serving.

INGREDIENT TIP: The small, savory capers we consume in many Mediterranean dishes are actually the small flower buds of the caper bush. Typically, they are pickled or packed in salt.

COCONUT-CRUSTED COD WITH MANGO-PINEAPPLE SALSA

DAIRY-FREE, GLUTEN-FREE, PALEO, SOY-FREE

SERVES 4 / PREP TIME: 15 MINUTES / COOK TIME: 7 MINUTES

Daily fish consumption is highly beneficial for our bodies because of its high omega-3 fatty acid content. These fatty acids in cod actually decrease the production of pro-inflammatory compounds in the body.

FOR THE SALSA

1 cup diced mango

1 cup diced pineapple

½ large avocado, diced

Juice of 1 lime

Dash salt

Dash chili powder

FOR THE COD

1 egg

1 cup unsweetened dried coconut

2 tablespoons avocado oil

4 (4-ounce) cod fillets

1 teaspoon salt

½ teaspoon garlic powder

¼ teaspoon cayenne pepper

PER SERVING Calories: 369; Total Fat: 27g; Saturated Fat: 14g; Cholesterol: 107mg; Carbohydrates: 18g; Fiber: 5g; Protein: 18g

TO MAKE THE SALSA

In a medium bowl, gently stir together the mango, pineapple, avocado, lime juice, salt, and chili powder.

TO MAKE THE COD

1. In a small shallow bowl, beat the egg. Put the coconut in another small shallow bowl.

2. Dip each cod fillet into the egg, then into the coconut until well coated, and place on a plate.

3. Sprinkle each fillet with the salt, garlic powder, and cayenne pepper.

4. In a large skillet over medium-high heat, heat the avocado oil.

5. Cook each fillet one at a time in the hot skillet for 4 to 5 minutes. Flip and cook on the other side for 1 to 2 minutes until the flesh begins to flake. Transfer to a plate.

6. Top each fillet with salsa and serve.

PREPARATION TIP: For extra lime flavor, add lime zest to the salsa.

FISH STICKS WITH AVOCADO DIPPING SAUCE

DAIRY-FREE, GLUTEN-FREE, PALEO, SOY-FREE

SERVES 4 / PREP TIME: 15 MINUTES / COOK TIME: 5 MINUTES

These simple fish sticks will please any crowd, without the inflammation-inducing ingredients of those frozen sticks you ate as a child. To make cutting the fish easier, cut it while partially frozen, then defrost the fish fully just before cooking. You can also freeze any finished sticks in a sealed container. Simply reheat on a foil-lined baking sheet at 400°F for about 10 minutes, or until cooked.

FOR THE AVOCADO DIPPING SAUCE

2 avocados

¼ cup freshly squeezed lime juice

2 tablespoons fresh cilantro leaves

2 tablespoons extra-virgin olive oil

1 teaspoon salt

1 teaspoon garlic powder

Dash ground cumin

Freshly ground black pepper

FOR THE FISH STICKS

1½ cups almond flour

1 teaspoon salt

½ teaspoon paprika

¼ teaspoon freshly ground black pepper

3 eggs

¼ cup coconut oil

1 pound cod fillets, cut into 4-inch-long, 1-inch-thick strips

Juice of 1 lemon

TO MAKE THE AVOCADO DIPPING SAUCE

In a food processor (or blender), add the avocados, lime juice, cilantro, olive oil, salt, garlic powder, and cumin, and season with pepper. Pulse until smooth.

TO MAKE THE FISH STICKS

1. In a small shallow bowl, mix the almond flour, salt, paprika, and pepper. Whisk the eggs in another small shallow bowl.

2. Dip the fish sticks into the egg, and then into the almond flour mixture until fully coated.

PER SERVING Calories: 583; Total Fat: 50g; Saturated Fat: 17g; Cholesterol: 200mg; Carbohydrates: 14g; Fiber: 8g; Protein: 25g

3. In a large skillet over medium-high heat, heat the coconut oil.

4. One at time, place the fish sticks in the skillet. Cook for about 2 minutes per side, until lightly browned. Transfer to 2 plates.

5. To serve, sprinkle with the lemon juice and serve alongside the avocado dipping sauce.

INGREDIENT TIP: Using refined coconut oil will cut out any coconut taste in the finished product. If you prefer some coconut flavor, choose unrefined coconut oil.

TILAPIA FISH TACOS WITH CILANTRO-LIME CREMA

GLUTEN-FREE, PROBIOTIC, SOY-FREE

SERVES 4 / PREP TIME: 15 MINUTES / COOK TIME: 8 MINUTES, WHILE THE TORTILLAS WARM

Tilapia is an easy-to-find, budget-friendly and tasty fish. It has sparked some controversy in the health world because it is a natural scavenger that cleans the water it lives in. This means it is particularly important to purchase tilapia from reliable sources that get their fish from clean, wild environments.

FOR THE CILANTRO-LIME CREMA
½ cup plain whole-milk Greek yogurt
2 tablespoons freshly squeezed lime juice
1 tablespoon minced fresh cilantro leaves
¼ teaspoon garlic powder
Dash salt

FOR THE FISH TACOS
8 small corn tortillas
1 teaspoon paprika
½ teaspoon salt
½ teaspoon garlic powder
½ teaspoon ground cumin
¼ teaspoon cayenne pepper
1 pound tilapia fillets
2 tablespoons avocado oil
1 large avocado, sliced

PER SERVING Calories: 363; Total Fat: 17g;
Saturated Fat: 3g; Cholesterol: 62mg;
Carbohydrates: 25g; Fiber: 6g; Protein: 27g

TO MAKE THE CILANTRO-LIME CREMA

In a small bowl, whisk the yogurt, lime juice, cilantro, garlic powder, and salt. Cover and chill until ready to serve.

TO MAKE THE FISH TACOS

1. Preheat the oven to 350°F.

2. Wrap the tortillas in aluminum foil and place them in the oven to warm for about 15 minutes.

3. Meanwhile, in a small bowl, mix the paprika, salt, garlic powder, cumin, and cayenne pepper.

4. Put the fish fillets on a plate, and sprinkle them with the seasoning mixture.

5. In a large skillet over medium-high heat, heat the avocado oil.

6. Add the fish fillets to the skillet. Cook for 3 minutes per side, or until flaky.

7. Lay the warm tortillas out on a work surface. Divide the fish among the tortillas.

8. Serve the fish tacos with the sliced avocado and cilantro-lime crema.

INGREDIENT TIP: Since corn is one of the most genetically modified crops in the United States, always choose organic. For an extra nutrient boost, look for sprouted corn tortillas, which are easier to digest and often have a higher content of amino acids, the building blocks of proteins.

OPEN-FACE AVOCADO TUNA MELTS

SOY-FREE

SERVES 4 / PREP TIME: 10 MINUTES / COOK TIME: 5 MINUTES

Tuna is well established as an excellent source of inflammation-fighting omega-3s. Canned albacore typically has more omega-3s than other types of lighter canned tuna. Choose brands with sustainability standards. The Marine Stewardship Council (MSC) certifies and labels tuna sold worldwide as sustainable, so look for the MSC label or ask your local fishery before purchasing.

4 slices sourdough bread

2 (5-ounce) cans wild-caught albacore tuna

¼ cup Paleo mayonnaise

2 tablespoons minced shallot

1 teaspoon freshly squeezed lemon juice

Dash garlic powder

Dash paprika

1 large avocado, cut in 8 slices

1 large tomato, cut in 8 slices

¼ cup shredded raw Parmesan
   cheese, divided

PER SERVING Calories: 471; Total Fat: 27g; Saturated Fat: 4g; Cholesterol: 40mg; Carbohydrates: 31g; Fiber: 4g; Protein: 27g

1. Preheat the broiler.

2. Line a baking sheet with aluminum foil.

3. Arrange the slices of bread in the prepared pan.

4. In a medium bowl, mix the tuna, mayonnaise, shallot, lemon juice, garlic powder, and paprika. Spread one-fourth of the tuna mixture on each slice of bread.

5. Top each with 2 of the avocado slices and 2 of the tomato slices.

6. Sprinkle each with 1 tablespoon of Parmesan cheese.

7. Broil for 3 to 4 minutes, watching carefully so they don't burn. Serve hot.

INGREDIENT TIP: There are plenty of "fake" sourdough bread substitutes in the grocery stores today. Look for sourdough bread with the ingredient "sourdough starter" in it, which can be a clue to the bread's fermentation process, making it much easier to digest.

AHI POKE WITH CUCUMBER

DAIRY-FREE, GLUTEN-FREE, PALEO, SOY-FREE

SERVES 4 / PREP TIME: 10 MINUTES, PLUS 15 MINUTES MARINATING

If you live near the ocean and can purchase fresh ahi from a fisherman you trust, do it! Otherwise, look for sushi-grade fish in your local grocery store, preferably frozen. Frozen can mean fresh, too, in the sense it may have been frozen immediately after being caught, as opposed to hanging around in the fish market for several days unfrozen. *Poke* is a Hawaiian raw fish salad.

1 pound sushi-grade ahi tuna, cut into 1-inch cubes

3 scallions, thinly sliced

1 serrano chile, seeded and minced (optional)

3 tablespoons coconut aminos

1 teaspoon rice vinegar

1 teaspoon sesame oil

1 teaspoon toasted sesame seeds

Dash ground ginger

1 large avocado, diced

1 cucumber, sliced into ½-inch-thick rounds

PER SERVING Calories: 214; Total Fat: 15g; Saturated Fat: 2g; Cholesterol: 68mg; Carbohydrates: 11g; Fiber: 4g; Protein: 10g

1. In a large bowl, gently mix the tuna, scallions, serrano chile, coconut aminos, vinegar, sesame oil, sesame seeds, and ginger until well combined. Cover and refrigerate to marinate for 15 minutes.

2. Stir in the avocado, gently incorporating the chunks into the ahi mixture.

3. Arrange the cucumber slices on a plate. Place a spoonful of the ahi *poke* on each cucumber slice and serve immediately.

PREPARATION TIP: If you hesitate to eat raw fish even when it's purchased from a fresh, local source, lightly sear the outside edges of the fish before using. This helps kill any possible microbial contamination on the surface of the fish.

SEARED HONEY-GARLIC SCALLOPS

DAIRY-FREE, GLUTEN-FREE, SOY-FREE

SERVES 4 / PREP TIME: 10 MINUTES / COOK TIME: 15 MINUTES

Scallops have a mild, sweet flavor usually enjoyed even by those who don't care for seafood. They're an excellent source of vitamin B_{12} (which supports the energy metabolism process), iodine (which supports healthy thyroid function), and phosphorous, on top of boasting a full amino acid profile. This means scallops contain every essential protein building block our bodies require. Because they cook quickly, have your sides ready before cooking them.

1 pound large scallops, rinsed

Dash salt

Dash freshly ground black pepper

2 tablespoons avocado oil

¼ cup raw honey

3 tablespoons coconut aminos

2 garlic cloves, minced

1 tablespoon apple cider vinegar

PER SERVING Calories: 383; Total Fat: 19g; Saturated Fat: 3g; Cholesterol: 64mg; Carbohydrates: 26g; Fiber: 1g; Protein: 21g

1. Pat the scallops dry with paper towels and sprinkle with the salt and pepper.

2. In a large skillet over medium-high heat, heat the avocado oil.

3. Place the scallops in the skillet, and cook for 2 to 3 minutes per side until golden. Transfer to a plate, tent loosely with aluminum foil to keep warm, and set aside.

4. In the same skillet, stir together the honey, coconut aminos, garlic, and vinegar. Bring to a simmer, and cook for 7 minutes, stirring occasionally as the liquid reduces.

5. Return the scallops to the skillet with the glaze. Toss gently to coat and serve warm.

INGREDIENT TIP: While pan-seared scallops sound decadent, they are simple and quick to prepare. Purchase "dry" scallops instead of "wet" scallops, which often have chemical additives.

COCONUT-CRUSTED SHRIMP

DAIRY-FREE, GLUTEN-FREE, PALEO, SOY-FREE

SERVES 4 / PREP TIME: 10 MINUTES / COOK TIME: 6 MINUTES

Serve these crunchy, coated shrimp as a tasty protein with just about any side dish or dipping sauce you like. Nutritionally, shrimp contain large amounts of a unique anti-oxidant called astaxanthin, which supports the nervous and musculoskeletal systems.

2 eggs

1 cup unsweetened dried coconut

¼ cup coconut flour

½ teaspoon salt

¼ teaspoon paprika

Dash cayenne pepper

Dash freshly ground black pepper

¼ cup coconut oil

1 pound raw shrimp, peeled and deveined

PER SERVING Calories: 279; Total Fat: 2 0g; Saturated Fat: 15g; Cholesterol: 258mg; Carbohydrates: 6g; Fiber: 3g; Protein: 19g

1. In a small shallow bowl, whisk the eggs.

2. In another small shallow bowl, mix the coconut, coconut flour, salt, paprika, cayenne pepper, and black pepper.

3. In a large skillet over medium-high heat, heat the coconut oil.

4. Pat the shrimp dry with a paper towel.

5. Working one at a time, hold each shrimp by the tail, dip it into the egg mixture, and then into the coconut mixture until coated. Place into the hot skillet. Cook for 1 to 3 minutes per side. Transfer to a paper towel–lined plate to drain excess oil.

6. Serve immediately.

COOKING TIP: You can use any size shrimp for this recipe. Just be aware of the extra cooking time that larger shrimp may require.

SALMON & ASPARAGUS SKEWERS

GLUTEN-FREE, LACTOSE-FREE, PALEO, SOY-FREE

MAKES 8 SKEWERS / PREP TIME: 15 MINUTES / COOK TIME: 10 MINUTES

Aside from salmon's incredible omega-3 content, it also contains bioactive protein molecules that have been shown to control inflammation in the digestive tract. You'll need eight skewers for this recipe.

2 tablespoons ghee, melted

1 teaspoon Dijon mustard

1 teaspoon garlic powder

½ teaspoon salt

¼ teaspoon red pepper flakes

1½ pounds boned skinless salmon, cut into 2-inch chunks

2 lemons, thinly sliced

1 bunch asparagus spears, tough ends trimmed, cut into 2-inch pieces

PER SERVING (2 skewers) Calories: 250; Total Fat: 9g; Saturated Fat: 5g; Cholesterol: 68mg; Carbohydrates: 4g; Fiber: 2g; Protein: 38g

1. Preheat the broiler.

2. Line a baking sheet with aluminum foil.

3. In a small saucepan over medium heat, heat the ghee.

4. Stir in the mustard, garlic powder, salt, and red pepper flakes.

5. On each skewer, thread 1 chunk of salmon, 1 lemon slice folded in half, and 2 pieces of asparagus. Repeat with the remaining skewers until all ingredients are used. Place the skewers on the prepared pan and brush each with the ghee-seasoning mixture.

6. Broil for 4 minutes. Turn the skewers and broil on the other side for about 4 minutes.

COOKING TIP: Using two skewers at a time makes turning and holding each skewer easier. If you are using bamboo skewers, soak them in water for 10 to 30 minutes before using to prevent burning.

SALMON BURGERS

DAIRY-FREE, GLUTEN-FREE, PALEO, SOY-FREE

SERVES 4 / PREP TIME: 15 MINUTES / COOK TIME: 10 MINUTES

To keep these burgers anti-inflammatory and Paleo, serve them over a bed of greens, chopped romaine lettuce, or on gluten-free buns. To help with prep, a sharp knife is your best friend. Don't be alarmed if the patties are crumbly before you cook them. Once cooked, they hold together well.

1 pound skinless boned salmon
 fillets, minced

½ cup almond flour

¼ cup minced sweet onion

2 eggs, whisked

2 garlic cloves, minced

1 tablespoon freshly squeezed lemon juice

1 teaspoon Dijon mustard

½ teaspoon salt

¼ teaspoon freshly ground black pepper

Dash red pepper flakes

1 tablespoon avocado oil

PER SERVING Calories: 250; Total Fat: 9g;
Saturated Fat: 5g; Cholesterol: 68mg;
Carbohydrates: 4g; Fiber: 2g; Protein: 38g

1. In a large bowl, mix the salmon, almond flour, onion, eggs, garlic, lemon juice, mustard, salt, black pepper, and red pepper flakes until combined. Let rest for 5 minutes.

2. In a large skillet over medium heat, heat the avocado oil.

3. Form the salmon mixture into 4 patties, each about ½ inch thick. Place them in the skillet. Cook for 4 to 5 minutes on each side, until lightly browned and firm.

INGREDIENT TIP: While many are concerned about salmon being full of pollutants, mercury, and pesticides, there are types from specific locations that remain highly recommended in the health community. Notably, wild-caught Alaskan salmon remains at the top of the low-risk list.

GRILLED SALMON PACKETS
WITH ASPARAGUS

DAIRY-FREE, GLUTEN-FREE, PALEO, SOY-FREE

SERVES 4 / PREP TIME: 10 MINUTES / COOK TIME: 20 MINUTES

This method of cooking food—called en *papillote*—is simply cooking in a folded pouch made from parchment paper or aluminum foil. Traditionally, many Asian countries use large banana leaves in the same way. While simple, this method allows flavors to combine into a mouthwatering meal fit for company.

4 (4-ounce) skinless salmon fillets

16 asparagus spears, tough ends trimmed

4 tablespoons avocado oil, divided

1 teaspoon garlic powder, divided

½ teaspoon salt, divided

Freshly ground black pepper

1 lemon, thinly sliced

PER SERVING Calories: 339; Total Fat: 23g;
Saturated Fat: 3g; Cholesterol: 80mg;
Carbohydrates: 1g; Fiber: 1g; Protein: 30g

1. Preheat the oven to 400°F.

2. Cut 4 (12-inch) squares of parchment paper or foil and put on a work surface.

3. Place 1 salmon fillet in the center of each square and 4 asparagus spears next to each fillet. Brush the fish and asparagus with 1 tablespoon of avocado oil.

4. Sprinkle each fillet with ¼ teaspoon garlic powder and ⅛ teaspoon salt, and season with pepper.

5. Place the lemon slices on top of the fillets. Close and seal the parchment around each fillet so it forms a sealed packet.

6. Place the parchment packets on a baking sheet. Bake for 20 minutes.

7. Place a sealed parchment packet on each of 4 plates and serve hot.

PREPARATION TIP: To break off the tough ends of the asparagus, take the bottom half of the spear between your thumb and forefinger and bend just above the woody part.

MISO-GLAZED SALMON

DAIRY-FREE, GLUTEN-FREE

SERVES 4 / PREP TIME: 5 MINUTES / COOKING TIME: 5 TO 10 MINUTES

Serving your family a hot, healthy, flavorful meal doesn't get easier than with this recipe. Miso is a traditional Japanese seasoning made with fermented soybeans. Fermentation breaks down the enzymes and anti-nutrients in the soy, making it much healthier and easier for the body to digest.

4 (4-ounce) salmon fillets

3 tablespoons miso paste

2 tablespoons raw honey

1 teaspoon coconut aminos

1 teaspoon rice vinegar

PER SERVING Calories: 264; Total Fat: 9g; Saturated Fat: 1g; Cholesterol: 80mg; Carbohydrates: 13g; Fiber: 0g; Protein: 30g

1. Preheat the broiler.

2. Line a baking dish with aluminum foil and place the salmon fillets in it.

3. In a small bowl, stir together the miso, honey, coconut aminos, and vinegar. Brush the glaze evenly over the top of each fillet. Broil for about 5 minutes. The fish is done when it flakes easily. The exact cooking time depends on its thickness.

4. Brush any remaining glaze over the fish, and continue to broil for 5 minutes, if needed.

INGREDIENT TIP: There is a wide range of types and colors of miso. Shiro miso, or white miso, is the most widely produced and typically contains fermented rice as well as soybeans. This is the kind I usually use.

MEDITERRANEAN BAKED SALMON

DAIRY-FREE, GLUTEN-FREE, SOY-FREE

SERVES 4 / PREP TIME: 5 MINUTES / COOK TIME: 20 MINUTES, PLUS 5 MINUTES RESTING

This salmon dish is stacked with Mediterranean delights. Sun-dried tomatoes are a delicious and concentrated source of nutrients, such as vitamin C, K, iron, and lycopene, which is a cancer-preventing antioxidant. Serve the salmon with a green salad or quinoa for a complete meal.

4 (4-ounce) salmon fillets

3 tablespoons Pistachio Pesto (page 32)

¼ cup chopped sun-dried tomatoes

¼ cup pitted, diced olives

2 tablespoons minced red onion

2 garlic cloves, minced

Dash salt

Fresh ground black pepper

1 tablespoon minced fresh basil

PER SERVING Calories: 301; Total Fat: 17g;
Saturated Fat: 2g; Cholesterol: 80mg;
Carbohydrates: 6g; Fiber: 1g; Protein: 31g

1. Preheat the oven to 400°F.

2. Line a baking sheet with aluminum foil.

3. Put the salmon fillets in the prepared pan, skin-side down.

4. Spread a thin layer of the pistachio pesto over the top of each fillet.

5. In a small bowl, mix the sun-dried tomatoes, olives, red onion, garlic, and salt, and season with pepper. Spread one-fourth of the tomato mixture over the pesto on each fillet.

6. Bake for 20 minutes. Remove from the oven and let rest for 5 minutes.

7. Sprinkle with the basil and serve immediately.

INGREDIENT TIP: Arctic char, trout, halibut, or bass would also work well in this recipe.

CURRIED POACHED HALIBUT

DAIRY-FREE, GLUTEN-FREE, PALEO, SOY-FREE

SERVES 4 / PREP TIME: 5 MINUTES / COOK TIME: 23 MINUTES

Poaching is a surprisingly quick and easy way to cook many foods, from eggs to fish. It simply involves simmering the food in a small amount of liquid until cooked. Depending on the recipe, you can use wine, broth, water, milk, or just about any liquid combination you prefer. Here I've created a coconut curry broth to flavor the delicate halibut.

1 tablespoon avocado oil

½ cup diced white onion

2 garlic cloves, minced

1 tablespoon red curry paste

1½ cups chicken broth

1 (14-ounce) can coconut milk

½ teaspoon coconut sugar

1 teaspoon salt

½ teaspoon freshly ground black pepper

4 (4-ounce) halibut fillets

PER SERVING Calories: 358; Total Fat: 22g; Saturated Fat: 17g; Cholesterol: 68mg; Carbohydrates: 10g; Fiber: 1g; Protein: 28g

1. In a large skillet over medium heat, heat the avocado oil.

2. Add the onion and garlic, and sauté for 2 to 3 minutes until the onions are translucent.

3. Stir in the curry paste until incorporated.

4. Add the broth, coconut milk, coconut sugar, salt, and pepper and stir to combine. Reduce the heat to medium-low and gently simmer for 10 minutes.

5. Pat the halibut dry with a paper towel. Place each fillet into the curried broth. Cover and poach for 10 minutes. Check the fish for doneness; if it flakes, it should be done. To speed the cooking time, occasionally spoon some broth over the halibut as it cooks.

6. Serve the fillets in four bowls with the curried broth spooned on top.

PREPARATION TIP: If you want more flavor and a thicker broth, add 1 to 2 tablespoons of tomato paste with the curry paste.

HERBED LAMB FILLETS WITH CAULIFLOWER MASH (PAGE 162)

Poultry & Meat Dishes

YELLOW CHICKEN CURRY

DAIRY-FREE, GLUTEN-FREE, PALEO, SOY-FREE

SERVES 6 / PREP TIME: 10 MINUTES / COOK TIME: 20 MINUTES

This aromatic dish is packed with nutritional goodness. Curry powder contains powerful antioxidants and anti-inflammatory compounds. The turmeric in curry powder, which gives it its yellow coloring, contains an active compound called curcumin that has been shown to be effective at reducing inflammation in the gut.

2 tablespoons coconut oil, divided

2 (4-ounce) boneless, skinless chicken breasts, cut into bite-size pieces

6 garlic cloves, minced

2 medium carrots, diced

1 small white onion, diced

1 tablespoon minced peeled fresh ginger

1 cup sugar snap peas, diced

1 cup chicken broth

½ cup canned diced tomatoes, with their juice

1 (5.4-ounce) can unsweetened coconut cream

¼ cup filtered water

1 tablespoon fish sauce

1 tablespoon Indian curry powder

¼ teaspoon salt

Pinch cayenne pepper

Freshly ground black pepper

PER SERVING Calories: 234; Total Fat: 11g; Saturated Fat: 10g; Cholesterol: 56mg; Carbohydrates: 7g; Fiber: 1g; Protein: 23g

1. In a large skillet over medium-high heat, heat 1 tablespoon of coconut oil. Add the chicken, and cook for about 15 minutes, until cooked through. Set aside.

2. Meanwhile, in another large skillet over medium heat, heat the remaining 1 tablespoon of coconut oil. Add the garlic, carrots, onion, and ginger, and sauté for 5 minutes, or until the onions soften.

3. Stir in the snap peas, broth, tomatoes, coconut cream, water, fish sauce, curry powder, salt, and cayenne pepper, and season with black pepper. Bring to a simmer, reduce the meat to medium-low, and cook for 10 minutes.

4. Add the cooked chicken and cook for 2 minutes until reheated through.

5. Serve hot over rice or quinoa, if desired.

PREPARATION TIP: If you prefer a thicker curry, add 1 tablespoon of arrowroot powder to the hot liquid and cook, stirring well to thicken.

CHICKEN BITES WITH AIOLI

DAIRY-FREE, GLUTEN-FREE, PALEO, SOY-FREE

SERVES 4 / PREP TIME: 10 MINUTES / COOK TIME: 10 MINUTES

Children and adults alike will love these chicken bites, and they're so easy to prepare and fun to dip! They make the perfect protein to serve alongside your favorite anti-inflammatory side dish or antioxidant-rich salad, such as the Massaged Kale Salad (page 90) or the Hearts of Romaine Caesar Salad (page 99).

FOR THE AIOLI

½ cup Paleo mayonnaise

1 tablespoon freshly squeezed lemon juice

¼ teaspoon garlic powder

Dash cayenne pepper

Dash salt

FOR THE CHICKEN

1 pound boneless skinless chicken breast, cut into 2-inch pieces

2 tablespoons avocado oil

½ teaspoon salt

½ teaspoon garlic powder

PER SERVING Calories: 383; Total Fat: 32g; Saturated Fat: 4g; Cholesterol: 105mg; Carbohydrates: 1g; Fiber: 0g; Protein: 26g

TO MAKE THE AIOLI

In a small bowl, stir together the mayonnaise, lemon juice, garlic powder, cayenne, and salt.

TO MAKE THE CHICKEN

1. Preheat the broiler.

2. Line a baking sheet with aluminum foil.

3. Spread out the chicken pieces on a plate. Brush with the avocado oil, and sprinkle with the salt and garlic powder.

4. Arrange the chicken on the prepared pan so the pieces are not touching. Broil for 7 to 10 minutes, turning halfway through.

5. Serve the chicken bites alongside the aioli sauce for dipping.

INGREDIENT TIP: Look for a Paleo mayonnaise made with avocado oil instead of canola oil. Canola oil is not heat stable, nor does it contain omega-3s after it has been heated and denatured. It also is highly refined using chemical solvents, lye, high pressure, and high heat.

BLACKENED CHICKEN WITH SUMMER VEGETABLE SAUTÉ

DAIRY-FREE, GLUTEN-FREE, PALEO, SOY-FREE

SERVES 4 / PREP TIME: 15 MINUTES / COOK TIME: 10 MINUTES

Traditionally, blackening a protein is done by dredging it in butter, dipping it in spices, and searing it over high heat until the butter and spices begin to char. Here it's lightened a bit using avocado oil instead of butter, but you still get a nice char with the ancho chili powder. This dish will spice up your weekly menu.

FOR THE VEGETABLE SAUTÉ

1 tablespoon avocado oil

3 garlic cloves, minced

2 cups non-GMO, organic sweet corn kernels

1 pint cherry tomatoes, halved

4 scallions, sliced

¼ cup fresh cilantro leaves, minced

FOR THE CHICKEN

2 teaspoons avocado oil

2 pounds boneless, skinless chicken breasts

2 teaspoons ancho chili powder

1 teaspoon salt

PER SERVING Calories: 253; Total Fat: 9g; Saturated Fat: 1g; Cholesterol: 65mg; Carbohydrates: 14g; Fiber: 3g; Protein: 29g

TO MAKE THE VEGETABLE SAUTÉ

1. In a large skillet over medium heat, heat the avocado oil. Add the garlic and cook for 2 minutes, stirring frequently.

2. Add the corn, tomatoes, and scallions, and cook for 5 to 7 minutes until the corn is cooked. Remove from heat and stir in the cilantro.

TO MAKE THE CHICKEN

1. In another large skillet over medium heat, heat the avocado oil.

2. Pat the chicken dry with paper towels and season with the ancho chili powder and salt.

3. Add the chicken to the skillet and cook each side for 4 to 5 minutes, until the spices have crusted and blackened to your liking. Remove from the heat when the chicken is cooked through.

4. Serve the blackened chicken alongside the vegetable sauté.

CHICKEN SALAD WITH GREEN APPLES & GRAPES

DAIRY-FREE, GLUTEN-FREE, PALEO, SOY-FREE

SERVES 4 / PREP TIME: 15 MINUTES / COOK TIME: 0 MINUTES

Serve this quick and easy chicken salad over a bed of mixed greens or by itself. Turn this into a curried chicken salad by adding 1 to 2 teaspoons of curry powder.

1 large avocado, diced

2 tablespoons Dijon mustard

½ teaspoon garlic powder

Dash salt

Dash freshly ground black pepper

2 (8-ounce) grilled boneless, skinless chicken breasts, chopped (see Ingredient Tip)

2 small green apples, diced

1 cup grapes, halved

¼ cup sliced scallions

2 tablespoons minced celery

1. In a large bowl, combine the avocado, mustard, garlic powder, salt, and pepper, stirring until creamy.

2. Add the chicken, apples, grapes, scallions, and celery. Stir well to combine.

3. Serve chilled, if desired.

INGREDIENT TIP: To add an easy flavor boost, use the Baked Chicken Breast with Lemon and Garlic (page 152).

PER SERVING Calories: 234; Total Fat: 7g; Saturated Fat: 1g; Cholesterol: 56mg; Carbohydrates: 19g; Fiber: 5g; Protein: 24g

CREAMY CHICKEN PESTO PASTA

GLUTEN-FREE, PROBIOTIC, SOY-FREE

SERVES 6 / PREP TIME: 10 MINUTES / COOK TIME: 10 MINUTES, PLUS CHILLING TIME

Brown rice pasta is a great alternative to wheat pasta when following an anti-inflammatory diet. It's generally higher in both protein and fiber. Pay attention to the specific cooking instructions the package provides, because each brand and grain has unique requirements.

3 cups brown rice fusilli

1 cup diced cooked chicken breast

1 cup Pistachio Pesto (page 32)

1 cup plain whole-milk Greek yogurt

1 red bell pepper, diced

1 tablespoon minced shallot

2 teaspoons freshly squeezed lemon juice

½ teaspoon salt

¼ teaspoon freshly ground black pepper

PER SERVING Calories: 286; Total Fat: 12g;
Saturated Fat: 3g; Cholesterol: 43mg;
Carbohydrates: 26g; Fiber: 2g; Protein: 20g

1. Cook the pasta according to the package instructions and drain. Transfer to a large bowl.

2. Add the chicken, pistachio pesto, yogurt, red bell pepper, shallot, lemon juice, salt, and pepper. Stir well.

3. Serve chilled, if desired.

INGREDIENT TIP: If you don't have Pistachio Pesto on hand, use purchased pesto. Read the ingredient list on the container to identify any inflammation-causing fillers, such as canola or soybean oil, potato flakes, yeast extract, or others.

GENERAL TSO'S CHICKEN

GLUTEN-FREE, LACTOSE-FREE, SOY-FREE

SERVES 4 / PREP TIME: 15 MINUTES / COOK TIME: 15 MINUTES

General Tso's Chicken is a popular dish in Chinese-American restaurants, and is named after the military leader from the Qing Dynasty. This tasty, sweet, and spicy chicken dish can be served over rice or alongside grilled vegetables.

FOR THE SAUCE

1 tablespoon ghee
¼ teaspoon ground ginger
2 garlic cloves, minced
3 tablespoons coconut sugar
3 tablespoons coconut aminos
2 tablespoons rice vinegar
1 tablespoon arrowroot powder
½ teaspoon red pepper flakes

FOR THE CHICKEN

2 tablespoons avocado oil
1 cup brown rice flour
¼ teaspoon salt
¼ teaspoon garlic powder
1 pound boneless, skinless chicken
    thighs, cut into 1-inch pieces

PER SERVING Calories: 436; Total Fat: 16g;
Saturated Fat: 3g; Cholesterol: 92mg;
Carbohydrates: 46g; Fiber: 2g; Protein: 27g

TO MAKE THE SAUCE

1. In a small saucepan over medium heat, stir together the ghee and ginger. Cook, stirring frequently, for 2 minutes.

2. Add the garlic, coconut sugar, coconut aminos, vinegar, arrowroot powder, and red pepper flakes. Stir well and bring to a simmer. Reduce the heat to medium-low and cook for 5 minutes until the sauce begins to thicken and reduce slightly.

TO MAKE THE CHICKEN

1. In a large skillet over medium-high heat, heat the avocado oil.

2. In a small bowl, mix the rice flour, salt, and garlic powder.

3. Dredge the chicken in the flour mixture and put in the hot skillet. Cook for 3 to 4 minutes per side. Transfer to a serving dish.

4. Pour the sauce over the chicken, and serve immediately.

INGREDIENT TIP: Substituting almond flour for the brown rice flour will give a slightly different coating texture, since the latter has a finer consistency.

BAKED CHICKEN BREAST WITH LEMON & GARLIC

DAIRY-FREE, GLUTEN-FREE, PALEO, SOY-FREE

SERVES 4 / PREP TIME: 5 MINUTES / COOK TIME: 20 TO 25 MINUTES

This is the perfect go-to chicken recipe. It's full of flavor and the ingredients blend subtly, making it go well with any side dish or allowing it to fit into another chicken dish. Coating the chicken with avocado oil helps seal in the moisture.

Juice of 1 lemon

Zest of 1 lemon

1 teaspoon garlic powder

½ teaspoon salt

3 tablespoons avocado oil

2 (8-ounce) boneless, skinless
    chicken breasts

PER SERVING Calories: 208; Total Fat: 12g;
Saturated Fat: 2g; Cholesterol: 56mg;
Carbohydrates: 2g; Fiber: 0g; Protein: 23g

1. Preheat the oven to 375°F.

2. In a small bowl, mix the lemon juice, lemon zest, garlic powder, and salt. Set aside.

3. With a basting brush, spread 1½ tablespoons of avocado oil on the bottom of a glass or ceramic baking dish and brush them thoroughly with the chicken breasts in the dish. Brush the remaining 1½ tablespoons of avocado oil.

4. With the brush, coat the chicken with the lemon-garlic mixture.

5. Bake for 20 to 25 minutes, or until the center of the chicken reaches 165°F on an instant-read thermometer.

PREPARATION TIP: For a little extra flavor, add 1 teaspoon of ground ginger to the lemon-garlic mixture.

RUSSIAN KOTLETI

GLUTEN-FREE, LACTOSE-FREE, SOY-FREE

SERVES 4 / PREP TIME: 10 MINUTES / COOK TIME: 10 MINUTES

Russian food is known for being hearty and filling. Luckily, with a few adjustments, it can be made without traditional inflammation-causing ingredients. Enjoy *kotleti*, a traditional Eastern European meat dish, described by many as a unique and flavorful cross between a meatball and hamburger patty.

¼ cup filtered water

1 pound ground chicken

½ small white onion, diced

1 egg, whisked

1 teaspoon salt

½ teaspoon garlic powder

½ teaspoon dried dill

½ teaspoon freshly ground black pepper

1 slice gluten-free bread

2 teaspoons ghee

PER SERVING (2 kotleti) Calories: 213; Total Fat: 9g; Saturated Fat: 3g; Cholesterol: 149mg; Carbohydrates: 9g; Fiber: 1g; Protein: 24g

1. In a medium bowl, combine the chicken, onion, egg, salt, garlic powder, dill, and pepper. Mix well with your hands.

2. In a small bowl, soak the bread in the water for 1 minute.

3. Add the soaked bread to the chicken mixture. With your hands, work to break it up as you mix it in. If you prefer, mix the ingredients in a stand mixer.

4. Divide the chicken mixture into 8 portions and roll each into a ball. Press them slightly to form short, thick patties.

5. In a large skillet over medium heat, heat the ghee. Place the patties in the pan so they do not touch, and cook for 5 minutes per side. Cut into one to check for doneness (no longer pink) before removing from the heat.

SUBSTITUTION TIP: This recipe can easily be made with other types of lean ground meat, such as beef or turkey.

CHICKEN SOUVLAKI WITH TZATZIKI SAUCE

GLUTEN-FREE, PROBIOTIC, SOY-FREE

SERVES 4 / PREP TIME: 15 MINUTES / COOK TIME: 15 MINUTES

Souvlaki is a popular Greek dish of skewered, bite-size pieces of meat and sometimes vegetables. It can be served alone or with rice or pita, and always with a sauce such as this fresh-tasting *tzatziki*.

FOR THE TZATZIKI

1 cup plain whole-milk Greek yogurt

½ cucumber, peeled and grated

1 tablespoon freshly squeezed lemon juice

1 garlic clove, minced

1 teaspoon fresh lemon zest

½ teaspoon minced fresh dill

¼ teaspoon salt

FOR THE SOUVLAKI

1 pound boneless, skinless chicken breasts, cut into bite-size pieces

2 small white onions, cut into bite-size pieces

2 green bell peppers, cut into bite-size pieces

2 tablespoons extra-virgin olive oil

2 teaspoons fresh lemon zest

2 teaspoons dried oregano

2 teaspoons garlic powder

1 teaspoon salt

TO MAKE THE TZATZIKI

In a medium bowl, stir together the yogurt, cucumber, lemon juice, garlic, lemon zest, dill, and salt. Set aside.

TO MAKE THE SOUVLAKI

1. Soak 8 bamboo skewers in water for 10 to 30 minutes before cooking.

2. Preheat a grill to medium-high heat, or place a grill pan over medium-high heat on the stove top.

3. In a large bowl, gently toss the chicken, onions, green bell peppers, and olive oil until coated.

PER SERVING (2 skewers) Calories: 332; Total Fat: 19g; Saturated Fat: 3g; Cholesterol: 69mg; Carbohydrates: 9g; Fiber: 1g; Protein: 32g

4. In a small bowl, combine the lemon zest, oregano, garlic powder, and salt.

5. On each skewer, alternate pieces of chicken, onion, and bell pepper. Sprinkle with the lemon-spice mixture. Transfer to the grill.

6. Cook for 10 to 15 minutes, or until the chicken is cooked through.

7. Serve with the *tzatziki* dip.

COOKING TIP: If you have time to marinate the chicken before cooking, add the juice of 1 lemon and ½ cup of extra-virgin olive oil to the spice mixture, add the chicken, cover, and let marinate in the refrigerator for up to 3 hours.

MEDITERRANEAN CHICKEN BAKE

DAIRY-FREE, GLUTEN-FREE, PALEO, SOY-FREE

SERVES 4 / PREP TIME: 10 MINUTES / COOK TIME: 20

Enjoy this juicy, flavorful dish with a large green salad, over gluten-free grains, or with a side of roasted vegetables. Genovese basil, one of the most commonly used types in the Mediterranean region, is milder than many Asian varieties. Basil's essential oil is known for its therapeutic properties, which are useful in treating indigestion and nausea. The cremini mushrooms, which are young portobello mushrooms and often called golden Italians or Italian browns, work well here; they are often used in Italian dishes.

4 (4-ounce) boneless, skinless chicken breasts

2 tablespoons avocado oil

1 pint cherry tomatoes, halved

1 cup packed chopped fresh spinach

1 cup sliced cremini mushrooms

½ red onion, thinly sliced

½ cup chopped fresh basil

4 garlic cloves, minced

2 teaspoons balsamic vinegar

PER SERVING Calories: 219; Total Fat: 9g; Saturated Fat: 1g; Cholesterol: 64mg; Carbohydrates: 7g; Fiber: 2g; Protein: 28g

1. Preheat the oven to 400°F.

2. Place the chicken breasts in a glass baking dish. Brush with the avocado oil.

3. In a medium bowl, stir together the tomatoes, spinach, mushrooms, red onion, basil, garlic, and vinegar.

4. Top each chicken breast with one-fourth of the vegetable mixture.

5. Bake for about 20 minutes, or until the chicken is cooked through.

COOKING TIP: To slice the basil into ribbons, use a technique called chiffonade. Lay the leaves flat on top of each other. Roll the pile of leaves into a tight bundle. With a sharp knife, make thin cuts crosswise.

TURKEY LARB LETTUCE WRAPS

DAIRY-FREE, GLUTEN-FREE, PALEO, SOY-FREE

SERVES 4 / PREP TIME: 10 MINUTES / COOK TIME: 20 MINUTES

Larb is a traditional meat salad from Laos, served in many Southeast Asian restaurants around the world. Typically, larb is made from ground meat, lime juice, fish sauce, and various herbs. Roughly ground toasted rice is included in most traditional recipes, but is omitted here for simplicity.

1 pound ground turkey

1 small red onion, diced

2 garlic cloves, minced

4 scallions, sliced

2 tablespoons freshly squeezed lime juice

2 tablespoons fish sauce

2 tablespoons minced fresh cilantro

1 tablespoon minced fresh mint (optional)

1 tablespoon coconut sugar

¼ teaspoon red pepper flakes

8 small romaine lettuce leaves

PER SERVING (2 wraps) Calories: 143;
Total Fat: 2g; Saturated Fat: 1g;
Cholesterol: 70mg; Carbohydrates: 9g;
Fiber: 1g; Protein: 24g

1. In a large skillet over medium-high heat, cook the turkey for 10 minutes, stirring and breaking up the meat.

2. Add the onion and garlic, and cook for about 10 minutes, stirring, until the onions soften and the meat is cooked.

3. Remove from the heat. Stir in the scallions, lime juice, fish sauce, cilantro, mint (if using), coconut sugar, and red pepper flakes until well incorporated.

4. Fill each romaine leaf with the meat mixture. Serve warm or cold.

SUBSTITUTION TIP: This recipe can be made with ground chicken, lean ground beef, or ground lamb, without changing any other ingredients or measurements.

SPICY SPINACH-TURKEY BURGERS

DAIRY-FREE, GLUTEN-FREE, PALEO, SOY-FREE

SERVES 4 / PREP TIME: 10 MINUTES / COOK TIME: 12 MINUTES

These burgers are ready to cook in a flash. If you don't have a food processor, you can still whip them up quickly with a little elbow grease. Simply mince the spinach and onion with a knife, and combine all the ingredients by hand. If serving these to kids, reduce or omit the red pepper flakes and cayenne pepper to tame the spiciness.

2 cups fresh spinach, washed

½ small white onion, diced

1 egg, whisked

1 pound ground turkey

1 teaspoon garlic powder

½ teaspoon dried oregano

½ teaspoon dried basil

½ teaspoon red pepper flakes

½ teaspoon salt

¼ teaspoon dried thyme

¼ teaspoon freshly ground black pepper

Dash cayenne pepper

1 tablespoon avocado oil

PER SERVING Calories: 197; Total Fat: 11g; Saturated Fat: 3g; Cholesterol: 133mg; Carbohydrates: 3g; Fiber: 1g; Protein: 23g

1. In a food processor (or blender), combine the spinach, onion, and egg. Pulse for about 15 seconds until the vegetables are minced.

2. Add the turkey, garlic powder, oregano, basil, red pepper flakes, salt, thyme, black pepper, and cayenne pepper. Pulse for 20 to 30 seconds until well combined.

3. Form the turkey mixture into 4 patties.

4. In a large skillet over medium heat, add the avocado oil. Cook the patties for about 6 minutes per side.

INGREDIENT TIP: To kick the spice level up, double the cayenne pepper, or add a few drops of your favorite hot sauce.

TURKEY MEATBALLS IN A MUFFIN TIN

DAIRY-FREE, GLUTEN-FREE, PALEO, SOY-FREE

MAKES 12 MEATBALLS / PREP TIME: 10 MINUTES / COOK TIME: 20 MINUTES

Keeping meatballs plump and round while cooking them in a skillet or baking dish can be tricky. Using a muffin tin helps portion the meat, while giving some structure to the finished dish. Serve these over zucchini noodles, buckwheat pasta, or as the main dish.

1½ pounds ground turkey

1 small white onion, minced

1 egg, whisked

¼ cup fresh mushrooms, minced

1 teaspoon garlic powder

½ teaspoon salt

½ teaspoon dried oregano

¼ teaspoon freshly ground black pepper

¼ teaspoon ground ginger

1 slice gluten-free bread, torn into
    small pieces

PER SERVING (1 meatball) Calories: 78;
Total Fat: 3g; Saturated Fat: 0g;
Cholesterol: 26mg; Carbohydrates: 3g;
Fiber: 0g; Protein: 15g

1. Preheat the oven to 400°F.

2. In a large bowl, add the turkey, onion, egg, mushrooms, garlic powder, salt, oregano, pepper, ginger, and bread, and mix thoroughly with your hands.

3. Form the turkey mixture into 12 balls and place 1 in each cup of a 12-cup muffin tin.

4. Bake for 20 minutes. Serve immediately.

INGREDIENT TIP: When choosing gluten-free bread, know that many brands use extra sugar and simple flours to make up for the lack of gluten. If you tolerate gluten, use a slice of traditional sourdough bread whose tougher proteins are broken down by the fermentation process.

SOUTHWEST TURKEY-STUFFED BELL PEPPERS

DAIRY-FREE, GLUTEN-FREE, PALEO, SOY-FREE

SERVES 6 / PREP TIME: 10 MINUTES / COOK TIME: 20 MINUTES

A family favorite, stuffed bell peppers usually require a lengthy cooking process. Here you get dinner on the table fast by cooking the peppers separately while the meat is browned. You can still feed the family quickly—and nutritiously—before your scheduled activities.

6 bell peppers, any color, tops and ribs removed, seeded

1 tablespoon avocado oil

1 pound ground turkey

1 small white onion, diced

2 garlic cloves, minced

1 (16-ounce) can diced tomatoes, drained

½ teaspoon ground cumin

½ teaspoon paprika

½ teaspoon dried oregano

½ teaspoon salt

Freshly ground black pepper

PER SERVING Calories: 188; Total Fat: 9g; Saturated Fat: 2g; Cholesterol: 60mg; Carbohydrates: 11g; Fiber: 4g; Protein: 15g

1. Preheat the oven to 400°F.

2. Line a baking sheet with aluminum foil.

3. Arrange the bell peppers on the prepared pan. Drizzle with the avocado oil.

4. Bake for 20 minutes, or until softened and cooked.

5. Meanwhile, in a large skillet over medium-high heat, brown the turkey for 5 minutes, breaking up the meat with a spoon.

6. Add the onion and garlic. Cook for 10 minutes, stirring frequently, until the turkey is cooked.

7. Stir in the tomatoes, cumin, paprika, oregano, and salt, and season with pepper.

8. Fill each cooked pepper with the meat mixture. Enjoy warm.

PREPARATION TIP: Make these peppers to suit your family's tastes by adding different ingredients to the filling, such as corn, Hatch chiles, or more spice.

LAMB & QUINOA SKILLET RAGÙ

DAIRY-FREE, GLUTEN-FREE, SOY-FREE

SERVES 6 / PREP TIME: 10 MINUTES / COOK TIME: 20 MINUTES

In Italian cooking, *ragù* is a sauce made from ground meat, onions, and tomato purée served over pasta. Here, I've upped the protein content and removed the gluten by substituting delicious quinoa for the traditional pasta (see Cooking Tip, Minestrone Soup with Quinoa, page 77).

1 cup quinoa, rinsed well

2 cups filtered water

1 pound ground lamb

3 garlic cloves, minced

1 yellow onion, diced

1 red bell pepper, diced

1 (28-ounce) can diced tomatoes
 with their juice

1 cup minced fresh spinach leaves

2 teaspoons chili powder

½ teaspoon ground cumin

½ teaspoon smoked paprika

Dash red pepper flakes

PER SERVING Calories: 306; Total Fat: 13g; Saturated Fat: 5g; Cholesterol: 50mg; Carbohydrates: 26g; Fiber: 5g; Protein: 19g

1. In a medium saucepan over high heat, bring the quinoa and the water to a boil. Cover the pan and reduce the heat to low. Simmer for 15 minutes. Remove from the heat and fluff with a fork.

2. Meanwhile, in a large skillet over medium heat, cook the lamb for 10 minutes, stirring occasionally to break up the meat.

3. Add the garlic, onion, and red bell pepper. Cook, stirring, for 5 minutes.

4. Stir in the tomatoes, spinach, chili powder, cumin, paprika, and red pepper flakes. Cover and cook for about 5 minutes, or until the lamb is fully cooked.

5. Remove the *ragù* from the heat and spoon over portions of quinoa.

COOKING TIP: Quinoa is an easy side to make, and it keeps well in the refrigerator for up to 1 week. Make a large batch at the beginning of the week to use in recipes like this one throughout the week.

HERBED LAMB FILLETS WITH CAULIFLOWER MASH

GLUTEN-FREE, LACTOSE-FREE, PALEO, SOY-FREE

SERVES 4 / PREP TIME: 10 MINUTES / COOK TIME: 15 MINUTES

It's important to choose grass-fed lamb, which has been shown to have a far better ratio of healthy omega-3s to less healthy omega-6s than conventionally raised lamb. These fatty acids work to lower inflammation in the body, such as the cardiovascular system, in turn, lowering heart disease risk.

FOR THE CAULIFLOWER MASH

1 large head cauliflower, florets broken into small chunks

Filtered water, for cooking the cauliflower

1 tablespoon ghee

½ teaspoon garlic powder

½ teaspoon salt

Dash cayenne pepper

FOR THE LAMB

2 (8-ounce) grass-fed lamb fillets

1 teaspoon salt

½ teaspoon freshly ground black pepper

2 tablespoons avocado oil

1 teaspoon dried rosemary

PER SERVING Calories: 289; Total Fat: 19g; Saturated Fat: 7g; Cholesterol: 74mg; Carbohydrates: 8g; Fiber: 3g; Protein: 34g

TO MAKE THE CAULIFLOWER MASH

1. In a large pot, combine the cauliflower and enough water to cover. Bring to a boil over high heat, and cook for 10 minutes. Drain, and transfer to a food processor (or blender).

2. Add the ghee, garlic powder, salt, and cayenne pepper. Pulse to a smooth consistency.

TO MAKE THE LAMB

1. Season the lamb with the salt and pepper.

2. In a large skillet over medium-high heat, add the avocado oil and rosemary.

3. Add the lamb fillets to the skillet, spaced so they are not touching. Sear for 5 minutes, spooning the rosemary oil from the bottom of the pan over the lamb halfway through. Flip and continue to cook the lamb for 5 minutes, basting with the rosemary oil after about 2 minutes.

4. Transfer to a plate, and let rest for 5 minutes.

5. Slice the lamb into coins and serve with the cauliflower mash.

INGREDIENT TIP: Lamb fillets are best served medium-rare or medium. If undercooked meat is something you avoid, buy local, organic meat from a trusted source.

PORK TENDERLOIN WITH DIJON-CIDER GLAZE

DAIRY-FREE, GLUTEN-FREE, SOY-FREE

SERVES 4 / PREP TIME: 5 MINUTES / COOK TIME: 25 MINUTES

Studies, like the one conducted in 2016 by the Weston A. Price Foundation, have shown that prepared pork (salt cured and smoked, or marinated raw in an acid like apple cider vinegar) has a much lower inflammatory response than plain pork. Adding an acidic ingredient while cooking can still reduce the inflammatory response.

¼ cup apple cider vinegar

¼ cup coconut sugar

3 tablespoons Dijon mustard

2 teaspoons garlic powder

Dash salt

1 (1½-pound) pork tenderloin

PER SERVING Calories: 268; Total Fat: 6g; Saturated Fat: 2g; Cholesterol: 110mg; Carbohydrates: 16g; Fiber: 0g; Protein: 36g

1. In a small bowl, stir together the vinegar, coconut sugar, mustard, garlic powder, and salt until the sugar dissolves. Brush this mixture over the pork loin.

2. Place a grill pan over medium-high heat and add the pork. Sear for 2 minutes per side.

3. Spoon half of the vinegar mixture over the pork and reduce the heat to medium. Cover the pan and cook for 10 minutes.

4. Spoon the remaining vinegar mixture over the pork. Cook for 5 minutes, or until the center of the pork reaches 145°F. Transfer the pork to a plate.

5. Bring the vinegar mixture remaining in the pan to a simmer. Cook for 5 minutes to reduce and thicken.

6. Serve the pork drizzled with the glaze.

PREPARATION TIP: To marinate: combine all the ingredients in a large resealable plastic bag. Turn to coat and refrigerate for up to 3 hours.

THAI GROUND BEEF WITH ASPARAGUS & CHILES

DAIRY-FREE, GLUTEN-FREE, PALEO, SOY-FREE

SERVES 6 / PREP TIME: 10 MINUTES / COOK TIME: 17 MINUTES

The cholesterol content of grass-fed beef has been shown to be between 22 and 39 percent lower than that of beef from conventionally fed animals. A study by the George Mateljan Foundation, 2016 shows that there are up to 3.5 grams of omega-3 fats in 4 ounces of grass-fed beef, which provides 100 percent of the recommended daily requirement. Blending that beef with these flavorful Thai-inspired ingredients combines great nutrition with great taste.

1 tablespoon plus 1 teaspoon fish sauce

1 tablespoon plus 1 teaspoon coconut aminos

1 teaspoon coconut sugar

1 tablespoon coconut oil

1 bunch asparagus, tough ends trimmed, shaved into ribbons with a vegetable peeler

3 garlic cloves, minced

3 red jalapeño chile peppers, seeded and sliced into 2-inch matchsticks

1¼ pounds lean ground beef

1 cup loosely packed fresh basil leaves

Lime wedges, for garnish

PER SERVING Calories: 214; Total Fat: 13g; Saturated Fat: 6g; Cholesterol: 59mg; Carbohydrates: 5g; Fiber: 2g; Protein: 21g

1. In a small bowl, stir together the fish sauce, coconut aminos, and coconut sugar. Set aside.

2. In a large skillet over medium heat, heat the coconut oil. Add the asparagus, and sauté for 1 minute. Transfer to a plate and set aside.

3. To the skillet, add the garlic and half of the jalapeño chiles. Cook for 15 seconds, stirring constantly.

4. Add the ground beef, and cook for about 15 minutes until cooked through and browned, breaking the meat up with a wooden spoon.

5. Stir in the sauce. Cook for 30 seconds.

6. Add the basil, cooked asparagus, and remaining half of the jalapeño chiles, and stir to combine.

7. Serve hot, garnished with lime wedges.

SPAGHETTI BOLOGNESE

GLUTEN-FREE, LACTOSE-FREE, SOY-FREE

SERVES 8 / PREP TIME: 10 MINUTES / COOK TIME: 20 MINUTES

Italian Bolognese sauce traditionally requires hours of cooking to develop its flavor. However, you can make a tasty, healthy Bolognese sauce in just 30 minutes! Enjoy the depth of flavor that comes with blending a touch of nutmeg with the classic vegetable trio of onion, carrot, and celery.

1 pound brown rice spaghetti

2 tablespoons ghee

3 garlic cloves, minced

½ cup chopped white onion

⅔ cup chopped celery

⅔ cup chopped carrot

1 pound lean ground beef

1 (14-ounce) can diced tomatoes with their juice

1 tablespoon white wine vinegar

½ teaspoon red pepper flakes

⅛ teaspoon ground nutmeg

Dash salt

Dash freshly ground black pepper

PER SERVING Calories: 358; Total Fat: 12g; Saturated Fat: 5g; Cholesterol: 33mg; Carbohydrates: 48g; Fiber: 3g; Protein: 14g

1. Cook the spaghetti according to the package instructions.

2. Meanwhile, in a large skillet over medium heat, heat the ghee.

3. Add the garlic and onion, and sauté for 5 minutes.

4. Add the celery and carrot, and sauté for 5 minutes. Push the vegetables to the side of the skillet.

5. Add the ground beef next to the vegetables. Sauté for 10 minutes, breaking up the meat as it begins to brown.

6. Stir in the tomatoes, vinegar, red pepper flakes, nutmeg, salt, and pepper, and bring to a simmer for 5 minutes.

7. Serve over the cooked noodles.

INGREDIENT TIP: In addition to brown rice pasta, there are other substitutes for wheat pasta at your grocery store, such as quinoa, lentil, or black bean pastas.

SESAME-GINGER BOK CHOY & BEEF STIR-FRY

DAIRY-FREE, GLUTEN-FREE, PALEO, SOY-FREE

SERVES 4 / PREP TIME: 10 MINUTES / COOK TIME: 10 MINUTES

Flank steak, a delicious cut, cooks quickly because of its thin structure. It pairs beautifully with stir-fried bok choy. A recent study shows that lutein, the beneficial carotenoid found in bok choy, is far more available to the body after stir-frying as opposed to steaming. It's all in how you cook it! Because this meal comes together quickly, there's no reason for that unhealthy takeout version.

12 ounces flank steak, cut into thin 2-inch strips

½ teaspoon salt

¼ teaspoon freshly ground black pepper

2 teaspoons avocado oil

1 tablespoon sesame oil

2 garlic cloves, minced

4 heads baby bok choy, quartered lengthwise

3 tablespoons coconut aminos

2 tablespoons rice vinegar

1 tablespoon grated peeled fresh ginger

1 tablespoon coconut sugar

¼ teaspoon red pepper flakes (optional)

PER SERVING Calories: 252; Total Fat: 13g; Saturated Fat: 4g; Cholesterol: 56mg; Carbohydrates: 12g; Fiber: 9g; Protein: 19g

1. Place a large skillet over medium-high heat. Season the steak strips with the salt and pepper. Add it to the skillet with the avocado oil, and stir-fry for 3 to 4 minutes until just cooked. Transfer to a plate.

2. Wipe out the skillet. Reduce the heat to medium and add the sesame oil and garlic. Cook, stirring occasionally, for 2 to 3 minutes.

3. Stir in the bok choy, coconut aminos, vinegar, ginger, coconut sugar, and red pepper flakes (if using) until well combined. Cover and cook for 2 minutes.

4. Add the steak to the skillet. Toss gently to combine and warm through, about 1 minute. Serve hot.

PREPARATION TIP: Grating ginger root can be done easily using a zester or even a cheese grater. Just peel back the tough skin first, and watch your fingers carefully!

CREAMY STRAWBERRY-BLUEBERRY ICE POPS (PAGE 170)

CHAPTER TEN

Desserts

CREAMY STRAWBERRY-BLUEBERRY ICE POPS

GLUTEN-FREE, PROBIOTIC, SOY-FREE, VEGETARIAN

MAKES 4 MEDIUM ICE POPS / PREP TIME: 5 MINUTES, PLUS FREEZING TIME

Ice pop molds are inexpensive kitchen tools, and they come in handy in the hot summer months for kids and adults alike! Taste the mixture before freezing to adjust the sweetness to your preference. These pops are a cooling, soothing treat anytime you need a quick pick-me-up.

1 cup strawberries, fresh or frozen

1 cup blueberries, fresh or frozen

2 cups plain whole-milk yogurt

¼ cup filtered water

2 tablespoons raw honey

1 teaspoon freshly squeezed lemon juice

PER SERVING Calories: 140; Total Fat: 4g; Saturated Fat: 3g; Cholesterol: 16mg; Carbohydrates: 23g; Fiber: 2g; Protein: 5g

1. In a blender, combine the strawberries, blueberries, yogurt, water, honey, and lemon juice. Blend until smooth.

2. Pour the mixture into the ice pop molds and freeze until solid, about 3 hours.

SUBSTITUTION TIP: If you avoid dairy, choose a coconut milk yogurt instead.

STONE FRUIT COBBLER

DAIRY-FREE, GLUTEN-FREE, SOY-FREE, VEGAN

SERVES 8 / PREP TIME: 10 MINUTES / COOK TIME: 20 MINUTES

Cobblers originated in the American colonies when the settlers didn't have access to many ingredients. This version layers premade biscuits on top of a stewed fruit filling. This lovely dessert will satisfy that sweet tooth with natural and naturally better for you, sugars.

1 teaspoon coconut oil plus ¼ cup, melted

2 cups sliced fresh peaches

2 cups sliced fresh nectarines

2 tablespoons freshly squeezed lemon juice

¾ cup almond flour

¾ cup rolled oats

¼ cup coconut sugar

1 teaspoon ground cinnamon

½ teaspoon vanilla extract

Dash salt

Filtered water, for mixing

PER SERVING Calories: 196; Total Fat: 12g; Saturated Fat: 6g; Cholesterol: 0mg; Carbohydrates: 15g; Fiber: 3g; Protein: 4g

1. Preheat the oven to 425°F.

2. Coat the bottom of a large cast-iron skillet with 1 teaspoon of coconut oil.

3. In the skillet, mix the peaches, nectarines, and lemon juice.

4. In a food processor or blender, add the almond flour, oats, coconut sugar, the ¼ cup of melted coconut oil, cinnamon, vanilla, and salt. Pulse until the oats are roughly broken up and the mixture resembles a dry dough.

5. If more moisture is needed to combine the ingredients, add some filtered water, 1 tablespoon at a time.

6. Pour the dough into a medium bowl. With your fingers, break the dough into large chunks and sprinkle across the top of the fruit.

7. Bake for 20 minutes. Serve warm.

INGREDIENT TIP: Make this cobbler seasonal by mixing in other fruits like blueberries and raspberries, depending on what is fresh that month.

MINI KEY LIME BARS

DAIRY-FREE, GLUTEN-FREE, SOY-FREE, VEGETARIAN

SERVES 8 / PREP TIME: 15 MINUTES, PLUS 2 HOURS FREEZING TIME

Ditch that thick, sugary (inflammatory) meringue and enjoy this no-bake, lighter version of Key lime pie that can be served as a snack or after-dinner dessert.

FOR THE CRUST
¾ cup almond flour
¾ cup rolled oats
¼ cup coconut oil, melted
2 tablespoons coconut sugar
1 teaspoon ground cinnamon
½ teaspoon vanilla extract
Dash salt
Filtered water, for mixing

FOR THE FILLING
2 cups coconut cream, chilled
¼ cup freshly squeezed lime juice
1 tablespoon fresh lime zest
3 tablespoons raw honey, or pure
　maple syrup

PER SERVING Calories: 309; Total Fat: 24g;
Saturated Fat: 18g; Cholesterol: 0mg;
Carbohydrates: 15g; Fiber: 2g; Protein: 5g

TO MAKE THE CRUST

1. Line the bottom of an 8-by-8-inch baking pan with parchment paper.

2. In a food processor or blender, add the almond flour, oats, coconut oil, coconut sugar, cinnamon, vanilla, and salt. Pulse until a sticky dough forms, adding 1 tablespoon of filtered water, if necessary, to help the ingredients combine fully.

3. Press the crust mixture evenly on the bottom of the prepared pan.

TO MAKE THE FILLING

1. In a medium bowl, whip the coconut cream with an electric hand mixer until it resembles whipped cream.

2. Add the lime juice, lime zest, and honey. Continue to mix until the ingredients are well incorporated. Spread the filling evenly over the crust.

3. Cover and place the baking dish in the freezer for up to 2 hours.

4. Slightly thaw and slice the bars before serving.

SUBSTITUTION TIP: For a vegan dessert, use maple syrup instead of honey.

BANANA "NICE" CREAM

DAIRY-FREE, GLUTEN-FREE, PALEO, SOY-FREE, VEGAN

SERVES 4 / PREP TIME: 5 MINUTES

It doesn't get any easier than a one-ingredient, one-step dessert! Keep a supply of frozen bananas on hand: Peel, chop, and freeze any extra ripe bananas you have before they go bad.

4 frozen, diced bananas

PER SERVING Calories: 112; Total Fat: 0g; Saturated Fat: 0g; Cholesterol: 0mg; Carbohydrates: 29g; Fiber: 3g; Protein: 1g

In a food processor or blender, blend the bananas for 3 to 5 minutes until they reach a whipped, creamy consistency. Depending on how frozen the bananas are, it may take a bit longer. Serve immediately.

VARIATION TIP: For a chocolate spin on this basic dessert, add ¼ teaspoon of vanilla extract and 1 tablespoon of cocoa powder.

BLUEBERRY PARFAIT WITH LEMON-COCONUT CREAM

DAIRY-FREE, GLUTEN-FREE, SOY-FREE, VEGAN

SERVES 4 / PREP TIME: 10 MINUTES

For a light treat that's anything but light on nutrients, lemony coconut cream is layered with fresh, plump blueberries for a healthy yet decadent parfait. Coconut cream contains some of the best plant-based saturated fats that the body easily translates into energy. Blueberries rank extremely high on the Oxygen Radical Absorbance Capacity (ORAC) scale that measures the antioxidant capacity of foods—the higher the better.

FOR THE CREAM

2 (14-ounce) cans coconut milk, chilled (see Preparation Tip)
1 tablespoon pure maple syrup
1 tablespoon fresh lemon zest
½ teaspoon vanilla extract
Dash salt

FOR THE PARFAIT

2½ cups fresh blueberries

PER SERVING Calories: 322; Total Fat: 24g; Saturated Fat: 23g; Cholesterol: 0mg; Carbohydrates: 23g; Fiber: 2g; Protein: 4g

TO MAKE THE CREAM

1. In a large bowl, whip the coconut cream with an electric hand mixer for 2 minutes until small peaks form.

2. Add the maple syrup, lemon zest, vanilla, and salt, and whip for a few more seconds.

TO MAKE THE PARFAIT

1. In 4 small glasses, alternate layers of whipped coconut cream and blueberries until the ingredients are all used.

2. Serve immediately.

PREPARATION TIP: Refrigerate the cans of coconut milk overnight so the coconut water and cream separate. Open the cans, and carefully scoop up the cream off the top to use in the recipe. Reserve the coconut water for use in smoothies.

SUPERFOOD HOT CHOCOLATE

DAIRY-FREE, GLUTEN-FREE, PALEO, SOY-FREE

SERVES 2 / PREP TIME: 5 MINUTES / COOK TIME: 8 MINUTES

Enjoy every ounce of this hot chocolate because it is packed with anti-inflammatory superfoods like collagen protein powder, ginger, turmeric, and coconut oil. Truly good for you to the last drop.

2 cups almond milk

1 tablespoon coconut oil

1 tablespoon collagen protein powder

2 teaspoons coconut sugar

2 tablespoons cocoa powder

1 teaspoon ground ginger

1 teaspoon ground cinnamon

1 teaspoon vanilla extract

½ teaspoon ground turmeric

Dash salt

Dash cayenne pepper (optional)

PER SERVING Calories: 216; Total Fat: 11g; Saturated Fat: 6g; Cholesterol: 0mg; Carbohydrates: 15g; Fiber: 6g; Protein: 11g

1. In a small saucepan over medium heat, warm the almond milk and coconut oil for about 7 minutes, stirring often. Add the protein powder, which will only properly dissolve in a heated liquid.

2. Stir in the coconut sugar and cocoa powder until melted and dissolved. Carefully pour the warm liquid into a blender.

3. Add the ginger, cinnamon, vanilla, turmeric, salt, and cayenne pepper (if using). Blend for 15 seconds until frothy.

4. Serve immediately.

INGREDIENT TIP: Collagen protein powder holds a wealth of goodness in its molecules. It's useful for lessening joint pain, tightening loose skin, strengthening hair and nails, and improving digestion.

ALMOND BUTTER FUDGE
WITH CHOCOLATE SAUCE

DAIRY-FREE, GLUTEN-FREE, SOY-FREE, PALEO, VEGETARIAN

MAKES 9 PIECES / PREP TIME: 5 MINUTES / COOK TIME: 7 MINUTES, PLUS 15 MINUTES FREEZING TIME

Sweet! No baking required for this freezer fudge. Enjoy this fudgy treat with plenty of healthy fats included to keep your blood sugar stable and balanced.

FOR THE CHOCOLATE SAUCE

3 tablespoons coconut oil

3 tablespoons cocoa powder

1½ tablespoons raw honey

Dash salt

FOR THE FUDGE

¼ cup coconut oil

2 tablespoons coconut sugar
(see Ingredient Tip)

1 cup natural almond butter

½ teaspoon vanilla extract

½ teaspoon salt

PER SERVING Calories: 288; Total Fat: 27g; Saturated Fat: 11g; Cholesterol: 0mg; Carbohydrates: 12g; Fiber: 3g; Protein: 7g

TO MAKE THE CHOCOLATE SAUCE

1. In a small saucepan over medium heat, stir together the coconut oil, cocoa powder, honey, and salt until dissolved and combined into a sauce, about 5 minutes. Remove from the heat.

2. Bring to room temperature before drizzling over the fudge.

TO MAKE THE FUDGE

1. Line a 9-by-5-inch loaf pan with parchment paper.

2. In a small saucepan over medium heat, warm the coconut oil just until melted. Remove from the heat, add the coconut sugar, and stir until dissolved.

3. In a small bowl, stir together the almond butter, warm coconut oil–coconut sugar mixture, vanilla, and salt until well combined.

4. Spread the fudge evenly over the bottom of the prepared pan.

5. Put in the freezer for 15 minutes, or until solid.

6. Cut into 9 pieces and serve drizzled with the chocolate sauce.

INGREDIENT TIP: If the brand of coconut sugar you use for the chocolate sauce doesn't dissolve well or remains too grainy, replace it with the same amount of pure maple syrup.

FLOURLESS BROWNIES WITH RASPBERRY SAUCE

DAIRY-FREE, GLUTEN-FREE, PALEO, SOY-FREE, VEGETARIAN

MAKES 9 BROWNIES / PREP TIME: 10 MINUTES / COOK TIME: 19 MINUTES

These are not your mother's brownies! With a base of almond butter, the nutty taste vanishes when combined with the rest of the gooey ingredients. Choose an extra-ripe banana for added sweetness.

FOR THE RASPBERRY SAUCE

1 cup fresh raspberries

2 teaspoons coconut sugar

1 tablespoon filtered water

FOR THE BROWNIES

Coconut oil, for the pan

¾ cup almond butter

½ cup cocoa powder

¼ cup coconut sugar

1 egg yolk, whisked

1 ripe banana, mashed well

1 teaspoon vanilla extract

½ teaspoon baking soda

¼ teaspoon salt

PER SERVING Calories: 186; Total Fat: 13g; Saturated Fat: 2g; Cholesterol: 20mg; Carbohydrates: 18g; Fiber: 5g; Protein: 7g

TO MAKE THE RASPBERRY SAUCE

In a small saucepan over medium heat, stir together the raspberries, coconut sugar, and water, mashing the raspberries as they cook, for 5 to 7 minutes, stirring often. Remove from the heat and set aside.

TO MAKE THE BROWNIES

1. Preheat the oven to 350°F.

2. Coat the bottom of an 8-by-8-inch baking pan with coconut oil.

3. In a medium bowl, stir together the almond butter, cocoa powder, and coconut sugar.

4. Add the egg yolk, banana, vanilla, baking soda, and salt. Stir together until a smooth batter forms. Spread the batter evenly in the prepared pan.

5. Bake for 12 minutes. Remove from oven and let cool for 5 minutes. Cut into 9 brownies.

6. Serve with the raspberry sauce drizzled over the top.

PREPARATION TIP: If you prefer a smooth sauce, blend the mixture in a food processor or blender, then press the mixture through a sieve into a small bowl.

MINI DARK CHOCOLATE-ALMOND BUTTER CUPS

DAIRY-FREE, GLUTEN-FREE, SOY-FREE, VEGETARIAN

MAKES 9 CUPS / PREP TIME: 10 MINUTES, PLUS 15 MINUTES CHILLING TIME / COOK TIME: 5 MINUTES

These homemade sweet and savory treats will put store-bought candies to shame! Choose a chocolate that is soy and dairy-free to melt down.

6 ounces dark chocolate, chopped

½ cup natural almond butter

2 tablespoons raw honey

½ teaspoon vanilla extract

Dash salt

PER SERVING Calories: 193; Total Fat: 16g; Saturated Fat: 6g; Cholesterol: 0mg; Carbohydrates: 14g; Fiber: 0g; Protein: 5g

1. Line 9 cups of a mini muffin tin with mini paper liners.

2. In a small saucepan over low heat, slowly melt the chocolate. Use half of the chocolate among the mini muffin cups. Set the rest of the chocolate aside.

3. In a small bowl, stir together the almond butter, honey, and vanilla. Divide the mixture into 9 portions and roll each into a small ball. Drop 1 ball into each muffin cup.

4. Drizzle the remaining chocolate into each cup, covering the almond butter balls.

5. Sprinkle each lightly with the salt.

6. Refrigerate until solid.

INGREDIENT TIP: If almond butter isn't your preference, try different types of nut or seed butters, such as cashew or sunflower seed.

CHEWY DOUBLE CHOCOLATE CHIP COOKIES

DAIRY-FREE, GLUTEN-FREE, SOY-FREE, VEGETARIAN

MAKES 12 COOKIES / PREP TIME: 15 MINUTES / COOK TIME:
10 MINUTES, PLUS 5 MINUTES RESTING TIME

Gluten-free with extra chocolate flavor, these cookies will please even the confirmed flourless skeptic. Experiment with other nut butters you prefer, such as cashew or hazelnut.

¾ cup creamy almond butter

½ cup coconut sugar

¼ cup cocoa powder

2 teaspoons vanilla extract

1 egg

1 egg yolk

1 teaspoon baking soda

¼ teaspoon salt

½ cup semi-sweet chocolate chips

Dash sea salt (optional)

PER SERVING Calories: 226; Total Fat: 15g;
Saturated Fat: 4g; Cholesterol: 31mg;
Carbohydrates: 20g; Fiber: 3g; Protein: 6g

1. Preheat the oven to 350°F.

2. Line 2 baking sheets with parchment paper.

3. In a medium bowl, cream together the almond butter, coconut sugar, cocoa powder, and vanilla.

4. In a small bowl, whisk the egg and egg yolk. Add the eggs to the almond butter mixture, and stir to combine.

5. Stir in the baking soda, salt, and chocolate chips until well mixed. Divide the dough into 12 pieces. Roll the dough into balls and put 6 on each prepared pan.

6. Bake for 9 to 10 minutes. Let the cookies rest on the pans for 5 minutes, where they'll continue to cook. Sprinkle each with a dash of sea salt (if using). Remove to a cooling rack.

PREPARATION TIP: These cookies are low in sugar. Topping each with sea salt plays up the salty vs. sweet factor, and can trick your taste buds into thinking there is more sweetness in each bite.

Measurement Conversions

VOLUME EQUIVALENTS (LIQUID)

US STANDARD	US STANDARD (ounces)	METRIC (approximate)
2 tablespoons	1 fl. oz.	30 mL
¼ cup	2 fl. oz.	60 mL
½ cup	4 fl. oz.	120 mL
1 cup	8 fl. oz.	240 mL
1½ cups	12 fl. oz.	355 mL
2 cups or 1 pint	16 fl. oz.	475 mL
4 cups or 1 quart	32 fl. oz.	1 L
1 gallon	128 fl. oz.	4 L

OVEN TEMPERATURES

FAHRENHEIT (F)	CELSIUS (C) (approximate)
250°F	120°C
300°F	150°C
325°F	165°C
350°F	180°C
375°F	190°C
400°F	200°C
425°F	220°C
450°F	230°C

VOLUME EQUIVALENTS (DRY)

US STANDARD	METRIC (approximate)
⅛ teaspoon	0.5 mL
¼ teaspoon	1 mL
½ teaspoon	2 mL
¾ teaspoon	4 mL
1 teaspoon	5 mL
1 tablespoon	15 mL
¼ cup	59 mL
⅓ cup	79 mL
½ cup	118 mL
⅔ cup	156 mL
¾ cup	177 mL
1 cup	235 mL
2 cups or 1 pint	475 mL
3 cups	700 mL
4 cups or 1 quart	1 L

WEIGHT EQUIVALENTS

US STANDARD	METRIC (approximate)
½ ounce	15 g
1 ounce	30 g
2 ounces	60 g
4 ounces	115 g
8 ounces	225 g
12 ounces	340 g
16 ounces or 1 pound	455 g

The Dirty Dozen and the Clean Fifteen

The Environmental Working Group (EWG) is a nonprofit, nonpartisan organization dedicated to protecting human health and the environment. Its mission is to empower people to live healthier lives in a healthier environment. This organization publishes an annual list of the twelve kinds of produce, in sequence, that have the highest amount of pesticide residue–the Dirty Dozen–as well as a list of the fifteen kinds of produce that have the least amount of pesticide residue–the Clean Fifteen.

THE DIRTY DOZEN

The 2016 Dirty Dozen includes the following produce. These are considered among this year's most important produce to buy organic:

1. Strawberries
2. Apples
3. Nectarines
4. Peaches
5. Celery
6. Grapes
7. Cherries
8. Spinach
9. Tomatoes
10. Bell peppers
11. Cherry tomatoes
12. Cucumbers
  + Kale/collard greens*
  + Hot peppers*

*The Dirty Dozen list contains two additional items—kale/collard greens and hot peppers—because they tend to contain trace levels of highly hazardous pesticides.

THE CLEAN FIFTEEN

The least critical to buy organically are the Clean Fifteen list. The following are on the 2016 list:

1. Avocados
2. Corn**
3. Pineapples
4. Cabbage
5. Sweet peas
6. Onions
7. Asparagus
8. Mangos
9. Papayas
10. Kiwi
11. Eggplant
12. Honeydew
13. Grapefruit
14. Cantaloupe
15. Cauliflower

** Some of the sweet corn sold in the United States are made from genetically engineered (GE) seedstock. Buy organic varieties of these crops to avoid GE produce.

References

Masterjohn, Christopher. "Fatty Acid Analysis of Grass-Fed and Grain-Fed Beef." Weston A. Price Foundation. January 21, 2014. www.westonaprice.org/know-your-fats/fatty-acid-analysis-of-grass-fed-and-grain-fed-beef-tallow/.

The George Mateljan Foundation. "The World's Healthiest Foods–Bok Choy." Accessed October 21, 2016. www.whfoods.com/genpage.php?tname=foodspice&dbid=152.

The George Mateljan Foundation. "The World's Healthiest Foods–Cabbage." Accessed October 21, 2016. www.whfoods.com/genpage.php?tname=foodspice&dbid=19.

The George Mateljan Foundation. "The World's Healthiest Foods–Squash, Summer." Accessed October 21, 2016. www.whfoods.com/genpage.php?tname=food spice&dbid=62.

The George Mateljan Foundation. "The World's Healthiest Foods–Beef, grass-fed." Accessed October 21, 2016. www.whfoods.com/genpage.php?tname=food spice&dbid=141.

National Center for Biotechnology Information (NCBI). "Anti-Oxidative and Anti-Inflammatory Effects of Ginger in Health and Physical Activity: Review of Current Evidence." April 4, 2013. www.ncbi.nlm.nih.gov/pmc/articles/PMC3665023.

National Center for Biotechnology Information (NCBI). "Randomized Double-Blind Crossover Study of the Efficacy of a Tart Cherry Juice Blend in Treatment of Osteo-arthritis (OA) of the Knee." August 21, 2013. www.ncbi.nlm.nih.gov/pubmed/23727631.

Rubik, Beverly. "How Does Pork Prepared in Various Ways Affect the Blood?" The Weston A. Price Foundation. October 12, 2011. Accessed October 21, 2016. www.westonaprice.org/health-topics/how-does-pork-prepared-in-various-ways-affect-the-blood.

Resources

THE WORLD'S HEALTHIEST FOODS IN CARE OF THE GEORGE MATELJAN FOUNDATION / WHFOODS.ORG The George Mateljan Foundation is a not-for-profit foundation whose mission is to help consumers eat and cook the healthiest way for optimal health.

THRIVE MARKET / THRIVEMARKET.COM
Buy healthy food from top-selling organic brands at wholesale prices. Shop for gluten-free, non-GMO, nontoxic products for a wide range of diets including the anti-inflammatory diet.

WESTON A. PRICE FOUNDATION / WESTONAPRICE.ORG
The Weston A. Price Foundation is a nonprofit, tax-exempt nutrition education foundation dedicated to restoring nutrient-dense foods to the human diet through education, research, and activism.

Recipe Index

Index